Missions and Unity

Missions and Unity
Lessons from History, 1792–2010

Norman E. Thomas

CASCADE Books • Eugene, Oregon

MISSIONS AND UNITY
Lessons from History, 1792–2010

American Society of Missiology Series 47

Copyright © 2010 Norman E. Thomas. All rights reserved. Except for brief quotations in critical publications or reviews, no part of this book may be reproduced in any manner without prior written permission from the publisher. Write: Permissions, Wipf and Stock Publishers, 199 W. 8th Ave., Suite 3, Eugene, OR 97401.

Cascade Books
An Imprint of Wipf and Stock Publishers
199 W. 8th Ave., Suite 3
Eugene, OR 97401

www.wipfandstock.com

ISBN 13: 978-1-60899-602-5

Cataloging-in-Publication data:

Thomas, Norman E.

    Missions and unity : Lessons from history, 1792–2010 / Norman E. Thomas.

    xxvi + 324 p. ; cm. 23 — Includes bibliographical references and indexes.

    American Society of Missiology Series 47

    ISBN 13: 978-1-60899-602-5

    1. Ecumenical movement. 2. Church—unity. 3. Missions. 4. Missions and Christian union. I. Title.

BX9.5 M5 T45 2010

Manufactured in the U.S.A.

Dedicated to

MAE GAUTIER

*My wife, who lives her
commitment to mission and unity*

Contents

Preface to the American Society of Missiology Series / ix

Foreword by Wilbert R. Shenk / xi

Acknowledgments / xv

Abbreviations / xvi

Introduction / xxi

PART ONE: Historical

1. William Carey's Pleasing Dream and Its Antecedents / 3
2. Evangelicals and Unity, 1792–1845 / 12
3. Cooperation in Mission, 1846–1909 / 27
4. Councils of Unity, 1910–1947 / 48
5. Multiple Unity Streams, 1948–2010 / 74

PART TWO: Ten Models of Unity

6. Unity through a Global Church / 85
7. World Conciliarism / 98
8. Christian World Communions / 121
9. World Associations / 136
10. Regional and National Voluntarism / 154
11. Regional and National Councils / 163
12. Towards Church Union / 187
13. "All in Each Place": Local Unity / 209

PART THREE: Wider Ecumenism

14. One World: The Secular Vision / 221
15. Christianity and Other Faiths / 241

Conclusion / 264

Bibliography / 273

Subject Index / 305

Name Index / 315

Preface to the American Society of Missiology Series

THE PURPOSE OF THE American Society of Missiology Series is to publish—without regard for disciplinary, national, or denominational boundaries—scholarly works of high quality and wide interest on missiological themes from the entire spectrum of scholarly pursuits relevant to Christian mission, which is always the focus of books in the Series.

By mission is meant the effort to effect passage over the boundary between faith in Jesus Christ and its absence. In this understanding of mission, the basic functions of Christian proclamation, dialogue, witness, service, worship, liberation, and nurture are of special concern. And in the context questions arise, including, How does the transition from one cultural context to another influence the shape and interaction between these dynamic functions, especially in regard to the cultural and religious plurality that comprises the global context of Christian life and mission.

The promotion of scholarly dialogue among missiologists, and among missiologists and scholars in other fields of inquiry, may involve the publication of views that some missiologists cannot accept, and with which members of the Editorial Committee themselves do not agree. Manuscripts published in the Series, accordingly, reflect the opinions of their authors and are not understood to represent the position of the American Society of Missiology or of the Editorial Committee. Selection is guided by such criteria as intrinsic worth, readability, coherence, and accessibility to a range of interested persons and not merely to experts or specialists.

The ASM Series seeks to publish scholarly works of high merit and wide interest on numerous aspects of missiology—the scholarly study of mission. Able presentation on new and creative approaches to the practice and understanding of mission will receive close attention.

The ASM Series Committee
Jonathan J. Bonk
Angelyn Dries, OSF
Scott W. Sunquist

Foreword

MISSIONS AND UNITY PROVIDES a comprehensive overview of the changes since 1800 in relationships not only between all Christian traditions—Protestant, Roman Catholic, Orthodox, Pentecostal, and indigenous Christian movements—but also interreligious and secular initiatives that seek to foster harmony and cooperation. Growing mutual respect and confidence led to the founding of new secular institutions and agencies, especially after World War II, that have worked to overcome entrenched prejudices and encourage cooperation in the struggle against poverty, disease, and ignorance. Indeed, historians have drawn attention to the interplay between multiple religious and secular groups and movements.

John King Fairbank, renowned Harvard Sinologist, pointed out in the 1960s that the secular historian can ill afford to neglect study of modern Christian missions because it is the largest and most sustained experiment in intercultural relations in human history.[1] One might add that it is also a movement that is richly documented with an abundance of archival material, much of it still waiting to be researched.

Although this book concentrates on developments since 1800, early impulses toward mission and unity are to be found in developments in the late seventeenth century. Between 1690 and 1710 several missionary societies were founded in Great Britain and in Germany. These new societies were the fruit of collaboration between European Pietists, some of whom were on assignment in London, and British and American Churchmen.[2] They maintained a lively correspondence in which they shared information, encouraged each other to action, and sought to promote missionary obedience and united Christian witness. As leader of the Moravian movement from 1722, Count Nicholas von Zinzendorf held that Christian unity and mission were of equal importance. A young

1. Fairbank," 861–79.
2. Brunner, *Halle Pietists*.

William Carey in the 1780s avidly read reports of Moravian missions and took this as his model for missionary action when he went to India in 1792.

Professor Norman E. Thomas's study is devoted to the development of missions and unity in the two centuries since 1800. Notwithstanding criticisms leveled against Christian missions, this has proved to be a seminal movement, for it unleashed creative energies that have spread out in many directions round the world. It is acknowledged, for example, that missions laid the foundation for public educational and healthcare systems in many countries. Missionaries championed the cause of the underclasses and women round the world. Historians credit Henry Venn, long-time leader of the Anglican Church Missionary Society in the mid-nineteenth century, with fostering development of the modern African nation-states through strategic initiatives he took as a mission strategist and administrator.

The missions and churches that were agents of the modern mission movement experienced creative change as well. Pent-up Christian energies were channeled into the founding of dozens of new societies between 1790 and 1830, on both sides of the Atlantic, for the purpose of sending missionaries to other continents, promoting the translation, production, and distribution of the Bible, organizing Sunday schools, working for the abolition of child labor, championing prison reform, campaigning for the abolition of slavery, and undertaking the publication of much literature for new literates in the homeland. All these societies were stepchildren to the churches that declined to acknowledge them as being legitimately integral to ecclesial life.

From the earliest stages promoters of these new initiatives sought to make common cause without regard to denomination. The London Missionary Society was founded in 1795 by "evangelical churchmen of many denominations to spread the knowledge of Christ among the heathen, and not to propagate Episcopacy, Presbyterianism or Independency, or any particular form of church government. They agreed to leave the persons converted 'to assume for themselves such form of church government as to them shall appear most agreeable to the Word of God.'"[3] This was called the LMS Fundamental Principle. It was in this environment that William Carey's "pleasing dream" occurred in 1806 in which

---

3. Latham, "London Missionary Society," 355–56.

he envisaged continuing consultation among missionaries and mission societies.

As this volume demonstrates, the practical need missionary pioneers felt for moral support and advice from their colleagues has spawned an impressive range of forms of cooperation across the world since 1800. The impulse toward mission and unity, if anything, has intensified over time. As parts II and III of this book show, the vision of unity has become more variegated over time to include interreligious coalitions and secular polities that seek to bring peoples together.

In 1800 less than 15 percent of all Christians were found beyond the boundaries of the historical Christian heartland. Two centuries later the preponderance of Christians is to be found in Asia, Africa, Latin America, and Oceania. This fact is a tribute to the power of mission and unity in the service of the gospel. Norman Thomas here provides a comprehensive, reliable, and imaginative map that will expand our understanding of these developments. At the same time he properly situates the narrative in the framework of the rapid globalization of the whole world community during these tumultuous two centuries.

Wilbert R. Shenk
Fuller Graduate School of Intercultural Studies

Acknowledgments

THE SEARCH FOR IMPORTANT library and archival material for this study was made possible by the kind assistance of staff at the following libraries and archives: Yale Divinity School, Yale University (Steven Peterson and Paul Stuehrenberg, librarians; Martha Smalley, archivist; Joan Duffy, assistant archivist), World Council of Churches Library (Pierre Beffa, librarian), School of Oriental and African Studies, University of London (Rosemary Seton, archivist), Selly Oak Colleges Library, Birmingham (Patrick Lambe, librarian), Basel Mission (Paul Jenkins, archivist), and Fuller Theological Seminary Library (David Bundy, librarian).

The author wishes to record his gratitude to the trustees of United Theological Seminary for providing the sabbatical needed for research and writing, to Yale Divinity School for appointment as a research fellow, and to the Overseas Ministries Study Center in New Haven, Connecticut, for housing and supportive community. Participants in two courses on "Ecumenism and Missions" at United Theological Seminary shared in development of case study materials. Wilbert Shenk read the entire manuscript and offered valuable critique and encouragement.

To the staff of United Theological Seminary Library goes special thanks for their support in the checking of references. My wife Mae Gautier helped make my English more readable. Without the emotional support of family members, the long separations and discipline of writing would have been impossible.

N. E. T.
Pasadena, California
February 2010

Abbreviations

A	Archives
AACC	All Africa Conference of Churches
ABS	American Bible Society
ABCFM	American Board of Commissioners for Foreign Missions
AEAM	Association of Evangelicals of Africa and Madagascar
AFER	*African Ecclesiastical Review*
AICs	African Initiated/Independent Churches
Amsterdam 1948	First Assembly of the WCC, Amsterdam, The Netherlands, 22 August—4 September 1948
ASMS	American Society of Missiology Series
Bangkok 1973	Meeting of the IMC, Bangkok, Thailand, January 1973
BBC	British Broadcasting Corporation
BCC	British Council of Churches
BDCM	*Biographical Dictionary of Christian Missions*, ed. Anderson (New York: Macmillan, 1998)
BEM	*Baptism, Eucharist and Ministry*, WCC/CFO (Geneva: WCC, 1982)
BWA	Baptist World Alliance
CADEC	Christian Action for Development in the Caribbean
Canberra 1991	Seventh Assembly of the WCC, Canberra, Australia, 3–25 February 1991
CBMS	Conference of British Missionary Societies
CC	*The Christian Century*
CCA	Christian Conference of Asia
CCBI	Council of Churches for Britain and Ireland
CCC	Church of Christ in China; also China Christian Council
CCIA	Commission of the Churches on International Affairs
CCJCA	Caribbean Committee for Joint Christian Action
CCLA	Committee on Cooperation in Latin America
CEC	Conference of European Churches
CELA	Conferencia Evangélica Latinoamericana (Latin America Protestant Conference)

Abbreviations

CELAM	Conferencia Episcopal Latinoamericana (Latin American Bishops Conference)
CLAI	Consejo Latinamericano de Iglesias (Latin American Council of Churches)
CLS	Christian Literature Society
CMS	Church Missionary Society
CMN	*Congo Mission News*
CONELA	Confederacion Evangélica Latinoamericana (Latin American Evangelical Confederation)
COPEC	CEC Conference on Christian Politics, Economics and Citizenship, Burmingham, USA, 5–12 April 1924
CSI	Church of South India
CT	*Christianity Today*
CWC	Christian World Communions
CWM	Council for World Mission
DI	*Dominus Iesus*
DP	*Dialogue and Proclamation*
EA	Evangelical Alliance
EACC	East Asia Christian Conference
EATWOT	Ecumenical Association of Third World Theologians
Edinburgh 1910	World Missionary Conference, Edinburgh, Scotland, 14–23 June 1910
EDWM	*Evangelical Dictionary of World Missions*, ed. Moreau (Grand Rapids: Baker, 2000)
EFMA	Evangelical Foreign Missions Association
ER	*Ecumenical Review*
ERT	*Evangelical Review of Theology*
Evanston 1954	Second Assembly of the WCC, Evanston, USA, 15–31 August 1954
Faith and Order	The World Conference on Faith and Order
FCC	Federal Council of the Churches of Christ in America
FMC	Foreign Missions Conference of North America
FOP	Faith and Order Papers
GCOWE	Global Consultation on World Evangelization
Ghana 1957–58	Meeting of the IMC, Accra, Ghana, 28 December 1957—8 January 1958
GOTR	*Greek Orthodox Theological Review*
HEM	*A History of the Ecumenical Movement*, 3 vols. (Geneva: WCC, 1986–2004)
IBMR	*International Bulletin of Missionary Research*
ICCC	International Council of Christian Churches
IFMA	Interdenominational Foreign Mission Association
IMC	International Missionary Council
IRM	*International Review of Mission*

ISAL	Movimiento de Iglesia y Sociedad en América Latina (Church and Society Movement in Latin America)
IVCF	Inter-Varsity Christian Fellowship
IWM	Interchurch World Movement
Jerusalem 1928	Meeting of the IMC, Jerusalem, 24 March—8 April 1928
JC&S	*Journal of Church and State*
JES	*Journal of Ecumenical Studies*
JPTSup	*Journal of Pentecostal Theology* Supplement Series
Lausanne 1974	International Congress on World Evangelization (Lausanne I), Lausanne, Switzerland, 16–25 July 1974
Lausanne II	See Manila 1989
LCWE	Lausanne Committee for World Evangelization
Life and Work	The Universal Christian Council for Life and Work
LMS	London Missionary Society
LW	*Lutheran World*
LWF	Lutheran World Federation
Madras 1938	Meeting of the IMC, Tambaram, Madras, India, 12–29 December 1938
Manila 1989	International Congress on World Evangelization (Lausanne II), Manila, The Philippines, July 1989
MARC	Missions Advanced Research and Communications Center
ME	*Mission and Evangelism: An Ecumenical Affirmation*, WCC (Geneva: WCC, 1983)
Melbourne 1980	World Conference on Mission and Evangelism, Melbourne, Australia, 12–25 May 1980
MS	*Mission Studies*
M-S	*Mid-Stream*
NAE	National Association of Evangelicals (USA)
Nairobi 1975	Fifth Assembly of the WCC, Nairobi, Kenya, 28 November—10 December 1975
NCCUSA	National Council of the Churches of Christ in the USA
New Delhi 1961	Third Assembly of the WCC, New Delhi, India, 19 November—5 December 1961
NGO	nongovernmental organization
Oxford 1937	World Conference on Church, Community, and State, Oxford, UK, July 1937
PCC	Pacific Conference of Churches
RCC	Roman Catholic Church
RM	*Redemptoris Missio*
San Antonio 1989	The Conference on World Mission and Evangelism, San Antonio, USA, 22 May—1 June 1989
SCM	Student Christian Movement
SHCM	Studies in the History of Christian Missions

Abbreviations

SODEPAX	The Committee on Society, Development and Peace
SPCK	Society for Promoting Christian Knowledge
SPG	Society for the Propagation of the Gospel in Foreign Parts
Stockholm 1925	First Meeting of the Universal Christian Council on Life and Work, Stockholm, Sweden, 19–30 August 1925
SVM	Student Volunteer Movement
SW	*Student World*
Tambaram	See Madras 1938
TSPM	Three-Self Patriotic Movement
UBS	United Bible Societies
UDHR	Universal Declaration of Human Rights
UN	United Nations Organization
UNELAM	Movimiento Latinoamericano Pro-Unidad Evangélica (Latin American Movement for Protestant Unity)
Uppsala 1968	Fourth Assembly of the WCC, Uppsala, Sweden, 4–20 July 1968
Vancouver 1983	Sixth Assembly of the WCC, Vancouver, Canada, 24 July—10 August 1983
Vatican 2	Second Vatican Council, held in several sessions, Vatican City, 12 October 1962—8 December 1965
WACC	World Association for Christian Communication
WARC	World Alliance of Reformed Churches
WCC	World Council of Churches
WCC/A	WCC Assembly
WCC/CC	WCC Central Committee
WCC/CFO	WCC Commission on Faith and Order
WCC/CWME	WCC Commission on World Mission and Evangelism
WCC/DWME	WCC Division on World Mission and Evangelism
WCE	*World Christian Encyclopedia*, ed. Barrett, Johnson, and Kurian, 2 vols. (2nd ed.; New York: Oxford University Press, 2001)
WEA	World Evangelical Alliance
WEF	World Evangelical Fellowship
Willingen 1952	Enlarged Meeting of the Committee of the IMC, Willingen, Germany, 1952
Whitby 1947	Enlarged Meeting of the IMC and of the Committee of the Council, Whitby, Canada, 5–24 July 1947
WMC	World Methodist Council
World Alliance	The World Alliance for Promoting International Friendship through the Churches
WSCF	World's Student Christian Federation
YDSL	Yale Divinity School Library
YMCA	The Young Men's Christian Association
YWCA	The Young Women's Christian Association

Introduction

WHAT THIS BOOK IS ABOUT

During the past two centuries two major developments of unprecedented proportion and power have given Christianity its distinctive character. One is the modern movement of Christian missions by which Christianity became a world faith. The second is the movement for Christian unity. This book is an analysis of the relationship between the two.

There is an inextricable link between these movements. Charles Ranson, in 1953 when he was general secretary of the International Missionary Council, expressed it well: "Wherever the Church recognizes itself as standing in a missionary situation, the question of unity becomes vital. The complacency of the Churches concerning their disunity can only be accounted for by the loss of the conviction that the Church exists to fulfill a mission. It was not an accident that the foundations of the modern ecumenical movement, with its concern for Christian unity, were laid by the organized missionary enterprise."[1]

What did the modern missionary movement contribute to understandings and work for Christian unity? How did it help persons to understand and accept their unity as part of one human family which includes persons of various faiths and ideologies? This study hopes to provide the first comprehensive answers to these questions. It is designed to be a history and reference work on mission and unity from 1792 to 2010.

HOW THIS BOOK IS STRUCTURED

Almost fifty years ago Henry Pitney Van Dusen wrote *One Great Ground of Hope: Christian Missions and Christian Unity*. A strong advocate for the ecumenical movement, Van Dusen took a normative approach to

1. Ranson, *World*, 123.

his subject, advocating two particular models of unity—the conciliar approach of interchurch cooperation with representation from each participating body, and organic church union. Most leaders from within mainline Protestantism have equated ecumenism with these two models of Christian unity.[2]

How have Christians cooperated or united in mission? This author began his twenty years of research for this study with this question. He chose a descriptive and analytical approach—not a normative one. This approach recognizes that multiple approaches to Christian unity have been tried in the past and are advocated today. Ecumenism in the Roman Catholic Church, the world confessional families, world evangelicalism, regional ecumenism, and the vibrant expressions of local ecumenism—all are significant models of Christian unity. Each of these has been deeply influenced by the missionary movement.

There are many variables that could be used for delineating models of Christian unity. This book focuses on two—the spatial (geographic) and the organizational. The spatial represents a continuum from local, to national/regional, to global. The organizational is a continuum from voluntary/informal, to cooperative/conciliar, to institutional/formal.[3]

Next, my study of the literature of ecumenism revealed ten models of Christian unity—one for each spatial/organizational alternative, with one exception. Both the world confessional and world conciliar models fall into the same square of the grid. This coalescence will be analyzed as competing models of Christian unity, with such competition both influenced by, and influencing, the modern missionary movement and the self-understanding of denominations including united churches.[4]

The following chart is a two-dimensional presentation of the ten models. The organizational dimension is on the horizontal axis, and the spatial is on the vertical. The numbers indicate the book chapters in which each model will be treated:

---

2. See Castro, *Sent Free*; and Neill, "Plans."

3. See *International Encyclopedia of the Sciences*, s.v. "Voluntary Associations: Sociological Analysis" for a parallel two-dimensional scheme.

4. Earlier delineations of the organizational typology of associational, confessional, conciliar, and unitary models can be found in Crow, "Ecumenics"; Crow, "Reflections"; A. Dulles, "Unity," 116–21.

TABLE: Models of Christian Unity

		ORGANIZATIONAL			
S		Voluntary/ Informal	Cooperative/ Conciliar		Institutional/ Formal
P A	World/ Global	(9) *World Associations* (e.g., LCWE, World Vision)	(8) *World Communions* (e.g., LWF)	(7) *World Conciliar* (e.g., WCC)	(6) *World Churches* (e.g., RCC, SDA)
T I	Regional/ National	(10) *Regional/ National Associations* (e.g., Third World missions)	(11) *Regional/ National Councils* (e.g., EACC, AACC)		(12) *Regional/ National United Churches* (e.g., CSI, CCC, ECZ)
A L	Local	(13) *Local Associations* (e.g., BCCs, Taizé)	(13) *Local Councils* (e.g., local councils of churches)		(13) *Local United Churches* (e.g., union churches)

This volume is not intended to be a history of the ecumenical movement. The three volumes entitled *A History of the Ecumenical Movement* remain a reliable source.[5] Instead, this study is an interpretive essay on the contribution of the missionary movement to understandings of Christian unity and work for common Christian witness. Central themes will be identified with selected case studies to represent them. Primary attention will be given to the work of Protestant missionary societies and the concerns for mission and unity of the churches that they spawned in six continents. Work for unity in mission among evangelical and Pentecostal Protestants, Orthodox churches, and the Roman Catholic Church are included. Recognizing that the missionary movement includes sectarian and anti-ecumenical elements, consideration

---

5. Vol. 1: *1517–1948*, ed. Rouse and Neill; vol. 2: *The Ecumenical Advance: 1948–1968*, ed. Fey; vol. 3: *1968–2000*, ed. Briggs, Oduyoye, Tsetsis.

will be given to these rip tides that appear to run counter to the prevailing tide of Christian missions towards unity.

WHAT THE READER SHOULD KNOW

By *missions* we shall refer to organized missionary work. Accepting that the mission of the universal church is to the whole inhabited world, and that all Christians in every continent are called to participate in that mission, often the term *mission* has replaced *missions*. In this study the older term shall be retained as it was commonly used throughout most of the history covered, but assuming the newer understanding of the church's mission as a mutual responsibility of all. The term *missionary movement* shall be used to refer to all efforts by the missions for joint planning and action.[6]

Unity shall refer to oneness, singleness, or accord among Christians of different traditions. Sometimes the result is *church union*, also called *organic union*, in which two or more previously separate denominations unite to become a single new denomination.[7]

The word *ecumenical* has multiple meanings. The original Greek word *oikoumene*, found in the New Testament, referred to the whole inhabited world or to the whole of the Roman Empire. In the early Christian church it came to mean the whole church. With the divisions of the Western and Eastern churches (Roman Catholic and Orthodox), and later the multiplication of denominations spawned by the Protestant Reformation, *ecumenical* came increasingly to refer to the goal and efforts to achieve worldwide Christian unity. To speak of being part of one human family is consistent with the original meaning of *oikoumene*. In this study the term *wider ecumenism* will be used for this connotation, and applied both to the secular efforts through the United Nations and other international bodies to strengthen organizations serving the global human family, and to the efforts of persons of differing faiths to understand and work with each other.[8]

The worldwide missionary movement, which is the subject of this volume, influenced three streams of world ecumenical cooperation in the twentieth century: Faith and Order, Life and Work, and the International

---

6. *Webster's Third New International Dictionary*, s.v. "missions"; Crane, "Dropping the S."
7. Barrett, ed., *World Christian Encyclopedia*, 847, 837.
8. For seven meanings of "ecumenical" see Visser t' Hooft, "Word 'Ecumenical.'"

Missionary Council. In the second half of the century their mergers in 1948 and 1961 became known as the *ecumenical movement*. It is that concerted effort "for cooperation and unity which seeks to manifest the fundamental unity and universality of the Church of Christ." The World Council of Churches is one part of that movement. Others are national and regional Christian fellowships and councils, world confessional bodies, and other associations for Christian fellowship, consultation, and joint action. Organic unions of churches are one conspicuous outcome. Unfortunately, the term *ecumenical movement* has been so identified with the WCC by its critics that they no longer accept it as expressing their own response to Christ's prayer that they may be one. The broader definition will be used in this study.[9]

Research for this study was exhausting but not exhaustive. Sources, both primary and secondary, are too numerous for full coverage. While indebted to many scholars for interpretations given, the totality of the argument is the author's own. It is hoped that this study, based on archival and library research, will provide readers with exposure to primary sources and case studies, and motivate some to engage in further research related to the themes presented.

---

9. Ibid., 740.

PART ONE
Historical

1

William Carey's Pleasing Dream and Its Antecedents

On May 15, 1806, William Carey, the pioneer Baptist missionary to India, wrote from Calcutta to Andrew Fuller, secretary of the Baptist Missionary Society:

> The Cape of Good Hope is now in the hands of the English; should it continue so, would it not be possible to have a general association of all denominations of Christians, from the four quarters of the world, kept there once in about ten years? I earnestly recommend this plan, let the first meeting be in the Year 1810, or 1812 at furthest. I have no doubt but it would be attended with very important effects; we could understand one another better, and more entirely enter into one another's views by two hours conversation than by two or three years epistolary correspondence.[1]

Two months later Carey outlined his plan to his neighbor Henry Martyn, the Anglican chaplain in Calcutta. Martyn was very much pleased with the idea "not on account of its practicality, but [because of] its grandeur."[2]

However, Andrew Fuller rejected the proposal, declaring that "in a meeting of all denominations, there would be no unity, without which we had better stay at home."[3] He represented the dominant view of the period that Christians of different denominations could not meet without quarreling and thereby intensifying their differences.

---

1. Quoted in Latourette, "Ecumenical Bearings," 355.
2. Martyn, *Journals and Letters*; quoted in Hogg, *Foundations*, 17.
3. Andrew Fuller to William Ward, Serampore, December 2, 1806; quoted in Rouse, "Voluntary Movements," 315.

The seed of what Ruth Rouse has called "the most startling missionary proposal of all time" had fallen on stony ground. Walls of division—the results of historic church conflicts—remained intact. Yet for missionaries working among the Bengalis of Calcutta, or later among the Chinese of Canton, or in other fields, such divisions increasingly were judged to be both unbiblical and unnecessary.[4]

REVOLUTION AND RELIGIOUS DISSENT

Carey was not the only visionary in 1806. In that year Napoleon Bonaparte had his own vision—that of military conquest. In 1806 sixteen minor German states formed the Confederation of the Rhine, throwing their futures in with Napoleon's ambitions. They were Napoleon's spoils of war following his victory at the battle of Austerlitz. Although the British had destroyed the French fleet at Trafalgar in 1805, Napoleon's army, which had swept eastward in Europe, could now move westward again. Until his final defeat at Waterloo in 1815, Napoleon was to convulse the continent with his ambitions of empire.[5]

Earlier the ideals of the French Revolution had been welcomed by English Dissenters at a time when they were battling for religious liberty. Carey, serving as secretary of the Dissenters' Committee in 1790, watched France's awesome drama with sympathy and hope as "a movement towards a completer humanity." At first he believed it was "God's answer" and that "a glorious door opened, and likely to be opened much wider, for the gospel, by the spread of civil and religious liberty, and by the diminution of the papal power." Carey hoped that religious liberty would spread from France to England. Parliament's rejection of a motion to repeal the detested Test and Corporation Acts, which placed restrictions on Dissenters, could only have reinforced Carey's radical opinions.[6]

Carey's "radicalism," however, was that of a stalwart defense of religious liberty, which had been and remained a hallmark of religious independency, especially among Quakers and Baptists. The old dissenting sects, which 140 years earlier had provided foot soldiers for Cromwell's army, had become more prosperous and less politically radi-

---

4. Rouse, "William Carey's 'Pleasing Dream,'" 181. Rouse's article is an imaginative projection of what might have happened in missions and unity *if* Carey's proposal had been implemented.

5. Semmel, *Revolution*, 111.

6. S. Carey, *Carey*, 7; Drewery, *Carey*, 34.

cal. Presbyterians and Independents were strongest in the commercial and wool manufacturing centers, while Baptists attracted small tradesmen, small farmers, and rural laborers. All these dissenters were inspired to holiness of life by reading John Bunyan's *Pilgrim's Progress* more than to political action by reading Thomas Paine's *Rights of Man*.[7]

Élie Halévy believed that England was spared a political revolution, toward which her contradictory polity and economy might have led her, through the stabilizing effect of evangelical religion. "The influence of Methodism," the French social historian wrote, "contributed a great deal, during the last years of the eighteenth century, to preventing the French Revolution from having an English counterpart."[8]

At the time, however, the jury was still out. On the one hand, John Wesley remained an Anglican clergyman and a good Tory throughout his life. In contrast to other Dissenters, he had defended Lord North against the American revolutionists at some considerable cost to his fledgling movement there. On the other hand, Methodism in England attracted many of the working class who shared political grievances and the appeals of the radicals. After Wesley's death in 1791, many politicians and Anglican clergy reacted with paranoia at the prospect of there being over 100,000 Methodists under the tight discipline of their Committee of One Hundred. They were the only body of organized people capable of making a revolution.

Halévy argued cogently that Methodism aroused the passions of England's working class, but for revival and reform—not political revolution. The concern for a new morality spread from them to other Dissenters, and through the evangelicals into the Church of England. The visible expression of this new persuasion was to be found in the activities of voluntary associations.[9]

On June 1, 1792, the Baptist Association, meeting in Nottingham, approved the groundbreaking proposition of Andrew Fuller "for forming a Baptist Society for propagating the Gospel among the Heathens." The next day the Nottingham weekly *Journal* was filled with the latest developments of the revolution in France, riots in Birmingham, and executions at Newgate. The action taken by the Baptist Association

---

7. Thompson, *Making*, 28–30.
8. Semmel, "Introduction," 1; Halévy, *Birth*, 51.
9. Simmel, "Introduction," 12, 18–19.

did not even rate a line, yet would be an event remembered over two hundred years.[10]

It is significant that the voluntary associations for missions developed in the eighteenth century in those states in Europe in which religious toleration had been accepted. The dream of a Christian society, a *corpus Christianum*, cherished by many throughout the Middle Ages, was not entirely shattered by the sixteenth-century Reformation. Calvin's Geneva, while a haven for oppressed Protestants, was also to be a holy commonwealth of those who believed in a common catechism. Dissenters were to be expelled or, like Servetus, exterminated. Menno Simons, the Anabaptist, faced persecution from both Roman Catholics and Lutherans. The turmoil of the Thirty Years War (1618–1648) was ended not by guarantees of religious freedom, but by the power of the ruler to determine the faith of all his subjects—the principle of *cujus regio, ejus religio*. The resulting state-church pattern, whether Protestant or Catholic, did not encourage independency.[11]

In the seventeenth and eighteenth centuries two new factors provided the seedbed for voluntarism in missions. The first was colonialism. Once European powers ventured to the East, where subject peoples could not be converted by the sword, they accepted a *de facto* religious plurality. British North America posed a special situation, where almost all the chief European strains of Christianity were present yet none was in the ascendancy. This provided a second seedbed—the recognition of a plurality of churches and ultimately a separation of church and state.[12]

CAREY'S MISSION ANTECEDENTS

His imagination fired by reports of the voyages of Captain Cook, William Carey hoped that he might serve his Master in the South Pacific. In doing so he was part of the long line of missionaries from St. Paul onwards who heard the call "to come over and help us." Since fifteenth-century explorations were sponsored largely by the rulers of Spain and Portugal, the first link of missions with colonialism was by Roman Catholics. By the seventeenth century, Dutch and English commercial companies joined in the competition for trade with the East, and added chaplains to

---

10. Drewery, *Carey*, 40.
11. Latourette, *History of Christianity*, 785, 884, 974.
12. Latourette, *History of Expansion*, 4:186–214; Neill, *Colonialism*, 70–77.

their payrolls. Initially they ministered to company employees, but often branched out to work with local peoples, as with the Dutch in Java.[13]

Royal and Company Initiatives

Anglicans led in ecumenical initiatives in mission in the eighteenth century. The Society for Promoting Christian Knowledge (SPCK), founded in 1698, maintained close connections in cooperation with Lutheran and Reformed churches on the continent and with their clergy who had recognition as Corresponding Members. Using the corporate model, Anglicans established in 1701 the Society for the Propagation of the Gospel in Foreign Parts (SPG). An incorporated society with royal charter, its main work was to care for Anglicans while overseas in the Caribbean or North America. However, missionaries were also to be sent to work with Native Americans, and with the slaves being brought from Africa. During the same period King Frederick IV of Denmark took royal initiative to send missionaries to the tiny Danish settlement of Tranquebar on India's southeast coast. Lacking Danes ready to serve, he asked the Pietist leader at the University of Halle in Germany, August Hermann Francke, to help. Bartholomäus Ziegenbalg and Henry Plütschau, Francke's former Halle students, responded, reaching India in 1706 as the first non-Roman Catholic missionaries there. From 1710 to 1728 the SPCK contributed financial support for them. From 1728 to 1825 it employed or partially supported some sixty missionaries to work in "the English mission"—all of whom had received Lutheran ordination. Another early form of cooperation was that of Lutherans Pietists from Halle serving a German-speaking parish in London in cooperation with Anglicans.[14]

Moravians

Count Nikolaus Ludwig von Zinzendorf, early leader of the Moravians, tied mission and unity together from the beginning of their missions. In 1742 the Moravians began missions to native North Americans in the New York colony. Their pacifism during years of war, and their identification with the people, led to the enmity of white settlers, clashes with civil authorities, and ultimately the massacres of the native peoples that

---

13. Drewery, *Carey*, 35; Neill, *History of Missions*, 140–209, 224.
14. Neill, *History of Missions*, 227–30; Sykes, "Ecumenical Movements," 160–61. See also Brunner, *Halle Pietists*, for a full historical account.

finally ended their creative mission effort.[15] James Hutton, an early associate of John Wesley and founder of English Moravianism, wrote in 1769 that the Moravians zeal for "conversion of the heathen" had its origin in their belief "that our Saviour had died for the whole world, and would have all men to be saved by the knowledge of the truth, which he had ordered to be preached to all nations." The Moravians were to exert a strong ecumenical impulse in Continental Europe, Great Britain, and North America in the decades that followed.[16]

Countess of Huntington

Often overlooked by historians is an influential yet failed mission sponsored by Selina Hastings, the Countess of Huntington and an evangelical member of the Church of England. After the death of her husband (in 1746 or 1747), Lady Huntingdon joined John Wesley and George Whitefield in the work of the Great Revival. Whitefield became her personal chaplain, who upon his death in 1770 bequeathed to her an orphanage and estate that he had founded in the colony of Georgia. Although a slave owner herself, having inherited overseas estates, Lady Huntington passionately supported freed slaves, and directed her missionary party of 1772 to reorganize Whitefield's orphanage and initiate new work among both slaves and Native Americans in the Georgia colony. A series of misfortunes, including the Revolutionary War, terminated the work. In 1787 Thomas Haweis served concurrently as rector of an Anglican parish and as chaplain to Lady Huntington's chapel in Bath, England. He proposed to her that she send graduates of the ministers' training college that she founded as pioneer missionaries to the South Seas. Her death in 1791 came too soon for her to carry out this dream, but Haweis became one of the four executors of her estate, and as cofounder of the London Missionary Society (LMS) in 1795 was instrumental in ensuring that Tahiti was their first field to be evangelized.[17]

Thomas Coke

As early as 1784 Thomas Coke, John Wesley's world evangelist, proposed the establishing of a charitable society for the promotion of foreign missions. It was designed to be undenominational and to act with the

---

15. For a full account see Westmeier, *Shekomeko*; idem., "Becoming."
16. Hutton, *Letter*, 4; quoted in Semmel, *Revolution*, 148.
17. Payne, *Church Awakes*, 103–5; Harding, *Countess*, 205–11.

freedom of a private voluntary company. No reference was made to Mr. Wesley or the Methodist Conference. Although predating Carey's movement by eight years, and the establishment of the similar London Missionary Society by eleven, it met with minimal response.

Undeterred, Coke began his own missionary labors. The intrepid voyager for Christ was driven by storms in 1786 from his course to Nova Scotia and landed instead on the island of Antigua where he succeeded in establishing a church. By 1790 Coke's mission had spread sufficiently to other Caribbean islands for the British Methodists to declare the West Indies a separate province.[18]

The ferment of Protestants for missions grew slowly but steadily in the eighteenth century in England and on the Continent, including cooperative efforts across sectarian lines. It was William Carey who would be the catalyst to spread that yeast throughout Protestantism with practical suggestions for action.

CAREY'S CONTRIBUTION

"Go into all the world, and preach the gospel to every creature." With this reminder of the Great Commission, Carey in 1792 began his book *An Enquiry into the Obligations of Christians to Use Means for the Conversion of the Heathens*. For him Jesus' Great Commission was "as extensive as possible." Christ's followers were "to disperse themselves into every country of the habitable globe, and preach to all the inhabitants, without exception, or limitation." What later became commonplace was radical in Carey's time. The existing mission societies had confined themselves to particular fields. In Kenneth Scott Latourette's judgment it was the young English shoemaker-teacher-clergyman "who first dreamed persistently of the needs of the entire human race and called upon his fellow Christians to make the dream come true."[19]

Theologically Carey favored a united effort, but he recognized the practical necessity of working through the prevailing sectarian structures. In proposing to form a voluntary mission society in 1792, he did not desire to confine it to one denomination. "I wish with all my heart," he wrote, "that everyone who loves our Lord Jesus Christ in sincerity, would in some way or other engage in it." But he went on to recognize "the present divided state of Christendom." More good would be done,

18. Findley and Holdsworth, *History*, 1:64–65; 2:27–62.
19. W. Carey, *Enquiry*, 7; Latourette, *History of Expansion*, 4:69.

he continued, by a united rather than separate effort. Competition should be avoided, with good will expressed to each other. Above all a concert of prayer should bind the hearts of Christians together, as prayer is "perhaps the only thing in which Christians of all denominations can cordially and unreservedly unite."[20]

Carey's conviction that prayer is the cement of Christian unity in mission came directly from the influence on him of the writings of Jonathan Edwards and David Brainerd. In response to Edwards' *Humble Attempt*,[21] Carey in 1784, with other Scottish evangelical pastors in fervent prayer for revival and mission, called at that time for a "Concert of Prayer." He also began to read Edwards' *An Account of the Life of the Late Reverend David Brainerd* (1749). During his first years in India, Carey was to read daily from this account of the pioneer missionary to Native Americans. For Carey, Brainerd was the exemplary missionary whose life was sustained by earnest prayer. Timothy George, in his biography of Carey, concluded that "in many respects the writings of Jonathan Edwards were the single most important theological influence on Fuller, Carey, and the English Baptists who launched the modern missionary movement."[22]

Carey, a convert from the Anglican Church through personal study of the Bible, believed that Baptists had a special contribution to make through their commitment to the authority of Scripture. His writings are replete with criticisms of various denominations. All fail to measure up. The solution of turning to prayer for guidance, however, was not a pious platitude for Carey. Instead he believed that prayer had the potential to unite the hearts of Christians so that they would be open to common action. "Were the whole body thus animated by one soul," he wrote, "with what pleasure would Christians attend on all the duties of religion." The missionary calling had prevailed over his proclivity to work solely with Baptists.[23]

20. W. Carey, *Enquiry*, 84, 81. For the relations with other groups of British Baptist missionaries in India see Potts, *Missionaries*, 49–61.
21. The full title gives a good idea of its contents: *An Humble Attempt to Promote an Explicit Agreement and Visible Union of God's People through the World, in Extraordinary Prayer, for the Revival of Religion, and the Advancement of Christ's Kingdom on Earth, Pursuant to Scripture-Promises and Prophecies Concerning the Last Time* (1747). It is reprinted in J. Edwards, *Apocalyptic Writings*. See Beaver, "Concert," for its wider influence on unity in missions.
22. George, *Witness*; Davies, "Edwards."
23. W. Carey, *Enquiry*, 81; Hinson, "Carey," 73–75. See also Stanley, *History*, 9–67, for a fuller account of Carey's contribution.

Carey envisioned a voluntary association of Christians committed to the church's mission. His model was that of a commercial trading company that obtains a charter, recruits partners, and selects with care goods to sell, ships, and crewmembers. Such companies sought every scrap of information required. They took risks and endured dangers because their minds were set on success. Likewise, Carey continued, Christians are a body "whose truest interest lies in the exaltation of the Messiah's kingdom." They too have a charter. Like a trading company they can carefully collect funds, select missionaries, and equip them for their work. An "instrumental" society would be required to do this, for existing church structures, whether Anglican parish or Free Church congregation, could not.[24]

Carey's "pleasing dream" of 1805 was a logical expansion of this commercial analogy. An association, once established, seeks partnership with others to fulfill its mission. The Kingdom task involves the acceptance of different denominations, the agreement to meet regularly with their representatives, and the cooperative use of scarce resources.

Toward the end of his missionary career, in 1822 Carey experienced a partial realization of his ecumenical vision in the founding of Serampore College. It was not just for Baptists, but open to every Christian denomination in Asia, "whether Protestant, Roman Catholic, the Greek or Armenian." For the purpose of study, it also included Muslim and Hindu youth.[25]

Carey's larger ecumenical vision, however, had been sown in rocky ground. Not until the nineteenth century would it begin to sprout in new forms of missionary cooperation, which in the twentieth century would achieve their full flowering.

---

24. W. Carey, *Enquiry*, 81–83; Walls, "Missionary Societies," 145–46.
25. Quoted in Champion, "Carey," 57; Potts, *Missionaries*, 129–35.

2

Evangelicals and Unity, 1792–1845

THE EVANGELICAL AWAKENING

To many observers Christianity had an insecure future in the closing years of the eighteenth century. Spain and Portugal, the countries chiefly responsible for Catholic expansion of Christianity to Asia, Africa, and the Americas, were in decline. The Society of Jesus was expelled from Portuguese, Spanish, and French territories, and then dissolved by Pope Clement XIV in 1773. New Christians in Japan were persecuted, while beachheads in China were eroded. In Europe the Enlightenment, with its rationalism antagonistic to Christianity, numbed religious conviction and cooled enthusiasm. Religious life declined in the American colonies following their rebellion from Great Britain, while the French Revolution and Napoleonic Wars destabilized church and state in Europe.[1]

Through the darkened skies, however, a light shone. A religious Awakening (*Erweckung*) took place from Eastern Europe to the American colonies. It differed from country to country, although communications and migrations extended its rays. Although origins and influences differed, the Awakening had a common spirit and motivation. Persons experienced the saving love of God in Jesus Christ. They felt that all persons everywhere had need of Christ. Their passion was evangelism—to share the Good News of salvation at home and to the ends of the earth.[2]

The Awakening created a sense of togetherness among Christians of different churches and nationalities. It was a pan-Protestant phenomenon. The redeemed shared a fundamental understanding of Christian

---

1. Latourette, *History of Expansion*, 3:454–57.
2. Rouse, "Voluntary Movements," 309. For details of the eighteenth-century Awakening from Eastern Europe to the American colonies see Ward, *Awakening*, 54–240.

unity. All saved persons shared a common life in Christ. They were one by virtue of this sharing. This oneness, they believed, was the essential Christian unity.

Wherever persons moved from their ancestral homelands they might become more receptive to interconfessional connections. In the northern German states, as well as Denmark and the Netherlands, persons of differing backgrounds lived side by side: Catholics, Lutherans, and Reformed—even Jews. Nowhere did the sense of denominational distinctiveness wane faster than in the colonies that would become the United States. Intermarriages became more frequent. The flame of the Awakening spread most rapidly there.[3]

THE RISE OF PROTESTANT MISSIONARY SOCIETIES

In 1837 Rufus Anderson, secretary of the American Board of Commissioners for Foreign Missions, described the unique features of the Protestant voluntary associations. They were not restricted to clergy or members of one profession. Instead all were free to join so long as they contributed their support. For Anderson "this Protestant form of association—free, open, responsible, embracing all classes, both sexes, all ages, the masses of the people—is peculiar to modern times, and almost to our age." In the recent judgment of Andrew Walls this development was the "fortunate subversion" of the church, enabling it to break out of the maintenance agendas of the parishes to be in mission.[4]

Great Britain

LONDON MISSIONARY SOCIETY (LMS)

William Carey, broadminded as he was, still thought it best to work on a denominational basis. Other British evangelicals disagreed. The LMS, formed in 1795 as The Missionary Society, was designed as an interdenominational organization. An organizing committee had sent letters "all over England to all the Evangelical Churches of different denominations" inviting them to the organizational meetings. They had been influenced in doing so by Melville Horne's *Letters on Mission*, published the previous year. Horne proposed forming a new missionary society that would exclude no evangelical: "Let liberal Churchmen

---

3. Rouse, "Voluntary Movements," 310; Ward, *Awakening*, 24–54.
4. R. Anderson, *Advance*, 65; Walls, *Missionary Movement*, 141–42.

and Conscientious Dissenters, pious Calvinists and pious Arminians, embrace with fraternal arms." The vision was to include evangelical Anglicans; that's why the new board decided "to wait on the Evangelical Clergy of the Establishment to request their support."[5]

With imagination the organizers launched the new Society at a series of public meetings. Reporters described the atmosphere as "a new Pentecost" and found "unspeakably delightful . . . the visible union of ministers and Christians of all denominations who, for the first time, forgetting their party prejudices and partialities, assembled in the same place, sang the same hymns, united in the same prayers, and felt themselves one in Christ." At the closing service, Dr. David Bogue exhorted "we are called together to *the funeral of bigotry*," and hoped that "it would be buried so deep as never to rise again," and with applause "the whole vast body of people manifested their concurrence, and could scarcely refrain from one general shout of joy."[6]

From its beginning the Society was distinctive in its intent to be nondenominational. Its "fundamental principle," adopted in 1795, was "that its design is not to send Presbyterianism, Independency, Episcopacy, or any other form of church order and government." Missionaries were free "to assume for themselves such a form of church government as to them shall appear most agreeable to the word of God."[7]

From the beginning, the Society tried to gain broad support for its work, not only in England, but elsewhere. It sent a full account of its founding to ministers and friends in Scotland and to churches on the Continent seeking their cooperation. Back came "letters of sympathy and liberal contributions from Rotterdam, Basel, Frankfurt, and Norrköping [Sweden]." Soon affiliates developed in Edinburgh, Rotterdam, East Friesland (Germany), and the Cape of Good Hope (South Africa). Each contributed generous support, with the South African affiliate supporting John T. Vanderkamp of Holland and other missionaries. Board minutes show that it accepted three German missionaries in 1801 for service in the Cape of Good Hope, and five from Berlin in 1810. In 1815, upon the opening of a missionary seminary in Basel, Switzerland, the Society sent financial support and began to consider sending its graduates, regardless of nationality or denomination, as the Society's missionaries.[8]

---

5. Quoted in Piggin, *Missionaries*, 108; A-CMS, W. Summer to Mr. Elliott.
6. Lovett, *History*, 1:35, 38.
7. Quoted in Thorogood, "Call," in *Gales*, 242.
8. Lovett, *History*, 1:75–77; A-CWM, "LMS: Board Minutes," boxes 3 (21 September 1801), 5 (19 November 1810), 7 (20 November 1815).

By 1818, when the Society began to call itself the London Missionary Society, it had become predominately a Congregational mission agency. Most evangelical Anglicans had switched their support to the Church Missionary Society upon its founding in 1799. Baptists and Methodists favored denominational missions. The majority of LMS missionaries to India before 1859 who were not Congregationalists were drawn from various Presbyterian churches in Scotland. As the rigidity of denominationalism increased, the ecumenical vision of the LMS remained a historical achievement of its founding, but not a continuing reality.[9]

Church Missionary Society (CMS)

Evangelical Anglicans in Britain, feeling that the SPG and SPCK represented the "High Church tendency," formed their own society in 1799. Called initially the Society for Missions to Africa and the East, it soon became the Church Missionary Society.[10]

During the next fifty years the CMS became a major project in intercultural Christian cooperation in missions. Of the twenty-four CMS missionaries sent out by 1816, seventeen were Germans and only three were ordained English clergy. In the most dangerous field, West Africa, the totals are even more striking—all missionaries sent, except one schoolmaster, were Germans. By 1824 the CMS had sent one hundred missionaries overseas, one third of whom were from the European mainland. Strikingly, of the seventy CMS missionaries with long service between 1824 and 1840, almost half were non-British by nationality. Among them were such noted pioneers as Johann Ludwig Krapf and Johannes Rebmann in East Africa, Samuel Gobat in Ethiopia (later the second Anglo-Prussian bishop of Jerusalem), David Hinderer among the Yoruba of Nigeria, and C. G. Pfander in northern India.[11]

The Basel Mission was the CMS's main partner, supplying one hundred missionaries from 1815 to 1860. The Evangelical Revival that spawned the formation of Protestant mission societies in Great Britain was also occurring all over Protestant Europe. In Basel, Switzerland, it found a receptive seedbed in the *Deutsche Christentumsgesellschaft* (German Christianity Society), which had begun in 1780 as a focus of Pietist thought and activity. It supported a number of philanthropic orga-

---

9. Piggin, *Missionaries*, 109–10.
10. Berg, *Constrained*, 134–37.
11. Walls, "Missionary Vocation," 151; Jenkins, "Church Missionary Society," 43–48.

nizations believed to carry out God's will through hospitals, orphanages, a Bible society, a teacher training college, two organizations for Christian witness to Jews, and the Basel Mission founded in 1815.[12]

Contact between Basel and London was facilitated by the German Lutheran pastor K. F. A. Steinkopf, who, after being secretary of the Basel *Christentumsgesellschaft* from 1795 to 1801, pastored for fifty-eight years a Lutheran parish in London, and from 1804 served as foreign secretary of the British and Foreign Bible Society.[13]

The CMS/Basel Mission agreement called for Basel to provide an agreed number of missionaries, with the CMS providing an agreed amount towards the cost of their training. CMS concern in the early 1820s for a stronger general, literary, and theological education (including Latin, Greek, and Hebrew) encouraged Basel to add to their post-primary vocational training a five-year mission seminary program.[14]

The cooperative venture waned in the 1860s as British recruitment of missionaries became more adequate, and Anglicans and Lutherans heightened their confessional consciousness. Nevertheless, the CMS sent jubilee greetings to the Basel Mission. Concerning their fifty years of relationship they wrote: "Our link to one another has been a witness for the power . . . of evangelical truth and life which enables Protestant churches, although different in the organisations of their churches, to unite in the work of the extension of the Kingdom of Christ."[15]

Continental Europe

As in Great Britain, missionary interest arose on the Continent in this period with significant cooperative efforts among the churches. Contact with the British missionary movement often was one impetus. Another came through indigenous sources largely of Pietist and Moravian origin.

HOLLAND

As early as 1797 Dutch Protestants launched the Netherlands Missionary Society (*Nederlandsche Zendelinggenootschap*) with strong connections with the LMS in England. John Theodore Vanderkemp, renewed in faith

---

12. Ibid., 51–52.
13. Q.v. "Steinkopf" in *BDCM*.
14. Jenkins, "Church Missionary Society," 53, 57–58.
15. Schlatter, *Geschichte*, 1:84.

following the tragic death by accident of his wife and daughter, offered to go to South Africa as an LMS missionary. Before departure he helped form the Society with members drawn principally from the Dutch Reformed Church, in close association with the LMS. It remained the only Dutch missionary society in the first half of the nineteenth century.

The British Baptist Missionary Society organized a network of continental colporteurs (literature distributors) and representatives in many countries on the Continent, including the Netherlands, with the NZ cooperating and giving its blessing to fundraising efforts. This example stimulated other European churches, such as the Dutch Mennonites, to organize their own missionary societies. Dutch Mennonites, in turn, were involved in the *Reveil* (Awakening), a pan-European movement. The feeling of "oneness in Spirit" enabled the ecumenical dynamic to cross both confessional and national boundaries.[16]

Germany

From those of the Pietist tradition arose renewed interest in missions in Germany in the early nineteenth century. The call by the LMS for recruits from the continent stimulated Pastor Johann Jänicke to found a missionary training school in Berlin in 1800. Quickly he became connected with the Moravians of Herrnhut, and with Halle and its mission in India. With support from earnest Protestants in various regions of Germany and Britain, he prepared missionaries to serve under the LMS, CMS, and the Netherlands Missionary Society.

After 1815 German Protestants established close links with the missionary training center in Basel, Switzerland. A number of regional and local mission societies formed as Basel auxiliaries. Several in the Rhineland merged in 1828 to form the Rhenish Missionary Society (*Rheinishe Missionsgesellschaft*), which brought together Lutheran and Reformed Christians. The auxiliary in Dresden in 1836 became the nucleus of the Evangelical Lutheran Mission there (later moved to Leipzig to become the *Evangelisch-lutherische Mission zu Leipzig*). It attempted, with only partial success, to unite Lutherans throughout Germany in support of its work. In 1838 several Basel affiliate societies combined to form the North German Missionary Society (*Norddeutsche Missionsgesellschaft*).

---

16. Shenk, *By Faith*, 36–37; Hoekema, *Dutch Mennonite*, 9–12.

Scandinavia

Among the rest of the new European mission societies formed during this period, that in Sweden was the most notable example of interdenominational cooperation. Formed in 1835, the Swedish Missionary Society (*Svenska Missionsförbundet*) included on its board Lutherans, Swedish Moravian Brethren, and English Wesleyans. It not only sponsored its own foreign missionaries, but also sent support to Moravians, the Basel Missionary Society, and the LMS and Wesleyan Methodists in England. The Danish Missionary Society (*Danske Missionsselskab*), during the first decade after its founding in 1821, supported not only clergy for Greenland, but also missionaries serving under the Basel Mission on the Gold Coast of West Africa. The Norwegian Missionary Society (*Det Norske Missionsselskab*), founded in 1842, established working relationships with the Moravians and with the Basel and Rhenish missionary societies. The Finnish and French Protestant societies, formed in the latter half of the nineteenth century, continued the pattern of sponsorship by various Protestant churches and support of various mission endeavors beyond their own.[17]

United States

Student Initiatives

The first major impetus to the foreign missionary enterprise in the United States arose out of student life. Although Massachusetts Baptists formed a missionary society in 1802, to be followed by that of Congregationalists in 1804, their constitutions emphasized home missions, with efforts outside the United States to be conducted "as circumstances invite and ability permits." D. L. Leonard wrote of this period that "the horizon is evidently receding" and that "for some years to come almost all movements towards organization will be but local, or bounded by state lines." At Williams College in western Massachusetts—a college known more for irreligion than evangelical piety—a small student group began to pray in 1806 about the missionary demands of the Christian religion. Led by Samuel J. Mills, they, from under a haystack while caught in a thunderstorm, made their commitment to missions. By 1808 they formally organized as the "Society of Brethren" with the object "to effect in the persons of its members a mission or missions to the heathen."[18]

---

17. Latourette, *History of Expansion*, 4:89–93; Hogg, *Foundations*, 13–14.
18. Leonard, *Hundred*, 100.

American Board of Commissioners for Foreign Missions (ABCFM)

In response to the missionary enthusiasm of the two Andover Seminary students, Samuel Mills and Adoniram Judson, the Congregational Association of Massachusetts, together with leaders from Connecticut, organized in 1810 the Board of Commissioners for Foreign Missions—renamed the American Board of Commissioners for Foreign Missions when legally incorporated in 1812. At first they inquired of the LMS directors what its relation should be to the older body. While receptive to having North Americans as its missionaries, LMS leaders felt joint control on both sides of the Atlantic was impractical.

Like the LMS, the ABCFM was at first interdenominational and established as an independent association of individuals committed to missions. For more than twenty-five years this broad ecumenical spirit remained strong. The General Assembly of the Presbyterian Church, having no board of missions of its own, voted in 1812 to recognize the American Board as its overseas missions society. In 1817, however, it voted to join with the Reformed Church in America and the Associate Reformed Church in forming the United Foreign Missionary Society to work among Native Americans, the peoples of Mexico and South America, and those in other parts of the world. In 1826, with the encouragement of its supporters, that body united with the American Board.

In the 1830s a tide of denominationalism swept in. In 1832 the Reformed Church in America arranged that their missionaries serving under the American Board could found churches according to their own polity, as did the German Reformed Church in 1838. In 1837 the General Assembly of the Presbyterian Church created its own Board of Foreign Missions, joined by several antecedent Presbyterian mission societies. Nevertheless, some Presbyterian churches continued to engage in foreign missions through the American Board. Eventually only the Congregational Church remained as a sponsoring body, although it continued to unite groups of several denominations in cooperative mission projects.[19]

---

19. Latourette, *History of Expansion*, 4:77–86; Hogg, *Foundations*, 11–13.

CAN THE WEST BE WON? FRONTIER UNITY

Unity and mission in the United States had a distinctive character during this period due to the expansion of the nation beyond its initial thirteen colonies. Following independence in 1783 migration west of the Alleghany Mountains accelerated—a dynamic that continues to this day. The Louisiana Purchase of 1803 doubled the size of the nation. Between 1845 and 1848 the territorial advance was larger than old and powerful European states (Texas in 1845, the Oregon Territory in 1846, and the Southwest ceded by Mexico from the Texas border to Colorado and California in 1848).

The unchurched character of Western society became a mission challenge and opportunity for the churches. In 1801 a Connecticut native wrote, "The American Church is placed in a new and interesting situation; and there is a new and more solemn obligation than was ever found on Christians before, arising from the removal of our children into the wilderness."[20]

For the next century the West was considered to be a home mission field. Much of the evangelization of the West was by Methodist and Baptist lay leaders, itinerant evangelists and camp meetings, and circuit riders. Church mission leaders faced a dual challenge. How were they to evangelize and teach the Christian faith in a new subculture marked by secularism? How were they to express and experience oneness in Christ in churches tempted by sectarianism? They considered this mission to be their particular calling. For historian Sidney E. Ahlstrom the frontier of the United States is not a geographic region, but rather a process that began with the arrival of the Pilgrims in Massachusetts in 1620 and continues until today. The phrase *manifest destiny* is first credited to John O'Sullivan, who in 1845 coined it to signify the mission of the United States "to overspread the continent allotted by Providence for the free development of our yearly multiplying millions."[21]

In most cases evangelism and mission on the frontier was a free-for-all in the effort to win souls for Christ—be they migrants from the East coast, immigrants from other countries, blacks, or Native Americans. Baptists were eager to immerse any wayward Methodists they could find, while Methodist circuit riders were glad to welcome Calvinists into their

---

20. *Connecticut Evangelical Magazine* 1 (1801) 324; quoted in Goodykoontz, *Home Missions*, 18.
21. Ahlstrom, *Religious History*, 452.

fellowships. Some Christian leaders, however, sought to unite in mission. Their united effort took three forms during this period: cooperation of sister denominations, nondenominational voluntary societies, and new churches based on the unity principle.

Cooperation of Sister Churches

To minister to New England settlers in the "Old Northwest" (upstate New York to Illinois and Minnesota), Congregationalists and Presbyterians agreed to form united parishes in new settler communities. The 1801 Plan of Union was the first sustained church union effort in the country. Urgency to minister to Western migrants of their traditions convinced these two strong churches that they needed each other. As a later report declared, "The wants of the mission field . . . demanded the united efforts. . . . It was of the highest importance that there should be no denominational conflict or collision. The claims of missionary evangelization were felt by all parties to be paramount to all denominational interests." While the two denominations moved westward hand in hand, setting up overlapping associations and presbyteries, local congregations could be united, choosing pastors and their style of organization and discipline from either the Congregation or Presbyterian tradition. Later, a heightened denominational consciousness caused Presbyterians to vote against the plan in 1837 and Congregationalists in 1852.[22]

Both the challenges of the frontier and the example of the 1817 Prussian Plan of Union between Reformed and Lutheran churches prompted leaders of German immigrant churches in the United States to seek for closer cooperation and union. They formed, especially from 1817 to 1837, a number of *union churches*—cooperative arrangements by which Lutheran and Reformed congregations shared ownership of property, often worshipping on alternative Sundays, but sharing a Sunday School, treasury, and even union services. Proposals for organic church union, receptive to many laity, were opposed in the 1830s by clergy who, educated in separate seminaries, emphasized their distinctive Lutheran or Reformed heritage.[23]

---

22. D. Yoder, "Unity"; Crow, "Impulses," 429–30.
23. Yoder, "Unity," 241–43.

Nondenominational Voluntary Societies

The Great Awakening, which gave Christians in Europe a passion for missions and experiences of oneness in Christ across denominational boundaries, spread to the United States with the same fruits. A parallel proliferation of voluntary societies took place there, bringing together Christians of many denominations to witness and work together on issues of common concern. Foremost among them were new societies to promote Christian mission.

To reach persons for Christ and his Church on the frontier, volunteers first formed local and state missionary societies to send and support missionaries. Soon these volunteers proved inadequate to address burgeoning needs in the new settlements. Churches of the Reformed tradition formed the United Domestic Missionary Society in 1821 to secure more adequate funds, prevent needless duplication of effort, and have a more efficient and economical administration. By 1826 it had 127 missionaries on its role—most of them serving in western New York State.

In 1826 prospective candidates from Andover Seminary advocated for a broader national missionary society. In response 126 clergy and laity, representing four denominations and at least 13 states and territories, met to form the American Home Missionary Society. It was designed to be an agency by which Christians of several denominations could engage together in comprehensive mission planning and action on a nationwide scale. It became "the most important single home missionary agency among Protestants in the United States before the Civil War." In its first 10 years it grew exponentially. In 1836 it exceeded $100,000 in income and had 755 missionaries on its rolls. It sent missionaries chiefly north of the Ohio River in the Midwest and on to the Rockies and the Pacific coast. Some went out as bands of graduating seniors from Yale Divinity School and Andover Theological Seminary. However, it was supported by only four denominations of the Reformed family, and it declined in strength as participating churches withdrew to support their own denominational societies.[24]

---

24. Latourette, *Expansion*, 4:209–12; Goodykoontz, *Home Missions*, 173–80, 243–44. By 1861 all but the Congregationalists withdrew their support.

Disciples of Christ

The third approach to mission and unity on the frontier was to form a new organic union apart from established denominations. Barton Warren Stone (1772–1844) migrated west to Kentucky with his family and led in the Cane Ridge Revival of 1801 that launched the Second Great Awakening in the West. Two brothers, Thomas (1763–1845) and Alexander Campbell (1788–1866), emigrated from Scotland by way of Ireland. They and Stone broke away from existing denominations and hoped to restore Christian unity by returning to New Testament faith and practices. They created separate movements called "Christians Only" (Stone) and "Disciples of Christ" (the Campbells), which had great appeal on the frontier. In 1832 the two movements merged as the Christian Church (Disciples of Christ).[25]

OTHER COOPERATIVE EFFORTS IN MISSION

Bible Societies

The founding of the British and Foreign Bible Society in 1804 was the beginning of cooperative effort in Europe and North America to respond to the crying need for new translations for mission work both at home and abroad. After 1804 national Bible societies were organized across Europe, all modeled on the British and Foreign Bible Society. As they multiplied translations of the Scriptures into languages needed in mission fields, they cooperated also there in both the translation and distribution of Bibles and Bible portions. This cooperation among Bible societies, though not always recognized, was a primary engine of ecumenical action.

Earlier Bible publishing and distribution was denominational in leadership. Both the SPCK, founded by Anglicans in 1698, and the Canstein Bible Institution of Halle, Germany, which since 1770 assisted Moravian missionaries, produced scriptures in various languages. The advantage of the nondenominational Bible societies of the early nineteenth century was that they could appeal to Protestants and Orthodox of various churches for support. This was the charter of both the Netherlands Bible Society, begun in 1814, and the American Bible Society (ABS),

---

25. Crow, "Impulses," 434–40. For more complete histories see Hughes, *Reviving*; Harrell, *Social History*.

which amalgamated the earlier work of older state and local societies in 1816.

Maintaining a nonpartisan approach to Bible translation was not easy. Bishop John Henry Hobart, of the Episcopal diocese of New York, in 1815 "viewed with alarm the avowed purpose of many of the Bible Societies to unite all Protestants in a common cause as an ignoring of essential difference of doctrine and polity." Earlier in 1822 the ABS, while honoring the heroic work of William Carey and his associates in Bible translation, hesitated to give financial support to Carey's all-Baptist work at Serampore because "it is of great consequence to the union and harmony of our operations, to adhere inviolably to the principles of indulging no Sectarian preferences."[26]

The *baptizo* controversy of 1827–37 illustrates the varied mission attitudes towards unity of the day. In 1827 Anglicans in Calcutta objected to William Carey's translation of the Greek *baptizo* as "immerse" and appealed successfully to the British and Foreign Bible Society to withdraw their support unless the word used for baptism did not suggest any particular form of ritual. Rebuffed in Britain, the Serampore Baptists appealed to the ABS in 1835 in which Baptists had a larger voice and vote. After a year's study the ABS by a bare majority voted to support only versions that all represented denominations could consistently use and translate. Angered by the rebuff, Baptists withheld funds and later formed a rival Bible society, making the issue of rival charters a bitter court battle in New York until 1848.[27]

Tract Societies

To further the evangelical revival, tract societies formed to provide a wide variety of religious literature—devotional writings, short evangelistic and moral tracts, hymns, and periodicals. Evangelicals of different denominations formed the pioneer Religious Tract Society in London in 1799. From the outset it was interdenominational in structure and support. Its board was to be half Anglican and half Nonconformist, with cosecretaries from those loyalties plus a third "foreign secretary" from the Continent. This connection influenced the beginning of the tract societies in Germany in 1811.[28]

26. Lacy, *Giant*, 31, 71.
27. Smalley, *Translation*, 21–81; Lacy, *Giant*, 87–92.
28. Rouse, "Voluntary Movements," 311; Mundt, *Sinners*, 32–40.

The society founded in Basel, Switzerland, in 1783, which became known as the *Deutsche Christenthums Gesellschaft* (German Christian Fellowship), pioneered in printing and distributing Christian literature for Protestants on the Continent. Karl Steinkopf, as its first secretary, extended its influence to England in the forming of the Bible Society and Religious Tract Society. Martin Schmidt judged it to be the first society definitely founded on an international and interchurch basis.[29]

The ecumenical dynamic continued as the movement spread to Germany. Steinkopf toured the German states from 1812 to 1816 as an ambassador for both the Bible and the Tract societies based in London, encouraging Germans to organize their own societies on the English model. The fourth major outcome, and most lasting of the German tract societies, was the *Niedersächsische Gesellschaft zur Verbreitung christlicher Erbauungsschriften* (Lower Saxony Society for the Distribution of Christian Devotional Materials), established in 1820 by English and French Christians in Hamburg as a daughter society of the Religious Tract Society.[30]

Formed in 1825, the American Tract Society was the first organization in the United States to publish and distribute the printed word on a mass scale. Its commitment to cooperation was clearly expressed in its statement of purpose—"To make Jesus Christ known in His redeeming grace and to promote the interests of vital godliness and sound morality, by the circulation of Religious Tracts, calculated to receive the approbation of all Evangelical Christians." Led by a diverse group of evangelical religious leaders from various denominations, the Society sought to consolidate the work of existing gospel tract ministries, and to efficiently and effectively share the gospel message especially with those on the frontier and new immigrants.[31]

Missionary Register

In 1813 Josiah Pratt, secretary of the CMS, launched the first of the great missionary magazines, the *Missionary Register*. He did it on his own initiative without financial support from the Society. The *Register* printed news from all around the world and from all missionary agencies. Pratt

---

29. Mundt, *Sinners*, 55–60; Schmidt, "Ecumenical Activity," 118.

30. Mundt, *Sinners*, is a full scholarly history and evaluation of the numerous German tract societies.

31. Twaddell, "American Tract Society," 121. In 2010 it celebrated the 185th anniversary of its cooperative publishing ministry.

attempted to report fully on missionary work regardless of denomination, including Roman Catholic missions. His was a remarkable example of "ecumenical sympathies." The *Missionary Register* became the magazine for the common people of Great Britain, many of whom had never before been readers of periodicals. It helped persons to be well informed about international issues of the day such as the burning (*sati*) of Hindu widows, the opium trade, and slave running.[32]

CONCLUSION

How shall we assess the state of unity in mission in 1845 as compared with 1792? Hugh McLeod, in his history, sees this period in Western Europe as both "the archetypal period of secularization, and a great age of religious revival."[33] The power and influence of state churches, under attack since the French Revolution of 1789, waned as large numbers were alienated from the churches of the establishment. Religion ceased to provide a societal focus of social unity. Instead, it became the glue that gave distinctive identity to specific communities of faith that found their loyalty to the churches intensified in the process. In the United States, where separation of church and state was codified in the Constitution in 1791, the Second Great Awakening revived the faith of millions, and motivated them to voluntarily support home and foreign missions.

Active cooperation by Protestant bodies led to a growing ecumenical spirit on both sides of the Atlantic. Friendly relations between Protestants and Roman Catholics increased. Nevertheless, old prejudices remained as sectarianism flourished alongside cooperative ventures. Various Protestant denominations felt that they could not pray together. The British and Foreign Bible Society, for example, although organized in 1804 on an interdenominational basis, did not have common prayer at its meetings until 1859. New denominational mission societies replaced former united efforts from 1835 onwards. New denominations appeared. However, the flame of revival and united missionary endeavor could not be extinguished by a narrow sectarian spirit. In 1846 it would be fanned into flame once more.[34]

---

32. Walls, *Missionary Movement*, 251–52.
33. McLeod, *Religion*, v.
34. Rouse, "Voluntary Movements," 315–16.

3

Cooperation in Mission, 1846–1909

COLONIES AND EMPIRES

THE UNPRECEDENTED EXPANSION OF Christianity in the nineteenth century coincided with the geographical expansion of European colonialism. In the late nineteenth century almost all of Africa, a large part of Asia, and most of the Pacific islands had come under the political control of Western European countries. Great Britain was leading, with France a distant second as a colonial power. Germany lagged because it did not achieve political unity until 1870, and Italy was still later in acquiring colonies for the same reason. Spain and Portugal, though long past their zenith as colonial powers, still were enlarging their holdings in Africa. Integral to territorial expansion was the imperialist spirit—a belief in the innate superiority of Caucasians, reinforced by social Darwinism.

Simultaneously the size and scope of Christian foreign missions increased greatly. The total number of foreign missionaries increased from 29,200 in 1800 to 62,000 in 1900.[1] However, in marked contrast to all other periods since Constantine, the initiative and financial support of mission, whether Protestant or Roman Catholic, came less from governments. The British government gave financial aid to mission schools in India and other British colonies, but they did so because of the desire to further education and not because these were Christian schools. The Tsarist Russian government gave more direct aid to Russian Orthodox missions, but within the Empire.

---

1. Barrett and Johnson, eds., *World Christian Trends*, 31. The best estimate in 1903 was that there were 13,371 Protestant and about 65,000 Roman Catholic missionaries working in cross-cultural missions (Dwight, Tupper, and Munsell, eds., *Encyclopedia of Missions*, 838, 851).

Important for the missions, nevertheless, was the official toleration and protection by colonial powers. For instance, the treaties of 1858, forced on the Chinese by Western powers, not only permitted foreign residence in selected cities, but also granted rights to travel freely anywhere in China to merchants and missionaries, and free exercise of the Christian faith to both foreign missionaries and Chinese believers. In other situations missionaries lobbied public opinion in England to support British colonial expansion, especially in Nyasaland (present Malawi) and Uganda in Africa.[2]

In mid-century many politicians and church leaders in Great Britain believed that Christianity, commerce, and civilization had interests in common and could unashamedly support one another. Where independent rulers in African and Pacific Island states needed to be convinced of the value of missions, proposals that missionaries help to develop cash crops and export outlets had an effect. British missionaries were more likely to assist with education and medicine, feeling that these efforts were more closely related to the evangelistic task. However, rarely did they criticize Britain's imperial ambitions during this period.[3]

German colonial imperialism had a slow start. Although Bismarck had united Germany in 1870, he regarded colonies as an expensive luxury. Public opinion favoring commercial and political expansion increased the nation's appetite for colonies in the 1880s and 1890s. German mission societies formed a standing committee (*Ausschuss*) in 1885 that by 1897 developed united policies affecting all societies and the Protestant churches on relations both with the government and with the Roman Catholic Church. It was instrumental in defeating the notion that only German missionaries ought to serve in German colonies.[4]

Although the overarching motive for missions in the United States in this period was the love of Christ and obedience to the Great Commission for the salvation of souls, another compelling vision gained prominence. After the 1840s a conviction developed that the nation had a divine manifest destiny to extend the blessings of the nation to other peoples. For fifty years it focused on "winning the West" and absorbing new territories and new immigrants into the nation's values and borders. During those years home missions were a major priority. The American

---

2. Latourette, "Colonialism and Missions," 333–37.
3. Walls, "British Missions," 162–64.
4. Hogg, *Foundations*, 70–73; see also Gensichen, "German."

Board (ABCFM) initially included both home and foreign missions in its purview. But with the nation's geographic boundaries established, a new goal emerged—described by one contemporary as the mission to fulfill "Anglo-Saxon destiny as a civilizing and Christianizing power." Citizens were "inordinately proud of themselves for avoiding colonial entanglement" while Christians poured enormous resources and leadership into "the fine spiritual imperialism of preaching the world-conquering Christ." It may be that without the ambiguities of colonial attachments, commitments to foreign missions in the U.S. did include "the almost universal tendency to accept *civilization* as intrinsic to evangelization and not inimical to it."[5]

DENOMINATIONS AND CONFESSIONS

Two countervailing tendencies existed in religious life in the period from 1846 to 1909: sectarianism and an ecumenical spirit. Social historians emphasize that in polarized societies sectarianism "provided for large numbers of people the strongest basis for their social identity." Religious groups often combined aggressive evangelism with attempts to mark out sharp and clear boundaries between their own religious group and the world beyond. In England Anglicans and Nonconformists heightened the barriers of separation. In France a "wave of dissidence" in the 1840s caused Methodists, Baptists, Plymouth Brethren, and Congregationalists to form denominations separate from the Reformed Church. Free churches separated from state churches in Scotland, Sweden, Norway, Switzerland, and The Netherlands.[6]

Such sectarianism often thwarted earlier cooperative missionary efforts such as the united international work through the Basel Missionary Society. German Lutherans formed separate regional bodies. Between 1857 and 1870 three denominational bodies that had been cooperating with the Congregationalists in the ABCFM in the United States (the Reformed Dutch, German Reformed, and the New School Presbyterian) all withdrew and formed separate denominational missions. Their motives included resentment at "outside" control, growing denominational self-confidence, practical issues of fundraising, relations with their own missionaries, and a growing desire to have "native" churches replicate the ones at home.[7]

---

5. G. Anderson, "American Protestants," 98; Hutchison, "Imperialism," 175–76.
6. McLeod, *Religion*, 36; Rouse, "Voluntary Movements," 316–17.
7. Rouse, "Voluntary Movements," 316; Hutchison, *Errand*, 95–96.

Two divergent views emerged as to the object of the missionary enterprise. One was that the object is to "extend the denomination throughout the world—its distinctive tenets and ecclesiastical forms." Rev. F. Schwager, SVD, gave clear expression to this perspective as he wrote, "Roman Catholics are firmly convinced that Christ Himself gave to [the Roman Catholic] Church alone the right and the duty of proclaiming the Gospel to the whole world." Protestant missionaries were proud to build churches overseas that were exact replicas of those in the sending countries, with vestments and liturgies, hymns and confessions that were exact copies of those of the mother church. The second view was that the object is "to communicate the essential truths of New Testament teaching without special reference to a denominational interpretation, leaving the churches in the mission field to develop their own creeds and forms of organization." Advocates of this viewpoint strongly opposed introduction of the sectarian divisions of Europe or North America into Africa and Asia. They asked, "Why should Christians of India be labeled English Wesleyans, German Lutherans and American Baptists?"[8]

THE EVANGELICAL ALLIANCE

The United States, England, Scotland, and the continent of Europe all make legitimate claims that the idea of an evangelical alliance originated in their area. One such claim is found in *Essays on Christian Union*, produced in 1845 largely by Scottish Presbyterians. It contains two visions that would characterize evangelicals' union concerns—for a spiritual union of individual Christians belonging to different churches, and for a federal or organic union of church institutions.[9]

The first vision—for union among individual Christians—received its international baptism in 1846. Eight hundred Christian leaders, from eleven countries in North America and Europe and from varied confessional backgrounds, met in London and resolved to form a confederation under the name of the Evangelical Alliance. To avoid ecclesiological controversy the doctoral Basis of the Alliance contained no mention of church. No administrative structure was set up. Instead national branches

---

8. Schwager, "Missionary Methods," 498; A. Brown, *Unity*, 239–40.
9. James, *Essays*; Rouse, "Voluntary Movements," 318–19; Randall and Hilborn, *One Body*, 18–44. For antecedents in the USA see Crow, "Impulses," 419–40.

and their auxiliaries were to send representatives to a general conference every seven years.[10]

The Alliance in its first fifty years pioneered in five dimensions of evangelical cooperation. First, it stimulated united prayer, including setting aside the first week of the year as a "call to prayer to Christians over all the world." Second, it provided increased awareness about the churches and conditions in various countries through publication of *Evangelical Christendom*. Third, it sponsored a series of international conferences that stimulated a sense of unity among Christians of various nations. Fourth, it championed religious liberty, defending oppressed religious groups and individuals by securing government action in their favor.

Finally, it was a powerful advocate for missions. At the London conference in 1854 there was "intense concern for greater unity in the whole missionary enterprise." A successor conference, the General Conference on Foreign Missions, was held in London in 1878. It and subsequent Alliance-sponsored conferences praised evidences of growing cooperation in missionary endeavors, and considered those richer because they transcended denominations, allowed for diversity of organization, and did not require organic uniformity.[11]

Nevertheless, the Alliance disappointed the hopes of those who sought a more tangible Christian union. It ignored church relations, remaining an association of individuals. Its rigid doctrinal basis was opposed by the French and others, and was to cause the practical disappearance of the branch in the U.S. in the 1890s. It lacked central leadership and organization. Its objective to unite Christians in the bonds of love was incompatible with its aim to combat popery and high Anglicanism.

Despite its weaknesses, the Alliance held a unique place in the nineteenth century Christianity. It was the preeminent international association founded with the express purpose of working towards Christian unity.[12]

---

10. See Rouse, "Voluntary Movements," 320n1 for the doctrinal Basis of the Alliance. Differences over admission of slaveholders as members caused the United States Alliance to organize separately. Jordan, *Alliance*, 33–67; Randall and Hilborn, *One Body*, 45–70.

11. Rouse, "Voluntary Movements," 321–22; see Hogg, *Foundations*, 36–50, for the content of specific conferences on cooperation in missions, and Ewing, *Fellowship*, for historical details.

12. Rouse, "Voluntary Movements," 322–24. For the later history of the Alliance to 2001 see Randall and Hilborn, *One Body*, 71–355, and J. Kessler, *Study*.

COMITY

The proliferation of missions in many fields in the latter half of the nineteenth century led to frequent chaos and overlap. Many missionaries abhorred the resulting waste of limited resources, as well as the confusion for those newly receiving the gospel. It was the Centenary Conference on the Protestant Missions of the World (London 1888) that first put *comity* on the agenda. Dr. A. C. Thompson of the AABCFM defined the term as "the observance of equity and Christian courtesy in foreign evangelization." Professor Gustaf Warneck of Germany in his paper presented at the conference called for a spiritual unity outwardly expressed as missionaries become mutually acquainted, bind themselves to avoid all overstepping of boundaries, and more constantly hold out helping hands to each other.[13]

The practice of comity in foreign missions, however, antedated the use of the term by more than sixty years. The first recorded example of a comity agreement occurred in the South Pacific. In 1830, Wesleyan missionaries Nathanael Turner and William Cross and London Missionary Society missionaries John Williams and Charles Barf agreed that Tonga and Fiji would be evangelized by the Methodists, while Samoa would be reached by the LMS. By 1836 the ABCFM had called on all missionary societies to make a global comity arrangement in order to speed the total evangelization of the world.[14]

Comity as a mission society policy had been generally accepted by the middle of the nineteenth century. It gained popular acceptance by mission supporters through the large missionary conferences. The Union Missionary Convention (New York 1854) unanimously adopted a resolution offered by Dr. Alexander Duff of Calcutta that fields previously occupied by an evangelical church or society, with the exception of great centers such as the capitals of powerful kingdoms, should be "respected by others, and left in their undisturbed possession." At the Ecumenical Mission Conference (New York 1900) twenty-five mission leaders spoke on various aspects of comity, including J. Hudson Taylor, superintendent of the China Inland Mission. His spirit was irenic: "Having been a pioneer mission we have had the privilege in many cases of leaving a field altogether when we found it would be sufficiently occupied by others...."

---

13. Centenary Conf., London 1888, *Report*, 1:429–47.
14. ABCFM, *Report*, 108–17; Beaver, *Beginnings*, 44–66.

When we get to heaven ... we shall belong to one society. We shall all be one happy family there."[15]

At the end of this period the Edinburgh 1910 conference highlighted the importance of comity agreements among the missions. Its conviction was that "the creation of as many opportunities as possible for those working in the same area to come into personal and friendly contact with one another will do more than anything else to further the cause of unity."[16]

In his history of comity R. Pierce Beaver wrote, "Comity is the bedrock foundation on which there has been built throughout Asia, Africa, Latin America, and the Pacific a Protestant community conscious of its unity." He concluded, "If the missionary enterprise could more than a century ago in an era of intense denominationalism achieve the unity that was expressed in its system of comity and cooperation, what greater and truer expression of spiritual unity ought not emerge in an ecumenical age!"[17]

EDUCATION

During this period most missionary societies devoted increasing resources of personnel and money to many types of educational work. Beginning in 1855 in North India, missionaries of various Protestant societies began to meet annually by region of service for Christian fellowship and the sharing of concerns. It is Richey Hogg's judgment that in the pre-1910 period "it seemed to be the missionaries, rather than the Christians among whom they worked, who took the initiative to foster concern for unity and cooperation."[18]

The large Anglo-American mission conferences of the period, however, gave scant evidence that cooperation by the missions in education was a priority. The Centenary Conference (London 1888) devoted a full session to missionary post-secondary education, but no presenter mentioned the need for cooperation. The Ecumenical Missionary Conference (New York 1900), attended by representatives of 162 missionary boards, gave opportunities to express such concerns. F. F. Ellinwood, secretary of

15. *Union Missionary Convention*, 16–17; Ecumenical Missionary Conference, *Report*, 1:271
16. *World Missionary Conference, 1910*, 8:12–26, 141.
17. Beaver, *Ecumenical Beginnings*, 40, 327; see also Goheen, "Mission."
18. Hogg, *Foundations*, 33.

the Board of Missions of the Presbyterian Church (USA), confessed that "there may be need of united action" in some special line of educational work, but generalized that "we have not favored union establishments with the mixed administration and control of different churches or societies." By contrast D. Stuart Dodge, secretary of the board of the Syrian Protestant College in Beirut, spoke in favor of nonsectarian colleges, which would, in the eyes of both nationals and missionaries, be "a singularly happy illustration of the direct advantage of missionary comity and co-operation."[19]

MEDICAL MISSIONS

The story of medical missions during this period is told primarily through the heroic work of the pioneers, among them Karl Gützlaff (1803–51) and Peter Parker (1804–88) in China, and John Scudder (1793–1855) and Clara Swain (1834–1910) in India. By 1887 there were 260 medical missionaries at work, with the majority sent by Protestant mission societies in the U.S. and Great Britain. In 1888 the Centenary Conference in London devoted two full sessions to medical missions. Outstanding medical doctors presented thrilling stories of their work but none called for cooperative action or united medical institutions.[20]

Nondenominational societies did emerge, however. The Medical Missionary Society in China, composed of medical personnel and their supporters both within China and outside, was formed in 1838 to give permanence to work begun and financed by individuals. Parallel bodies developed during the century in the sending countries, with focus on recruitment and training of qualified personnel. The Edinburgh Medical Missionary Society, formed in 1841, was the most prominent of these bodies. The Medical Missionary Association, founded in London in 1878, later became the prototype for many societies in the United States, Great Britain, and Continental Europe that were concerned not only for recruitment and training of medical personnel, but also for their financial and material support.[21]

---

19. Ecumenical Missionary Conference, *Report*, 1:242, 2:145.
20. Grundmann, "Role," 45 n. 4; Centenary Conf., London 1888, *Report*, 2:101–39. See Ecumenical Missionary Conference, *Report*, 2:188–229, for reports by medical missionaries that rarely mention cooperative efforts.
21. Grundmann, *Sent*, 65–71, 96–124.

FAITH MISSIONS

A new type of mission society developed in the latter half of the nineteenth century. Often they have been called "faith missions" because they believe in the faith principle that God will provide financial support even when it appears that no money is available. They also are referred to as "independent, interdenominational, or nondenominational." They developed first in Great Britain with the founding of the China Inland Mission (CIM) in 1865. In the United States the largest early sending groups were the Christian and Missionary Alliance (1887), the Evangelical Alliance Mission (1890), the Sudan Interior Mission (1893), and the Africa Inland Mission (1895). The main motives for their founding "were not theological or sectarian but practical—to decentralize missionary responsibility for greater efficiency, to overcome denominational separatism, and to supplement the work of denominational agencies." Demands for more missionaries, the personal magnetism of their founders, and new mission theories based on premillennial beliefs were other causative factors.[22]

Hudson Taylor, founder of the CIM, was exemplary in his ecumenical and generous spirit. His vision, Arthur T. Pierson contended, was that CIM would be "interdenominational—Catholic, evangelical, and so both inviting and embracing all sympathetic disciples who were willing to cooperate." On his world tours he appealed to mission-minded people to support more actively their own churches' programs with gifts and prayers. In the last decades of the nineteenth century Taylor attended the great mission conferences, sharing the platform with such ecumenical leaders as Dwight L. Moody, A. T. Pierson, John R. Mott, Robert Wilder, and Robert Speer.[23]

The CIM pioneered also in being both international in sponsorship yet very local in its chosen field of service. By 1905 it had stationed eight hundred missionaries in forty-five mission stations in fifteen provinces of China. Its international headquarters was in Shanghai, with national branches in England, Scotland, Canada, the United States, and Australia, plus cooperative missions in Sweden, Norway, Germany, and Finland. "May the good Lord mix us up more and more!" Henry T. Frost enthused when he visited the CIM's language schools in China where new mission-

---

22. *EDWM*, s.v. "Faith Missions"; G. Anderson, "American Protestants," 99; Robert, "Crisis," 30–31.
23. Pierson, *Movements*, 274; Kane, "Taylor," 199.

aries of eight to ten nationalities studied together. He noted that the CIM missionaries included every kind of evangelicals, but also Pentecostals and Protestant liberals—all desiring to emulate their founder's ecumenical and generous spirit.[24]

More than the winds of the Spirit of unity, however, were blowing on the CIM during this period. By the early 1900s many faith mission leaders had embraced a premillennial dispensationalism, a theology of the end times believed by many conservative evangelicals who opposed cooperation with Christians who did not share this view. Frost, the North American director of the CIM, was strong enough as a fundamentalist in 1915 to force the CIM to withdraw from the Continuation Committee of the Edinburgh Missionary Conference.[25]

MOTT AND THE STUDENT MOVEMENT

Arthur Pierson, in his reflection on missions of this period, devoted a chapter to the "World-Wide Uprising of Christian Students." He identified four stages. First, the YMCA introduced chapters into the universities and colleges of Christian lands, organized them into a national and international alliance, and extended them to other lands. Second, summer schools and conventions brought these enthusiastic young Christians together, cementing their bonds of personal friendship. Third, the Student Volunteer Movement (SVM) motivated and recruited thousands to go as foreign missionaries. Finally, the World Student Christian Federation (WSCF) united Christian students across the world.[26]

Nonsectarian at their core, these movements inspired students to be committed to Christian unity, trained as leaders, and passionate about the Church's mission. John R. Mott, who has been called the "architect of Co-operation and unity," was an influential leader in all four stages identified by Pierson.[27]

YMCA and YWCA

The Young Men's Christian Association (YMCA) and the Young Women's Christian Association (YWCA) began in England in 1844 and 1854 respectively, and quickly spread to North America. It is recorded that

24. Austin, "Only Connect," 282, 313.
25. Austin, "Blessed Adversity," 307–9.
26. Pierson, *Movements*, 218–29.
27. Fisher, *Mott*.

George Williams, founder of the YMCA, exclaimed to three interested young men, "Here we are, an Episcopalian, a Methodist, a Baptist, and a Congregationalist—four believers but a single faith in Christ. Forward together!" Henri Dunant of Geneva, founder of the Red Cross, wrote on behalf of the Geneva "Y" to invite all associations of the world to the first international YMCA conference in Paris in 1855. He said their aim must be "to spread abroad that ecumenical spirit which transcends nationalities, languages, denominations, ecclesiastical problems, ranks and occupations." By 1885 the YMCA was the largest "foreign" mission of its day, sending hundreds of their missionaries (called "secretaries") from Great Britain to the college campuses of the United States and the British Empire.[28]

John R. Mott, as president of the Cornell University Christian Association, built it into the largest and most active student "Y" in the nation. Upon graduation in 1888 Mott visited campuses in the U.S. and Canada as travelling secretary with the Intercollegiate YMCA. In an 1899 address entitled "The Two Hundred Million Young Men in Non-Christian Lands," Mott emphasized his linkage of unity and mission: "We owe it to the best life of our Associations to fill them with the missionary spirit. Eleven years travelling among the Associations in different countries has led me to form the conclusion that without doubt the most spiritual and most fruitful Associations are those in which the missionary spirit most abounds." As associate general secretary for its foreign department (1901–15), Mott was the catalyst for the YMCA's "foreign work," building global linkages.[29]

Student Volunteer Movement (SVM)

In 1886–87, before the SVM was organized, Presbyterians Robert P. Wilder and John N. Forman visited American and Canadian universities encouraging students to volunteer for missionary service.[30] In July of 1886, 251 students responded to an invitation by Dwight L. Moody to come to his center at Mt. Hermon near Northfield, Massachusetts, for a

---

28. Rouse, "Voluntary Movements," 327; Austin, "Only Connect," 283; See Shedd, *Two Centuries*, for a detailed history.

29. Mott, *Addresses and Papers*, 6:269. Later Mott served as the "Y"s Secretary of the Home Base (1901–28), President of the World YMCA Alliance (1926), and national General Secretary of the International Committee of the YMCA and President of its World Alliance (1928).

30. Later they served as the SVM's first traveling secretaries.

month of Bible study and shared Christian living. After extended prayer one hundred students, among them John R. Mott, declared themselves "Willing and desirous, God permitting, to become foreign missionaries." Formally organized in 1888, the SVM adopted as its watchword "The Evangelization of the World in This Generation."[31]

By 1898 Mott could declare, "Interest in the missionary enterprise is greater, more intelligent and more powerful among students than among any other class of Christians (not even excepting clergymen). This revolution—for it has been nothing less—has taken place within ten years ... not simply to North America but to other lands as well, and notably to the Continent and Australasia." He continued, "the Volunteer Movement ... has been the greatest unifying force, under the influence of the Spirit, not only in the student world but also in the Christian Church."[32]

Quadrennial conventions were one means by which the SVM helped college students to unite and commit themselves to missions. In February 1906, 4,235 student delegates gathered in Nashville, Tennessee, the largest SVM conference of the period. In his opening address Mott, the conference organizer, reported that 2,953 Volunteers had sailed for overseas mission assignments with various mission boards in the SVM's first twenty years, constituting two-thirds of new Protestant missionaries.[33]

The SVM's dual commitment to missions and unity, and its evangelical theology, piety, and enthusiasm, also influenced other nondenominational associations. Although organized as a distinct movement, it was closely tied at its founding with the college YMCAs and YWCAs and to the Interseminary Missionary Alliance, each of which had representatives on its executive committee in 1889. The SVM also influenced the development of national SCMs in the United States, Great Britain, Ireland, and other countries, and the formation of the World Student Christian Federation. It has been called "one of the most influential mission movements in history."[34]

---

31. Hogg, *Foundations*, 885–87. See also Parker, *Kingdom*; Robert, "Origin," 146–49.

32. Mott, "Great Facts about the S.V.M." in A-YDSL/SVM, "SVM History."

33. Hopkins, *Mott*, 280–81; Harder, "SVM," 143. By 1909 the British SVM had pledges from 3,360 volunteers and 1,400 had sailed for overseas assignments.

34. Hogg, *Foundations*, 86–87; Robert, "Origin," 146.

World Student Christian Federation (WSCF)

During the 1880s Christian associations were formed in continental Europe, Asia, and Australasia. Luther D. Wishard became a firm believer in international conferences and movements after attending the International YMCA Convention in 1872. From 1877 to 1884 he was the only SCM secretary in the world. Through his foresight the first student YMCA outside the U.S. was formed in India in 1884. In that year he wrote of the need for Christian students in all lands to be united in "one world-wide movement, whose purpose shall be *Christ for the Students of the world, and the Students of the World for Christ*." By 1894 Mott also was convinced that the time was ripe to form a "world-wide union of Christian students."[35]

From Japan came the spark to ignite the fire. In 1889 500 Japanese students, meeting in Kyoto at Doshisha, the oldest Christian college in Japan, sent greetings to the Student Conference of the YMCA in the U.S. with the theme words of their conference in Japan, "Make Christ King," meeting at the same time. When read to student delegates at the Scandinavian Missionary Conference one replied, "If students can gather round Jesus Christ as their King over there in the Far East, why not also here in the North?" With a new vision Scandinavian student movements formed national organizations. Joined by American, British, and German delegates at their third meeting at Vadstena Castle in Sweden in 1895, they voted together to launch a world federation with the aim "to unite student Christian movements or organizations throughout the world." The "Student Christian Movement in Mission Lands" (those in countries of Asia not closely organized at the time) also was represented. From the start the WSCF gave an importance to the smaller student movements, including those of the Majority World (Africa, Asia, Latin America, and Oceania), by giving every national or international organization in the WSCF one vote on the general committee.[36]

Mott perceived immediately the importance of this radical step towards ecumenical cooperation. He reported, "There has been no more hopeful development towards the real spiritual union of Christendom than the World's Student Christian Federation which unites in common purpose and work the coming leaders of Church and State in all lands." Later he would add that "the chief significance of the Federation

---

35. Rouse, *WSCF*, 26–29, 53.
36. Rouse, *WSCF*, 44–47; Parker, *Kingdom*, 92–96.

is in its unifying power [in] plans and methods of Christian work among students in different countries ... [in] uniting in effort and in spirit as never before the students of the world ... [in] helping to unite the nations." Finally, "the Federation, by uniting the students of some seventy leading branches of the all-embracing Church of Christ, is demonstrating in the most practical manner that 'there is one body, and one Spirit (Eph. 4:4).'"[37]

For its first twenty years the WSCF focused its energies on the formation and strengthening of national student movements, calling students to the Christian faith and to the mission of world evangelization. As the WSCF's first general secretary (1895–97), Mott visited the world's major universities, and stimulated the founding of seventy student Christian associations. After the North American and European members, the next national associations to join were the SCMs of Australasia, South Africa, China, and Japan, and the Intercollegiate YMCA of India and Ceylon.

Conferences, Ruth Rouse reports, were "the warp and woof of Federation growth." In them "diverse threads of nationality, faith and practice, race and language, were woven into the ecumenical pattern." Unlike the immense missionary conferences and SVM quadrennials of the period, the WSCF conferences were smaller gatherings of representatives from member bodies, each preceded by an executive committee meeting. The WSCF model influenced the structure and organization of later ecumenical conferences beginning with Edinburgh 1910, as well as the components of the ecumenical movement that joined to form the World Council of Churches in 1948.[38]

The seventh conference (Tokyo, 1907) was a unique pioneer event, "the first international conference of any kind, secular or religious, to be held in the East." The 700 assembled students were guests of the Japanese SCM, including 443 delegates from Japan, 74 from China, 15 from India, and others from lands of Asia and Oceania. It was in striking contrast to the Centennial Conference of Christian Missions in China held that year, attended by hundreds of missionaries from Europe and the U.S. but only nine, non-voting Chinese. The sixth conference (Zeist, Holland, 1905) was equally a breakthrough in relating women students

---

37. Report Letter from John R. Mott, Constantinople, October 4, 1895; quoted in Rouse, *WSCF*, 64; Mott, *Addresses and Papers*, 2:4–5.

38. Rouse, *WSCF*, 68; Hopkins, *Mott*, 242–43.

to the Federation. Women participated in many sessions and Ruth Rouse was appointed Secretary for Work amongst Women Students. Two years later at Tokyo the WSCF Constitution was amended to permit member movements to have one woman representative as well as two men on the governing General Committee.[39]

The Mott Legacy

Upon the close of Mott's illustrious career John Mackay wrote, "In his spirit and life he incarnated the double commitment to mission and unity. . . . In the thought, the experience and the activity of Mott, unity was always for the sake of mission. His interest was that the followers of the Risen Christ should become one in order that the world might believe that the Father had sent the Son to be the world's Saviour."[40]

Mott's commitment was to unity but not conformity. He did not favor "undenominationalism," which called Christians to reduce themselves to the lowest common denominator. Instead, he supported "interdenominationalism"—a unity in diversity whereby a Christian develops loyalty to one's own Christian communion while bringing to an ecumenical body their own discovery of Christian truth. His contribution to the movement for greater Christian unity was global and lay-centered rather that ecclesiastical and church-centered.[41]

Mott was one of the first to grasp that there ought to be a give-and-take among all Christians of the world. "I have a debt of gratitude to all Christian confessions," he once said and then added, "and especially to the Orthodox and the Quakers." From his first meeting with the Russian Orthodox missionary Bishop Nicolai in Tokyo in 1897, he grew to have a deep love affair with Orthodoxy, enhanced by its music and its central emphasis on the resurrection, central also in Mott's faith. He assured Roman Catholics that they were welcome in the WSCF, and found ways to work with Catholics in Latin America at a time of intense Catholic/Protestant antagonisms on that continent. "I have known no one whose foresight and achievement in promoting inter-racial understanding and cooperation in any way equaled that of Mott," J. H. Oldham wrote upon Mott's death. He continued, "The WSCF was inter-racial from the start,

---

39. Rouse, *WSCF*, 124–26, 103–4; Hogg, *Foundations*, 94.
40. Mackey, "John R. Mott," 334.
41. Mott, *Addresses and Papers*, 2:5; Hopkins, *Mott*, 82; Mott, quoted in Visser t' Hooft, "John R. Mott," 290.

and was a most powerful agency in breaking down racial barriers." Mott emphasized that a "major interest has been that of helping to weave together in closer co-operation and unity the Christians of all nations, races, and communions."[42]

WOMEN IN MISSION

"The women created the first international ecumenical missionary agency intended to be universal in scope." This was the assessment of R. Pierce Beaver in his history of American Protestant women in world mission. Twenty-two years before the World Missionary Conference at Edinburgh in 1910, thirty-six leaders of women's boards of mission in the U.S. and Canada formed the World's Missionary Committee of Christian Women, and invited their British sisters to join them. Their object was "to secure concerted action on the part of all Women's, General, Foreign, and Home Missionary Societies."[43]

From the early nineteenth century women were a significant part of foreign missions from the United States. As early as 1830 they comprised 49 percent of the Protestant missionary force. By 1880 they reached 57 percent, and by 1929 they were 67 percent of the Protestant missionaries from the U.S. In the four decades after 1886 women responded more than men to the call for missionaries by the SVM, the largest Protestant recruiting agency. By 1905 they were the majority of SVM members who annually sailed as missionaries.[44]

Prior to the United States Civil War in 1860 the missionary roles of women were largely confined to those of wife or teacher. After 1860 they developed "women's work for women," adding the roles of nurse, social worker, and even evangelist. New women's missionary boards were established under women's leadership. The first was the nondenominational (or interdenominational) Woman's Union Missionary Society incorporated in 1861. In the years to follow women established more independent boards (twenty by 1880; forty-one by 1900). Some were designed to supplement the denominations' mission boards. Others, like

---

42. Visser t' Hooft, "John R. Mott," 289; Marty, *Pilgrims*, 345; Oldham, "John R. Mott," 258.
43. Beaver, *American Protestant Women*, 145, 146.
44. Parker, *Kingdom*, 50, 43.

the Methodist Episcopal women's agency, were to be on a par with the denominational board.[45]

The high tide of women's mission boards in North America coincided with their ecumenical priorities. Women mission leaders, including Helen Barrett Montgomery and Lucy Waterbury Peabody, gained a strong sense of unity and common identity through their participation in the World's Missionary Committee of Christian Women. It had three major achievements following its founding at the London Missionary Conference of 1888. First, it organized a Woman's Congress of Missions in conjunction with the Chicago World's Fair of 1893. Next, it planned the women's work programs of the Ecumenical Missionary Conference in New York in 1900. Third, as a follow-up of that conference, it organized the Central Committee for the United Study of Foreign Missions. In the next thirty-eight years the Committee published more than four million textbooks for use in schools of mission that became an important means of mission education in North America.[46]

NATIONAL COORDINATION IN MISSIONS

The London Secretaries Association

This, the earliest and least formal of national associations, began in 1819 as the secretaries of London-based foreign mission boards agreed to form an association for "mutual counsel and fellowship." As trust deepened the societies engaged in more cooperative projects including some launched by the Association. It was the Association that initiated plans for the large international missionary conferences held in England (Liverpool 1860, London 1878, and London 1888.) On several occasions, especially after 1900, the Association made general appeals to government on behalf of missions.[47]

---

45. Ibid., 50-51; Beaver, *American Protestant Women*, 87-115. See Robert, *American Women*, 1-254, for a detailed social history of these developments.

46. Robert, *American Women*, 257-69; Beaver, *American Protestant Women*, 148-49; Catton, *Lamps*, 36-47. There were no corresponding women's missionary societies in Europe. For a history of Roman Catholic women's orders in Europe see Goyau, *La femme*.

47. Hogg, *Foundations*, 51-53.

Cooperation on the Continent

As early as 1842 Hartwig Brauer of the Bremen Mission had proposed a continental conference of representatives of mission societies. Not until 1866, however, was the first Continental Missions Conference held in Bremen, with thirty participants from eight German societies, and from societies in France, Holland, Denmark, Sweden, and Norway. It continued to meet every four or five years. Upon the unification of the German states in 1871 and the development of German colonies beginning in 1884, mission societies faced the need to develop a united approach to government on mission issues. In 1885 Gusfav Warneck proposed the establishment of a *Missionsbund* (Missions Alliance) to handle problems common to all mission societies. Formally established as the *Ausschuss* (Standing Committee) in 1885, it represented fourteen German societies of the Lutheran, Reformed, Moravian, and Union State Church confessions. It recommended policies concerning the relation of the societies to the churches, the government, and the Roman Catholic Church. It was both the primary mission agency to negotiate upon behalf of its members with the government, and the body that mediated problems between mission societies.[48]

The Foreign Missions Conference of North America (FMC)

In 1893 representatives of twenty-three North American mission agencies, including John R. Mott and Robert Speer, met in New York on invitation of the Committee on Cooperation in Foreign Mission Work of the Alliance of Reformed Churches. Those who attended, predominately executives of mission boards, hoped that their "striving to learn from each other" would constitute "an object-lesson in Christian unity." Little did they realize that they were inaugurating a pattern of annual gatherings, known as the Foreign Missions Conference of North America, which would last for fifty-eight years. The FMC contributed substantially to the Ecumenical Missionary Conference in 1900.[49]

Stimulated by patterns of mission cooperation in other countries, most notably the *Ausschuss* (Standing Committee) of German missionary societies begun in 1885, the Conference in 1907 established a Committee on Reference and Counsel. It was to lead in joint action be-

---

48. Ibid., 60–73.
49. FMC, *Report*, 4; Hogg, *Foundations*, 74–75; Mott, "Gains," 26.

tween the annual conferences, including negotiations with government and other issues of cooperation and comity, but not to interfere "in the internal administration of any Board or Society."

THE HIGH TIDE OF MISSION CONFERENCES

Both colonial powers and Christian missions were in expansion modes in the last two decades of the nineteenth century. Cooperation between governments and missions increased. Missionaries increasingly felt that cooperation, rather than competition, would increase their effectiveness. Large international mission conferences were an important means by which to share concerns and increase commitment to unity in mission.

London 1888

Ten years after the London missionary conference of 1878, secretaries of the mission boards based in London convened what they called the "Centenary Conference" on foreign missions. It was "the largest, most representative interdenominational, international assembly to that date." The 1,579 attendees represented 139 missionary societies—the majority from Great Britain and her colonies, but with significant participation from North America and continental Europe. All the British Protestant societies, except those of High Church Anglicans and the Salvation Army, sent participants.

Missionary comity and mutual relations was the theme of several sessions, but no resolutions touching missions policy were allowed since no authority existed to act upon them. That was unfortunate as Gustav Warneck, the outstanding German professor of missions, presented a concrete proposal to create a "Standing Central Committee" composed of delegates from all Protestant missionary societies to act "where the united action of all Missionary Societies is desirable" and to arbitrate differences among them. Essentially it was the plan adopted thirty-three years later by the International Missionary Council upon its formation.[50]

---

50. Hogg, *Foundations*, 42–45; Askew, "1888 London." See Centenary Conf., London 1888, *Report*, for the full report and papers.

New York 1900

The Ecumenical Missionary Conference of 1900 was the largest missionary conference ever held. It is estimated that in 10 days 170,000–200,000 people attended its various meetings. The core meeting included 2,500 delegates representing 162 mission boards in the U.S., Great Britain, and Continental Europe, with 13 from other regions. Of the 500 speakers at the multiple sessions for the vast audience, only eight came from the Majority World.[51]

One stated goal was "To demonstrate a unified church and manifest the oneness in mission of Protestant Christianity, resulting in greater comity between the denominations in reaching the world for Christ." Despite this lofty intention the 1900 conference had little lasting impact. It passed no resolutions and took no actions for further cooperation, leaving it to be remembered primarily for its goal "to mobilize congregations and Christian public opinion toward greater mission commitment, financial support, and increased missionary recruits."[52]

CONCLUSION

How shall we assess the global state of Christian unity and missions at the end of this period? The pioneer historian of world Christianity, Kenneth Scott Latourette, called the period from 1800 to 1914 the "Great Century," when mission frontiers were greatly expanded and new initiatives gave rise to the ecumenical movement. Some assessments from continental Europe, however, were less sanguine. "Unfortunately," Gustav Warneck noted in 1901, "it is not a united Christendom that is engaged at present in the propagation of the Gospel." He found in the many divisions of evangelical missions "a confusing tendency, even when the missionaries of the various societies do not compete with each other." A French historian judged the Protestant missionary movement to be largely independent of the churches.[53]

---

51. Hogg, *Foundations*, 45–48. For the first time the word "ecumenical" was used in a title, but to mean "the common commitment of all concerned to carry the Gospel to the whole world"—not to seek any ecclesiastical unity. See Ecumenical Missionary Conference, *Report*, for the full report and papers.

52. Askew, "New York," 146.

53. Latourette, *Christian Outlook*, 155; Warneck, *Outline*, 345; Le Guillou, *Mission*, 2:42.

With a longer historical perspective on this period, Jan van Butselaar judged that the modern missionary movement marked an end to the narrow thinking that the church is just "my" church or "my" confessional group. Christians met across church boundaries more and more as they proclaimed the gospel, denounced injustice, consoled each other in adversity, and celebrated their oneness in Christ. He continued, "It made the pain of Christian division deeply felt, brought Christians together, and made them long for Christian unity . . . in small parishes, in the forests of Africa, and in the wilderness of nineteenth century Europe, missionaries, through their stories and reports, made people aware of the worldwide character of humanity." This was "a spontaneous, worldwide missionary education programme." The first ecumenical world missionary conference (Edinburgh 1910) was to be a logical outcome of this process.[54]

---

54. Butselaar, "Thinking," 364.

4

Councils of Unity, 1910–1947

ADVANCE THROUGH STORM

Kenneth Scott Latourette entitled the final volume of his monumental *A History of the Expansion of Christianity* "Advance through Storm: AD 1914 and After." Within thirty years two world wars devastated many nations and disrupted most nations and peoples. Humans caused wholesale destruction on a massive scale as never before in history. Following the first world conflict, revolutions toppled traditional rulers in Russia, Germany, and Italy. As a result of the Great Depression of the 1930s world trade shrank, financial institutions collapsed, personal savings eroded, and millions lost their jobs. Shifting populations lost their rootedness in communities and in their faith communities. Worldwide populations increased, and with that came demands for more jobs, housing, education, and medical care.

Especially in Europe, people spoke of the age as the "post-Christian era." Threats to the faith from secular ideologies led them to predict that Christianity was doomed. By contrast, Latourette and others took the opposite viewpoint, arguing that "Christianity was putting forth fresh movements, was becoming more widely spread, more deeply rooted among more peoples, and more nearly united on a world scale."[1]

In this chapter we will trace the strands interweaving missions and unity during this period. We will highlight their rapid progress in periods of relative political and economic stability, as well as their slower but steady development as adversities impelled Christians in mission to respond with united action.

---

1. Latourette, *History of Christianity*, 1349–57.

EDINBURGH 1910

Mission secretaries in both North America and Great Britain proposed holding a third "Ecumenical Conference" in 1910, and Scottish mission leaders nominated Edinburgh as the site. Reflecting on the earlier massive London 1888 and New York 1900 conferences, John R. Mott's spoke for North Americans when he said that it "should not be devoted primarily to education and inspirational purposes," but instead a "thorough consultation and study" of the "most vital questions of missionary opportunity and policy." The official delegates should be restricted in number to 1,200 sent from as many Protestant foreign mission agencies as possible. Under Joseph H. Oldham's thorough leadership as full-time secretary, eight study commissions worked for two years before the Conference. Their findings, based on detailed surveys with data from 1,000 returned questionnaires, provided substance both in conference deliberations and in the Conference's nine-volume report.[2]

Participants came to Edinburgh not as interested individuals, but as officially accredited delegates of their churches or mission boards, setting a new model for such conferences in the twentieth century. It was unique in that delegates covered the full theological spectrum of Protestantism in North America and Europe, "from the most conservative of evangelicals to committed Anglo-Catholics." No attempt was made to include Roman Catholic representatives, although it was the bishop of Cremona who "expressed most clearly of all" the basis of delegate participation as "representatives of all the Christian denominations." Latin America was excluded as being nominally part of Christendom, but Robert Speer organized two unofficial sessions on missions there.[3]

Issues of mission and unity received thoughtful treatment. Commission 2, "The Church in the Mission Field," began its report suggesting that the very title was erroneous as "the whole world is the mission field, and there is not a church that is not a church in the mission field. Some Christian communities are younger and some are older, but that is all the difference." Commission 8, on "Co-operation and the Promotion of Unity," agreed that mission and unity is "the concern of the whole Church of Christ." It faced thoroughly and honestly all forms of cooperation among Christians both in the South and in the North, encouraged all

2. FMC, *Report*, 108–10; Stanley, ed., *World*, 18–48.
3. Stanley, ed., *World*, 320; Gairdner, *Edinburgh*, 200, 210; Hogg, *Foundations*, 120–21.

movements toward church union on "the mission field," and recognized that churches there "may lead the way to unity; but they cannot move far and move safely without the co-operation of the Church at home." The supreme need, they concluded, is not for schemes of union, but rather "apostles of unity." Cheng Jingyi of China electrified the hall as he said, "Speaking plainly we hope to see, in the near future, a united Christian church without any denominational distinctions."[4]

How has Edinburgh 1910 been judged by historians in the past century? For Latourette it was "the birthplace of the modern ecumenical movement." Stephen Neill called it "a landmark in church history" that "led on to the first permanent ecumenical organization ever to exist in the non-Roman Christian world." Richey Hogg rated it "an ecumenical keystone" that with the Second Vatican Council will be considered "one of the two most decisive church councils in the first seven decades of the 20th century."[5]

On June 21 Edinburgh delegates gathered to discuss and vote on the only proposed decision of the Conference—to establish a Continuation Committee on an international and representative basis. Its responsibilities would be to maintain the cooperative work and spirit of the Conference, and "to confer with the Societies and Boards as to the best method of working towards the formation" of a "permanent International Missionary Committee." The vote, after discussion, was a unanimous "Aye," followed by a spontaneous singing of the doxology in relief and jubilation. Two days later the Committee met for the first time and elected Mott as its chairman, and subsequently confirmed Oldham as its full-time salaried secretary—the first for any ecumenical body. That Committee and secretariat would enable Mott, Oldham, and others to hold conferences in Asia to promote the ecumenical vision, to create the *International Review of Missions*, to survive the trauma of the Great War, and to work for the formation of the International Missionary Council in 1921.[6]

---

4. *World Missionary Conference, 1910*, 2:4–6; 8:138, 196; see Stanley, ed., *World*, 91–131, on the voice of the younger churches at Edinburgh.

5. Latourette, "Ecumenical Bearings," 1:362; Neill, "Missionary," 243; Neill, G. Anderson, and Goodwin, eds., *Concise Dictionary*, s.v. "Conferences, World Missionary." For 2009 reflections see Kerr and K. Ross, *Edinburgh 2010*.

6. Stanley, ed., *World*, 297–302; Oldham, "Reflections," 333.

THE TRAVAIL OF WAR

It is striking that Edinburgh 1910, inspired by the vision and purpose of bringing all humanity to oneness in Christ, was to be followed just four years later by the most widespread and destructive war the world had ever known. That war did not break out in non-Christian lands, but rather rent the heartland of Christianity with devastating destruction conceived and executed by those professing the Christian faith.[7]

To that world of colossal suffering people of faith responded with programs of healing and relief on a scale never experienced before. Some were led by united Christian organizations. YMCAs aided prisoners of war. The American Friends Service Committee, supported by Christians of many persuasions, led in relief work, as did *Hilfswerk* from the German side. Other organizations that had their origin in Christian faith and caring but did not bear a Christian name, such as Near East Relief and the International Red Cross, were major players.[8]

German missions gave a special challenge. At the war's outbreak nearly 1,900 Germans, including wives, served overseas as missionaries, most of them outside the few Germany colonies. They ministered to about 630,000 baptized Christians, with about 215,000 pupils attending their mission schools. In their largest fields of service, the National Missionary Council of India and the China Continuation Committee, with financial support from Great Britain and the U.S., helped to fill the void. Where German missionaries were repatriated, as in Togo and the Gold Coast (now Ghana) in Africa, other missions stepped up to provide personnel and financial support.[9]

Is the church supra-national? If so, can church mission work claim a right to continue irrespective of political conditions? This was the position of the Conference of Swedish Missionary Societies in 1915, and the hopes of German missions during World War II. Mott, from a non-belligerent country, in 1914 visited Germany and agreed to pursue negotiations for the release of interned missionaries, and to look for ways by which German Christians could send money to support missionaries working in British possessions. He became the "remnant-symbol of the Continuation Committee" and symbolically a "board of international appeal." Later Oldham lobbied with others successfully for a clause in-

---

7. Latourette, *Christianity in a Revolutionary Age*, 3:490.
8. Latourette, *History of Christianity*, 1357.
9. Hogg, *Foundations*, 167-68.

serted in the Treaty of Versailles that exempted mission properties from confiscation, placing them under one of two Commonwealth trusts prior to their return to the Continental mission agencies.[10]

CONTRASTING VISIONS OF UNITY

Oldham issued this caution during World War I, using the metaphor from war of the imperative of a united effort: "If the hundred or more Protestant Missionary Societies continue . . . to make their plans independently of what others are doing, we may do some splendid and heroic work but we are not going to win the [spiritual] war."[11]

Mainline denominations were not the only ones feeling the urgency to cooperate during this period. In 1917 conservative faith missions formed the Interdenominational Foreign Mission Association (IFMA) as a "fellowship of missions without denominational affiliation" but with an agreed statement of faith adhering to "the fundamental doctrines of the historic Christian faith." Among the founding agencies were the Africa Inland Mission, the China Inland Mission (now Overseas Missionary Fellowship, or OMF International), the Inland South America Missionary Union (South American Indian Mission), South Africa General Mission (now Africa Evangelical Fellowship), and the Women's Union Missionary Society of America. Their primary concern was to reach "hidden" inland people groups. From the 1920s to 1950s the IFMA added about ten new member agencies each decade who also desired closer mission cooperation.[12]

Christians who placed more emphasis on spiritual than institutional unity tended to break away during this period from the more inclusive conciliar movement. The fundamentalist-modernist controversy in the U.S. during the 1920s precipitated breaks in previously united efforts, not only in that country but among Christians in other parts of the world. For example the CIM had been strongly represented at the national conference (Shanghai 1913), forming a Continuation Committee for the Edinburgh 1910 Conference, and was a member of the National Christian Council of China from its formation in 1922. Beginning in

---

10. Ibid., 174–89; Pierard, "Mott," 604–9; Goodall, *Second Fiddle*, 81–82; see also "Survey."

11. "Co-operative Work," in A-WCC/IMC, "IMC General."

12. *EDWM*, s.v. "IFMA"; G. Anderson, "American Protestants," 105. For a comprehensive history see Frizen, *75 Years*.

1926, however, it ceased to participate in any broadly based ecumenical groups. Henry W. Frost, head of the CIM North American division, was cofounder in 1917 of the IFMA and led the CIM into it.[13]

THE INTERNATIONAL MISSIONARY COUNCIL (IMC)

Oldham stressed the importance of cooperation from the beginning of the IMC. In 1916 he wrote, "If co-operative work is to have any future, it must not be an outside subject, but must become an integral part of the work of all Missionary Societies. . . . international co-operation is the order of the day." In 1921 sixty-one representatives from fourteen countries met at Lake Mohonk in New York to constitute formally the IMC. Only seven members of the younger churches came, and German mission leaders were conspicuous by their absence. Those present reaffirmed the Hague Principle, first enunciated in 1885 by the *Ausschuss*, the Standing Committee of German Protestant Missions, that the only bodies authorized to determine missions policy were the boards, missions, and the churches themselves. That principle has been called "the very genius of Protestant and Protestant-Orthodox co-operation."[14]

Among the functions defined in 1921 for the IMC were the following:

> To stimulate thinking and investigation on missionary questions;
> To bring about united action where necessary in missionary matters;
> To help unite the Christian forces of the world in seeking justice in international and inter-racial relations; and
> To call a world missionary conference if and when this should be deemed desirable.

Initially the IMC's member bodies were national missionary organizations that in later years were succeeded by national councils of churches in many countries. Mott's post-Edinburgh visits to Asia stimulated their development, with the formation of the IMC having a similar motivating influence in the 1920s. For years no other organization existed to knit the churches of the Majority World into the organized fabric of world Christianity. In that particular sense the IMC "for a time was the Ecumenical Movement."[15]

---

13. Austin, "Blessed Adversity," 68. The flowering of the cooperative agencies among evangelical Protestant missions will be elucidated in the next chapter.
14. "Co-operative Work," in A-WCC/IMC, "IMC General"; Hogg, *Foundations*, 70–71, 358–59.
15. IMC meetings, *Minutes*, 36; Hogg, *Foundations*, 205–6, 210–15, 283.

Approach to Unity

One appeal of the IMC, Latourette believed, was that it permitted wide variations in creed and polity among its constituent bodies. Deliberately it avoided any effort to bring about an organic union of the churches. As a result it brought together "more of Protestantism than has ever before cooperated through any one agency." Yet even this "great internal freedom" was not sufficient for some major missions to participate, such as the CIM, the largest in China in 1936.[16]

Jerusalem 1928

The IMC's progress in fostering worldwide fellowship among Christians and united planning and action for world mission was in clear evidence at the enlarged meetings of the Council at Jerusalem 1928 and Tambaram (Madras, India) in 1938. Jerusalem was the first global assembly of non-Roman Christians. Of its 231 members nearly one-fourth represented the churches of Asia, Africa, and Latin America. It was the first international Christian meeting to discuss the issue of race, and to lift up secularism as the great new challenge to Christians and those of other faiths. Concerning unity and mission, it appealed to the older churches "to encourage and support the younger churches when, in facing the challenging task of evangelizing the non-Christian world, they take steps according to their ability, to solve what perhaps is the greatest problem of the Universal Church of Christ."[17]

In 1932 John R. Mott divided the modern movement of missions and unity into three periods. He characterized the first, or pre-Edinburgh period as one of "countless detached pieces or demonstrations of co-operative or united effort on the part of Christians of different denominations or races." The second period, between Edinburgh and Jerusalem, was for the great ecumenist the time of "the development of interdenominational and international machinery designed to foster united thinking, planning and action." Noteworthy was the increase in the number of national Christian councils during this period from two to twenty-eight, and the formation and development of the IMC. The third period just dawning, Mott believed, would require the Christian forces for unity to launch out from their bodies of international coop-

---

16. Latourette, *Missions Tomorrow*, 193, 200.
17. Hogg, *Foundations*, 244–58; IMC Conf., Jerusalem *1928, Meeting*, 3:172.

eration into a world of race conflict, international misunderstandings, and threats of war. He called for a transparent Christian fellowship able to transcend all national and racial boundaries.[18]

Tambaram/Madras 1938

Ten years after Jerusalem the churches of Asia, Africa, and Latin America came into their own at Tambaram. A majority of the 471 delegates from 69 countries were from these churches, most of them in their forties. D. T. Niles of Ceylon (now Sri Lanka) called it a "miracle because at a time when national boundaries were bristling with guns . . . Christian men and women still held true to the conviction that they belonged together and to each other." He believed that this conference "decently buried the old distinction between Christian and non-Christian lands." For the delegates the whole world was now a mission field, with the churches challenged to be a true partnership in mission in which the selfhood of every member body is the goal.[19]

The Conference in its report commended spiritual unity and cooperation. That did not satisfy representatives of the younger churches, who unanimously approved their own statement included in the report. They believed that "disunion is both a stumbling block to the faithful and a mockery to those without." Insisting that "visible and organic union must be our goal," they appealed to established missionary societies and boards "to support and encourage us in all our efforts to put an end to the scandalous effects of our divisions, and to lead us in the path of union."[20]

Achievements

In 1947 at Whitby near Toronto, Canada, 112 persons from 40 countries surveyed the state of the worldwide church and its mission emerging from the ashes of war. They approved an important document on "The Supranationality of Missions," which effectively buried the older categories of older and younger churches. It called on churches everywhere to "expectant and world-wide evangelism" in the spirit of "partnership in obedience." In three decades the IMC had brought into being a worldwide Christian fellowship that survived the trauma of war. It had in-

18. Mott, *Addresses and Papers*, 1:240–42.
19. Hogg, *Foundations*, 290–303; Niles, *World Mission*, 18, 23.
20. IMC Conf., Madras 1938, *World Mission*, 151–56.

vested the word "ecumenical," which in the North had been equated with "interdenominational," with a fuller meaning.[21]

MISSION IMPACT ON FAITH AND ORDER, LIFE AND WORK

Three streams of Christian unity flowed out of Edinburgh 1910. While only one focused on missions—the IMC—the other two made important contributions from their perspectives on issues of mission and unity, and were the parent movements of the World Council of Churches.

Faith and Order

This stream sought to have the churches come closer together on issues of doctrine, the ministry, and the sacraments. Its first world conference was held in Lausanne, Switzerland, August 3–21, 1927. The vast majority of the 604 attendees, who represented 108 churches, came from Europe and North America, with smaller numbers from Africa and the Middle East, and only six delegates from Asia. Bishop Charles Henry Brent, a Canadian who served as Anglican bishop of the Philippines, and as bishop in western New York after 1918, had attended Edinburgh 1910, and worked prodigiously to ensure the success of the conference. Its report on "The Call to Unity," drafted by Brent, was unanimously accepted by the delegates. "God wills unity," it declared, but we must "labour in penitence and faith, to build up our broken walls." It reflected the vision of the younger churches in its statement that "already the mission field is impatiently revolting from the divisions of the Western Church to make bold adventure for unity in its own right."[22]

The Second Faith and Order Conference (Edinburgh 1937) fittingly met in the same assembly hall of the Church of Scotland that had been the venue of the World Missionary Conference of 1910. The 443 delegates, plus eight guests and 53 youth participants, came from 43 countries and 123 churches. As in his Lausanne 1927 address on "The Necessity of Christian Unity for the Missionary Enterprise of the Church," Bishop Azariah of Dornakal, India, spoke with penetrating insight and passion on the obstacles to mission caused by Christian disunity. He quoted a leader of the Depressed Class (now called Dalits) who said that his people, when invited to become Christians, respond, "We

---

21. IMC Conf., Whitby 1947, *Renewal*, 335–42, 368–69.
22. Faith and Order, Lausanne 1927, *Faith and Order*, 460–61.

are united in Hinduism ... and we shall become divided in Christianity." And the bishop said, "I had no answer to give." Azariah continued: "The mission field *does* present the greatest opportunity for the achievement of unity; and relatively, unity movements have been most successful in non-Christian areas." "Why do they not go forward at greater pace?" he asked. The answer is simple, he continued. Unless a union "radically alters the relation of similar churches in the home field," no union worth having will be possible among the younger churches because of their continued dependency on the older churches for "spiritual leadership and financial support." The conference "Affirmation," even with Bishop Azariah and a Chinese delegate on the drafting committee, was timid in comparison. It excelled in contrition, acknowledging "that our divisions are contrary to the will of Christ," but called only for prayer that God will "shorten the days of our separation" and "guide us by His Spirit into fullness of unity."[23]

Life and Work

The aim of the first Conference on Life and Work (Stockholm 1925) was "to unite the different churches in common practical work ... applied to the solution of contemporary social and international problems." Its genesis was in the groundswell among the churches after World War I to find a common vision for action. It neither dealt directly with missionary questions nor deliberated on Faith and Order issues. The 600 delegates from 37 countries included for the first time in an ecumenical conference a strong delegation from the Orthodox churches. Only six nationals were present from China, India, and Japan. Although it did not produce any ecumenical social creed or solve any controversial social problems, its symbol of reconciliation among the nations would be the principle reason why the Nobel Peace Prize of 1930 was awarded to its inspired leader, Archbishop Nathan Söderblom of Sweden.[24]

Oldham, as secretary of the Continuation Committee from Edinburgh 1910, worked during World War I to preserve the essential freedom of the whole missionary enterprise. He had maintained that

---

23. Faith and Order, Edinburgh 1937, *Second*, 49–55, 275. For fuller treatment of Faith and Order see Tatlow, "World Conference."
24. Universal Christian Conf., *Stockholm*, 1; Ehrenström, "Movements," 545–52. For Söderblom's personal impact on mission thought see Sharpe, "Legacy," 65–70, and Sundkler, *Nathan Söderblom*.

the less missions have to do with governments the better. As the IMC secretary in the 1920s, however, he gained insight concerning the inextricable relations of missions to colonial governments in Africa. To Mott he wrote in 1928, "Unless, therefore, missions are content to be little more than driftwood on the main stream of human progress in Africa, they must take full account of the policies of government, criticizing them when they believe them to be wrong in order that they may be changed, and co-operating whole-heartedly in the carrying out of the policies when they are right."[25]

New challenges arose in 1935 when Oldham was invited by Life and Work to chair its Research Committee in preparation for its second conference (Oxford 1937), which would focus on issues of "Church, Community, and State." Despite Mott's opposition, Oldham accepted the invitation and became responsible more than any other person for organizing the preparatory studies, the conference itself, and its report. The preparatory studies, involving 300–400 contributors, were later judged "in thoroughness and range of cooperation" to be "unequaled by previous Christian world gatherings."[26]

Oxford's 425 registered members included 300 delegates from 120 communions, plus 100 specialists in various fields recruited by the Universal Christian Council for Life and Work, formed after Lausanne 1927. It was "an ecumenical study conference on a world scale," with Mott as chair and Archbishop William Temple heading the Conference Message Committee. The Message tried "to look without illusion at the chaos and disintegration of the world, the injustices of the social order, and the menace and horror of war." It condemned war and reasserted the churches' "obligation to seek the way of freeing [humankind] from its physical, moral and spiritual ravages." It called upon Christians to "do all in their power to promote among the nations justice and peaceful cooperation," and to "press the demand for justice on behalf of the less fortunate."[27]

---

25. Hogg, *Foundations*, 178–82; Oldham to Mott, September 17, 1928, in A-WCC/IMC, "Letters."

26. Hogg, *Foundations*, 284–85, 421–22; Oldham to Mott, November 14, 1935, and Mott to Oldham, December 15, 1935, in A-WCC/IMC, "Letters"; Ehrenström, "Movements," 585.

27. Ehrenström, "Movements," 589; World Conf., *Oxford Conference*, 47–51. For the conference papers see World Conf., *Universal Church*.

OTHER COOPERATIVE EFFORTS

Student Movements

As in the late nineteenth century, Christian students continued to provide missionary vision and commitment, and their organizations a training ground for future leaders able to work across social, political, and religious boundaries.

STUDENT VOLUNTEER MOVEMENT (SVM)

The SVM shared the buoyant optimism of the pre-World War years, only to be buffeted by the winds of isolationism and economic depression, and the subsequent international tensions. The Mott imprint of world vision with optimism characterized the Eighth SVM Quadrennial in Des Moines, Iowa, in 1920 with its theme, "Students and World Advance." The venerable SVM chairman of thirty-two years challenged students to "common understanding and triumphant unity of action." Concerning the accomplishments for unity of the Movement, he wrote, "It may be questioned whether there is any other one unifying influence among Christians which is today more potent than that of the life and work of the 8,000 American and Canadian student volunteers and the nearly 3,000 British, Australasian, South African and Continental European volunteers, who constitute over one-third of the foreign missionaries of the world."[28]

The spirit of reaction and disillusionment following the First World War deeply affected the student associations, most notably the SVM. Other factors were the revolt of youth, the rise of nationalism, and the decline of the small college in the U.S. Francis F. Miller assessed the pulse of the nation in 1936 and declared that "we have perhaps never, in the past thirty years, been more isolated from the rest of the world than we are at the present time."[29] The number of active student unions with SVM groups in the U.S. dwindled from 41 in 1925 to 13 in 1937. In contrast to the 1920 SVM Quadrennial, at which 2,783 participants signed decision cards indicating willingness to be foreign missionaries, only 25 signed cards in 1938. The national program had virtually collapsed.[30]

---

28. SVM, *Achievements*, 20.
29. Beahm, "Factors," 312; SVM Conv., *Students*, 229.
30. Beahm, "Factors," 275–76; Winter, *Twenty-Five*, 55. For a detailed history see Parker, *Kingdom*.

Inter-Varsity Christian Fellowship (IVCF)

As the SVM declined and changed its priorities in the 1930s from missions to ecumenism, evangelicals formed the Student Foreign Missions Fellowship (SFMF) in 1936. In 1939 the first IVCF chapters began in the U.S. In 1945 these two movements merged as the SFMF became the missionary arm of the IVCF. At the first IVCF convention (Toronto 1946) Samuel Zwemer reminded the students that they were meeting on the sixtieth anniversary of the Mount Hermon gathering that launched the SVM with the watchword of the "Evangelization of the World in This Generation." Thereafter, the IVCF considered itself to be the group providing authentic continuity in student fervor for evangelization and missions. Succeeding conventions, held every three years at the University of Illinois Urbana campus, grew to attendances of almost 20,000 students. All went home with pledge cards to be signed after prayer by those willing to serve overseas as missionaries. Follow up on those making written commitments has been facilitated in recent years through use of computers to store data about the interested students, matching their interests with needs expressed by mission agencies.[31]

World Student Christian Federation (WSCF)

The WSCF pioneered in bringing the Eastern and Oriental Orthodox churches into the ecumenical movement. The first contacts were with the Syrian Orthodox in India. In 1911, led by Mott, the WSCF took an "adventure in faith" and held its conference in Constantinople, Turkey, where the threat of war was imminent and no SCMs or national student organizations existed to be hosts. Mott wrote, "The ecumenical character of the conference was unique, for not since the early church councils in this part of the world, has there been an assembly so representative of the entire Church. Practically all the great Communions were represented. Delegates were present from the various Eastern churches, the Orthodox churches of Greece, Russia, Rumania, Bulgaria and Serbia; as well as the Gregorian, Syrian, Maronite, and Coptic churches."

The Ecumenical Patriarch gave the conference his blessing: "I consider such a conference to draw Christians into fellowship and cooperation as one of the most sacred causes, and I will help it in any way in my power." After these contacts the patriarch was emboldened in 1920 to propose the formation of a world league of churches.[32]

---

31. G. Anderson, "American Protestants," 106; Escobar, "Recruitment," 538–39.
32. Quoted in Rouse, *WSCF*, 154; Potter, "Third World," 59.

Participation in the WSCF was in the resume of almost everyone who helped form the World Council of Churches. The WSCF was also formative for many participants in the first WCC assembly in 1948.

Laymen United for Missions

Many lay men and women shared the passion for missions with cooperative effort during this period. For example, John B. Sleman, a young Washington D.C. businessman, attended the 1906 SVM conference. Deeply impressed by the commitment of college students to missionary service, he presented to another Congregationalist businessman, Samuel B. Capen, the idea of forming a parallel movement of businessmen to provide the finance and administration "to make the work of these young men effective." Later that year Capen led in forming the Laymen's Missionary Movement, served as its chairman, with John R. Mott and Robert E. Speer on the board to inspire and link the new body to the SVM. This was but the first of several organizations of laymen united for missions from 1910 to 1947.[33]

LAYMEN'S MISSIONARY MOVEMENT

The Movement's goal was "to enlist all men of all branches of the Church in cordial and active support of the mission work of their own missionary organizations." Soon parallel movements began in Canada (1907), Scotland (1907), Ireland (1908), and England (1909).[34]

The objective of the Movement, as stated at the Boston conference of 1908, was that "every Christian man [be] a giver to mission." In 1909 and 1910 three- to four-day conventions were held in more than 50 cities. An estimated 250,000, including many women, attended 425 shorter interdenominational conferences in 1912–13. Solicited pledges for foreign missions were to be paid through the churches. Measured by dollars given for mission, no other institution had such a great impact on the foreign mission work of the Protestant churches from 1906 to 1913, the years of its greatest influence.[35]

MEN AND RELIGION FORWARD MOVEMENT

While the Laymen's Missionary Movement motivated support for foreign missions across denominational lines, the Men and Religion Forward

---

33. L. Carey, *Capen*, 164–78.
34. Maclennan, *Laymen's*, 23–24.
35. Dawson, "Funding," 156–57.

Movement of 1911–12 sought to educate Christians about social conditions in their own communities and to motivate and equip them to improve those conditions. Its key leaders, Fred B. Smith, Charles Stelzle, and Raymond Robins, all were leaders in the YMCA nationally and internationally. Mass meetings and seminars held in seventy cities promoted both evangelism and social service. Speakers included a cross-section of Protestant luminaries, including William Jennings Bryan, John R. Mott, Gypsy Smith, Booker T. Washington, and Jane Addams. Although Walter Rauschenbusch, a leading proponent of the Social Gospel, insisted that this enterprise was the "most comprehensive evangelistic movement undertaken in this country," the popular enthusiasm bore few lasting results.[36]

Inter-Church World Movement (IWM)

The end of World War I and the plans to form the League of Nations inspired Protestant church leaders in North America to unite in cooperative fundraising to meet the providential opportunities of the post-war era. The IWM began the very week that John R. Mott, missionary leader and head of the YMCA, launched the United War Work Campaign, which he was to call the "largest voluntary offering in history." The Campaign raised $230,000,000 to assist servicemen in their transition to civilian life.

Supporting the foreign missionary enterprise was the focus of the IWM. While soliciting financial support in North America, leaders communicated their plans and activities to missionary organizations in Britain, Continental Europe, Asia, and Africa. Mission executives from thirty denominations, representing about 60 percent of Protestant church membership, shaped the joint budget. With Mott, the master fundraiser, as its chair, the executive committee agreed on a first-year goal of $336,000,000. They were encouraged by the active participation of John D. Rockefeller Jr., who predicted that "it will become the greatest force for righteousness in this whole world." Convinced that Christian businessmen, even those not active in churches, would support this movement as they had the war effort, they secured a bank loan and a five-story office building to house the Movement's 2,612 employees.

Within a year, however, the plan failed. Although 176 million dollars was raised in the first year (the largest sum ever raised interdenomi-

---

36. G. Smith, "Men," 95–107.

nationally), it met only 52 percent of its goal. With debts outstanding it was regarded by the general public as a colossal failure. Mott, in his 1939 post-mortem, however, felt that the Movement "made a tremendous appeal to the imagination, quickened the conscience, and stimulated sacrificial action." Fresh and comprehensive social surveys completed by the staff were an ongoing contribution—a work continued in subsequent years by the Institute of Social and Religious Research funded by Rockefeller.[37]

Laymen's Foreign Mission Inquiry

The vision of a united Protestant effort in missions did not die with the collapse of the Inter-Church World Movement. In 1930 Baptist laymen, meeting with Rockefeller and Mott, proposed a major new evaluation of Protestant missions. The "Laymen's Inquiry," as the overall project was called, was financed by Rockefeller, blessed by seven of the major denominational mission boards, and carried out by the Institute of Social and Religious Research. Staff visited India, Burma, Japan, and China to conduct interviews and collect data. A fifteen-member Commission of Appraisal, representing major denominations but independent of their mission boards, visited mission areas and composed with staff the seven-volume final report.[38]

The one-volume summary, entitled *Rethinking Missions*, attracted unusual attention. Much controversy ensued over its redefinition of mission as "preparation for world unity in civilization" by Christians joining together with those of other faiths to discover the foundation of religiosity shared by all. Largely lost was its cogent analysis of the "evils of disunion" in which union projects are "hampered and nullified" by having to appeal to multiple mission agencies for support and personnel. Their visionary proposal for unity in mission on a comprehensive scale included transfer of mission responsibility to the hands of the nationals, and the channeling of resources through "a single organization for Christian service abroad."[39]

---

37. Hopkins, *Mott*, 569–74; FMC, *Report*, 179–82; Mott, *Five Decades*, 63–67; Ernst, *Moment*, 69–75; Harvey, "Rockefeller." The Institute of Social and Religious Research sponsored not only important social surveys in North America, but also IMC-sponsored projects, including J. Waskom Pickett's study of the mass movements toward Christianity in India.

38. *Laymen's Inquiry*.

39. Laymen's Inquiry, *Re-thinking*, 313–29; for the debate see Hutchison, *Errand*, 158–75.

Women United for Mission

Two great missionary gatherings took place in 1910—the World Missionary Conference in Edinburgh and the Women's Missionary Jubilee. The latter was inspired by Helen Barrett Montgomery's *Western Women in Eastern Lands*, a fifty-year history of the woman's missionary movement that was a religious bestseller in 1910. The Jubilee of 1910–11 included celebrations in forty-eight major cities attended by thousands of women. Thank offerings raised a million dollars for projects that would unite all women. To perpetuate the cooperative spirit, women's mission boards formed the Federation of Woman's Boards of Foreign Missions in North America, and pledged to form local federated missionary societies. Realizing that women around the world were eager for higher education, they raised three million dollars to support seven ecumenical colleges for women in China, India, and Japan. Lucy Peabody, in her 1927 retrospective on these years, concluded, "Directly or indirectly women's missionary societies have made a great contribution to the world and have strengthened the Church by this contribution."[40]

The World Day of Prayer was another important innovation and lasting contribution. In 1919 the Federation of Women's Boards agreed to combine their separate observances and promote this united Day of Prayer. Increasingly the program became more international in character, with women named by the International Missionary Council as advisory members. By 1930 women in forty countries participated.[41]

Education

Edinburgh 1910 was a watershed for cooperation in education by missions. Many survey respondents believed united efforts to be a necessity, not a mission luxury. "The only hope of the survival of Christian schools in China," Bishop Bashford wrote, "lies in such federation, co-operation, or union as will enable them to furnish a better equipment for the present life, as well as for the life that is to come, than the government schools

---

40. Peabody, "Woman's Place," 910; Montgomery, *Western Women*; Robert, "Introduction," 506. See Robert, *American Women*, 255–316, for the Jubilee event and later twentieth-century developments, and 317–407 for the history of Roman Catholic women in overseas mission from the United States.

41. Beaver, *American Protestant Women*, 159–62. In 1951 sponsorship was transferred to the United Council of Church Women of the NCC, which became Church Women United in 1966.

can furnish." The report of Commission 8 on "Co-operation and Unity" cited the Institution at Lovedale, South Africa, as a model. Although founded and maintained by one mission society (the United Free Church of Scotland), it "trained students connected with every denomination in South Africa." The Madras Christian College in India took the next step—shifting ultimate control from the United Free Church to a college council with official representatives from seven churches. Other union institutions in 1910 included the North China Education Union and the Shantung Christian University. The United Missionary Training College for Women in Calcutta was but one of several joint ventures in India. United Theological College in Bangalore, founded in 1910, was the pioneer cooperative venture in that country in theological education.[42]

How would Anglicans or Baptists or Presbyterians inculcate their denominational emphases in united institutions? Commission 8 favored the plan in which an educational institution would be under the joint control of several missions, with provision for religious teaching in denominational hostels. The Commission said concerning this solution, "Co-operation is so essential to educational efficiency . . . where denominational differences prevent any other plan being adopted." The report concluded that in colleges of art, medicine, teaching, and theology "it seems to us a duty to take steps wherever circumstances make it possible to secure increased efficiency by cooperative action. . . . There is probably no branch of missionary work, in respect of which joint action is so feasible and so manifestly desirable, if not absolutely necessary, as in educational work." Commission 3 on education came to the same conclusion and proposed that united Christian colleges be established in India, China, and Japan. As a direct result of this recommendation six collaborating missions opened Fukien Christian College in China in 1915.[43]

The Edinburgh vision for cooperation and united effort in educational mission flowered with increasingly urgency from 1910 to 1947. The IMC's next conference (Jerusalem 1928) reported that "a large and rich experience in international cooperation is being worked out" embracing institutions of higher learning. By 1935 there were twenty-two

---

42. *World Missionary Conference, 1910*, 8:62-71.
43. Ibid., 8:68, 73; 3:56-57, 121, 164-65; Stanley, ed., *World*, 200. For further development of these concepts after Edinburgh see A. Brown, *Unity*, 158-65; and Burton, "Findings," 670-82.

union colleges and fifteen professional schools of collegiate rank. The next international IMC conference (Madras 1938) expressed alarm that "the present condition of theological training is one of the greatest weaknesses in the whole Christian enterprise." They emphasized particularly "the need for cooperative and united effort."[44]

Higher education came later in Africa, but with it a rapid concern for cooperative and united effort by mission agencies. Through the initiative of the Foreign Missions Conference (USA) and the Phelps-Stokes Fund, a survey commission on educational conditions and needs went to Central, West, and South Africa in 1920–21 with the purpose "to enable missionary societies to plan a more effective strategy." A second commission, stimulated by the Conference of British Missionary Societies and J. H. Oldham of the IMC, went to East Africa in 1923–24. Both reports urged cooperation in education between missions and the governments, and cooperative efforts in higher education by the missions.[45]

Medical Missions

The World Missionary Conference (Edinburgh 1910) gave a dynamic push for cooperation in medical work. A sectional conference of medical delegates resolved "that co-operation in the Mission field is of the highest importance." They recognized that the training facilities for national medical personnel should be cooperative ventures "for the purpose of economy, efficiency, and permanence." They gave high approval to the model of the Union Medical College in Peking with faculty from eleven different missionary societies. Another model commended by Commission 8 on "Cooperation and Unity" was that of the Mission to Lepers, an interdenominational society that worked cooperatively with other mission agencies.[46]

The impetus for cooperative effort continued after Edinburgh. Three years later Arthur T. Brown wrote in *Unity and Missions*, "Medical work presents another attractive opportunity for union effort. Disease is not denominational, and there is no good reason why its treatment should be." He argued that union hospitals are already in successful

---

44. IMC Conf., Jerusalem 1928, *Meeting*, 7:22–23; Fahs and H. Davis, *Conspectus*, 111–87. The IMC's Theological Education Fund, created in 1957, was an outgrowth of these recommendations. See Lienemann-Perrin, *Training*, 4–7.

45. Hogg, *Foundations*, 231–32, and 414 n. 88–89, for the full reports.

46. *World Missionary Conference, 1910*, 8:73–74, 9:113–20.

operation in various cities of Asia, and that "missionary societies have agreed upon the policy of union medical colleges and nurses' training schools . . . turning a deaf ear to appeals for denominational schools." The Rockefeller Foundation added its weight in 1916 when asked to fund the building of higher quality medical centers in Peking and Shanghai. Determined "to secure efficiency if it should cost us millions," the Foundation called for the establishment of the China Medical Board, and urged "team work upon the part of the representatives of the various Boards and Societies." A mission executive concluded that "the union medical colleges . . . stand today as the greatest hope of the future of medical missions in the Orient."[47]

The peak of medical missions may have come in 1928 with 1,307 medical missionaries at work. Already by 1925 China had nearly 600 medical missionaries working in 200 hospitals and dispensaries. In the next 35 years in that country, buffeted by civil war and the Japanese invasion, leadership shifted dramatically. By 1948 the membership of the Chinese Medical Association included about 350 foreign doctors but over 5,000 Chinese physicians. Even before the Peoples Republic of China was established, the government raised educational standards and pushed for united efforts. While mission leaders approved of such cooperation, with many regarding it as "essential for the progress and permanence of Christian medical work," the change was difficult to apply in practice.[48]

Cooperation in medical missions shifted after World War II as many newly independent nations placed a priority on higher levels of medical training in government institutions. Dr. Stanley Browne wrote in 1956, "But a few short years ago, Christian missions offered the only or the best training available in medicine or in nursing. Now, except for a few well-known exceptions, missions are still training the lower-grade medical auxiliaries only, while recently developed government institutions are coping with the more expensive higher training." He predicted that "missions must work together, or wane in separation [because] circumstances, financial and strategic, are making more obviously necessary some form of co-operation."[49]

47. A. Brown, *Unity*, 166–67; Lambuth, *Medical*, 185–87; Moorshead, "Church," 283.
48. H. Chapman, "Co-operation." Not until 1944 did missions in India form the Union Christian College, Vellore. For its history see McGilvray, "Vellore."
49. Browne, "Crossroads," 279–81.

Increasingly, preventive medicine became a priority area for united effort. The IMC Conference (Madras 1938) gave "a clear call to give greater attention to preventive medicine," saying that "this will mean active sharing in all forms of health and welfare work and health teaching in schools." P. V. Benjamin in 1939 called this "a new emphasis" in which "cooperation is especially important." The Christian Medical Commission, founded in 1967 by the WCC to coordinate church-related medical work on six continents, set a missional priority of "Christian responsibility for the development of health care to the total population of the area they serve." It conceived of its role to be "to stimulate and help establish national agencies for the coordination and joint planning of health care offered by both Protestants and Roman Catholics" and to build a close working relationship with the World Health Organization.[50]

Rural Development

Once again John R. Mott was the catalyst for a significant new cooperative development in missions. In 1928 he called together thirty-eight rural workers in India, among them seven full-time agriculturists, and said, "We must have a world movement by the churches. Thoroughgoing rural reconstruction is basic to the permanent well-being of . . . nations. The churches have, by proclaiming the Good News of Christ, set the arena for a *good revolution*. The widely scattered people like yourselves and the variety of creative endeavours that you represent must be unified into a world agricultural movement . . . strong enough to make its impact felt."

Two year's later Mott met with a group of U.S. laymen and church leaders in New York to organize Agricultural Missions, Inc. Its purpose and policy was "to aid churches, selected persons, institutions, and agencies in any part of the world which are in any way related to agriculture and country life; to facilitate the interchange of agricultural knowledge and experience among the nations." The new cooperative body began to assist Protestant agricultural missionaries who increased in number from 50 to 104 during the years 1930–36.[51]

Since World War II, Agricultural Missions, Inc. has focused on practical programs including provision of services and supplies to rural

50. IMC Conf., Madras 1938, *World Mission*, 81; Benjamin, "Outlook," 565; WCC/CC, *Uppsala to Nairobi*, 96–97.
51. Moomaw, *Crusade*, 198.

development programs in many countries, along with Heifer Project, CROP, and Church World Service in the U.S. Increasingly it gave priority to the training of national colleagues within Africa, Asia, the Middle East, and Latin America. In 1965 it formally affiliated with the NCCUSA and its Church World Service program, and welcomed Roman Catholic agencies as full members. On June 6, 1965, the National Council issued its own statement on world hunger. In it the council

> *Recognizes* that "... one billion people are living under conditions of crippling hunger."
> *Calls* for "... denominational and concerted action."
> *Hopes to see* "... coordination with churches that are not members of the National Council and discussions with representatives of the Vatican, with Jewish, and other, voluntary organizations."[52]

Christian Literature and Media

From their founding the IMC and member national councils of churches took a keen interest in promoting and producing Christian literature for Christians in the Majority World. "The production and circulation of Christian literature is an outstanding example of the value of cooperation," the Jerusalem 1928 conference declared. Madras 1938 called for a "drastic overhaul of the methods and means of producing and selling Christian literature." It recommended "that each National Christian Council or regional conference of missions should work for an effective co-operative union or federation of the Christian literature agencies and presses within the area it serves."[53]

Special cooperative agencies developed to serve the needs of Africa, and of women and children. Recognizing Africa's special need for Christian literature, the Conference of British Missionary Societies in 1923 established its Africa Literature Committee. In 1929 the IMC expanded the work by establishing the International Committee on Christian Literature for Africa, with membership of most of the Protestant missions and literature societies at work on that continent. Its sole aim was to "promote the production, publication, and distribution of literature for use in connection with missionary work in Africa."

---

52. Rhoades, "Agricultural Missions," 346–53.
53. IMC Conf., Jerusalem 1928, *Meeting*, 7:53; IMC Conf., Madras 1938, *"Madras Series,"* 4:292–93; IMC Conf., Madras 1938, *World Mission*, 96. See also Ury, *Highway*.

Books for Africa, a quarterly bulletin begun in 1931, was distributed freely to all Africa missionaries sharing news of available publications and literature plans.

Women's boards of foreign missions in North America led in concern for Christian literature for women and children. They formed in 1912 the Interdenominational Committee on Christian Literature for Oriental Women, supporting its program from their own resources, and from 1925 by the World Day of Prayer offerings. Incorporated in 1934 as the Committee of Christian Literature for Women and Children in Mission Fields, it subsidized popular magazines for women and children in Japan, India, and Korea, picture books for African children, and the Home Library of more than 100 small books for Africa. Upon the formation of the NCCUSA in 1950, this was the only program of the Division of Overseas Ministries carried over from the earlier ecumenical sponsorship.[54]

Frank Laubach, called the "Apostle to the Silent Billion," developed his "each one teach one" approach to literacy as an American Board missionary to the Moros of Mindanao Island in the Philippines beginning in 1929. Convinced that his method had worldwide application, Laubach formed a World Literacy Committee in 1935. In 1941 the Foreign Missions Conference of North America began to sponsor this ministry, with Laubach as staff person teaching literacy methods and promoting literacy campaigns. By his death in 1970 he had carried his literacy ministry to 103 countries with literacy primers embodying his principles for 313 languages.[55]

Christian radio broadcasts are as old as the medium itself. The first wireless broadcast sent across the world was an informal Christian program on Christmas Eve, 1906. HCJB, "The Voice of the Andes," was the first of many evangelical mission radio stations. It began broadcasting from Ecuador in 1931. The Far East Broadcasting Company began programs from Shanghai in 1945 and Manila in 1948.

Conciliar Protestants and Roman Catholics chose to work through secular broadcast companies. In 1928 the NBC network in North America established a Religious Advisory Council of Protestant, Roman Catholic, and Jewish leaders to formulate policies for free air time for

---

54. Hogg, *Foundations*, 277–78; Beaver, *American Protestant Women*, 163–65, 194–97.

55. Gowing, "Laubach," 500–507.

religious broadcasts. The national ecumenical organizations (FCC succeeded by NCCUSA) developed joint nonsectarian programming. In the 1940s Margaret Wong, secretary of the International Committee on Christian Literature for Africa, prepared scripts and recordings on behalf of the churches for broadcast to Africa by the BBC.[56]

ORPHANED MISSIONS

As early as 1934 Oldham, secretary of the IMC, had written, "I am giving a good deal of time to the question of the future of German missions." In the summer of 1939 Mott, the IMC chairman, and A. L. Warnshuis, its U.S. secretary, visited German and other missionary leaders in Berlin and worked out plans for safeguarding missionary work in the likely event of war. In September Dr. Karl Hartenstein resigned as director of the Basel Mission because he expected "to be called for military service in Germany," and expressed thanks to William Paton, then IMC secretary, "for all you can do to maintain the work and the missionary fields of the German missions."[57]

Before war broke out Mott wrote that "the overwhelming demands of war relief can never be met by divided counsels and action." The rapid German occupation of Norway, Holland, Belgium, and the partition of France, caught the ecumenical agencies with no plans in place. In Asia and Africa the affected missions, including the German boards, totaled 168 missions, with 3,500 missionaries and $4.5 million in annual contributions from Europe disrupted by the war. Even the Basel Mission, headquartered in neutral Switzerland, was profoundly affected. Its purpose since its founding in 1815 was to be a transnational mission agency. By 1941, however, the Basel Mission found it impossible to work as a transnational mission "in a time like ours."[58]

Christians around the world responded with great generosity. From 1939 to 1947 churches contributed almost $6.5 million to support the orphaned missions. They channeled $1.5 million through the IMC, and an additional $2.5 million through the Lutheran World Federation to as-

56. Voskuil, "Reaching," 81–84; Hogg, *Foundations*, 332.
57. J. H. Oldham to John R. Mott, November 14, 1934, in A-WCC/GS, "IMC Correspondence," doc 26133.14; Goodall, *Second Fiddle*, 82; Hartenstein to Paton, September 5 and October 26, 1939, in A-Basel, "IMC," QK 4.9.
58. Mott, *Five Decades*, 60; Warnshuis, "The Story," 23; "Report on the Situation of the Basel Mission, Nov. 10, 1939," Letter A. Koechlin to Warnshuis, Sept. 26, 1941, A-Basel Box QK-4.9.

sist orphaned Lutheran missions. No Protestant mission anywhere in the world had to be suspended or abandoned, with aid sent to every one of the 112 missions in distress. Christians in Africa, Asia, and Oceania not only contributed funds, but also gave material support to missionaries left penniless. The Norwegian government in exile in London contributed, and the Chinese doubled the exchange rate for mission relief funds from outside.[59]

In the darkest hours of 1942 Latourette wrote that "quite conceivably it will be the Oecumenical Movement through which, while the nations of the world have been pulling apart, the Christians of the world have been coming together." In 1944 Warnshuis concluded that this united effort "forged a fellowship that is standing the strain of war today and is functioning across the frontiers of nations and also over the barriers of denominations." It is "the miracle of the realized oneness." C. W. Ranson predicted that when the full story is told "it will be recognized as one of the most impressive episodes in the annals of the Christian Church." "In conception and achievement the project was unique in the history of the Christian church," Richey Hogg wrote, and continued, "Here was the actual proof of a Christian world fellowship transcending nation and denomination and uniting its members in faith and love."[60]

CONCLUSION

After surveying nearly 140 years of Protestant missions, Kenneth Scott Latourette concluded that "never has so much of Protestantism been drawn together for common action as through the International Missionary Council and its constituent bodies." Through it Christians were "being knit together consciously into a world-embracing fellowship and reaching out in friendly fashion to non-Protestant Christians." Archbishop William Temple in 1942, upon becoming archbishop of Canterbury, gave an equally sanguine assessment: "God has been building up a Christian fellowship which now extends into almost every nation, and binds citizens of them all together in true unity and mutual love. No human agency has planned this. It is the result of the great mis-

---

59. IMC (Whitby 1950), *Minutes*, 47–51; Hogg, *Foundations*, 309–12.
60. Latourette, "Missions and Wars," 399; Warnshuis, "Story," 31; Ranson, in IMC Conf., Whitby 1947, *Renewal*, 4; Hogg, *Foundations*, 316.

sionary enterprise of the last hundred and fifty years . . . it is the great new fact of our era."[61]

Yet missionary leaders of wide vision like Latourette felt the continuing impulse of the Spirit for a wider unity. "Remember the 'invisible Christians,'" the Yale historian urged, referring to those thousands in every land, most notably in India, who regarded themselves as followers of Christ without ever being baptized. Rejoicing in the communion of love which binds Christians together, yet saddened by barriers to sacramental unity, Latourette argued that the real unity is one of the Spirit and "cannot be insured by intellectual formulas, organization, or even intercommunion."[62]

---

61. Latourette, "Distinctive Features," 443; Latourette, *Missions Tomorrow*, 197; Temple, *Forward*, 2.

62. Latourette, *Missions Tomorrow*, 195-96.

5

Multiple Unity Streams, 1948–2010

A REVOLUTIONARY AGE

WHEN THE UNITED NATIONS was founded in 1945, some 750 million people, nearly a third of the world's population, lived in territories that were dependent on colonial powers. In the next 25 years 63 nations received their independence from colonial rule. This wave of decolonization changed the face of the planet. "Never before have so many millions of people taken part in such a rapid and radical social upheaval," Rajah Manikam wrote from India in 1957. "In the last ten years, nearly 700 millions have gained their independence." He called it "a revolution of the people, of the masses who are demanding political independence, economic justice, social equality and religious motivation of life." While the new nationalism of Asian countries could be cemented by political and cultural traditions of long standing, African national units were more the creations of European colonialism. Political boundaries on that continent divided approximately one-third of all the indigenous tribal peoples among two or more nation states. However, by 2010 fewer than two million people continued to live under colonial rule in the sixteen remaining non-self-governing territories.[1]

"One Zambia, One Nation!" was shouted over and over at political rallies attended by this author in that nation following the granting of black majority rule in 1964. The division of colonial India into the separate nations of India and Pakistan caused a greater migration of peoples than World War II. In Africa national boundaries remained intact while people groups fought for separate identities from Biafra to Sudan, and naked power struggles in Liberia, Sierra Leone, Angola, and the Congo

---

1. United Nations, "Decolonization"; Manikam, "New Era," 32.

engulfed peoples in seemingly unending warfare and suffering. "Ethnic cleansing" became a living nightmare for millions from Bosnia and Rwanda to Darfur and Iraq.

In 2010 the United Nations worked for peace with justice within 192 member nations. While wars between nation-states had declined dramatically since its founding, internal violence and denial of human rights within states had increased. Terrorism proliferated diverting scarce resources away from noble international goals of "Health for All by the Year 2000," eradicating poverty, providing universal education, and combating climate change. Many whose nations had gained political independence felt strongly that globalization threatened their economic and cultural independence.

This was the political and cultural milieu in which for over fifty years Christians found new frontiers for mission and unity. The WCC's conference on rapid social change in 1959 included a timely probe into "the dynamics of nationalism in areas of rapid social change today." It declared that the church's participation in nationalism must be positive and responsible. One special contribution "to the development of a healthy nationalism" is "the Church's struggle for the freedom to worship and witness to Christ as Lord of the nation, to keep its fellowship open to all men [and women] irrespective of colour or other communal affiliation, and to have relations with churches outside the nation." A 1963 conference found the church's primary missionary challenge around the world in "the line that separates belief from unbelief." But other frontiers existed. The most important of these, it declared, "are between nations and races, between ideological and cultural groups." It recognized that "many of these nations are newly independent and are struggling for selfhood and a better way of life than they have known." It identified a "secular ecumenical movement" in the "growing sense of common humanity or human solidarity in the world which finds its expression in mutual concern, a sense of participation in the struggles of others for their fundamental rights, and a common endeavour in building structures of a world community and search for an ethos to make them stable." "How are secular ecumenism and Christian ecumenism related to each other?" the conference asked. "What is the peculiar Christian witness of missions to and within secular ecumenism?"[2]

2. International Ecumenical Conf., *Dilemmas*, 54–61; WCC/DMWE Conf., Mexico City 1963, *Witness*, 161, 15.

PART ONE: Historical

VITALITY AND PLURALISM

Because Christianity had been associated with imperialism and colonialism, scholars predicted that many Christian communities in newly independent countries would wane as alien enclaves. Initially in China under communism that thesis appeared to be substantiated. However, by 1965 Latourette noted the indigenous strength of the Christian movement in the non-Western world. He wrote that "the revolt among non-Europeans against imperialism and colonialism was accompanied by the deepened rootage of Christianity.... In land after land, the Christian churches grew and were increasingly self-governing, self-supporting, and self-propagating, as the long-cherished dream of Western missionaries had envisioned them." Later evidence at the turn of the century showed that Christianity in China was flourishing as never before. Globally it was estimated in 2008 that affiliated Christians increased 77,000 in number each day, with 91 percent of that increase taking place in Africa, Asia, and Latin America. Barrett judged that "the perception of Christianity as a Western religion is disintegrating" now that a growing majority of Christians are in the Global South.[3]

Pluralism of religious loyalties—both with Christianity and with other faiths—became the defining reality of the age. Although the United States had excelled in having a multiplicity of religious loyalties, Hutchison found by 1960 "an epochal and quite fundamental transition" from a Protestant hegemony to a more widespread pluralism. In the same period McLeod found a fragmentation of religious life in Western Europe. Churches that historically had helped bind societies together were rapidly losing their influence. Simultaneously, new sect-like groups, although small in numbers, became highly active. Even the more church-like religious institutions contained renewal movements that took on a more sectarian character.[4]

Evangelicals, characterized by emphasizing the Bible as their authority, the new birth as the normative religious experience, and evangelization as their mission, grew in numbers on every continent. Evangelicalism is a kaleidoscope of resilient new and older spiritual movements. Outside of North America and Europe evangelical Christianity has grown significantly in the last forty years. It has two components. Membership

---

3. Latourette, *Christianity through the Ages*, 299; Barrett, Johnson, and Crossing, "Missiometrics," 28.

4. Hutchison, "Preface, vii–viii; McLeod, *Religion*, 140–43.

of evangelical churches or denominations grew globally from 93.4 million in 1970 to 210.6 million in 2000. The larger number of Christians who call themselves "evangelicals" grew from 277.1 million in 1970 to 647.8 million in 2000. Evangelicals also are called "Great Commission Christians" because they profess obedience to Christ's commission to witness to all peoples.[5]

Dynamic growth, diversity, and pluralism also characterized missions in this half-century. By 2000 the number of full-time Christian workers sent as foreign missionaries totaled 419,524. This total included 91,956 foreign missionaries sent by churches of the Majority World—22 percent of the global total. Churches of Africa sent 17,406, Asia 24,504, Latin America 41,544, and Oceania 8,502. The numbers of Protestant foreign missionaries sent from North America increased 776 percent between 1972 and 2005. The largest increases were in short-termers serving two weeks to one year (5,000 to 147,852) and in non-North Americans (0 to 88,500). Many of the latter were workers in Majority World churches supported by North American funding.[6]

Side by side with increasing pluralism and diversity among Christians came a growing willingness to cooperate and work together. From 1970 to 2005 there was a greater annual growth worldwide of the number of local councils of churches than was the percentage increase in numbers of both denominations and congregations. At the world level Christian world communions more than doubled in number.

The WCC's Lund Conference on Faith and Order held in 1952 raised four questions concerning unity that remained relevant throughout this period:

1. Should our Churches "ask themselves whether they are showing sufficient eagerness to enter into conversation with other Churches?"
2. Should they "act together in all matters except those in which deep differences of conviction compel them to act separately?"
3. Should they "acknowledge the fact that they often allow themselves to be separated from each other by secular forces and influences?"
4. Should they instead be "witnessing together to the sole Lordship of Christ who gathers His people out of all nations, races and tongues?"[7]

---

5. T. Smith, "Perspective"; *EDWM*, s.v. "Evangelical Movement;" *WCE*, 1:9, 2:660.
6. *WCE* 1:843; Jaffarian, "Statistical."
7. Barrett et al., "Missiometrics," 30; WCC/CFO Conf., Lund 1952, *Report*, 16.

PENTECOSTALISM

Two forms of Christianity mushroomed between 1948 and 2010—Pentecostalism and Independency. They deserve special attention before we go on to consider ten models of unity in Part II.

The Pentecostal movement has been described as "the most rapidly growing missionary movement in the world and in the history of Christendom." David Barrett estimates that in 1900 there were about 2.5 million mainline Protestants who were "pre-pentecostals," plus 1.2 million "denominational Pentecostals"—just 0.7 percent of the world's Christians. By 1970 Pentecostals and charismatics numbered an estimated 75 million, 6 percent of the world's Christian population. By the year 2000 they had grown to an estimated 562 million or 28.6 percent of the world's Christians.[8]

South Korea, Sub-Saharan Africa, Southeast Asia, and Latin America have been the country and regions of greatest Pentecostal growth in recent years. In 1999 Pentecostals were 20 percent of the population of Brazil and Nicaragua, and 30 percent of Guatemala's population. The largest Christian congregations in the world were Pentecostal.[9]

Phenomenal has been the growth also of mission work by Pentecostals in Africa, Asia, and Latin America. Since 1970 some 800 new Pentecostal/charismatic agencies for foreign mission have begun on those continents. By 1990 these Pentecostals fielded almost 30,000 full-time foreign missionaries. However, their prevailing pattern has been initially to serve Christian migrant workers in North America and Europe from Third World countries. It is Barrett's judgment that 97 percent of these Third World missionaries are living among Christian populations in the Western world, with few in contact with persons of other faiths in non-Christian countries.[10]

Although organized Pentecostal/charismatic missions have been frustrated in outreach to un-evangelized countries, the Spirit has not been left without a witness. Migrant Korean construction workers in the Middle East witness for Christ in and through their labor. Where human missionary organization has failed, God has called God's people to be witnesses. Many testify to signs and wonders, personal miracles, healings, and theophanies. Unorganized mission is taking place. Thriving

---

8. Kärkkäinen, "Pentecostal Missiology," 207; Barrett, "Twentieth-Century," 120–21.
9. A. Anderson, "Introduction," 25–28.
10. Barrett, "Signs," 194. See also Pate, "Pentecostal Missions"; and McGee, *Miracles*.

Pentecostal indigenous churches are being established in many parts of the world without the help of any foreign missionaries.[11]

"The origins of Pentecostalism are ecumenical," a leading Pentecostal scholar asserts. Walter Hollenweger finds its origins in an ecumenical renewal movement in mainline churches in the early twentieth century. Most early Pentecostals believed in the invisible as well as visible church, and that the true unity of believers was accomplished by the work of the cross.[12]

By the 1940s, however, most North American Pentecostals allied themselves with evangelicals, and even fundamentalists. They feared a compromise of faith on essential doctrines. An exception was the Assemblies of God, which joined the FMC in 1920 and the IMC in 1921. Attitudes shifted by 1965, however, when the Assembly's General Council passed a resolution disapproving "of ministers or churches participating in any of the modern ecumenical organizations on a local, national, or international level in such a manner as to promote the Ecumenical Movement."[13]

Not all Pentecostals, however, took a negative view of the ecumenical movement. David J. de Plessis of South Africa and Donald Gee of Great Britain attended WCC meetings and urged their churches to become more involved in the movement. At the WCC's New Delhi Assembly in 1961 two Pentecostal denominations joined that body— the *Iglesia Pentecostal de Chile* (Pentecostal Church of Chile) and *Misión Iglesia Pentecostal* (Pentecostal Mission Church). Their number swelled to twelve by 1997, according to Hollenweger, including three of the largest African-initiated churches.[14]

The main contribution of Pentecostalism has been described as the "reintroduction of charismatic spirituality, with emphasis on the baptism with the Holy Spirit, as empowerment for witness and service." Both the charismatic movement within historic Protestant churches and the Roman Catholic Church, and the WCC's Pentecostal member churches, have strengthened the WCC's interest in charismatic spirituality.[15] As for the Pentecostal movement, Vinay Samuel of India identifies this challenge: "Global Pentecostalism can bring a new impetus to the movement

 11. Barrett, "Signs," 194; A. Anderson, "Global Pentecostalism," 221.
 12. Kärkkäinen, "Pentecostal Missiology," 208; Hollenweger, *Pentecostalism*, 334–49.
 13. Robeck, "Pentecostals," 342–43; Assemblies of God GC, *Minutes*, 133.
 14. Sandidge, "WCC."
 15. Ibid., 902–3; Kärkkäinen, "Pentecostal Missiology," 216.

for Christian unity with its commitment to mission. Its experience of the ministry of the Holy Spirit brings a much-needed dimension to the movement for unity. The democratic principle that shapes Pentecostal church polity and the [indigenous] nature of Pentecostal Churches have much to contribute to the shaping of a new twenty-first century definition for Christian unity. A commitment to Christian unity must become intentional in Pentecostal Churches."[16]

INDEPENDENCY

In 2001 the editors of the *World Christian Encyclopedia* added a sixth global megablock of Christians to their previous groupings of Orthodox, Roman Catholic, Anglican, Protestant, and marginal Christian. They grouped these Christians as Independents, or "post-denominationalists." This major trend by 2000 included over 385 million Christians "who have discarded historic denominationalism and even any dependence on historic Christianity."[17]

Two main types of independency have emerged. The first, comprising non-white indigenous Christians, are growing most rapidly both in Asia and Africa. They include the Han Chinese churches (80 million members), and the African independent churches (55 million members). The other type, white-led Independents, are of more recent origin (1940–2000). The largest of these is the Fullness/Praise Network of Churches in the United States (an estimated 6,000 churches, with 3.3 million members).[18]

David Barrett and Todd Johnson rate this megablock of Christianity to be the fastest growing in the world. In 1970 their numbers were half the size of Protestantism. By 2025, however, Independents may outnumber Protestants by nearly 115 million members and comprise 22 percent of the Christians in the world.[19]

---

16. Samuel, "Pentecostalism," 254–55. For a less sanguine viewpoint see Robeck, "A Pentecostal."

17. *WCE* 1:16–18; Barrett and Johnson, eds., *World Christian Trends*, 292. The term *independent* for such churches has not gained full acceptance, with writers on African Christianity preferring the terms "African initiated" or "African indigenous" churches.

18. Barrett and Johnson, "Annual," 24.

19. Ibid.; see idem., *World Christian Trends*, 291–309, for a detailed analysis of independency.

Are African-initiated/Independent churches (AICs) protest movements or mission churches? Inus Daneel raised this question in a stimulating article on these churches in southern Africa.[20]

Daneel argues that although few observers have applied the term "mission church" to the AICs; they have developed many indigenous models of mission, and have equipped their members to be persons in mission. They have not institutionalized their mission outreach in mission boards and agencies, as many of the "daughter" Protestant churches of Western missions have done in Africa, Latin America, and Asia. Instead, their models of mission are "diffuse and integral to holistic patterns of church life."[21]

Many of the "Spirit-type" AICs in Zimbabwe build their evangelistic and mission outreach around their annual paschal celebrations. These may last for two to seventeen days. After spiritual cleansing through confession of sins, fasting, and prayer, the faith community is renewed through preaching and song. The climax, the Eucharist, becomes the commissioning service to go out and witness for Christ, convert, and baptize people. Since 1972 the African Independent Church Conference (AICC), popularly called *Fambidzano* (lit. "co-operative of churches"), concludes its meetings with a "Eucharist-in-mission." Considering the doctrinal differences among participating AICs this is a remarkable achievement. Contrast this with the conviction of most Orthodox Christians who refuse to participate in the so-called practice of "inter-communion" because they believe that "there can be no such thing as the 'inter-communion' of divided churches."[22]

In contrast to Eucharistic celebrations in many Pentecostal and charismatic churches, which focus on the individual's need to "be right with God," the paschal services in African AICs witness to holistic understandings of mission. A second AIC ecumenical movement in Zimbabwe, the Association of African Earthkeeping Churches (AAEC), has promoted the giving of a seedling tree to each worshipper. Daneel believes that the tree-planting Eucharist is in itself "the witnessing event, the proclamation of good news to all creation. The sacrament integrates the healing of earth and humans as witness of Christ's good news to the

---

20. Daneel, "African Initiated Churches"; see 185–90 for Daneel's differentiation of these "Spirit-type" churches from Pentecostalism.

21. Ibid., 201.

22. Ibid., 201–6; Saayman, *Unity*, 95. For a fuller analysis see Daneel, *Fambidzano*, 127–46.

world." The AAEC and AICC also have enabled rural communities to engage in development projects—often with development funds from international donor agencies. Unity in mission—often a peripheral concern of Protestant mainline local churches—can be central to the life of African independent churches.[23]

CONCLUSION

This chapter is just an introduction to the rich variety of expressions of Christian unity and mission during this period. The rest is contained in the remaining chapters of this book presented as ten models of Christian unity and two forms of wider ecumenism.

Monophysitism was an ancient Christian heresy of the fifth century CE. It's adherents argued that Christ had only a divine *physis* or nature. They denied or considered unimportant his humanity. The Ebionites, on the other hand, believed that Jesus was only human. Like these contending groups, Christians in the twenty-first century are in constant danger of being like either Monophysites or Ebionites, by defining the Christian faith according to the one element that they regard as non-negotiable, often to the practical exclusion of all others. Another metaphor is that they are like the six blind men of the Indian fable who each gave a different description of the elephant—a tree, a rope, a wall, a snake, a sword, or a fan—depending on the part of the elephant's body each had touched. David Bosch contended that what was needed instead is "'pan-Christians', people who stand for the wholeness and fullness of the gospel and refuse to allow phrases such as 'evangelical', 'ecumenical', 'catholic', and 'charismatic' to be downgraded to party terms and become the monopoly of only one group." Look for stories of pan-Christians who worked for mission and unity across the social and religious divisions of their time in the chapters to come.[24]

---

23. Daneel, "African Initiated Churches," 208; also 195–200, 207–13. See also Daneel, *African Earthkeepers*.

24. Bosch, "'Ecumenicals,'" 472.

PART TWO
Ten Models of Unity

6

Unity through a Global Church

UNA SANCTA: IDEALS AND REALITIES

CHRISTIANS OF ALL PERSUASIONS pray for Christian unity, believing that it is God's will for God's people. The Lambeth Conference of Anglican bishops in 1920 issued "An Appeal to All Christian People." In it they shared that "the vision which rises before us is that of a Church, genuinely catholic, loyal to all Truth, and gathering into its fellowship all 'who profess and call themselves Christians.'" Pope John Paul II, in his 1995 encyclical *Ut Unum Sint* ("That All May Be One"), reaffirmed that the Catholic Church "bases upon God's plan her ecumenical commitment to gather all Christians into unity . . . that there may be one visible Church of God."[1]

How then do Christians reconcile this God-given vision with the visible reality of divisions among Christians? Some resolve the dilemma by declaring that theirs is the only true church. Others answer, as did Kenneth Scott Latourette, the Baptist historian, that "In theory there was only one Church, the 'body of Christ,' but in actuality there were several churches. One of them, which claimed to be catholic and the custodian of the faith as taught by Jesus and the apostles, was the largest." Knowing the deep divisions that existed among Christians and their churches when the New Testament was written, he believed that a truly universal or catholic church never existed. Still others, like Henry P. Van Dusen, the Presbyterian ecumenist, held to the hope that "the dawn of the second Christian millennium might witness an approximation of the two-fold

---

1. Kinnamon and Cope, eds., *Ecumenical Movement*, 81; *Ut Unam Sint*, art. 5, 7, quoted from Catholic Church, *Encyclicals*.

goal of the acknowledgment of Christ throughout the earth, and of the unity of a majority of his followers in one 'great church.'"[2]

ROME AND CHRISTENDOM

Rome and Orthodoxy

For the first thirteen centuries Christians affirmed one holy catholic church, though with two wings: the Western, with allegiance to the Bishop of Rome as Pope, and the Eastern (Greek or Byzantine), with the Patriarch of Constantinople as the ranking bishop of the Byzantine Church. In the four centuries between 950 and 1350, however, the two wings drifted apart due to doctrinal differences, rivalries between the Holy Roman and Byzantine Empires, and the Crusades. Despite efforts for reunion, by 1350 the rupture was final.[3]

Pre-Vatican II [4]

The prevailing official concept of unity in the Roman Catholic Church before Vatican II was that it was the only true church of Christ. Pope Pius XI declared in 1928, in his encyclical *Mortalium Animos*, that "the Apostolic See can by no means take part in [ecumenical] assemblies" since "the unity of Christians can come about only by furthering the return to the one true Church of Christ of those who are separated from it." Before 1959 the Catholic view of its annual Week of Prayer for Christian Unity was to pray for Protestants to return to the one true church, and that the Orthodox would end their schism.[5]

Nineteenth-century Protestant-Catholic relations in missions were antagonistic in almost every country. Protestant missionaries, including both bishops of the "high church" Society for the Propagation of the Gospel and those of the Society of Friends, complained bitterly of the imperialistic ambitions of the Church of Rome, and of Catholic opposition and interference in their work. Catholic mission theory lumped Protestants with Muslims and heathen as objects of missions since they

---

2. Latourette, *History of Christianity*, 1464; Lindgren, *Unity*, 288; Van Dusen, *One Great Ground*, 93.
3. Latourette, *History of Christianity*, 571–75.
4. For the historical attitudes of Rome to the Eastern churches and to Protestants see Tillard, "Roman Catholic."
5. Quoted in Saayman, *Unity*, 56–57; Vatican Council, *Documents*, 336.

were considered to be heretics and schismatics. Protestants expected no comity agreements dividing mission territory with Roman Catholics unless imposed by government. With the proclamation by John R. Mott and others of the Student Volunteer Movement that "for the first time in the history of the Church practically the whole world is open," and the sending of increased numbers of missionaries to Latin America, many Catholic missionaries reacted with dismay to the influx of Protestants. One significant exception was the proposal by R. M. Cust on behalf of the Church Missionary Society to Cardinal Lavigerie of the White Fathers in 1878 to prevent competition in Uganda. Without cooperation there would be four mutually hostile religious systems in Buganda, including traditional religion and Islam, the latter having been welcomed by the powerful King Mutesa.[6]

By the twentieth century more irenic voices could be heard. In 1936, Baptist historian Latourette recognized that "the Roman Catholic Church officially looks upon sincere Protestants as belonging to her soul although now severed from her body." He hoped, however, that the stress of anti-Christian movements of the day "may well bring to both great bodies the consciousness of a common faith and a joint cause." Although Protestants remained "a competitive reality" for most Catholic missionaries, "modest occasions for ecumenism" occurred. Some came through shared imprisonment and other circumstances of war.[7]

Vatican II[8]

What influenced Pope John XXIII to call together the bishops to the Second Vatican Council, with the resulting new understands of unity and mission? Willem Saayman wrote that in contrast to Protestant churches, whose ecumenical impulse came from the "mission field," the Roman Catholic initiative for change came in response to the Protestant and Orthodox momentum in the ecumenical movement.[9]

---

6. R. Oliver, *Missionary Factor*, 47–48; Beaver, *Ecumenical Beginnings*, 203; Mott, *Evangelization*, 15; Dries, *Missionary Movement*, 63.

7. Latourette, *Missions Tomorrow*, 191; Dries, *Missionary Movement*, 147. For other developments see Tomkins, "Roman Catholic"; and Vischer, "Ecumenical Movement," 311–22.

8. For documents cited in this section and Catholic commentary, see Vatican Council, *Documents*. For the mission of the Roman Catholic Church in relation to Vatican II see Le Guillou, *Mission*; and Achútegui, "Missions." For Protestant analyses see Saayman, *Unity*, 58–67, and Vischer, "Ecumenical Movement," 2:322–43.

9. Saayman, *Unity*, 58.

In *Lumen Gentium* I.8 ("Dogmatic Constitution on the Church") it is stated that "the Church, organized in the world as a society, subsists in the Catholic Church." The new understanding was that "many elements of sanctification and truth" exist outside the Roman Catholic Church. Thus, in *Unitatis Redintegratio* I.3 ("Decree on Ecumenism") reference is made to "churches and ecclesial bodies" that the Catholic Church accepts "with respect and affection as brothers." The Decree continues: "The Spirit of Christ has not refrained from using them as means of salvation." This shift opened the door for Catholics to work together with others as sisters and brothers in Christ for the unity of the church and as partners in mission.[10]

Vatican II was a continuing event over five years with significant changes taking place during that period. For example, chapter 2 of *Unitatis Redintegratio* was entitled "Principles of Catholic Ecumenism" in the first draft, as if there were more than one ecumenical movement. In the final document it is changed to "Catholic Principles of Ecumenism." The change reflected the understanding that there could be but one ecumenical movement for all Christians (Catholic, Protestant, and Orthodox). The relationship between unity and mission was stated in these words: "almost everyone (i.e. every Christian), though in different ways, longs that there may be one visible Church of God, a Church truly universal and sent forth to the whole world that the world may be converted to the gospel and so be saved, to the glory of God."[11]

Ad Gentes II.15 ("Decree on the Missionary Activity of the Church") further set out guidelines for ecumenical cooperation. Among the obligations of missionaries was that "The ecumenical spirit too should be nurtured in the neophytes. They should rightly consider that the brethren who believe in Christ are Christ's disciples." In accordance with "the norms of the Decree on Ecumenism," Catholics can cooperate "in a brotherly spirit with their separated brethren" and "can collaborate in social and in technical projects as well as in cultural and religious ones ... for the sake of Christ, their common Lord." Cooperation is to be undertaken "not only among private persons, but also ... among Churches or ecclesial Communities and their enterprises."[12]

---

10. Vatican Council, *Documents*, 23, 345.
11. Saayman, *Unity*, 60–61; Vatican Council, *Documents*, 343.
12. Vatican Council, *Documents*, 602–3.

Reactions to Vatican II

In his reflection on Vatican II and ecumenism, Catholic theologian Raymond Brown wrote in 1967, "Thus the ecumenical future, on the basis of the ecumenism decree, is an open future. What direction the future takes depends not only on what Catholics do with the decree, but on how Protestants respond to it as well." Lukas Vischer, the WCC's secretary for Faith and Order, judged that "Once the Decree on Ecumenism had been promulgated . . . ecumenism had become the task of the Church as a whole."[13]

Relations with the Ecumenical Movement[14]

In the post-Vatican II period Pope Paul VI often acknowledged that the whole church was committed to the ecumenical movement. The Secretariat for Christian Unity, originally created for Vatican II, continued and steadily increased its relationships with various Christian confessional groups and the WCC. The Joint Working Group of the Roman Catholic Church and the WCC began to meet twice yearly, beginning in 1965 during Vatican II. In addition to theological work on unity issues, it was able to initiate a wide network of relationships between corresponding departments of the Vatican and the WCC. In the next twenty years areas of cooperation expanded from theological conversations to development aid, cooperation among women's organizations, and combined efforts to fix a common date for Easter.[15]

MEMBERSHIP IN THE WCC

This issue received active consideration beginning in 1964 during Vatican II. Both sides acknowledged from the start the uphill climb ahead. Protestant participants felt, on the one hand, that "The Roman Catholic Church needs the World Council if it is to deepen its relationships with the other churches of Christendom, and the World Council needs close contact with the Roman Catholic Church if it is not to lose sight of the totality of Christendom." On the other hand, it recognized that the Catholic Church and WCC "are not comparable entities" for the former is "a church" while the latter "is an inter-church organization." They "are not partners on the same level."[16]

---

13. R. Brown, *Ecumenical Revolution*, 207; Vischer, "Ecumenical Movement," 346.
14. For an overview see McDonnell, *WCC*.
15. Vischer, "Ecumenical Movement," 346–49; Raiser, "Thirty Years," 430–32.
16. A-WCC/GS, "Working Paper."

The real launching of the membership question took place at the WCC's Fourth Assembly (Uppsala 1968). Although Catholics only had observer status, Father Roberto Tucci's call for ecumenical fellowship received rapt attention. "The Church of Rome," Tucci began, "has no desire but to develop more and more dynamic and more intimate relations with the World Council, which it recognizes as an institution set up by Providence and an instrument privileged to serve the ecumenical movement." He noted the developing mutual relations on the levels of national and regional councils, and through special organs of the WCC, and gave his judgment that "the difficulties which might be raised by Roman ecclesiology do not constitute an insuperable obstacle" to Roman Catholic membership in the WCC. In response, the WCC Assembly made it clear that from their side there was, in principle, no obstacle to Roman Catholic membership in the Council. These were years of high hopes for ecumenically minded Roman Catholics. Thomas F. Stransky, CSP, of the staff of the Vatican Secretariat for Promoting Christian Unity, asked, "Have not the WCC and the RCC arrived at that stage of pro-existence where RCC membership is recommended, if not required?"[17]

In the next four years both parties discussed the issues at the highest levels. Early optimism faded by 1970, although the decisive criterion for the Roman Catholic Church was what solution would render the best possible service to the cause of unity of all Christians. Fr. Jerome Hamer, secretary of the Secretariat for the Promotion of Christian Unity, expressed the problems as:

1. The question of *priorities*: what place does the search for visible unity occupy among the activities of the WCC?
2. The question of *efficacy*: what is the influence of the WCC on the thought, general lines of policy and programs of the member churches?
3. The question of *relevance*: what is the impact of WCC membership on the internal crisis through which most Christian churches are passing?
4. The question of *"pastoral realism"*: to what extent is membership of the WCC a real and concrete question for Catholics on the national and local levels and could it be of positive value for pastoral life?

---

17. WCC/A, Nairobi 1975, *Breaking Barriers,* 328–29; Vischer, "Ecumenical Movement," 349–52; Stransky, "Membership," 204.

Sensing this hesitancy, the Joint Working Group in 1972, in its "Patterns of Relationship" report, suggested three possibilities for closer RCC-WCC relations:

1. The evolution of coordinated structures for increasing collaboration;
2. The formation of a new fellowship, differently constituted; or
3. Membership of the Roman Catholic Church in the WCC.

Three suggestions were offered on the second option: (1) that the WCC be reorganized to be an organization of confessional families, (2) that it become a fellowship based on national or regional Christian councils, or (3) that it become a fellowship of Christian movements and organizations. None of these alternatives received support. When Roman Catholic Church membership was also rejected, it left only the first possibility then described as "increasing cooperation, collaboration and participation."[18]

Why did the plans for Catholic Church membership fail? Some blamed a "lack of democratic openness" in Rome. Others noted that the high Roman Catholic view of what unity requires differed from the low views of many Protestant WCC members. Willem Visser 't Hooft, an architect of the WCC and its first General Secretary, reflected that "the structural problem of bringing the RCC into WCC membership was insoluble unless either the RCC or the WCC made radical changes in its own structure."[19]

SODEPAX

The Joint Committee on Society, Development and Peace was the only program agency responsible both to the WCC and the Vatican. Formed in 1965 and jointly staffed, SODEPAX helped bring thought of the WCC on social issues into encounter with Catholic reflection and practice. It made significant contributions in research on economic development, communications, and peace. Pedro Achútegui, SJ, found its main beneficiaries in the Third World where most of the missions are. He felt that "the impact of this organization for ecumenical cooperation in the missions cannot be emphasized enough." Marc Reuver of the Vatican Commission on Justice and Peace contended that it was "the best outcome of the Vatican Council, of renewal in the church, and of

---

18. For a full account see Grootaers, "Unfinished Agenda"; Houtepen, "Collaboration," 482.
19. Visser 't Hooft, "WCC-RC Relations," 341.

ecumenism." Philip Potter, the WCC's general secretary, wrote in 1973 that the activities of SODEPAX "have shown the truly universal nature of the ecumenical movement today."[20]

SODEPAX helped to disclose the remarkable areas of agreement between the Vatican and the WCC on human rights, religious liberty, economic development, and racism. Tensions between the two sponsors arose, however, that caused its demise in 1980. Reuver believed that "the real war between the Vatican and the WCC on SODEPAX was that it held consultations and made statements that went further than the Vatican could support, especially in areas of justice, peace, and human rights." Thomas Derr attributed the downfall to differences both of doctrine and of style. The Vatican was accustomed to speaking cautiously and in generalities after long and careful study of an issue. The WCC, by contrast, let WCC-sponsored conferences speak specifically and prophetically, even when their views had not been tested for consensus among WCC members.[21]

Cooperation in Mission

In mission the Roman Catholic Church and the WCC have achieved increasing cooperation. Desiring to deepen its relationship to the Catholic Church, the WCC's Commission on World Mission and Evangelism (CWME), at its 1973 meeting, amended its constitution to allow for the consultative relation of non-member bodies. As early as 1963 Roman Catholics participated in the WCC's world mission conferences as observers. After 1973 Catholic consultants became as active in drafting conference documents as representatives of member bodies, and the WCC's world mission conferences became significant points for greater cooperation. Four mission-sending Catholic institutes sent consultants to CWME meetings beginning in 1974. Sister Joan Delaney, MM, was employed by the Catholic Secretariat and seconded to the CWME to work on its staff beginning in January 1984. Her participation deepened communication and collaboration, and facilitated actual experiences of common witness. All this was consistent with the 1974 Declaration by the Synod of Bishops that "we intend to collaborate more diligently with those of our Christian brothers with whom we are not yet in the union of

---

20. Achútegui, "Missions," 144; Reuver interview; Potter, "Report," 416.
21. Reuver interview; Derr, *Barriers*, 30–31.

a perfect communion . . . we can henceforth render to the world a much broader common witness of Christ."[22]

Extended cooperation characterized RCC-WCC relations in the decades that followed. The Joint Working Group report for 1990 gave an extended list of WCC activities in which Catholic representatives were present and contributed. The general secretary noted that "with few exceptions, all programmatic activities of the WCC are included in this register." Both parties, WCC general secretary Konrad Raiser believed, "look at this relationship with realism. We know on both sides that we must move forward, but we also know much better what are the points of difficulty for each of the two partners." Saayman believed "that Rome is firmly established as a 'partner' in ecumenical discussions on unity and mission." Visser 't Hooft concluded his assessment: "We must not only talk about common witness; we must render common witness. Not just the skeptical world but even the millions of church members will take us really seriously only when the WCC and the RCC speak and act together in the name of Christ, bringing new hope to a world threatened by meaninglessness, self-destruction, violence and poverty."[23]

Relations with Protestant Evangelicals

A remarkable convergence in understanding the nature of evangelization took place in 1974–75 as evangelicals published the "Lausanne Covenant" and the Pope made his apostolic exhortation entitled *Evangelii Nuntiandi*. Stimulated by it, the two streams of Christianity agreed to hold an Evangelical-Roman Catholic Dialogue on Mission from 1977 to 1984. Participants were theologians and missiologists from many parts of the world. Evangelical members were drawn from various churches and Christian organizations. The Vatican Secretariat for Promoting Christian Unity named the Catholic participants. In the final report participants agreed that "deep truths already unite us in Christ, yet real and important convictions still divide us." They agreed that common witness in Bible translation and publishing is "extremely important" as divergent texts breed mutual suspicion. They also favored common community service including response to natural disasters, the hungry, and the refugees.[24]

22. Meeking, "Vatican II," 61; Delaney, "Relationship"; Saayman, *Unity*, 69.
23. Raiser, "Thirty Years," 437–38; Visser 't Hooft, "WCC-RC Relations," 344; Saayman, *Unity*, 72.
24. Meeking, and Stott, eds., *Dialogue on Mission*, 7–9, 82–85.

PART TWO: TEN MODELS OF UNITY

PROTESTANT WORLD CHURCHES

Most Protestants base their aspiration for Christian unity upon Jesus' prayer "that they may be one" (John 17:22). In contrast to Roman Catholics, they do not envision an institutional unified structure, but rather sing, "Bless be the tie that binds our hearts in Christian love; the fellowship of kindred minds is like to that above."[25] A few Protestant denominations, instead of encouraging their former missions to seek autonomy as national churches, retain structure as world churches. Two examples are the Seventh-Day Adventist Church and the Church of the Nazarene. A third, the United Methodist Church, is significant because it is in transition.

Seventh-Day Adventist Church

This denomination arose out of the Millerite movement of the 1840s which awaited the imminent second coming of Christ. Formally organized in 1863, its work was confined to North America until 1874. With urgency it then carried across the globe what it calls "the everlasting gospel"—the basic Christian message of salvation through Christ, Sabbath worship, and righteous living in expectation of the second coming of Christ. The Church grew rapidly worldwide to reach a membership of 15,660,000 in 2007, making it the eighth largest international body of Christians. Present in 201 countries and organized into 13 geographic divisions, the North Americans represent but 11 percent of the total world membership. Seventh-Day Adventists are organized not as a series of separate national or regional churches "but as one worldwide, unified, international church."[26]

At the beginning of the twentieth century the Seventh-Day Adventist Church was predominately a U.S. denomination, with 80 percent of the membership in that country, and had foreign missions in other parts of the world. In 2000, by contrast, the denomination had become internationalized. Almost all geographic divisions of the church were now administered by leaders indigenous to each respective region. In relations the Adventist Church was like the zebra, whose young fend for themselves almost from birth. "From everywhere to everywhere" is the present understanding by which missionaries are sent between re-

---

25. Hymn written by John Fawcett (1782); music by Johann G. Nägeli (1828); arranged by Lowell Mason (1845).
26. Seventh-Day Adventist, "Statistics."

gions, with Adventist churches in Africa, Asia, India, and Latin America sending "missionaries" to Europe and the United States.

Adventists live with a dynamic balance in their polity between unity and diversity as core values. Unity is expressed as a prerequisite of mission, with denominational leaders desiring to preserve unity and central direction in the church. Diversity is expressed through a congregational form of local organization, and through considerable independence given to the various geographic regions. [27]

No Adventist can be opposed to the unity that Christ himself prayed for, for they believe "that all sincere Christians, of whatever communion, constitute the people of God." They seek to work in fellowship with other Christians in ways that "do not involve a compromise of what they understand to be their mission as a people." They prefer an observer-consultant status with councils of churches at all levels, feeling that their imperative to emphasize distinctive Adventist doctrines prevents their full membership.[28]

Church of the Nazarene

From its founding in 1908 by the merger of two Holiness groups, the Church of the Nazarene has been mission focused. Even before 1908 the founder groups had sent missionaries to Cape Verde, Japan, Guatemala, India, and China. By the denomination's centennial in 2008, 63 percent of the Church's members were in 155 "world areas" outside the U.S. These experienced a 77 percent growth in the previous decade compared with 2.8 percent growth in U.S. membership.

The Nazarene Church has encouraged congregations in world areas to be self-supporting and self-governing but tied closely by organization in the world body. Representation by the former mission areas in the denomination's General Assembly, meeting every four years, grew exponentially. By 2001 over 40 percent of the voting delegates either spoke English as their second language or did not speak it at all. Denominational leadership, however, has remained overwhelmingly from the U.S. until very recently. This polity resembles more the kangaroo, which nurtures its young in a pouch until almost full grown. In 2008 Eugénio R. Duarte from Cape Verde, director of the Africa Region, was elected a general

---

27. Land, *Dictionary*, 7–9; Knight, *History*, 144–45; B. Oliver, *SDA*, 270, 338–46.
28. *Seventh-Day Adventist Encyclopedia*, s. v. "Ecumenism."

superintendent of the Church, the first leader from outside Canada and the U.S. to hold that important post.[29]

In 1980 the General Assembly accepted "internationalization" as a philosophy to guide the denomination's development. Nazarenes committed themselves to transcending the social and national lines that divide people. In 1985 the Assembly authorized the formation of regional councils. The 2008 *Manual* permitted restructuring "according to the particular needs, potential problems, existing realities, and diverse cultural and educational backgrounds in particular geographic areas of the world." All this is to take place within the strong global church. Although Nazarenes are members both of the World Methodist Council and of the National Association of Evangelicals in the U.S., they have no expressed urgency to cooperate or unite in joint action with other churches beyond what may take place at a local level.[30]

United Methodist Church

This denomination is the result of a succession of mergers of denominations of the Wesleyan heritage. Methodism grew in its first seventy-five years in North America from a small number of Wesley's followers in the New York area in 1775 to become by 1850 the largest Protestant family in the United States. In the twentieth century the forerunner denominations of the United Methodist Church were all founder members and active participants in the ecumenical movement both nationally and worldwide.

Tracey Jones, a Methodist mission executive, expressed well the prevailing sentiment of Methodists in 1965 that his church "is increasingly being drawn into the main stream of the ecumenical dialogue regarding mission and unity." In the denomination's mission and church extension work, both nationally and internationally, the consistent goal was to develop churches and not missions. "We have never seen our 'sister churches' as a mission field, but as Annual Conferences within one world Church," Jones wrote. Consistent with the WCC's decision in 1961 to encourage formation of united churches within countries, Methodist conferences in Asia and Latin America requested the autonomous status "recognized as a direct or transitional step toward church union." Most

---

29. Church of the Nazarene, *Journal*, 294.
30. Church of the Nazarene, *Manual*, 166; "Church of the Nazarene."

conferences in Europe and Africa chose to remain part of the Methodist Church.[31]

Since the merger of the Methodist and the Evangelical United Brethren churches to form the United Methodist Church in 1968, the denomination has wrestled with the four options for institutional reconciliation of the goals both of unity and mission proposed by Jones: (1) Remain one denomination but give wider freedom to member churches in Europe, Asia, Africa, and Latin America "to satisfy their selfhood;" (2) encourage each national part of the denomination to seek autonomy so as to enter into union with other Protestants; (3) have a "decentralized world church" with the U.S. United Methodists as one regional conference within it; or (4) develop a World Conference of Methodist churches. The denomination is more like a lumbering rhino than a mobile gazelle or fleet cheetah. Since 1968 none of the proposals for structural change mandated by study commissions and the Council of Bishops have been adopted. "Our current infrastructure is unable to carry the weight of a truly just and sustainable global church," wrote the former general secretary of the Church's Commission on Christian Unity in 2004. Bruce W. Robbins expressed the aspiration of many United Methodists that "Now is the time to create a structure for a global church."[32]

CONCLUSION

"Jesus wills the growth of his people and perfects their fellowship in unity." With these words Vatican II expressed a consensus that all Christians can agree upon. *Unitatis Redintegratio* I.2 ("Decree on Ecumenism") continued that Christians manifest this unity "in the confession of one faith, in their common celebration of divine worship, and in the fraternal harmony of God's family." Avery Dulles, SJ, added: "Within this unity of faith, worship, and polity, considerable scope is allowed for diversity of styles and practices. This variety, far from impairing the unity, enriches it." To achieve "the unity for which we hope" remains the ongoing task, not just of those churches that seek unity through a global church, but of all Christians.[33]

31. T. Jones, "Mission."
32. Ibid., 176–77; Robbins, *World Parish?*, 15. See Robbins for a fuller account of the denomination's struggles over these issues.
33. Vatican Council, *Documents*, 344; Dulles, "Unity," 134.

7

World Conciliarism

THE GOAL

"LET THE CHURCH LIVE on the frontier," John Mackay challenged church leaders in his 1944 address. After discussing political and cultural frontiers, Mackay zeroed in on "the missionary frontier [for] that is where the ultimate problems of the Christian Church are today." He called for the church to deal with "an adequate missionary approach to the world. Basic to any such approach is Christian unity." Anticipating a new world order after World War II, Mackay emphasized that "the physical unity of the world, and the international character of contemporary problems, make the unity of the Christian Church still more imperative." But Christian unity is not enough to "lead the Church to the missionary Frontier and keep it there." In his judgment "evangelistic fervor is needed, a passion to make Jesus Christ known, and loved, and obeyed."[1]

Four years later, just before the WCC's First Assembly in Amsterdam, Mackay reframed his vision as one of "evangelical catholicity." The new chairman of the International Missionary Council, who would be a key voice at Amsterdam, elaborated:

> The Church must ever move outward and onward toward the great frontiers of life, proclaiming the Gospel and living the Gospel both within its own borders and in the secular order. The Church of Jesus Christ must be a pilgrim Church, whose discovery and proclamation of Christ and his Gospel must lead it to live on the missionary road.[2]

---

1. Mackay, "Let the Church," 149, 150.
2. Mackay, "Theological Foreword," 149, 150. See Van Dusen, "Christian Missions," for an assessment of Mackay's contribution and leadership.

This chapter is about the responses to that vision by those churches that work together through the WCC.

Amsterdam 1948[3]

In his address at the Amsterdam Assembly on "The Missionary Legacy to the Church Universal," John Mackay linked the desire for Christian unity with the fact that "today in all the representative regions of the globe and in every land save three[4] . . . there are organized Christian churches." He continued: "For the first time in Christian history the church has become 'ecumenical' in the literal meaning of that word. Its boundaries are co-extensive with the inhabited globe." Henry P. Van Dusen, another active participant, concluded that "The Amsterdam Assembly revealed a vaster sweep and depth of underlying unity than had been foreseen, a unity more profound and powerful than had been evident in any previous comparable gathering in Christian history."[5]

At Amsterdam the churches had their first opportunity to express their collective view on the interrelationship of unity and mission. The report of Section 2 on "The Church's Witness to God's Design" addressed the logic that "if we take seriously our world-wide task, we are certain to be driven to think again of our divisions." The message of the Assembly to the churches picked up the urgency of unity for effective witness, confessing that "our coming together to form a World Council will be in vain unless Christians and Christian congregations everywhere commit themselves to the Lord of the Church in a new effort to seek together, where they live, to be His witnesses and servants among their neighbors."[6]

The Calling to Mission and to Unity

At its next meeting at Rolle, Germany, in 1951, the WCC's Central Committee made its most profound statement on the interrelationship between unity and mission. First, it declared "that it is impossible to say simply that the IMC represents the calling of the Church to evangelism, and the WCC it's calling to unity." The missionary movement from its beginning has been "imbued with a deep sense of the calling to unity."

---

3. For further discussion of the unity and mission statements of ecumenical conferences see Bassham, *Mission Theology*, 27–121; and Saayman, *Unity*, 13–55, 105–30.
4. No countries were named, but possibly Nepal, Bhutan, and Mongolia.
5. Mackay, "Missionary Legacy," 369; Van Dusen, "United Strategy," 222.
6. WCC/A, Amsterdam 1948, *First Assembly*, 10, 69.

For too long, it declared, churches unmindful of their missionary calling have been content to live with their divisions, blind to the reality that it blunted their "duty to take the Gospel to the whole world." They stated clearly the theological basis of unity in mission as they declared:

> The obligation to take the Gospel to the whole world, and the obligation to draw all Christ's people together both rest upon Christ's whole work, and are indissolubly connected. Every attempt to separate these two tasks violates the wholeness of Christ's ministry to the world. Both of them are, in the strict sense of the word, essential to the being of the Church and the fulfillment of its function as the Body of Christ.[7]

Whereas the WCC Central Committee at Rolle gave a christological basis for unity and mission, the next IMC Conference (Willingen 1952) affirmed that "the calling of the Church to mission and unity issues from the nature of God." The statement concluded that "we can no longer be content to accept our divisions as normal. We believe that in the ecumenical movement God has provided a way of cooperation in witness and service, and also the means for the removal of much that mars such witness and service." By this concurrence on the theological basis for unity and mission, the IMC and WCC together had a joint conviction to present to their constituencies—the member churches, national Christian councils, and missionary societies—as they were to advocate for closer cooperation and joint action.[8]

Later Refinements

At its Second Assembly (Evanston 1954) the WCC declared that "our divided witness is a necessarily defective witness, and indeed a scandal in the face of the non-Christian world." It admitted that "we have scarcely begun to work out the essential connection between 'mission' and 'unity.'" The report on evangelism struck the same chord, saying, "Unity is destroyed where there are confessional antagonisms, nor will unity of faith and life among Christians be achieved except as churches increasingly work together to bring the gospel to the whole world."[9]

---

7. WCC/CC, "Calling," 13, 16.
8. IMC Conf., Willingen 1952, *Missions*, 193–94.
9. WCC/A, Evanston 1954, *Report*, 91, 100.

THE IMC-WCC INTEGRATION DEBATE

Like a prism refracting light into its spectrum of colors, so the IMC-WCC integration debate disclosed the varied understandings of mission and unity. From its very first meeting in 1946, the Joint Commission of the IMC and the WCC Provisional Committee gave its judgment that "the World Council cannot leave outside its purview the missionary enterprise of the Churches." Out of the "present crisis which confronts humanity" comes the imperative for the whole Christian community to give "the clearest possible manifestation of its essential unity and of its common eagerness to carry out the Great Commission of our Lord." It recognized also that the churches need the IMC with its wider membership and particular responsibilities, but that "their common Christian interests and purposes will require that they be increasingly united in vision, plan, and sacrificial action." Each body included in their constitution the statement that they were "in association" with the other.[10]

In the next years the two bodies increasingly collaborated in programming for unity in mission. At a consultation in Bangkok in 1949 they created a joint East Asia secretariat. In 1952 the WCC's Division of Inter-Church Aid was authorized to act for both bodies in administering relief and emergency aid to individuals and churches. In 1954 they unified their research and study programs in the WCC's Division of Studies. In that year the Joint Committee of the WCC and IMC was reconstituted and enlarged, providing for a full-time secretary in the person of Norman Goodhall. It was charged with the duty "to study the advantages, disadvantages, and implications of a full integration" of the IMC and the WCC.[11]

Arguments for Integration

As early as 1947 Goodhall drafted a proposal that the IMC become the Missionary Council of the WCC. He believed that by doing so the WCC would explicitly acknowledge "that the world mission of the Church ... is integral to its own life and calling." In 1952 he added to the rationale a renewed concern "that this fundamental identity of our calling to mission and unity shall find more vivid and dynamic expression than commonly belongs to it today." Lesslie Newbigin, responding from India,

---

10. WCC, *Ten Formative Years*, 73; "Report of the Joint Committee 1946," in A-WCC/IMC, "Joint Committee," box 27001.
11. Van Dusen, "Christian Missions," 319–21; Goodall, "Limits," 449–50.

agreed that the full integration of the IMC and WCC "is the goal that we must work for," but echoed the concerns of Baptists and Pentecostals in the discussion with the question, "What is the form of visible unity which the Lord wants for his people? That is the question upon which we cannot be neutral."[12]

In 1955 the WCC-IMC Joint Committee focused on "Inter-Church Aid and the Mission of the Church." They agreed that both the WCC and the IMC needed to articulate more clearly, "both in their own life and in their developing relationships with one another, the inseparable character of the Church's witness to the Word (*apostole*) and its witness through service (*diakonia*)." They concluded that "it is most desirable that the organizations of the churches concerned with missions and inter-church aid should be seen to be part of one integrated whole, so that the total task of the Church may be conceived and fulfilled in its unity." After vigorous debate the Committee voted to recommend to its parent bodies consideration of the possibility of full WCC-IMC integration "subject to an adequate safeguarding ... of the distinctive expression of the mission of the Church" as embodied in the IMC.[13]

Debate continued the next year over the "Draft Plan of Integration." From Asia came "insistence from churches and councils which desire to be related to a single organization concerned with both the mission and unity of the church." "A basic theological truth is being rediscovered in our time," the Plan stated. "The *unity* of the Church and the *mission* of the Church both belong, in equal degree, to the *essence* of the Church. If Christian churches would be in very truth the Church, they must carry the Gospel into all the world. They must also strive to achieve the unity of all those throughout the world for whom Jesus Christ is Lord."[14]

Max Warren, secretary of the Anglican Church Missionary Society, gave the most probing arguments against integration. He opposed the viewpoint that mission can only be fulfilled in unity. For Warren that perspective "does not correspond with the facts ... mission can be pursued without an equal preoccupation with unity." It may even be pursued

---

12. Goodhall, "The International Missionary Council and the World Council of Churches" (1947), box 270006; "Comments on WCC/IMC Relationships," box 270006; Goodhall, "The Calling of the Church to Mission and to Unity" (1952), box 270001. All in A-WCC/IMC, "Joint Committee."

13. "Minutes and Papers" (1956), in A-WCC/IMC, "Joint Committee," box 270006.

14. "Minutes of the Joint Committee, 1957," in A-WCC/IMC, "Joint Committee," box 270005. See also WCC, "Report of the Joint Committee."

in disunity! "Mission and Unity are not the same thing and they do not call for similar forms of expression," he continued. His preference was for "a multiplicity of organs of initiative, linked together by bonds of association rather than by constitutional structures."[15]

Deciding on Integration

Debate on the proposed WCC-IMC integration dominated the discussions at the next IMC Conference (Ghana 1958) under the theme "The Christian Mission at This Hour." Proponents stressed that since the concern of both bodies was for "unity and mission," their integration would put mission at the heart of the ecumenical movement. Opponents of the merger argued that agreement that mission and unity belong together does not necessarily involve the administrative unity of the two organizations. The prevailing conviction became that "mission and unity belong together." After heartfelt discussion the IMC voted to recommend IMC-WCC integration to its members, although it was not until 1961 at the WCC Assembly in New Delhi that the decision became final.[16]

At New Delhi both the Section on Unity and that on Witness stressed the theological interrelation of unity and mission. The report from the Section on Unity stated, "In the fulfillment of our missionary obedience the call to unity is seen to be imperative, the vision of one Church proclaiming one Gospel to the whole world becomes more vivid, and the experience and expression of our given unity more real." It continued, "There is an inescapable relation between the fulfillment of the Church's missionary obligation and the recovery of her visible unity." Noting the interrelationship in the reports on Witness, Unity, and Service, the report from the Section on Witness stressed that these three themes "are in the last resort not three but one." After the vote for integration at New Delhi, D. T. Niles, secretary of the East Asia Christian Conference, considered this action to be "the most significant expression of the growth of the churches together into selfhood." He continued, "It is the instrument of the resolve to be churches together in the World. It is to be the means by which the churches enter into a meaningful participation in the missionary task of the Church."[17]

15. See A-WCC/IMC, box 270006; quoted in Hoekstra, *Demise*, 40–46.
16. For the debate see IMC Conf., Ghana 1957–58, *Ghana Assembly*, 156–67; Bassham, *Mission Theology*, 40–45; Winter, "Ghana."
17. WCC/A (New Delhi 1961), *Report*, 78, 121; Niles, *Earth*, 169. The WCC created

Later Reflections

Lesslie Newbigin, writing in 1962 as director of the new Division on World Mission and Evangelism (DWME), found that with the merger member churches could no longer view mission to be an ancillary concern. He wrote, "For the churches which constitute the World Council this means the acknowledgment that the missionary task is no less central to the life of the Church than the pursuit of renewal and unity." He reiterated his conviction that "no movement is entitled to the use of the word ecumenical which is not concerned that witness be borne to the Gospel throughout the whole earth, and which is not committed to taking its share in bearing that witness." Philip Potter, Newbigin's successor a decade later, added that the integration "certainly challenged the churches to rethink their missionary character and not leave missionary activity to para-ecclesiastical groups." Russell Chandran of India concurred, adding his judgment that "the integration of the IMC with the WCC was a fulfillment of the vision of the wholeness of the ecumenical movement based on the conviction that mission and unity were integrally related to each other and both together were of the very essence of the church."[18]

Twenty years after integration, Emilio Castro, then director of the CWME, focused on the theological underpinnings of the merger. He began with his conviction that both the IMC and the WCC were "instruments in God's hands to advance the cause of the unity of the Church in the fulfillment of its mission." However, Castro noted with concern that in the last twenty years "we have seen a gap growing between new agencies created by the churches in the West and the missionary dimension of the Church's life." He emphasized that "the Gospel of Jesus Christ is the total invasion of God's love manifested fully in the cross of Jesus Christ. The Christian community as a worshipping, proclaiming, teaching, serving reality is an indivisible unity that should be both at the root of our missionary sending and the aim of our missionary concern."[19]

Shortly before his death in 1977, Max Warren gave final reflections on the debate, in which he had been a most active participant. He re-

---

a Division of World Mission and Evangelism (DWME) in 1961, which became in 1971 the Commission on World Mission and Evangelism (CWME).

18. Newbigin, "Missionary Dimension," 245–46; Potter, "Christ's Mission," 59; Chandran, "Merger," 426.

19. Castro, "Editorial," 233, 234.

turned to the "fear that there was a great danger in centralizing the direction of missionary strategy." Being responsive to the "unpredictability of the Holy Spirit" requires maximum flexibility. One IMC success, he reflected, "was its success in drawing into consultation and into increasingly mutual respect and trust an extremely wide section of Christian thinking." While recognizing the positive benefit of the new structure in involving Orthodox churches in discussions on mission and unity, he cited many examples of "the existence of a powerful source of spiritual energy directed explicitly toward the missionary enterprise, which is outside the purview of the WCC in general, and of the CWME in particular." Harvey Hoekstra summed up the consensus of critics of integration that "the WCC promised that the missionary and evangelistic commitment would now become central to its life and work. The outcome, however, proved otherwise." In 1981 Newbigin affirmed again that the IMC-WCC merger was "the right and necessary action," but confessed that the hopes have not been realized "that integration would bring the missionary and evangelistic concern into the heart of the WCC so that all its activities would in future be infused by that concern."[20]

UNITY IN MISSION

At the WCC's Third Assembly (New Delhi 1961) the Section on Unity stated that "in the fulfillment of our missionary obedience the call to unity is seen to be imperative." In it "the vision of one Church proclaiming one Gospel to the whole world becomes more vivid and the experience and expression of our given unity more real." Those at New Delhi believed that "there is an inescapable relation between the fulfillment of the Church's missionary obligation and the recovery of her visible unity."[21]

The distinctive contribution of the next Assembly (Uppsala 1968) was its discussion of mission and unity in terms of catholicity. There was a sense in which "catholicity" could not be confined to the church, but rather attained its true and full meaning only in relation to the unity of all humanity. For example, how was the church to be authentic in repudiating racism and political and economic exploitation unless it was obedient to God's call to express in its own life "the fullness, the integrity, and the totality of life in Christ"? Thus "the catholicity of the Church

20. Warren, "Fusion," 104, 105, 108; Hoekstra, *Demise*, 36; "Integration," 248, 250.
21. WCC/A, New Delhi 1961, *Report*, 121.

is taken up and carried into her apostolicity, her mission." A tension between the visions of the unity of humanity and the proclamation of the gospel to those who have not heard remained. The WCC's Central Committee reported in 1975 that the "CWME has been concerned about the extent to which the missionary imperative could avoid being a disruptive factor in the search for unity."[22]

By the Fifth Assembly (Nairobi 1975) the WCC was ready to underline the close relationship of mission and unity by amending the first clause of its Constitution on "Functions and Purposes" to read: "to call the churches to the goal of visible unity in one faith and in one Eucharistic fellowship ... and to advance towards that unity in order that the world may believe." Section I on "Confessing Christ Today" outlined the purpose of mission to be the whole church bringing the whole gospel to the whole person in the whole world.[23]

The Broadening Vision

The next world mission conference (Melbourne 1980) had as its theme "Your Kingdom Come" from the Lord's Prayer. Melbourne related God's "option for the poor" to the theme "Your Kingdom Come." Rather than recipients of mission, the poor become God's agents in mission. Section 3 on "The Church Witnesses to the Kingdom" related emerging ecological concerns to unity in mission. It declared, "Mission in Christ's way must extend to God's creation. Because the earth is the Lord's the responsibility of the church towards the earth is a crucial part of the church's mission." In 1983 the WCC Central Committee, expressing as much its own convictions as those of Melbourne, wrote, "The churches were called to recognize the relationship between mission and unity. Unless the pilgrimage route leads the churches to visible unity in the one God, the one Christ, and the one Holy Spirit, the mission entrusted to us in this world will always be questioned, and rightly so."[24]

Finally, the climax of thirty-five years of search for a common understanding of unity and mission came in 1983. In that year the WCC adopted *Mission and Evangelism: An Ecumenical Affirmation*. The state-

---

22. WCC/A, Uppsala 1968, *Report*, 7, 13; WCC/CC, *Uppsala to Nairobi*, 71.

23. WCC/A, Nairobi 1975, *Breaking Barriers*, 22–24, 317–18. See Bassham, *Mission Theology*, 98–106, for extended commentary and analysis.

24. WCC/CWME Conf., Melbourne 1980, *Kingdom*, 373; WCC/CC, *Nairobi to Vancouver*, 91.

ment found that authentic unity in mission is "in the action of the body of Christ in the history of humankind—a continuation of Pentecost." Common unity for Christians was to be "the natural consequence of their unity with Christ in his mission." Recognizing the plurality of cultures in which that unity finds expression, the document stated that "the unity we look for is not uniformity but the multiple expressions of common faith and a common mission." This was to remain the Council's definitive statement for the next several decades.[25]

The next world mission conference (San Antonio 1989) incorporated in its theme, "Your Will Be Done: Mission in Christ's Way," another phrase from the Lord's Prayer. It appropriated the theology contained in *Mission and Evangelism* and challenged the churches to make it their own "and give expression to the holistic understanding of mission reflected in it." Concerning mission and unity, Section I on "Turning to the Living God" declared that the conference theme "sets unity and mission in an inseparable relation." Mission in Christ's way involves "becoming a community that transcends in its life the barriers and brokenness in the world." It continued, "The search for visible unity in one faith and in one Eucharistic fellowship, and the struggle to overcome injustice and alienation in the human family, are one single response to the gospel." The conference message reinforced this linkage of concerns for unity, mission, and justice as it said, "To churches and nations where divisions, barriers and enmities prevail: Mission in Christ's Way calls us to strive for unity with justice as a basis for effective mission."[26]

The Central Committee, in its report to the Seventh Assembly (Canberra 1991), stressed that "the WCC's commitment to the visible unity of the church, the renewal of humankind, and its work for justice, peace and the integrity of creation, is today a major context of CWME's programme, as are the involvement of women and youth and the search for an authentic spirituality." Canberra added its conviction that "a reconciled and renewed creation is the goal of the church's mission. The vision of God uniting all things in Christ (Eph. 1:10) is the driving force of the church's life of sharing, motivating all efforts to overcome economic inequality and social division." It reiterated that "our mission needs to be 'in Christ's way,'" and stated that "wholeness of mission demands a will

---

25. WCC, *Mission and Evangelism*, ¶ 20, 23, 27. For later developments see Castro, "New Perspectives," 77–88.
26. WCC/CWME Conf., San Antonio 1989, *Report*, 23, 28, 35.

to break down barriers at every level, and involves the whole people of God in sharing, serving and renewal in a spirit of love and respect." It affirmed the prophetic witness of local ecumenical endeavors believing that "each church acting in mission is acting on behalf of the whole body of Christ."[27]

The Compelling Vision

In 2000 the WCC's Commission on World Mission and Evangelism adopted an important statement on "Mission and Evangelism in Unity Today." The section on "Called to Witness in Unity" noted, "In recent decades the churches have become ever more aware of the necessity to engage in mission *together*, in cooperation and mutual accountability." Simultaneously, there has been "an escalation of confessional rivalries and competition in mission in many parts of the world." These "compel the ecumenical family to re-examine issues of mission in unity."[28]

Delegates to the Eighth Assembly (Harare 1998) celebrated the WCC's fiftieth anniversary. At the closing recommitment service they reaffirmed a holistic statement of mission and unity, saying:

> We long for the visible oneness of the body of Christ, affirming the gifts of all, young and old, women and men, lay and ordained. We expect the healing of human community, the wholeness of God's entire creation. We trust in the liberating power of forgiveness, transforming enmity into friendship and breaking the spiral of violence. We open ourselves for a culture of dialogue and solidarity, sharing life with strangers and seeking encounter with those of other faiths.[29]

At the Ninth Assembly (Porto Alegre 2006) moderator Aram Keshishian, Catholicos of Cilicia, reminded delegates that the WCC Constitution states clearly that the primary purpose of the WCC fellowship of churches is "to call one another to visible unity in one faith and in one Eucharistic fellowship, expressed in worship and common life in Christ, through witness and service in the world, and to advance towards that unity in order that the world may believe." He continued, "*Being church* is a missiological issue; it means redefining and rearticulating

---

27. WCC/CC, *Vancouver to Canberra*, 103; WCC/A, Canberra 1991, *Signs*, 251.
28. WCC/CWME, "Unity Today," 84. See Matthey, "Missiology," for background and analysis.
29. WCC/A, Harare 1998, *Together*, 4.

the *esse* of the church as a missionary reality.... It means rediscovering the centrality of unity. Speaking with one voice and assuming together the church's prophetic vocation are, indeed, essential requirements of 'being church' in a polarized world." In his introduction to the official report, editor Luis Rivera-Pagán wrote, "The Porto Alegre assembly also reaffirmed the integral relationship of the three traditional ecumenical concerns: the quest for church unity, the missionary proclamation of the gospel, the prophetic struggle for justice and peace. Unity, mission and justice were again conceived as indissoluble and indispensable dimensions of the ecumenical movement. The pressures to downgrade any of them were resisted."[30]

The centenary of Edinburgh 1910 was an occasion that challenged the global missionary movement to re-gather and take stock of where it stood in relation to its task. A new Global Christian Forum was its sponsor rather than the WCC. The General Council that prepared for the Edinburgh 2010 Conference included not only representatives of WCC-member bodies, but also Roman Catholic, Pentecostal, and African independent church leaders. They comprised "a broader cross-section of World Christianity" than had "ever before come together in a purposeful way." Eight study commissions wrestled with "the great challenges facing church and mission in the 21st century." The Conference searched for "new ways to express the unity and common mission of the churches."[31]

UNITY IN EVANGELISM

In 1974 Philip Potter, WCC general secretary, addressed the Roman Catholic Synod of Bishops in Rome on "Evangelization in the Modern World." In his address he spoke clearly on the WCC and unity in evangelism: "The ecumenical movement finds its origin, among other things, in the requirements of evangelization that call for unity among Christians. ... The conviction of the World Council of Churches has been that evangelization is the ecumenical theme *par excellence* ... Evangelization ... can only be conceived and carried out in an ecumenical perspective and fellowship." Methodist bishop Mortimer Arias of Bolivia, addressing the WCC's Assembly in Nairobi the next year, quoted Potter's statement and then added, "This means that from the perspective of the Church's mission, unity is not merely an eschatological hope, a spiritual reality or an

30. WCC/A, Porto Alegre 2006, *God*, 48, 118–19.
31. Kerr and K. Ross, *Edinburgh*, 42–44.

inter-ecclesiastical aim; it is an actual prerequisite of mission. We are not seeking unity *per se*, but rather, as in the prayer of Jesus, '*that the world may believe.*'"[32]

In confession Arias said, "above all we must admit with shame that evangelism has been the Cinderella of the WCC, at least to judge by the extent to which it appears in its structure, where it figures as nothing more than one office with a single occupant, in a sub-structure which is itself merely part of a unit, and with no more than a monthly letter by which to communicate with the churches of the whole world."[33]

Earlier Statements

In their clear statements on unity in evangelism, the WCC's First and Fifth Assemblies (Amsterdam 1948 and Nairobi 1975) appear like oases in a desert.[34] Amsterdam, after grasping the situation of the world and the church, declared, "The evident demand of God in this situation is that the whole Church set itself to the total task of winning the whole world for Christ." The Central Committee in 1951 reminded the churches that the word *ecumenical* "is properly used to describe everything that relates to the whole task of the whole Church to bring the Gospel to the whole world."[35]

The "most comprehensive ecumenical statement" on a theology of evangelism was "A Theological Reflection on the Work of Evangelism," produced by the WCC's Department of Evangelism in 1959. Foundational for the WCC's position on unity and evangelism was its Trinitarian theology: "God is a missionary God. In Jesus Christ He came into the world to save it.... For the meantime, He created a people to carry on His missionary task. Of this people Christ is the Head, and of their work and witness the Holy Spirit is the reality." It is the Triune God who empowers the church to evangelize.[36]

---

32. Potter, "Evangelization," 163; Arias, "Believe," 13.
33. Arias, "Believe," 16–17.
34. See Pope-Levison's three-part history of "Evangelism in the WCC" from 1948 to 1991. See also Werner, "Evangelism," and the documented critical assessment in Hoekstra, *Demise*.
35. WCC/A, Amsterdam 1948, *Man's Disorder*, 2:216; WCC/CC, "Calling," 15.
36. WCC Division of Studies, "Theological Reflection," 15; Pope-Levison, "Part Three," 102–6.

God-World-Church

Around the triad God-church-world revolved the ongoing theological reflections of the WCC on unity in evangelism. Beginning with the Third Assembly (New Delhi 1961), focus shifted to the third leg, the world. Evangelism was again defined by the phrase, "a commission given to the whole Church to take the whole Gospel to the whole world." Witness to the gospel (with "witness" used synonymously with "evangelism") was expressed as engagement "in the struggle for social justice and for peace; it will have to take the form of humble service and of a practical ministry of reconciliation amidst the actual conflict of our times."[37]

Studies in preparation for the WCC's next Assembly (Uppsala 1968) focused on what God is doing in the world to bring humanization, with no mention made of the earlier conviction at the Amsterdam Assembly that God demands that the "whole Church set itself to the total task of winning the whole world for Christ." This brought a chorus of protests against the new perspective led by Donald McGavran of Fuller Theological Seminary in the U.S., in his oft-quoted article, "Will Uppsala Betray the Two Billion?," and in the "Frankfurt Declaration on the Fundamental Crisis in Christian Missions," drafted by Peter Beyerhaus, professor of mission at Tübingen, Germany.[38]

Reflecting later on the Uppsala Assembly, Lesslie Newbigin recalled his "most painful experience of that assembly" to be the struggle to overcome "the almost implacable resistance" of the group drafting the section on mission "to include any reference whatever to the duty of the church to bring the Gospel to those who had not heard it." Vigorous debate between those who would stress mission as evangelization, and those emphasizing mission as humanization, continued in the WCC as well as outside among Protestant evangelicals, Roman Catholics, and those of the Orthodox churches.[39]

An Inclusive Theology

In response to criticism, and in a desire to seek common ground with other Christians, the WCC sought for a more inclusive theology in 1975.

37. WCC/A, New Delhi 1961, *Report*, 85, 86.
38. McGavran, "Will Uppsala Betray"; "Frankfurt Decleration" in Beyerhaus, *Missions*. See Bassham, *Mission Theology*, 278–80, Stott, "Rise and Fall," 60–63, Hutchison, *Errand*, 186–89, and McGavran, *Conciliar-Evangelical Debate*, for analysis.
39. Newbigin, "Ecumenical Amnesia," 4. This review of Konrad Raiser's *Ecumenism in Transition*, amplifies his debate on this issue with the then general secretary of the WCC.

M. M. Thomas of India, in his official report as WCC moderator at the WCC's Fifth Assembly (Nairobi 1975), described the growing consensus between understandings of evangelism in the Lausanne Covenant (1974), the declaration of the Catholic Synod of Bishops (1974) and Pope Paul VI's apostolic exhortation *Evangelii nuntiandi* (1975), and that of the WCC.[40] Bishop Arias, in his keynote address on evangelism, called for a holistic or integral approach. He gave the model of the statement on evangelism by the Evangelical Methodist Church in Bolivia. Nairobi, that lifted up God's love for the whole world as the basic motivation for the church's concern for all people in this way: "Our obedience to God and our solidarity with the human family demand that we obey God's command to proclaim and demonstrate God's love to every person of every class and race, on every continent, in every culture, in every setting and historical context."[41]

The holistic approach to evangelism and unity came to a culmination in the WCC's "Mission and Evangelism: An Ecumenical Affirmation," the official statement adopted by the WCC's Central Committee in 1982. It read: "Churches are called to unity.... Common witness should be the natural consequence of their unity with Christ in his mission.... Witness that dares to be common is a powerful sign of unity coming directly and visibly from Christ and a glimpse of his kingdom."[42] This remained the WCC's position in the years that followed. The 2000 statement on "Mission and Evangelism in Unity Today" reiterated positions taken in 1982, adding particular applications to the proselytism debate that had been a serious concern of the Orthodox churches, and the gospel and culture debate highlighted at the CWME conference in San Salvador in 1996.[43]

The Ongoing Challenge

Critics of the WCC's approach to evangelism are numerous, and not just from those outside the WCC. In 1957 Keith R. Bridston, WCC's Faith and Order secretary, presented to representatives of the five world ecumeni-

---

40. WCC/A, Nairobi 1975, *Breaking Barriers*, 231; "Lausanne Covenant," in LCWE, Lausanne I, *Let the Earth*, 3-9; Catholic Church, Pope Paul VI, *Evangelization* (*Evangelii nuntiandi*).
41. WCC/A, Nairobi 1975, *Breaking Barriers*, 53.
42. WCC/CWME, "Mission and Evangelism: An Ecumenical Affirmation," 18.
43. WCC/CWME, *"You Are the Light"*, 59-89; WCC/CWME Conf., Salvador 1996, *One Hope*.

cal bodies that participate in the World Christian Youth Commission[44] an intentionally provocative paper entitled "Is Ecumenism a Hindrance to Evangelism?" He contended that "the ecumenical community should not be one which is striving to synthesize mission and unity, but one which recognizes the inevitable dialectic tension between mission and unity." He interpreted that tension as arising from "the centrifugal and disintegrating pressures of evangelism running into the centripetal and integrating forces of unity." The result, he believed, is the delusion that "ecumenism *is* evangelism" and that "unity guarantees evangelism."[45]

In 1987 the CWME invited forty-five Christian leaders from around the world to consider evangelism. They addressed unity and evangelism, and affirmed "that unity, important as it is, must never be a unity for its own sake. It is a unity so that all may believe, and in harmony with a mission in Christ's way on behalf of, and in identification with, the poor, the lost, and the least in God's creation." They urged the WCC again to "stimulate theological reflection on the nature of evangelism and its relationship to the nature of the Church."[46] That has remained an ongoing task for the WCC in the twenty-first century.

In 2007 Jacques Matthey, director of the WCC's renamed Programme on Unity, Mission, Evangelism, and Spirituality, elaborated on the holistic approach to mission and unity as he wrote, "we must hold together our passion for salvation and our passion for unity, which will obviously be a unity in diversity. One without the other is a partial and indeed defective witness to the gospel."[47]

UNITY AND MISSION IN FAITH AND ORDER

From the beginning the WCC connected mission and unity. At its first meeting the WCC Central Committee emphatically declared that unity and mission are "indissolubly connected."[48]

At the third world conference on Faith and Order (Lund 1952) the world mission of the church was one of five central themes. In his public address Henry Smith Leiper, the WCC's associate general

---

44. These include the World Alliance of YMCAs, the World YWCA, the World Council of Christian Education and Sunday Schools Association, the World Student Christian Federation, and the WCC.
45. Bridston, "Hindrance," 358–60.
46. WCC/CWME, "Statement," 220, 223.
47. Matthey, "Evangelism," 366.
48. WCC/CC, "Calling," 16.

secretary, stressed his conviction that "a world mission without an urge to unity is unthinkable; a Christian Church without a consciousness of world mission ought to be also unthinkable." The world needs to hear our conviction, he continued, "that a Church without a world mission is not a Christian Church." In its report to the churches the Lund conference spoke of the inextricable link between unity and mission: "Many of our differences arise from a false antithesis between the Church's being in Christ and its mission in the world." They declared, "obedience to God demands also that the churches seek unity in their mission to the world."[49]

This emphasis gained wider agreement at the WCC's Second Assembly (Evanston 1954) with its declaration that the church's task is to manifest unity "not for the sake of the Church as a historical society, but for the sake of the world. The being and unity of the Church belong to Christ and therefore to His mission."[50]

At the fourth world conference on Faith and Order (Montreal 1963) a central issue was how the historic tradition of the Christian faith should be transmitted through the life of the church in particular languages and traditions. Facing the reality of Christian divisions, the conference was asked: in the building up of new nations "are Christians, to whom the ministry of reconciliation has been committed, to be a factor of division at such a time?" They addressed the dialectic of the church's mission in both to relate "the Tradition as completely as possible to every separate cultural situation" and at the same time demonstrate its transcendence of all human divisions. William Stringfellow, out of the struggles of the racial crisis in the United States, challenged the conference to recognize that "the real issues of Faith and Order are simply the ordinary issues of life or death in the world, and that baptism is "not merely the sacrament of unity of the church, but the sacrament of the unity—reconciliation—of all persons and all creation in the life of God."[51]

In the 1970s Faith and Order discussed the sacraments as signs both of unity and of mission. A 1971 document entitled "Beyond Communion" declared that "communion is missionary ... a celebration of God's reconciling work in the life of the world." It raised the question, "How can we restrict the fellowship of worship to a circle narrower

---

49. WCC/CFO Conf., Lund 1952, *Report*, 16, 18, 205.
50. WCC/A, Evanston 1954, *Report*, 85.
51. WCC/CFO Conf., Montreal 1963, *Fourth Conference*, 58–59; Crow, "Legacy," 25.

than that appropriate for mission?" Can persons of other faiths, with whom Christians in missionary obedience frequently share a common purpose, occasionally be "drawn into the fellowship with Christ instead of being estranged from it?"[52]

In 1989 Aram Keshishian addressed the Faith and Order Commission on "the intimate interwovenness of unity and mission." He contended that "to draw a line of demarcation between the two is simply a new heresy. A divided church cannot have a united mission. Mission without unity is void of any ecclesiological basis." He regretted that plans for a world conference on unity and mission, jointly sponsored by the WCC's program units of Faith and Order and of Mission and Evangelism, had been replaced with joint theological reflection.[53]

At the fifth world conference on Faith and Order (Santiago de Compostela 1993) Archbishop Desmond Tutu of South Africa spoke out of the crucible of the struggle against apartheid the finding "that a united church is a far more effective agent for justice and peace against oppression and injustice." In response the report urged Faith and Order to explore more fully "three issues that can be barriers to common witness in mission and evangelism: proselytism, denials of religious liberty, and the false proclamation of cultural values and habits as Gospel truth." Throughout the conference participants prayed for the church that God would "empower its witness; heal its division; make visible its unity." The Faith and Order movement continues its pilgrimage "towards the visible unity of the church for the sake of God's saving purpose for all humanity and creation."[54]

UNITY AND MISSION IN SERVICE (*DIAKONIA*)

In his epilogue to *A History of the Ecumenical Movement: 1517–1948* Bishop Stephen Neill wrote, "It [the WCC] makes possible corporate charitable action on a scale never previously considered possible, and unsurpassed as a means of creating genuine Christian fellowship. It has taken the first steps in corporate witness to the whole body of the churches and to the world."[55] In 1944 the work of the European Central Bureau for Inter-Church Aid became the responsibility of the world fellowship

---

52. "Beyond Intercommunion," in WCC/CFO, *Documentary History*, 93, 96.
53. WCC/CFO Conf., Budapest 1989, *Faith and Order*, 263–64.
54. WCC/CFO Conf., Santiago de Compostela 1993, *Koinonia*, xii, xvii, 97, 256–57.
55. Neill, "Epilogue," 728.

of churches, which was in the process of formation. Europe in 1945 was confronted with the staggering needs of an estimated 12,500,000 refugees, and the new Department of Reconstruction and Inter-Church Aid began to work alongside national agencies offering refugee and resettlement services. As the program developed churches "found it easier to act together in relieving human suffering than to act together in any other cause." Their experience was that joint action creates genuine Christian fellowship.[56]

The resettlement of Old Believers[57] from China to Brazil is one example, among many, of how through unity in mission churches working together can meet human needs beyond their own national or confessional priorities. The Old Believers fled to China at the time of the 1917 Russian Revolution and there became self-contained, self-supporting communities. Their situation became precarious after China became communist. With the cooperation and assistance of the United Nations' High Commissioner for Refugees, Inter-Church Aid helped more than one thousand Old Believers to emigrate to Brazil, providing transport, materials, seeds, livestock, and tools with which to begin again. Once self-supporting, this community with WCC assistance helped other Old Believers to resettle in Argentina, Australia, and New Zealand.[58]

After the WCC's Third Assembly (New Delhi 1961) Inter-Church Aid included new responsibilities. When newer churches of Africa and Asia, as well as Orthodox churches, joined the WCC, the previous project system, initiated after World War II in the rebuilding of Europe, came into serious question. Many persons, both donors and recipients, felt that it perpetuated patterns of power, domination, and dependence. Under their prodding the WCC launched new and controversial programs of participation in peoples' struggles for development and liberation, including aid to those in rebellion in the Nigeria-Biafra War (1968–69), and solidarity with the racially oppressed in southern Africa through the Program to Combat Racism.

In response to its critics the Commission[59] declared in 1978 that "our commitment to seek justice in relationships in the human family

56. G. Murray, "Joint Service," 202, 204–6.
57. A seventeenth-century schism from the Russian Orthodox Church.
58. G. Murray, "Joint Service," 220.
59. At the WCC's Fourth Assembly (Uppsala 1968), the Division of Inter-Church Aid, Refugee and World Service (DICARWS) became the Commission on Inter-Church Aid (CICARWS).

brings tensions and pain to our search for and experience of unity." Their response was to reaffirm their conviction that "unity is the work of the Holy Spirit," and to relocate the vocation of service at the very center of Christian faith, that is, unity in Jesus Christ and eucharistic fellowship.[60]

Jean Fischer, director of CICARWS, reminded the Commission that the first Christians appointed as deacons were to address a situation of injustice, because "widows were being neglected in the daily distribution of food" (Acts 6:1). In our world of unjust distribution "our diakonia must aim to re-establish justice, not [just] to distribute the leftovers to those who are neglected, discriminated against, marginalized." Such inter-church action, Fischer continued, must go far beyond charity, for "our diaconal service must actively oppose the forces which are seeking to destroy life." It must be "a total service, intended for the whole of humanity, affirming the forces of life."[61]

The CICARWS Commission in 1987 expressed well this obligation: "Diakonia is service to the whole human being, to all humanity, and to the whole creation. . . . Diaconal action will therefore demand suffering and self-emptying (*kenosis*) but always celebrating the hope of the resurrection."[62]

Visser 't Hooft recalled in 1984, near the end of his life, that he had written in 1944 at the height of the suffering in World War II that the way churches would act in service to refugees would become the test of the ecumenical movement. Would it be shown to exist as a living, caring organism? Or, if denominational and confessional individualism triumph, will it be shown to be just "a matter of theory"? He concluded that "churches have begun to learn the lesson of the coherence of the body of Christ. As one member suffers, all suffer." Inter-Church Aid, working across national and confessional frontiers, enabled ecumenical partners to realize that "the *familia Dei* is not just a beautiful dream." For many it was their only form of "concrete and personal participation in the ecumenical movement."[63]

THE ICCC, A RIVAL COUNCIL

From 1948 to at least 1999 fundamentalist opponents of the WCC have picketed at every assembly. With placards they circled the bastion of ecu-

60. Quoted in Fischer, "Inter-Church Aid," 130.
61. Ibid., 132.
62. "Minutes of the CICARWS Commission" (June 23–27, 1987), 32; quoted in Dickinson, "Diakonia," 430.
63. Visser 't Hooft, "Inter-Church Aid," 10–11.

menism like the army of Joshua around Jericho, led by Carl McIntire, president of the rival International Council of Christian Churches (ICCC).

McIntire was an old warrior whose animosities were honed in the fundamentalist-modernist controversies of the 1920s. When his mentor, J. Gresham Machen, withdrew from Princeton Theological Seminary to found Westminster Seminary in 1929, the seminarian McIntire followed him. Together they were tried as schismatics and dismissed from the Presbyterian Church (USA) in 1936. From his base as pastor of the Bible Presbyterian Church of Collingwood, New Jersey, a suburb of Philadelphia, McIntire went on to found the Bible Presbyterian Synod in 1937 and Faith Theological Seminary in Philadelphia. Denouncing the "dark record and paganizing influence" of the Federal Council of Churches, he became the first president of the rival American Council of Christian Churches. From this base he attacked not only the liberal Council, but also the "One Great Hour of Sharing," which raised funds for the hungry and homeless overseas. Two weeks before the WCC formed in 1948 he launched the rival International Council of Christian Churches and became its first president.[64]

"Two movements of a world-wide nature have arisen within this twentieth century to challenge and command the Christian churches," McIntire wrote in 1955, referring to the WCC and the IMC as the first, and the "Twentieth Century Reformation movement, represented in the International Council of Christian Churches and its related organizations" as the second. To further the ICCC's crusade against modernism and ecumenism in the mission fields, McIntire encouraged the formation of regional affiliates: the Latin American Alliance of Christian Churches (1951), the Far Eastern Council of Christian Churches (1951), and the Central Christian Council (1969).[65]

The WCC "represents a false concept of Christian unity and has no Biblical basis," charged the ICCC in its 1965 Congress. Furthermore, it "acts as an instrument for building of an apostate super-church." Since the goal of the ecumenical movement from its very beginning, the delegates continued, has been the formation of one visible church, it would, if it comes into being, "have no Biblical creed or confession of faith!" It would make room "for the denials of Unitarians, liberals

---

64. Russell, *Voices*, 155–57; Roy, *Apostles*, 186–202.
65. McIntire, *Servants*, 1; A-YDSL/ICCC, "East Africa Christian Alliance."

and neo-orthodox" and for Orthodox and Roman Catholic false teachings. In 1983 the ICCC chose to send a letter to the WCC Assembly at Vancouver. In it they reiterated their premillennial belief "that the stage is being set in Roman Catholicism and Communism to join together in helping to bring to power both the world Babylon church and the world super state."[66]

In 1990 Carl McIntire began his fifty-fifth year as editor of the *Christian Beacon* and forty-second year as president of the ICCC with the headline, "Marxist Philosophy Has Become Ecumenical Theology for the WCC." He claimed that the political changes in Eastern Europe vindicated the ICCC's anti-communism stance. Meanwhile the old warrior repeated his charge of the World Council's identification with Karl Marx. Claiming allegiance of member bodies in more than one hundred nations, McIntire addressed the thirteenth ICCC Congress in 1990, meeting in the hall where the WCC Vancouver Assembly was held in 1983. The rhetoric was as vitriolic as ever: "We are at war with the WCC ... for it has come into being by the power of Satan." But the faithful were but a remnant of six hundred as the Canadian government had denied visas to an equal number.[67]

HOPE FOR WIDER UNITY

In 1982 José Miguez-Bonino presented to the WCC's Commission on Faith and Order his prescient view of "a new ecumenical reality." "In faith we can claim the eschatological unity," he declared, "the unity that God wills for the church and that he has promised to it." By that standard "the authenticity of church unity" is judged "in the light of God's promised kingdom of peace and justice." Our "prophetic-missionary impulse," however, interacts with historical forms of injustice, institutionalized in our churches, which produces conflict. For Miquez-Bonino ecumenism is "the struggle for creation of a new oikoumene in justice." In the tension between the historical present of the struggle and the final future of a "land where justice dwells, we find our ecumenism in its ambiguity and its promise."[68]

---

66. *Reformation Review* 13 (1965) 54–55; 28 (1983) 195. See also McIntire, "Critique."
67. *Christian Beacon*, September 6, 1990.
68. Miguez-Bonino, "'Third World' Perspective," 122–24.

Others hoped for a future in which the conciliar expression of ecumenism through the WCC would contribute to a wider unity. Stephen Neill wrote in 1954, "The ecumenical movement today is not to be identified with the World Council of Churches. Many older movements, such as the voluntary Christian lay movements, continue their separate existence, and make their fruitful contribution along their own lines. Some Churches which are not members of the World Council have also a sense of ecumenical vocation and in their own way work for unity." Bethuel Kiplagat of Kenya found it to be "a mistake to equate the World Council of Churches with ecumenism or the ecumenical movement." He affirmed the WCC as "but one of the expressions of this search for unity of the people of God."[69]

Jan van Butselaar of the Netherlands in 1992 called for a new ecumenical movement that "should take far more seriously the local and regional expressions of the faith." What is needed is a "place where all those local, regional, confessional expressions of faith in Jesus Christ, of all mission in his name, may come together" with all, including Roman Catholics and evangelicals, participating fully, "respecting each other's tradition, each other's understanding of faith." His vision was of a WCC guided by the Spirit that would become "a real World Council of Churches, a World Council of Christians, a World Council of Diversity that does not direct the ecumenical movement, but is guided by it."[70]

In that spirit the message from the WCC's Ninth Assembly (Porto Alegre, 2006) ended with this prayer: "God in your grace, transform the world. Transform us in the offering of ourselves so that we may be your partners in transformation to strive for the full, visible unity of the one Church of Jesus Christ, to become neighbours to all, as we await with eager longing the full revelation of your rule in the coming of a new heaven and a new earth. Amen."[71]

---

69. Neill, "Epilogue," 728; Kiplagat, "Ecumenism," 243.

70. Butselaar, "Thinking," 371–72. In 1999 Konrad Raiser, WCC general secretary, helped in the formation of the Global Christian Forum. Informally representatives of a wide spectrum of Christian groups began meeting, and then later in larger consultations. At the 2007 consultation in Limuru, Kenya, the Forum's stated Guiding Purpose was: "To create an open space wherein representatives from a broad range of Christian churches and interchurch organizations . . . can gather to foster mutual respect, to explore and address together common challenges" (Global Christian Forum, "Proposals"). See also van Beek, ed., *Revisioning Christian Unity*; and "The Global Christian Forum."

71. WCC/A, Porto Alegre 2006, *God*, 50.

8

Christian World Communions

THE ALTERNATIVE

IN 1924 FINDLEY AND Holdsworth reported that by the 1920s there was a widespread sentiment among Chinese Christians, faced with the plethora of denominational missions in their country, that these "are not the stigmata of Jesus, but the marks of a foreign Church." While commending the diligent efforts of Anglicans, Lutherans, Methodists, and Presbyterians to unite churches of their confessional traditions, the Chinese praised also the vision of one united Chinese church. While the latter might end in a "merely national unity," the former "might belt the globe with strips of catholicity without securing unity in any single locality.[1]

The confessional issue also arose as student Christian movements sought a wider unity. In 1926 the World Student Christian Federation faced the issue of what was to be their attitude toward confessional groups. Their "Interconfessional Commission," while recognizing that national bodies may desire to approve confessional groups, wished to make "absolutely clear, both in principle and in particular cases" that the WSCF's aim is "to encourage ecumenism, and not to foster an exclusive confessionalism."[2]

Early world confessionalism[3] had modest beginnings. In 1867 Anglican bishops met in the first Lambeth Conference—the first world gathering of representatives of a particular faith tradition. Others followed as world alliances were formed of Reformed churches (1877),

---

1. Findley and Holdsworth, *History*, 559–60.
2. A-YDSL/WSCF, "Report of Interconfessional Commission," box 39.
3. The term "confession," used synonymously with "communion," denotes churches grouped on the basis of a common profession of some one form of the Christian faith.

121

Methodists (1881), Congregationalists (1891), Baptists (1905), and Lutherans (1923). Prior to the formation of the World Council of Churches, however, each remained a periodic meeting without ongoing programs or secretariats.

Early planning to form the WCC included the issue of the place of confessionalism. Lutherans advocated allocating seats in the WCC's Assembly and Central Committee on a confessional basis. Henry Pitney Van Dusen, president of Union Theological Seminary in the U.S., wrote that the confessional issue would be "much the most explosive issue" at the inaugural Amsterdam Assembly because of the tension between regionalism and nationalism on the one hand, and denominationalism or confessionalism on the other. The decision to make the WCC a council of autonomous churches, however, did not provide a structural means by which world confessional groups could participate in its deliberations.[4]

In the 1950s and 1960s both the WCC and the world confessional bodies grew in programs and institutional structures. Relief, refugees, and inter-church aid—all were needs that could be met creatively through parallel cooperative efforts among churches. Would the strengthened world confessional bodies also seek a "distinctive witness" resulting in "institutional introversion?" asked Norman Goodall, an IMC secretary.[5]

Lutherans in 1976 raised the same issue. At the final consultation of their major study on "The Identity of the Church and Its Service of the Whole Human Being," delegates from forty-six member churches of the Lutheran World Federation (LWF) raised the question, "Do we Lutherans faithfully represent the unity of the Church which has been *given* in Christ and in the Gospel, or do we allow the Christian identity to be 'overshadowed' by other identities?" They concluded that inter-Lutheran relationships present "a particular ecumenical challenge, because they can become anti-ecumenical." They affirmed the need for common worship and struggle with churches of different backgrounds in order to take seriously the call to the church to be one and find its identity in Christ.[6]

LUTHERAN WORLD FEDERATION (LWF)

Today the LWF is the strongest in staff and program of the various world confessional bodies. Its search for a distinctive, yet representative, un-

---

4. Van Dusen, "Amsterdam," 50; Fey, "Confessional," 117–18.
5. Goodall, *Ecumenical Movement*, 168.
6. Duchrow, *Conflict*, 139; LWF, *Identity*, 140.

derstanding of the church—its unity and mission—therefore provides a useful case study.[7]

Open Hostility (1923–46)

Prior to and during the First World War German Lutherans were the unchallenged leaders within world Lutheranism. An important part of their history had been the continued advocacy of regional Lutheran churches within Germany after the unification of the several states to form the German Empire in 1871. Then, following the First World War, world Lutheran leadership shifted to the North American Lutherans with their massive aid program for Lutherans on the continent. The North Americans took over leadership in the first Lutheran World Conference of 1923 with a pan-Lutheran agenda. They rejected as unionism and a liberal heresy the ecumenical vision of Archbishop Söderblom of Sweden of "evangelical Catholicity" that would concentrate "on a common source of revelation, strength, and inspiration, and not a tacit agreement to eliminate everything in the tradition that might give offense." The earlier Lutheran World Convention, at its founding in 1923, had an "openly anti-ecumenical tendency."[8]

Interconfessionalism (1947–70)

A significant shift took place after 1947 as the former mission churches of the Majority World (Africa, Asia, Latin America, and Oceania) contributed their understandings of unity. Whereas draft constitutions for the LWF prepared by the North American and European sections contained only general references to the ecumenical movement, the final text of the LWF Constitution, upon its founding in 1947, included the function "to foster Lutheran participation in ecumenical movements."[9]

The Fourth LWF Assembly (Helsinki 1963) took place during Vatican II. In response, world Lutherans commenced bilateral conversations with leaders of the Roman Catholic Church, and later with Presbyterians, Anglicans, and others that have become an important program for the world confessional movements.

---

7. See Scherer, *Mission*, for a detailed history of mission and unity in the LWF's program and pronouncements.
8. Duchrow, *Conflict*, 163–69; Sharpe, "Legacy," 69. See also Schmidt-Clausen, "Launching."
9. LWF Assembly, Lund 1947, *Proceedings*, 260.

The next LWF Assembly (Evian 1970) faced a distinct challenge from member churches in South India and East Africa. Each had been involved in church union negotiations that had achieved significant doctrinal agreement but *not* organic union. Would the LWF shift from its historic anti-unionist stance to support organic union? The reply opened new doors as the 1970 assembly declared, "A union of churches must be seen as a proper expression of the unity of the Church when uniting churches have agreed upon a confessional statement of faith that witnesses to a right understanding of the Gospel to serve as a guide for preaching and the administration of the sacraments."[10] Further evidence of the influence at Evian of the churches of the Majority World on issues of mission and ecumenism can be found in three new points of agreement: (1) that the unity of the church was to be seen "within the horizon of the common mission in the world;" (2) that LWF cooperation with the WCC, rather than competition, was to be intensified and extended; and (3) that the LWF was to support "the responsible union of Lutheran churches with other churches."[11]

Reconciled Diversity (1970–)

Since 1970 the LWF's focus in Faith and Order has been on bilateral conversations between confessional bodies. Conducted largely by male theologians from the North Atlantic region, they have centered on concerns for confessional traditions and identities more than imperatives of mission. Meanwhile the LWF's Life and Work foci have been upon strengthening the relief and development resources provided through the LWF to member churches. One consequence has been that member churches, such as those in South India and Tanzania, fear losing the material advantages of LWF ties if they enter into organic unions on the national level. The concept of *reconciled diversity*, first articulated in 1974 and used increasingly by Lutherans in bilateral and LWF-WCC conversations, has become the prevailing rationale for strengthening the LWF and other world confessional bodies.[12]

"Much of today's local ecumenical activity in mission is quite unrelated to worldwide inter-confessional dialogues or to programs of ecumenical world organizations." The LWF included this confession in their

---

10. LWF Assembly, Evian 1970, *Sent*, 142.
11. Duchrow, *Conflict*, 182.
12. Ibid., 182–204.

policy statement on mission in 1988. This lack, they recognized, "presents a challenge to Lutheran churches for whom the local congregation is a cornerstone of mission, who by their very confession are committed to the unity and renewal of the church." To redress the balance, the LWF reaffirmed that "participation in the mission of God is the central purpose of the church" and that "faithfulness in mission implies pursuit of the unity of the church." The Constitution as amended in 1990 stated explicitly that the LWF "furthers the united witness to the gospel of Jesus Christ and strengthens member churches in carrying out the missionary command and in their efforts towards Christian unity worldwide."[13]

In 2004 the LWF made its finest statement on the imperative of unity in mission. It confessed that "the inability of churches to achieve unity in diversity or to engage in joint mission ventures has undermined the credibility of the church in mission." It outlined a broad range of priorities for "a missional church as an *oikoumene* community," including "bringing peace, justice, health, and abundant life" and engaging "prophetically with the increasing political and social instability and violence in different places in the world." It stated clearly that "while church unity is one of the aims of mission, ecumenical dialogues between Christian denominations need to have mission at their center."[14]

WORLD CONFESSIONS AND MAJORITY WORLD CHURCHES

In 1952 the WCC's Study Department (later named the "Division of Studies") convened an ecumenical study conference for East Asia in Lucknow, India, in preparation for the world body's Second Assembly (Evanston, 1954). David G. Moses of India, in his keynote address, reflected on the "tremendous spiritual significance" of the union of Christians of various denominations in the church of South India, and questioned whether the creation of worldwide denominations is a step toward the actual unity of the churches. Such developments "make the task of real organic unity between the denominations more remote and formidable," Moses declared. For him the critical issue was one of mission. He believed that there was "a growing realization that Christians

---

13. LWF, "Together," 27, 5, 9; LWF Assembly, Curitiba 1990, *I Have Heard*, 141–44.
14. LWF, Dept. for Mission and Development, *Mission*, 30, 53.

who are unreconciled with one another can never be fit to witness to the gospel of reconciliation."[15]

As for world confessionalism, study conference delegates said that it is a phenomenon that holds "great promise as well as great danger." They expressed appreciation for its role in conserving and sharing a heritage, but considered world confessional bodies a danger insofar as they "plan the extension and imposition of their confessionalism in the lands of the younger churches." They considered regional church unity as their top priority and feared that world confessionalism might jeopardize its realization.[16]

Moves to strengthen world confessionalism continued to receive their strongest opposition from Asia. The launching of the East Asia Christian Conference (EACC) in 1959, with delegates from forty-eight churches in fourteen countries at the inaugural assembly, was based on the conviction "that the purpose of God for the Churches in East Asia is life together in a common obedience to Him for the doing of His will in the world." Admittedly, leaders grew up in areas where often missionaries only of one denomination had worked, be it Anglican, Lutheran, Baptist, or Methodist. Many through the student movements had experienced oneness in Christ for the first time, and thereafter objected to being defined and classified according to historic Western church divisions.[17]

In 1961 Asian concerns for mission and unity gained a global hearing at the WCC's Third Assembly (New Delhi, India). Beforehand, the EACC convened in Bangalore its own conference on "World Confessional Development and the Younger Churches." The conference expressed "fear and anxiety" that "the expression of world confessionalism in increasingly complex institutional structures results in the perpetuation and reinforcement of patterns of paternalism and continued exercise of control." To these Asian leaders the world confessional organizations stood for "rival loyalties to particular forms of Christianity." They felt that within them the younger churches will remain "almost permanently weaker partners."

The Asian perspective was heard loudly next at the WCC's conference in Geneva in 1963 on "The Confessional Movements and Mission and Unity." Present were representatives from all the major Protestant

---

15. Ecumenical Study Conference, *Christ*, 9–10.
16. Ibid., 25.
17. Weber, *Asia*, 288, 304.

world confessional bodies, the Orthodox churches, the WCC, and the churches of Asia and Africa. It was Shoki Coe (C. H. Hwang) of Taiwan who raised the concern of Majority World churches that questions regarding *mission, unity,* and *truth* must be interrelated. First, he said that the churches' greatest need is "to become confessing churches in a missionary situation" in which Christians are often a small minority. Second, these churches can witness to the power of Christ to bring unity within nations and cultures *only* if "unity becomes an important part of the witness of the Church." Finally, Coe would examine truth in relation to mission and unity, seeking insights from many Christians, and not only those of one's own confessional background. He feared that *confessionalism* would be the inheritor or protector of truth as understood in a particular period of history, rather than being appropriate for the life of a developing church.[18]

Coe's presentation stimulated discussion on three issues of concern to participants from Asia and Africa: (1) Are churches free to make their own confessions of faith as the indigenous Batak Church of Indonesia has done? (2) Do we want a national or a world fellowship? (3) If my brother is the one confessing Christ at my side, what does this say to the priorities of national versus world confessional fellowship?[19]

A second major Asian consultation met in 1964 prior to the EACC assembly at Bangkok, Thailand. With the theme "Confessional Families and the Churches in Asia," the emphasis was on enabling Asian churches to find their own selfhood along with other churches in mission in the same situation. They called upon the world confessional bodies to make plans that "strengthen and do not weaken the movements toward larger cooperation, closer coordination, [and] joint action for mission and unity." At the EACC's consultation on "Confessing the Faith in Asia Today" (Hong Kong, 1966) participants declared that "the confessional need of the churches of Asia is primarily in relation to their mission in the world," rather than focusing on things in which the churches differ from one another.[20]

18. "Report of Proceedings," in A-WCC/GS, "World Confessional Bodies."
19. A-WCC/GS "World Confessional Bodies, 2."
20. Fey, "Confessional," 125; EACC, *Confessional Families*, 9.

PART TWO: TEN MODELS OF UNITY

WORLD COMMUNIONS AND THE WCC

Challenge from New Delhi 1961

The younger churches were not the only source of challenge to the understandings of unity and mission in world confessional bodies. At its New Delhi Assembly in 1961, the WCC adopted its famous statement concerning "the centrality of unity of all Christians *in each place*."

World Confessional Leaders Respond

The response by leaders of world confessional organizations, in conversation with WCC leaders, can best be traced through the papers of what came to be known as the Conference of Secretaries of World Confessional Families. The specific purpose of their third meeting in Geneva in 1962 was "to allay suspicion and eradicate misunderstanding between them as a group, the WCC, and the critics of 'world confessionalism' in the younger churches of Asia." Kurt Schmidt-Clausen, executive secretary of the Lutheran World Federation, presented the LWF as the means by which Lutheran churches have stepped out of traditional isolationism, have rediscovered the ecumenical and catholic orientations of the Augsburg Confession, and have taken on worldwide responsibilities in common. Its leaders "saw no contradiction between their 'ecumenical' and their 'Lutheran' efforts." He argued that diaconal, social, and relief activities should be coordinated globally through groups like the LWF, leaving the WCC free for its "primary obligation: namely to work towards consensus in truth among the separated churches." As for organic unions of "all in each place," Schmidt-Clausen contended that they are in danger "of relativizing biblical truth" and of becoming "an isolated body without any internationally accepted doctrinal ties."[21]

The sharpest attack on the WCC's priority for unity of *all in each place* was delivered at the secretaries' 1965 meeting, in a paper by W. von Krause entitled "Engagement in the Mission and Unity of the Church." Remembering that Adolf Hitler wanted to unite all Protestant churches in Germany under the banner of nationalism, von Krause, the director of the Neuendettelsau Mission of the Evangelical-Lutheran Church in Bavaria, denounced unity of *all in each place* as unecumenical, dangerous, and positively bad! "I am not convinced," he wrote, "that Union Churches with vague dogmatic beliefs and a faded, insipid confession

---

21. Schmidt-Clausen, "World," 35, 38, 40, 42. See also Martensen, "Federation."

are more zealous or more successful in evangelism than confessional Churches with a clear confessional basis and clearly-defined beliefs about dogma." "Regional unionism (on a world scale)," he concluded, "is the worst form of ecumenical sin because it endangers or destroys the world-wide unity which already exists." This polemic was too provocative to be included in the conference statement or to be published with other conference papers.[22]

New Structures?

Discussion of the WCC's relationship with world confessional bodies gained new saliency in the 1960s as Orthodox member churches became more vocal in the WCC, and Roman Catholics opened new doors following Vatican II. In 1968, at the WCC's Fourth Assembly in Uppsala, a committee was formed to re-examine the WCC's structure, including its relations with non-member churches and confessional bodies. Should the confessional families have a policy-making function within the WCC? This question, first raised in 1948, arose again. Once again the WCC's decision was to keep the relationship consultative. To leaders of the confessional families, however, the rationale seemed more one of fear "in order not to perpetuate these families as such." Their deliberations, however, included neither leaders from the Majority World nor specific missional issues.[23]

Reconciled Diversity

A central issue remained: Is the identity as "Christian" to be one's primary identity, or is it in confessionalism overshadowed by other identities? Earlier we saw that Lutherans wrestled with this issue. But the issue of competing understandings of unity could not be papered over by mutual assent to "cooperative working relationships." In 1974 a new concept, *reconciled diversity*, was introduced at the Conference of Secretaries of World Confessional Families in a paper on "The Ecumenical Role of the World Confessional Families in the One Ecumenical Movement." The argument presented was that confessional identity is a legitimate form of diversity in the church of Christ, corresponding to the diversity of spiritual gifts and the diversity of creation and history. As for church

---

22. A-WCC/GS, "Gen. Sec."; Scherer, *Mission*, 121–22. See "Statement" and *IRM* 55 (1966) 145–88 for other papers of this conference.

23. WCC/CC, *Minutes* (1971), 183–84; A-WCC/GS, "World Confessional Families/Bodies."

unity, the variety of denominational heritages was justified as "legitimate insofar as the truth of the one faith explicates itself in history in a variety of expressions." The staff of the Lutheran Ecumenical Research Institute in Strasburg, who originated the concept, went further to argue that *reconciled diversity* had as much validity as the WCC's principles of *conciliar fellowship* or *organic union*. In reconciled diversity confessional membership is vital argued Vilmos Vajta, Director of the Institute.[24]

Christian World Communions

In 1980 the Conference of Secretaries of World Confessional Families became one of "Christian World Communions." They felt that their former designation, "World Confessional Families," emphasized the distinctiveness of each. Instead, they wish to begin with their unity in Christ, and only secondarily mention their given names of Baptist, Lutheran, Methodist, etc. They followed the model of the LWF which in 1979 changed from calling itself "a free association of Lutheran churches" to "a communion of churches" with a common confession of faith. By 2000 there were 250 distinct Christian traditions that had organized themselves into what Barrett calls "worldwide geo-renewals."[25]

PARTNERS IN MISSION

"How are the world confessional organizations contributing to a genuine *partnership in obedience*?" asked Norman Goodall in 1962. The answer can be found in a multiplicity of partnerships in mission stimulated by world confessional bodies, and in the common ties evolving out of historic mission societies.[26]

Twinning

Anglicans have been among the leaders in linking or "twinning" dioceses from the North with those of the South. Often twinning begins with exchange visits, but grows through shared ministries to meet human needs, or common witness for justice and peace. The 10th Lambeth Conference

---

24. Duchrow, *Conflict*, 185–92.
25. Meyer, "Identity and Calling," 389; Meyer, "Christian World Communions," 110; Barrett and Johnson, eds., *World Christian Trends*, 269. By 2000 seventeen CWCs were represented in the Conference, including the Vatican and the Pentecostal World Fellowship. See also Barrett et al., "Missiometrics," 27–30.
26. Goodall, "World Confessionalism," 57.

in 1968, for example, gave to the Anglican Consultative Council the function to develop as far as possible agreed Anglican policies in the world mission of the church, and to encourage national and regional churches to engage together in developing and implementing such policies by sharing their resources of manpower, money, and experience to the best advantage of all.[27]

Lambeth, the conference of Anglican primates, met but once in each decade. Desiring to bind Anglicans more closely together, the bishops established in 1968 the Anglican Consultative Council. It was to meet every two to three years, include laity and priests as well as bishops, and represent all parts of the communion. In 1976 Archbishop Runcie proposed that Anglican bishops meet in alternate years. Increasingly bishops of the Majority World have found opportunities at these meetings to speak with boldness of the concerns of their dioceses. In a surprising development, bishops of united churches in South India, North India, Pakistan, and Bangladesh have since 1988 become regular participants and full voting members of this Anglican body.[28]

CEVAA

Another new structure for mutuality in mission between churches of the North and the South has been the evolution of certain mission societies in Europe into representative councils for mission. CEVAA is one example of this approach to unity in mission.

In 1964 Jean Kotto, general secretary of the Evangelical Church of the Cameroon, gave a challenge to leaders of churches linked to the Paris Evangelical Mission Society in Africa, Madagascar, the Pacific, France, and Switzerland. Mission, he declared, can no longer go in one direction. Ever since its inception at the beginning of the nineteenth century, the *Société des missions évangélique de Paris* had sought to be broadly interconfessional and international. "A church which does not evangelize," Kotto said, "wastes away and dies." In response, the churches in 1967 pledged themselves to "joint apostolic action" in a rural area of Dahomey in West Africa.

Four years later representatives from thirteen denominations on three continents formed the Communauté Évangélique d'Action Apos-

---

27. Adegbola, "Ecumenism," 58–59; Wright, "Mission," 104; for a Roman Catholic parallel linking 1,100 Franciscan sisters of the United States and the Cameroon, see Dries, "U.S. Catholic Women," 305–7.

28. Hastings, *Runcie*, 141–45. See also Meyer, "Relations," 101–20.

tolique (CEVAA) "with a view to assuming together some of the responsibilities which fall to them in fulfilling the mission which Jesus Christ allots to them." They met regularly to choose joint mission projects, allocate funds, and reflect on their understandings of mission. Although a majority of participants were from churches in the Reformed tradition, mutuality in mission, rather than confessionalism, was the bonding glue. As early as 1972 the CEVAA council stated, "We all have one thing in common: our relationship to Jesus Christ. Consequently, in spite of the differences between us, we can understand one another, and live and work together to carry out the mission of the Church." In 2010 the group had thirteen participating churches including some Methodists, Baptists, Lutherans, and the United Church of Zambia.[29]

Council for World Mission (CWM)

This body is a parallel development out of the former London Missionary Society. Formed in 1977 by twenty-two churches (four from the United Kingdom and eighteen from the global South), mostly of the Congregational or Reformed tradition, it also includes united churches from India, Hong Kong, Papua New Guinea, and Zambia. The new structure was designed to be light, flexible, interim, and open to ecumenical developments, and not to "have a confessional basis for outreach." The essential missionary movement was to be "from the circle of friends to the world of need," always carrying the marks of Christ (incarnation, conversation, teaching, sacrifice, and resurrection). In missionary service each receiving or host church was to have full pastoral and financial care for those who came from other countries to serve, contributing to their stipends, with the CWM covering other costs.

The CWM was "a serious attempt to deal with power sharing" in a world in which the "historic imbalance of power is very much with us still." Nevertheless, participating in a family-like international relationship with others may lead to neglect of "problems of church relationships next door." Focus may remain more on declaring needs than on sacrificial sharing of a significant proportion of a church's income through fully ecumenical channels.[30]

---

29. Rakotoarimanana, "CEVAA," 407–9; Blanc, "Experiment," 108, 111.
30. Thorogood, "Towards Mutuality;" idem, "Sharing," 448–50. For a critical evaluation of these partnerships see Funkschmidt, "New Models."

TOWARDS THE FUTURE

Does the strengthening of world confessional ties weaken local unity efforts? What should be the place of world confessional groups in the ecumenical movement?

In 1962 the WCC asked five world mission leaders to give their answers.[31] Gordon Rupp recalled that the conciliar movement of the late Middle Ages hoped to mend existing schisms yet floundered on the rock of nationalism. It was "salutary and inevitable" that twentieth-century ecumenism "threw people back upon their own loyalties and traditions." Does world denominationalism "open doors to wider unities or does it close them?" Rupp asked. His judgment was that world confessionalism "is at heart sectarian, the very antithesis of the Catholic church."

Hendrik Kraemer concurred. While world confessional bodies profess an intention to promote wider Christian unity, they in fact block it by "fostering in their constituencies . . . a strong sense of confessional solidarity and power as the *pre-eminent* aspect of their Christian consciousness."

Paul Devanandan identified unity, indigenization, and evangelism as concerns of pressing urgency for Asian and African churches in societies facing nationalism, the resurgence of non-Christian religions, and social revolution. In the face of those challenges, Devanandan wrote, any church that focuses on confessional loyalties is in danger "of becoming isolated, introspective and pietistic."[32]

It is those deeply involved in mission who raised the loudest voices of alarm. R. Pierce Beaver recalled that after World War II the world confessional bodies reached out into the lives of young churches as never before. Often material aid was made available in such volume "as firmly to tie the young churches into the confessional bloc." Majority World leaders, desiring international recognition and leadership, often found it first in world confessional assemblies. The result, Beaver concluded, was that world confessionalism "has set in motion separatist forces that run counter to the two-century-long trend toward regional unity and union in the lands of the young churches."[33]

---

31. P. D. Devanandan (India), Benjamin I. Guansing (The Philippines), Hendrik Kraemer (Netherlands), Gordon Rupp (England), and W. G. Wickramasinghe (Sri Lanka).
32. A-WCC/GS, "Gen. Sec."
33. Beaver, *Ecumenical Beginnings*, 281.

Lesslie Newbigin, out of the urgency for common witness to Christ in India, asked, "How will a Hindu recognize the name of Jesus as supreme above every name, if those who bear his name define their own identity not by reference to it, but by reference to the name which evokes the memory of their special religious and cultural histories?"[34]

Others, like Kenneth Scott Latourette, saw ahead "an emerging world culture" and believed that Christianity "must be built into the heart of this culture." He found denominations out of step with this yearning. While not advocating their demise, he would subordinate them to "a higher, larger, more inclusive community—the Universal Church of Christ."[35]

This book presents ten models of Christian unity.[36] Both their variety and differences are highlighted. Advocates for each model agree that Christians should seek that unity for which Jesus earnestly prayed (John 17:11). But both Roman Catholic and Orthodox Christians lay claim to being the "true church" on historical and theological grounds. Protestant Reformers initially sought renewal of the Roman Church, but the Church proved resistant to most efforts at renewal and reconciliation. In the past century Christians seeking in mission to reach those outside the faith, and for maturity in life together, have advocated various models of unity. At the global level the WCC seeks through representation by member bodies to work toward a restored union and to work together in mission. World Communions, on the other hand, seek to unite Christians of only one historic confessional tradition. This chapter has highlighted the inherent tension between two models of Christian global unity—the *world conciliar*, and that of *world communions*.

Is *reconciled diversity* to be a permissible goal for a world confessional model of Christian unity? Ulrich Duchrow answered that the concept is ambiguous and must be critically examined "in the light of the Church's calling to confess the one Christ." The Nairobi Assembly of the WCC declared in 1975, "We *deplore* also that our confessing Christ today is hindered by the different denominations which split the confessing community of the Church." Lukas Vischer believed that the role of the world communions in the ecumenical movement "had to be

---

34. Newbigin, "All," 294.
35. A-YDSL/WSCF, "Report of Interconfessional Commission," box 39.
36. The schema is found in table form in the Introduction, with both spatial (World to Local) and organizational (Voluntary to Institutional) dimensions.

re-examined and discussed from decade to decade" and that "no solution fully satisfactory to all parties was ever found." Persistent issues of church and mission will fan the flames of this debate in the twenty-first century.[37]

---

37. Duchrow, *Conflict*, 204, 359; WCC/A, Nairobi 1975, *Breaking Barriers*, 45; Vischer, "World Communions," 142.

9

World Associations

MODALITIES AND SODALITIES

In 1973 Ralph Winter, general director of the Frontier Mission Fellowship and founder of the U.S. Center for World Mission in Pasadena, California, gave an important address at the All-Asia Mission Consultation in Seoul, Korea. He titled it "The Two Structures of God's Redemptive Mission." In the apostolic age the church began as a Christian synagogue. Over time it developed parishes and dioceses, priests and bishops. Winter called these structured fellowships, in which there was no distinction based on sex or age, *modalities*. Side by side with church structures, intentional communities formed of persons engaged in mission. The Apostle Paul and his band were the first, to be followed in later centuries by associations of men, or women, in monastic orders. Such groupings Winter called *sodalities*.

Protestantism began in the sixteenth century, Winter contended, with modalities but not sodalities. "In failing to exploit the power of the sodality," he wrote, "the Protestants had no mechanism for missions for almost 300 years." It was the Evangelical Awakening in the late eighteenth and nineteenth century, as noted in chapter 2, which spawned the missionary societies that spread the gospel to every continent. What began as voluntary associations, however, often were absorbed back into the modalities as denominational missionary boards and agencies in the late nineteenth century. The resulting structural vacuum was to be filled in the twentieth century by the faith missions and parachurch[1] agencies.

---

1. "Parachurch" (from the Greek preposition *para* meaning "beside" or "alongside") is a convenient but imprecise descriptor for those institutions that draw participation and funds from Christians and Christian churches, but are not under the control of institutional churches. Winter calls them "sodalities." *EDWM*, s.v. "Parachurch

Winter challenged the non-Western churches to encourage the formation of new sodalities—associations of believers committed to exercise their missionary responsibility.[2] Sodalities operating worldwide are the focus of this chapter.

WORLD EVANGELICALISM

Evangelicals in the twentieth century, desiring unity in mission, have looked to the Evangelical Alliance begun in 1846 as their prototype. They could affirm the words of the 1846 Statement of Faith that "as soon as a sinner accepts Christ as Saviour, he becomes one with all members of the Body of Christ throughout the earth." Since the 1846 Basis contained no reference to the church, evangelicals could avoid their ecclesiological differences and have a broad basis for association. They also eschewed use of the term "ecumenical," which earlier evangelicals commonly used.[3]

World Evangelical Alliance (WEA)

In 1946 an important centennial was honored, that of the Evangelical Alliance begun in 1846. Although moribund as an international body, a remnant remained as the World Evangelical Alliance of Great Britain, which promoted for one hundred years the Universal Week of Prayer. A visit to the Alliance by Dr. J. Elwin Wright, representing the National Association of Evangelicals in the United States, led to a shared dream of reviving a world movement of evangelicals. A second concern was to provide an alternative for evangelicals to the WCC which was in process of formation.[4]

WORLD EVANGELICAL FELLOWSHIP (WEF)

After two preparatory conferences in 1950, ninety-one men and women from twenty-one countries met near Zeist, Holland, in 1951 to establish the World Evangelical Fellowship. It was to be a global administrative body to provide "the umbrella that national fellowships have lacked for

---

Agencies and Mission"; Dwight, Tupper, and Munsell, eds., *Encyclopedia of Missions*, s.v. "Parachurch."

2. Winter, "Two Structures"; *EDWM*, s.v. "Sodality and Modality."

3. J. Kessler, *Study*, 62. Rouse, "Voluntary Movements," 320. For a concise introduction see the *Encyclopedia of Christianity*, s.v. "Evangelical and Fundamental Christianity."

4. Murch, *Cooperation*, 178–79; see ch. 3 on the Evangelical Alliance's earlier history.

over a century." Because some present were wary of joining a group opposed to ecumenical endeavor, it was stated that the WEF was "not a council of churches, nor is it in opposition to any other international or interdenominational organization. It seeks to work and witness in a constructive manner, ever maintaining the truth in love."[5] Doctrinal issues were not divisive as the world body took over the conservative evangelical Statement of Faith of the WEA.

Gilbert Kirby served first as general secretary of the EA of Great Britain, and then in the same capacity for the WEF from 1966 to 1970. He coined the phrase "Spiritual Unity in Action" and declared, "We have so often protested that we already know the meaning of spiritual unity and that we do not need to strive for it. Now it is high time that this unity be expressed in effective action." To implement this goal the WEF formed international commissions on theology, missions, communications, women's concerns, religious liberties, youth, church renewal, theological education, and international relief and development. These provided much creative thinking on mission and unity.[6]

By 1992 the WEF had grown to include 62 associations representing 120 million evangelical Christians. The selection in 1992 of Agustin B. Vencer Jr. of the Philippines as its first international secretary from the non-Western world was consistent with the WEF's membership strength as the majority of member national associations were in Africa, Asia, Latin America, and Oceania. His vision was "to establish 237 viable and vital national evangelical fellowships in the world," and for each to have the full range of concerns from prayer and renewal, to mission and church growth, to national relief and development that are expressed through the nine commissions of the WEF. "If all are "working in concert," Vencer believed, they become "a global network for Christ!"[7]

Adopting a Historic Name

At its Kuala Lumpur 2001 General Assembly in Malaysia, the WEF chose to adopt a new but historic name (from 1846)—the World Evangelical

---

5. Randall and Hilborn, *One Body*, 237–41; Goodall, *Ecumenical Movement*, 153. Later anti-ecumenical statements, and inclusion of the word "infallible" concerning Scripture in the doctrinal statement, kept most European evangelical associations out of the WEF until 1968.

6. Howard, *Dream*, 47; *EDWM*, s.v. "World Evangelical Fellowship." For a detailed history of the work of the Theology Commission see Nicholls, "WEF."

7. *EDWM*, s.v. "WEF"; Fuller, *People*, 196.

Alliance. By 2009 the WEA had seven regional organizations plus 121 national evangelical alliances as its full members. It existed "to foster Christian unity and to provide a worldwide identity, voice and platform to Evangelical Christians."[8]

Lausanne Committee for World Evangelization (LCWE)

THE PREDECESSORS (WHEATON AND BERLIN CONGRESSES 1966)

The integration of the WCC and IMC in 1961 did not meet with agreement by many evangelicals within the WCC's member churches, as well as those affiliated with the IMC through their national councils. Two congresses in 1966 with international participation provided platforms for evangelicals to express their views on mission and unity: the Wheaton and the Berlin congresses.

Wheaton 1966. In April 1966 at Wheaton College, Wheaton, Illinois, 938 missionaries and mission leaders from 71 countries attended the Congress on the Church's Worldwide Mission. It was jointly sponsored by the Evangelical Foreign Missions Association (EFMA) and the Interdenominational Foreign Mission Association (IFMA).[9] "The Call to the Congress" gave dissatisfaction with ecumenical mission theology and practice as an impetus, and voiced the conviction that the time had come for "evangelical leadership to make plain to the world their theory, strategy and practice of the church's universal mission."[10]

The "Wheaton Declaration" of the congress stated concisely the prevailing sentiment on unity and mission. The unity expressed was a biblical oneness of spirit, not unity within any organizational. Delegates declared "That we will endeavour to keep the unity of the Spirit in the bond of peace so that the world may believe." The definition of religious liberty as "freedom to propagate and to change one's faith or church affiliation, as well as the freedom to worship God," also called for "resisting the monopolistic tendencies both within and without Christendom that seek to stifle evangelical witness to Jesus Christ." Harold Lindsell, in his overview of the congress, pointed to a strong suspicion of the WCC, the Orthodox churches, and the Roman Catholic Church that pervaded the congress.[11]

---

8. http://www.worldevangelicals.org.
9. Ch. 10 contains a short history of the EFMA and IFMA.
10. Congress, *Worldwide Mission*, 3. Bassham, *Mission Theology*, 210–20, and Saayman, *Unity*, 74–78, for summary and evaluation of the Congress.
11. Congress, *Worldwide Mission*, 10–11, 226–28.

Wheaton promoted cooperation rather than unity for the furtherance of the missionary mandate to evangelize. Other declarations were "That we will encourage and assist in the organization of evangelical fellowships among churches and missionary societies at national, regional and international levels," and "That we will encourage evangelical mission mergers when such will eliminate duplication of administration, produce more efficient stewardship of personnel and resources and strengthen their ministries." Evangelicals were cautioned "to avoid establishing new churches or organizations where existing groups of like precious faith satisfactorily fill the role."[12]

Berlin 1966. Six months after the Wheaton Congress, an even larger assembly of evangelicals with some 1,100 leaders from more than 100 countries, met in Berlin under the theme "One Race, One Gospel, One Task." Billy Graham, who first envisioned the congress, served as its honorary chairman with Carl F. H. Henry, editor of *Christianity Today*, as the executive chairman. In its closing statement the congress, echoing the opening address by Billy Graham, claimed to be the true successor of the World Missionary Conference of 1910 by setting a goal that is "nothing short of the evangelization of the human race in this generation."[13]

Billy Graham echoed the prevailing concepts of unity and mission of the congress in his closing message. He strongly emphasized spiritual unity: "We have said to the world that we are a spiritually united fellowship regardless of *race, culture, language, denominational or ecclesiastical affiliation . . . This is the* spiritual unity of the Church." In this assertion Graham reemphasized what he had declared in his opening speech that "our greatest need is *not* organizational unity," but "spiritual unity in the Gospel" and "for the Church to be baptized with the fire of the Holy Ghost and to go out proclaiming the Gospel everywhere." The intention both at Wheaton and at Berlin was to lay the foundation for "the evangelical alternative to the ecumenical concepts of unity and mission."[14]

Lausanne I

The Lausanne Congress on World Evangelization of 1974, now known as Lausanne I, has been heralded as "by far the most significant meeting of evangelicals" since the integration of the IMC into the WCC in

---

12. Ibid., 22.
13. World Congress on Evangelism, *One Race*, 1:5, 22.
14. Ibid., 1:32, 151; Saayman, *Unity*, 78.

1961. Among its surprises has been the long-standing influence of the Lausanne Covenant, signed by 2,200 participants. Over the years it has been widely accepted as the consensus statement by evangelicals on mission and evangelism.[15]

Billy Graham, in his opening address to the congress, presented Lausanne as the heir of the "evangelical stream" of the missionary movement that flowed out of the Edinburgh World Missionary Conference of 1910. "We come to the task of evangelism," he declared, "as one Church, one body, one company of the redeemed, proclaiming the Lord Jesus Christ." The Lausanne Covenant amplified this understanding in its section on "Cooperation in Evangelism." It said: "We affirm that the church's visible unity in truth is God's purpose. Evangelism also summons us to unity, because our oneness strengthens our witness, just as our disunity undermines our gospel of reconciliation." C. Peter Wagner of Fuller Seminary felt that "for a significant number of Lausanne participants, the congress as *koinonia* was its outstanding characteristic." There was a dynamism in the witness of so many evangelicals of "all colors and sizes and costumes and languages" talking, praying, eating, and rooming together. This unity was expressed when more than 3,000 participants shared the Lord's Supper together. Harold Lindsell noted that this was "a spiritual unity unknown to the ecumenical movement even in its heyday."[16]

In contrast to the WEF, an umbrella for the national evangelical associations and other evangelical institutions, the LCWE, as formed in 1975, was a voluntary network of individuals and groups that affirmed the Lausanne Covenant. Their common commitment was to support the cause of world evangelization wherever it is done in a way true to Scripture. John Capon, a British evangelical participant, reported that "July 1974 saw the emergence of the Lausanne person—a new breed of evangelical, committed to genuinely biblical evangelism, radical discipleship, intense social involvement, sacrificial living, mature partnership and authentic faith." Willem Saayman of South Africa concluded that "With Lausanne 1974 the Evangelicals firmly established themselves as a force to be reckoned with in ecumenical discussions on unity and mission."[17]

---

15. Saayman, *Unity*, 81.
16. LCWE, Lausanne I, *Let the Earth*, 26–27, 5; Wagner, "Lausanne," 962; Lindsell, "Lausanne 74," 1332.
17. Quoted in Glasser, "Evangelicals," 8; Saayman, *Unity*, 86.

Pattaya 1980

"How Shall They Hear?" was the theme of a large LCWE global consultation held in Pattaya, Thailand, in 1980. More than 900 persons attended of whom 650 were voting participants. A large number were related to parachurch agencies.

One of the goals of the consultation was to "develop specific evangelistic strategies related to different unreached people." To achieve this goal seventeen mini-consultations built their discussions and reports upon a lengthy study program in which hundreds of groups around the world had been involved. Each concentrated on Christian witness to a particular people. Concerning unity, the consultation in its final statement reaffirmed the words of the Lausanne Covenant of 1974 "to seek a deeper unity in truth, worship, holiness and mission." It added: "While a true unity in Christ is not necessarily incompatible with organizational diversity, we must nevertheless strive for a visible expression of our oneness."[18]

It has been judged that a major opportunity for greater unity in mission and evangelization was missed in 1980 as the WCC and LCWE held separate large world consultations three weeks apart in the same quadrant of the earth (Melbourne, Australia, and Pattaya, Thailand). Those who attended both conferences gave probing assessments. Fr. Thomas Stransky, CSP, judged both conferences to have been "missed opportunities." David J. Bosch, the South African missiologist, found that both conferences failed to produce a truly comprehensive definition of mission and evangelism. Waldron Scott, then general secretary of the World Evangelical Fellowship, saw "little evidence of evangelical/ecumenical convergence."[19]

Lausanne II

Held in Manila in 1989, Lausanne II was an even larger witness to evangelical unity, attended by over 4,000 participants and observers from 186 countries. Unity and cooperation related directly to one of the key themes of Manila, "the whole church proclaiming the whole gospel to the whole world." Its Manifesto reinforced the Lausanne Covenant's

---

18. Scott, "Significance," 60–61; LCWE Cons., Pattaya 1980, "Thailand Statement," 30–31. See the Pattaya consultation's seventeen Lausanne Occasional Papers, nos. 5–19, 22–23.

19. Stransky, "Reflection," 51; Bosch, "Search"; Scott, "Significance," 66.

urgency of cooperation in evangelism. With contrition, signers confessed "our own share of responsibility for the brokenness of the body of Christ, which is a major stumbling-block to world evangelization." They reaffirmed their commitment "to go on seeking that unity in truth for which Christ prayed."[20]

Electric moments symbolized the unity manifested in Manila. The torch, ignited a year earlier and carried through fifty countries, arrived on opening night to a standing ovation. More than sixty Soviet believers, delayed by authorities in Moscow for two days, received a rousing welcome upon their late arrival. However, three unity issues that surfaced remained unresolved: How will charismatics and non-charismatics, as well as evangelicals and Roman Catholics, work together? To what extent will social justice concerns characterize evangelical missions? How will the predominately middle-aged Western leadership of Lausanne respond to the growing vitality of Majority World churches in mission?[21]

Peter Beyerhaus, the German missiologist, has described the LCWF's multifaceted ministry as acting "like the head of a flying arrow." On the one hand, it encouraged Lausanne I and II participants to convene congresses on the Lausanne pattern at national or regional levels. On the other, it sponsored a series of significant consultations on the theology and strategies of mission, publishing many consultation reports as Lausanne Occasional Papers.[22]

At the turn of the century the LCWF was not the only voice for unity and mission of evangelicals worldwide. It had served, nevertheless, as "the essential mouthpiece of those Protestant missionary movements which were not Pentecostal nor associated with the WCC."[23]

"The Challenge of AD 2000 and Beyond"

This was the title of section 11 of the 1989 "Manila Manifesto." It expressed deep shame "that nearly two millennia have passed since the death and resurrection of Jesus, and still two-thirds of the world's population have not yet acknowledged him.... 2000 has become for many a challenging milestone," it continued, and challenged Christians to "com-

---

20. LCWE, Lausanne II, *Proclaim Christ*, 35.
21. Cryderman, "Camp Meeting," 39; Coote, "Lausanne II."
22. Beyerhaus, "Evangelicals," 174.
23. Matthey, "Milestones," 293; *EDWM*, s.v. "Lausanne Movement."

mit themselves to evangelize the world during the last decade of this millennium."[24]

In 1987 Thomas Wang, LCWE's international director, canvassed world mission leaders to assess interest in an AD2000 Program. In the next two years scholars identified more than two thousand plans focused on global evangelism by the year 2000. Wang convened the first Global Consultation on World Evangelization (GCOWE) in January 1989 in Singapore. There 314 mission leaders from 50 countries, mostly from the Majority World, formed the AD2000 and Beyond Movement. Its purpose was to motivate, network, and inspire leaders with the goal of "a church for every people and the gospel for every person by the year 2000."[25]

Through three global conferences and numerous national conferences the AD2000 Movement both mobilized leaders and facilitated reconciliations. The first, in Singapore, included Roman Catholic representatives who shared Pope John Paul II's 1987 proclamation of 1990–2000 as the "Universal Decade of Evangelization." The second, GCOWE '95 in Seoul, Korea, attended by 4,000 delegates from 186 countries, was the largest and most widely representative international Christian gathering held to date. There the Israeli delegation, composed both of Arab Christians of Palestine and Israel and Messianic Jews, experienced a new oneness and pledged to work together in their homeland. GCOWE '97, the next global conference held in Pretoria, South Africa, attended by 4,000 delegates from 133 countries, focused on adoption of 1,739 designated "people groups" for church planting efforts. Racial reconciliation was another focus, with recognition that reconciliation was a prerequisite for world evangelization. Delegates were moved as an official leader of the South African Dutch Reformed Church read a formal statement of repentance with request for forgiveness, paving the way for ongoing multiracial initiatives in that country.[26]

In the twelve years (1989–2001) of its existence, AD2000 and Beyond lived out the evangelical concept of unity in mission articulated at Lausanne I by Billy Graham, who had said that Christians are "one body, obeying one Lord, facing one world, with one task . . . to proclaim the message of salvation in Jesus Christ." Prayer was a major priority

---

24. LCWE, Lausanne II, *Proclaim Christ*, 37.
25. Barrett, *Seven Hundred Plans*; Bush, "AD2000," 17–19.
26. Bush, "Catalyst," 30–32.

in this movement to bring the gospel to the world's unreached peoples. The geographic area in which most of them lived was labeled the "10/40 Window"—the 60 countries located between 10 degrees and 40 degrees latitude above the equator. A "Praying through the Window" initiative began in 1993 with 21 leaders praying for specific unreached people groups. Later it mushroomed to involve more than 40 million evangelicals praying in over 100 countries. With a networking priority, the movement linked hundreds of mission organizations in international task forces for prayer, translation, Gospel recordings, mobilization, unreached peoples, and saturation church planting.[27]

PATTAYA 2004

"A New Vision, a New Heart, a Renewed Call" was the theme of the 2004 Forum for World Evangelization held in Pattaya, Thailand. This, the fourth of the LCWE's international consultations, was attended by 1,517 delegates from some 130 nations, with 58 percent coming from the Majority World of Africa, Asia, Latin America, and the Pacific. René Padilla of Argentina, in his paper on "Holistic Mission," presented a vision of the church as "a true agent of transformation in its own context." Such a church would not only have the essential marks of being "one, holy, and catholic," but also a life of "Kingdom mission"—of "a love that is translated into action on behalf of the needy."[28]

LAUSANNE III

At the urging of evangelical leaders worldwide, the Lausanne Movement planned to hold the Third Congress on World Evangelization (Lausanne III) in Cape Town, South Africa, for ten days in October 2010, with more than 4,000 delegates. The Congress' goal was to re-stimulate the spirit of Lausanne represented in the Lausanne Covenant: to promote unity, humbleness in service, and a call to action for global evangelization.[29]

---

27. Intl. Congress, Lausanne I, *Let the Earth*, 27–28; Bush, "AD2000," 24–28; Coote, "'AD 2000'"; Wood, "Baton."
28. LCWE, Forum, Pattaya 2004, *New Vision*, 1:227.
29. Lausanne Movement, "About."

PARACHURCH ORGANIZATIONS IN MISSION

Bible Societies[30]

The first modern Bible society, the British and Foreign Bible Society, was formed in Great Britain in 1804. From its founding it was intended to serve in the wider circulation of Holy Scriptures in missionary outreach. The first volume it published was not for the poor people of Wales, the focus of concern at its founding, but rather for the Mohawk Indians of North America. The American Bible Society, founded in 1816, served more than the American churches as it provided missionaries with copies of the Bible in the languages of the people they sought to evangelize.[31]

The Bible societies were to be nondenominational and predominately led by laypersons. Each was a voluntary association that encouraged cooperative efforts among local or regional Bible societies. A symbiotic relationship existed from the start between the Bible societies and the missionary societies. Bible societies relied on missionaries for both translation and dissemination of Scripture portions and Bibles. The missionaries from their side "depend upon the Bible Societies for a supply of the Scriptures, without which their work could hardly go on. Nine-tenths of our successes are the result of the Bible Society work," a Korea missionary reported in 1904. From Sidon, Lebanon, another reported, "If there were no Bible Society, we might as well pack up and go home."[32]

Following World War II the work of the Bible societies increased exponentially in size and scope. "Times have changed," the general secretary of United Bible Societies reported in 1954. "Representatives of the most diverse theologies and confessions are sometimes at work together" in Bible translation. As new nations of Asia and Africa achieved independence and autonomy, new national Bible societies developed. By 1970 the UBS grew to have thirty-three full national societies as members and eleven associate members.[33]

The concern at the grassroots level, however, was for the distribution of the Scriptures as "an essential part of the missionary activity of the Church." Each congregation, or group of congregations, was encouraged

---

30. See Smalley, *Translation*, for the only comprehensive history of the Bible societies.
31. Robertson, *Word*, x–xi; Tigert, "Bible Society," 397.
32. Ibid., 399, 400.
33. Béguin, "Weakness," 413; Robertson, *Word*, 281.

to have some distributing agency of its own. The century-old practice of Bible distribution by workers called *colporteurs* (sellers of religious books) expanded. Leaders encouraged members of youth organizations "to bring the Scriptures into the hands of non-Christians."[34]

New developments had unexpected impact on the circulation of the Scriptures. One was the new openness of the Roman Catholic Church to cooperative work in Bible translation and dissemination. From their earliest years Bible societies had published Scriptures "without note or comment." Until Vatican II Catholics declined participation in Bible societies because of their insistence on always publishing with official Church commentary. A breakthrough on this issue took place as the bishops at Vatican II declared in *Dei Verbum* ("On Divine Revelation") that "access to sacred scripture ought to be widely available to the Christian faithful," and that Catholics could cooperate with the "separated brethren" in the production and distribution of scriptures. By 1968 the UBS and Roman Catholic Church agreed on guiding principles for Hebrew and Greek texts and modern translations. Their clear goal was to make "a common witness to the Word of God in the world of today."[35]

Another was new openness to the printing of the Bible in China, with the Amity Foundation approved by the government to carry out this responsibility. In February 2010 Amity marked the publication of fifty million Bibles in the country. Of these, forty-three million had been made for believers on the Chinese mainline, including editions in Braille and eight minority languages. Production had been increased to over three million Bibles each year.[36]

World Vision International

Bob Pierce, an evangelist with Youth for Christ, began World Vision in 1950 to help children orphaned in the Korean War, and in 1953 developed a sponsorship program to provide long-term, ongoing care for Korean orphans. World Vision next expanded its program into other Asian countries and eventually into Latin America and Africa.

Initially, Pierce led World Vision in sponsoring evangelistic crusades and paid-for Christian radio broadcasts. By the 1960s, however, World

---

34. IMC (Willingen 1952), *Missions,* 219; Béguin, "Weakness," 406–09.

35. Ibid, 115. Vatican Council, *Constitution*, 112. For the history of Roman Catholic cooperation with the Bible societies see Robertson, *Word*, 103–22, and Abbott "Cooperation."

36. China Book, "Official Pledges."

Vision began its relief efforts, delivering food, clothing, and medical supplies to desperate people. A devastating earthquake shook northern Iran in 1962, killing 120,000 people and causing untold human suffering. Determined to offer major assistance, but inhibited by limited resources, World Vision created World Vision Relief Organization, a separate nonsectarian agency able to secure grants for ocean freight and food from the U.S. government. Now called World Vision Relief & Development (WVRD), this organization also solicited clothing and other merchandise from corporations. Such gift-in-kind donations in 2009 accounted for more than 25 percent of World Vision's income.[37]

In its early years the policies, program, funding, and staffing of World Vision came from the U.S. and its evangelical core constituency. This began to change in the late 1970s under the leadership of its second president, W. Stanley Mooneyham. In every major Asian country in which it worked, World Vision developed a locally organized and legally registered board of directors composed of both clergy and lay persons. By 2005 more than fifty national World Visions entities were incorporated, each with its own autonomous board and national director.[38]

As World Vision grew, it found working exclusively through the churches to be impractical and to lead to charges of discrimination and sectarianism from others. "We work with all the churches in the community—Orthodox, Catholic, Protestant." That was the pledge of Dean Hirsch, World Vision's president in 2005. Locally, World Vision desires to work with an entire community, including people of other faiths.[39]

By 2005 World Vision had become one of the largest Christian organizations in the world, employing 22,000 people in 100 countries. It raised only $500 million in 1996, but $1.5 billion in 2004. Its budget is roughly three times that of CARE, and thirty times that of World Relief. Still true to its original structure, much of its funding for child support comes in small monthly gifts that sponsor 2.2 million individual children.

As World Vision grew it become an increasingly important player in world humanitarian aid. As its international president, Dean Hirsch was able to address the U.N. General Assembly, the World Bank, and the World Trade Organization. A U.S. ambassador once exclaimed,

---

37. World Vision, "History." See also Stafford, "Colossus."
38. Mooneyham, "World Vision," 707; Stafford, "Colossus," 53, 55.
39. Stafford, "Colossus," 52.

"You've got more people in Mozambique than the U.S. government has in all of Africa!"[40]

Media and Mission

In 1968 representatives of Protestant churches, both conciliar and evangelical, joined with Roman Catholics and Orthodox Christians to form the World Association for Christian Communication (WACC). Multimedia in orientation, WACC included twenty public corporations as members by 1971, including Australian, Canadian, Norwegian, Dutch, and British radio and TV broadcasting services, and the leading Arabic evening newspaper in Beirut. Its training programs prepared men and women for secular as well as church-related employment.

WACC's specific instrument of mission was its Department of Church-Related Communication, composed of two representatives from each regional council or conference of churches. This Department began as an interdenominational partner committee to advise the Lutheran World Federation Broadcast Service in the work of "Radio Voice of the Gospel" broadcasting from Addis Ababa in Arabic and Persian to the Middle East.[41]

By 2010 WACC had grown to have 1,500 corporate, personal, and affiliate members in 120 countries. Genuinely ecumenical in membership and communication activities, it encouraged cooperation between Protestant, Anglican, Orthodox, and Roman Catholic communicators, as well as cooperation between persons of other faiths. WACC's mission in 2010 was to "promote mission for social change." It stated "that communication is a basic human right that defines people's common humanity, strengthens cultures, enables participation, creates community, and challenges tyranny and oppression."[42]

World Radio Missionary Fellowship Inc., commonly known as HCJB World Radio, is the oldest interdenominational missionary broadcast organization. In 2009 it had radio ministries in more than one hundred countries and more than one hundred languages and dialects. In 1985 it joined with Far East Broadcasting Company, Trans World Radio, and the Sudan Interior Mission to launch the "World by 2000" initiative

---

40. Ibid., 51.
41. Johnson, "Communication," 492–94. The International Christian Media Commission, an association of media professionals and trainers from around the world established in the 1980s, provides consultancy, training, and coordination services.
42. WACC, "About."

with the goal to provide Christian broadcasts to each person on earth in a language each could understand. Other mission organizations including Sudan Interior Mission, FEBA Radio, and Words of Hope later joined the partnership, now named "World by Radio," which continues to seek out and work with local partners to meet this goal.[43]

ECUMENICAL ASSOCIATION OF THIRD WORLD THEOLOGIANS (EATWOT)

The 1960s and 70s were years of awakening and promise for peoples of the Third World, now called Majority World.[44] The United Nations had declared two development decades, and proposed in 1974–75 a New International Economic Order. Major pronouncements, both by the Vatican and the WCC, had stressed the rights of peoples to self-development, national self-determination, social justice, and human dignity. Catholic bishops of Latin America in 1968 at Medellin focused on concern for the poor, later described as the "preferential option for the poor."[45] The Medellin documents gave evidence of the emerging theology of liberation. This paralleled the emergence of new contextual theologies after 1972. Both movements gave legitimacy to the indigenous and local to a degree never known before. In time they became mutually reinforcing. In this milieu theologians of Africa, Asia, and Latin America felt the need for an international dialogue.[46]

The Ecumenical Association of Third World Theologians was born in Dar es Salaam, Tanzania, on August 12, 1976. Founding members defined their aim to be "the continuing development of Third World Christian theologies which will serve the church's mission in the world and witness to the new humanity in Christ expressed in the struggle for a just society." They agreed that only through comprehension of their socioeconomic, political, and cultural realities could they interpret God's will in a meaningful way for their societies. They embraced a theological method that placed commitment and involvement in the struggle

43. *EDWM*, s.v. "Radio Mission Work."
44. The term "Third World" has acquired layers of meaning, including geographic ("the South"), socioeconomic ("poor," "underdeveloped"), political ("non-aligned"), and even theological ("from the underside of history"). EATWOT, New Delhi 1981, *Irruption*, xii.
45. Oduyoye, "Reflections," 61.
46. Fabella, *Bonding*, 7–12. See WCC Theological Education Fund, *Ministry in Context*.

for a just society as an act of theology prior to reflection. Burgess Carr, general secretary of the All-Africa Conference of Churches, affirmed his understanding that "African theology and the unity of the Church are interdependent," and that they can be based on a three-fold traditional emphasis on corporateness, community, and celebration.[47]

Initially, the association planned for a series of intercontinental conferences as the major means to achieve its objectives. The second, third, and fourth EATWOT conferences focused successively on the realities of particular continents.[48] The fifth (New Delhi 1983), appropriately titled "Irruption of the Third World," was to synthesize the findings of the preceding conferences and serve as EATWOT's first general assembly. Delegates concluded that "the irruption of the poor and oppressed does not automatically lead to the victory of justice." They renewed their pledge "to stand with our people ... for the greater realization of justice and freedom in our world." They affirmed that to do so "is to participate actively in the liberating mission of Jesus." Their new priorities included supporting women in their struggles for equality and dialogue with First World theologians on liberation themes.[49]

The Women's Commission, established in 1983, enabled women theologians to move from marginality to full participation in EATWOT. Beginning with their own series of regional conferences, women became 45 percent of delegates to the EATWOT Third Assembly (Nairobi 1992). The spirit was one of "openness, cooperation, and mutual respect."[50]

In its self-evaluation in 1996, EATWOT affirmed that it began and developed in the context of two processes—"the crisis of the prevailing economic and inter-state system" and the self-affirmation of Christian communities on six continents. They understood liberation to include not just socioeconomic and political justice, but also gender, ethnicity and race, cultural, and ecological dimensions, declaring that "liberation should be perceived as the defense and promotion of life." They affirmed that liberation of the poor involves not just economic betterment, but also affirmation of their humanity and place in societies in which they

---

47. Ecumenical Dialogue, Dar es Salaam 1976, *Emergent Gospel*, 273; Fabella, "Bonding," 16–17; Carr, "Relation," 163.

48. Africa (Accra, Ghana, 1977), Asia (Wennappuwa, Sri Lanka, 1979), Latin America (São Paulo, Brazil, 1980).

49. EATWOT, New Delhi 1981, *Irruption*, 205.

50. Fabella, "Bonding," 115, and 67–91 for the individual journeys of EATWOT women.

have been excluded and oppressed. They favored a wider understanding of ecumenism. Dialogue should include not just the present partners from Roman Catholic, Protestant and Orthodox churches, but also thoughtful persons of other world religions and leaders of indigenous peoples. The 2001 assembly affirmed EATWOT's "macro ecumenical vocation towards unity between Christian denominations and all religions of the earth."[51]

During its short history EATWOT has provided regional and global forums in which participants share theologies that are contextual, liberational, and ecumenical. In the twenty-first century they aim to be more inclusive and "to integrate other theological voices" of women, younger persons, non-academics, and indigenous peoples.[52]

CONCLUSION

In January 2010 a massive earthquake devastated Haiti, destroying the capital city, killing more than 230,000 people, and leaving more than one million persons homeless. Christian sodalities like World Vision, along with Doctors without Borders and other agencies, acted quickly to provide relief. In the gravity of the situation Gerald Granado, general secretary of the Caribbean Conference of Churches, asked, "Was all the destruction, death and distress experienced the result of the 7.0 earthquake *per se*, or was not the factor of an over-crowded city with weak and compromised structures—all due to decades of continued impoverishment and underdevelopment—a major factor in the equation of devastation?" While appreciating the aid contributions of the sodalities, he called on modalities (governments, the United Nations, and the churches) to devote all available resources to "genuine development cooperation."[53]

Anglicans John Stott of England and John Reid of Australia are representative of persons conversant with the modality/sodality dichotomy. "We need a greater unity," John Stott wrote in 1995. He recalled that the Lausanne Covenant of 1974 had declared that "unity strengthens our witness while disunity undermines it." The section on "Cooperation in Evangelism" expressed penitence for our "sinful individualism" and "needless duplication," and pledged to "seek a deeper unity in truth, wor-

51. Santa Ana, "Evaluation."
52. EATWOT, New Delhi 1981, "Message of Hope," 42.
53. Caribbean Conference, "Statement."

ship, holiness and mission." Looking forward, Stott saw few signs of such penitence and commitment to unity among evangelicals. He regretted the "tendency to individualism and empire building" that took place as Eastern Europe and the former Soviet Union opened up to new initiatives, the multiplication of global missionary movements, and the virtual absence of an ongoing Catholic-Evangelical dialogue.[54]

The analysis of John R. Reid of Sydney, Australia, coincides with the analysis of sodalities by Ralph Winter with which we began this chapter. Voluntary societies possess an inherent flexibility and freedom that church structures often lack. As a consequence they frequently "revitalize the sending churches with missionary vision." They mobilize like-minded Christians to further the church's mission apart from official synods and conferences. But Bishop Reid also warned that we cannot be blind "to the problems which can be created by such missionary work." Placing a high priority on evangelism can fail "to give appropriate expression to the formation of the church and order in the churches." Voluntary mission agencies "may stifle the development of the emerging churches." They "may stand as an obstacle to fellowship between churches." They "may act recklessly in disregarding comity of missions and bring unnecessary duplication." These potential weaknesses, the bishop believed, "illustrate the great need for consultation and mutual co-operation."[55]

---

54. Stott, "Twenty Years," 53.
55. Reid, "Voluntary."

10

Regional and National Voluntarism

PARTNERSHIP

A NEW REALITY EXISTED in many church-to-church relations after World War II. Where missionaries had been evacuated, national leaders assumed new leadership roles. The clamor for independence from foreign control first came from the Asian colonies, among them India, Indonesia, and the Philippines.

The first IMC conference following WWII (Whitby 1947) had representatives of the older and of the younger churches meet separately to prepare drafts for a statement on partnership. Not one single major difference of opinion came to light. In the agreed-upon statement they rejoiced "to find that in the years of separation, and especially through the testing of war, we have been brought nearer to one another." They also rejoiced over "the developing partnership of the younger churches one with another." "Real partnership," they declared, "involves the grace of receiving as well as the grace of giving." They emphasized the urgent need of partnership in establishing "pioneer work in all those parts of the world in which the Gospel has not yet been preached and where the Church has not yet taken root."[1]

In 1955 Max Warren, general secretary of the Church Missionary Society, defined partnership in relation to two complementary ideas of Christian unity—the organic and the covenantal. He believed that a growing "togetherness" among Christians will come through the dynamic interplay of the two, with "a developing freedom, a unity in diversity." In the light of past divisions among Christians, Warren advised mission

---

1. IMC Conf., Whitby 1947, *Minutes*, 173, 175, 179.

leaders "to speak less about unity and to think more about partnership, seeking with God's help to marry thought to action."[2]

The 1990s were marked by renewed interest in North America in new mission opportunities in Eastern Europe, and the rapid growth of Majority World missions. The 1991 "Working Consultation on Partnership for World Evangelism," sponsored by the Billy Graham Center in Wheaton, Illinois, affirmed:

1. The interdependence of all parts of the Body of Jesus Christ, the Church, and the reciprocal nature of all partnerships;
2. The viability of many models of partnerships;
3. The necessity to change long-standing indifference toward partnerships, so they will be seen not as luxuries but as utter necessities.

The participants recognized that various types of partnerships will be needed—in training missionaries, in pioneer missions, and within denominations "to pursue valid cross-cultural ministry tasks." They will include various mission agencies associated for coordinated ministries within geographic areas, information partnerships, and partnerships among Majority World missions.[3]

PARTNERSHIPS IN MISSION

United Mission to Nepal

In 1954 King Tribhuvan invited Robert Fleming to open a hospital in Tansen and to start women's and children's welfare clinics in the Katmandu Valley. At the time there were no public schools in Nepal, and only one small military hospital to provide modern health care. Eight mission societies had been at work in India along the border with Nepal thus making it possible to serve Nepalese who crossed the border. They agreed in 1954 to form together the United Mission to Nepal (UMN). Each society would be responsible for the support of their missionaries, while the UMN would coordinate all mission activities in Nepal.[4]

---

2. Warren, *Partnership*, 71, 81.
3. Keyes and Pate, "Two-Thirds," 203–5.
4. The eight founding organizations were the Regions Beyond Missionary Union, Church of Scotland Mission, American Presbyterian Church, Methodist Church in Southern Asia, Zanana Bible and Medical Mission, World Mission Prayer League, Swedish Baptist Mission, and the United Christian Missionary Society. Lindell, *Nepal*, 147.

One of the fruits of this united mission approach has been the oneness of the Christian Church in Nepal. Essentially it is free from imported denominational differences. Congregations are linked loosely in the Nepal Christian Fellowship. Such united witness is important in a country with restrictions on religious freedom. Since 1959 the constitution has forbidden citizens to change their religion, and prohibited proselytizing. Converts could be taken to court; more often they were shunned by their families. Despite these restrictions the Nepal Christian community grew to 50,000 by 1990, although still less than half a percent of the nation's population.

By 1990 the UMN had grown to include thirty-nine member societies from nineteen different countries in Europe, the Americas, Asia, and Australia. Together they employed six hundred workers. The central mission of the UMN was to enhance the people's capacity for self-development. When the National Education Policy was established in 1970, the UMN gave its schools to the government. Since then it has worked to train teachers for government schools. Similarly, the national health services expanded rapidly so that the four UMN-administered hospitals were but a fraction of the total. The United Mission's major contribution in health was its training of nurses and other medical staff.

How shall one assess this "unique cooperative approach to mission"? Del Haug, a former UMN medical missionary, judged that "together with the aim of empowerment of indigenous leadership," it "has proved beneficial to the church and people of Nepal."[5]

Mindolo Ecumenical Foundation

The world's largest Christian lay training center is located not in the United States or Europe, but rather outside the copper mining city of Kitwe, Zambia. There 150 acres have been the site of two unique ecumenical partnerships for the nation and Africa.

The first began after Merle Davis and a team of sociologists sent by the International Missionary Council surveyed in 1932 how the churches cooperatively might serve migrants attracted by the new copper mines. Missionary societies agreed that only a united effort could confront creatively the social consequences of rapid industrialization. Together they formed the United Mission to the Copperbelt. Working

---

5. Haug, "Cooperative." See Lindell, *Nepal* for a narrative history of the United Mission's first twenty-five years.

closely with both the colonial government and the mining companies from its center in Kitwe, the Mission developed by 1942 four schools which grew to 6,000 pupils, and a variety of social welfare ministries. In 1950 it handed over its work to the government and the mining companies, feeling that it had done its pioneering work in areas that should be governmental responsibilities.[6]

Was joint action in mission still needed in a British colony moving towards independence? Although the United Mission closed in 1955, participating mission societies agreed in 1957 to continue joint work under the new banner of the Copperbelt Christian Service Council. E. J. Peter Mathews, an Australian Congregational minister, came as organizing secretary to survey local needs. At that time studies by the WCC and IMC highlighted the importance of creative joint ministries in areas of rapid social change.[7]

Mindolo Ecumenical Center began in 1958, with Peter Mathews as its first director. It was conceived to be for Africa what the WCC's ecumenical center in Bossey, Switzerland, and the German lay academies were for the churches of Europe—centers of creative Christian thought and action outside the churches' parish structures. Mindolo was established "to serve the Christian Church and community at large as a centre of study, worship and consultation where men and women may deepen their understanding of questions affecting the unity and renewal of the Church and its responsibilities in the life of the community."[8]

During its first six years, Mindolo held consultations on race relations, political change, and church and state as the struggle for nationhood intensified. With the independent state of Zambia a reality in 1964, Mindolo partnered with government, industry, and the churches in leadership training. An Industry and Commerce program offered a Top Management course for senior managers in government, industry, and the churches, plus short courses in basic supervision, secretarial skills, marketing and sales, and union leadership. Barclays Bank located their training program on the campus. Betty Kaunda, wife of the president, joined the eleven-month Women's Training Course, and supported "Mindolo-on-Wheels," an extension program offering three-to-

6. J. Davis, *Industry*; J. V. Taylor and Lehmann, *Copperbelt*, 37–50.
7. M'Passou, *Mindolo*, 8–22; J. V. Taylor and Lehmann, *Copperbelt*; Van Doorn and Van Doorn-Snijders, *Churches*.
8. "Statement by Fr. F. T. Sillett," February 3, 1961; quoted in H. Andrews and L. Andrews, "Birth," 197.

six-month-long women's courses in rural areas. In the 1970s Mindolo added an eleven-months-long Pan-African courses for both women and youth leaders. Other programs included a two-year course for preschool teachers and trainers, appropriate technology and community development programs, and conferences and consultations on church and national development themes. The Swedish government donated the Dag Hammarskjold Memorial Library.[9]

Archbishop of Canterbury Robert Runcie, during his June 1989 visit to Mindolo, commented, "As I see so many different areas of discipline and study all together on this beautiful campus, I also see a rare thing: the bringing together of action and contemplation. There are not many places in the world where students from so many different backgrounds and with so many different vocations study alongside one another."[10]

EVANGELICAL ASSOCIATIONS

Evangelical Foreign Missions Association (EFMA)

Mission boards of the churches affiliated with the National Association of Evangelicals (NAE) in the U.S. formed in 1945 the EFMA to "provide a medium of voluntary united action." It was unique in serving both the denominational, and the non-denominational or faith missions, that were affiliated to the NAE. From an initial membership of fifteen mission agencies, the EFMA grew by 1965 to include ninety participating mission boards responsible for more than one-fourth of all Protestant missionaries sent from the United States.

After initial tensions with the older Interdenominational Foreign Mission Association (IFMA) founded in 1917, the two agencies in the 1960s began fruitful cooperation. They formed a joint Latin America Committee, and in 1964 the Evangelical Missions Information Service (EMIS), responsible for joint publication of the *Evangelical Missions Quarterly*. They cosponsored the 1966 Congress on the Church's Worldwide Mission, which in its "Wheaton Declaration" agreed "that the proper relationship between churches and missions can only be realized in a cooperative partnership in order to fulfill the mission of the Church to evangelize the world in this generation." While advocating partnership among evangelicals, they opposed what they called "ecumenical

---

9. M'Passou, *Mindolo*, 46–96.
10. Phiri, "Mindolo."

unity," fearing that it could lead to "that type of union which syncretizes doctrine and ignores polity and distinctives."[11]

New mission realities caused both IFMA and the EFMA to change their names in 2007. Increasingly, North American mission initiatives had begun in local congregations that supported and funded cross-cultural missionaries. Linkages multiplied with churches and mission associations in the Majority World. Executive director Marv Newell, in announcing that the IFMA had been renamed CrossGlobal Link, interpreted the change as a "deliberate new effort to link with North American churches, especially churches bypassing agencies as they do mission." In 2009 it joined together 90 mission agencies and over 15,500 missionaries. Steve Moore, president and CEO of EFMA, said that his organization changed its name to The Mission Exchange because "we believe it captures the sense of dynamic, interactive relationships between missional entities . . . that is at the heart of our vision and identity." He added that "while local churches have always been the primary stakeholders in the Great Commission, globalization has enabled them to take more aggressive action." To facilitate this, The Mission Exchange added to its network more than 100 organizations representing approximately 20,000 missionaries in nearly every country of the world. It also added an affiliate membership status for churches and small organizations.[12]

In Search of Identity

In 1976 Carl Henry, former editor of *Christianity Today*, called upon evangelicals to find renewal through "recovery of the larger sense of evangelical family, in which fellow believers recognize their common answerability to God in his scripturally given Word and their responsibility for and to one another within the body of faith." The next year Waldron Scott, the World Evangelical Fellowship's general secretary, shared his conviction "that strong national evangelical associations provide the only viable basis for a more comprehensive continental and global cooperation."[13]

---

11. *EDWM*, s.v. "Evangelical Fellowship of Mission Agencies"; Congress, Wheaton 1966, *Worldwide Mission*, 230, 169.

12. Nicholas, "IFMA and EFMA." For their developing programs see http://www.crossgloballink.org and http://www.themissionexchange.org.

13. Henry, "Brighter Day," 1140; Scott, "Evangelical Cooperation," 71.

INITIATIVES BY MAJORITY WORLD MISSIONS

In 1956 Max Warren of the Church Missionary Society wrote to Norman Goodall, the IMC secretary, concerning "the crucial part which must be played by the younger churches themselves, rather than the missionary societies, in the next great outreach of the Christian mission." In fact that outreach had its beginnings more than a century earlier. Before Alexander Duff of the Church of Scotland reached Calcutta as a pioneer missionary, eight Tahitian missionaries were telling Samoan island villagers about Christ. The first European missionaries arrived five years later to find 2,000 Christians meeting in small groups in 65 villages. Over 1,000 Pacific Islanders went out as cross-cultural missionaries in Oceania in the next 100 years.[14]

India

An indigenous missionary movement flourished in India before 1900. Its watchword was "the evangelization of India in this generation." The Native Evangelistic Society had existed in South India since 1853. In 1904 V. S. Azariah led in reorganizing it as the National Missionary Society of India, and became its first secretary. Azariah worked closely with missionary Sherwood Eddy in promoting evangelization by Indians—both through the Society and through the YMCA in which both men were secretaries. After his Anglican ordination as deacon and priest, Azariah himself went as a missionary to the remote Dornakal district of South India. In 1912 he was chosen and consecrated as bishop of Dornakal. The work begun by the National Missionary Society flourished. In thirty years the diocese grew from 50,000 to 150,000 Christians.[15]

Explosive Growth

From 1970 to 2010 the number of missionaries from the churches of the Majority World of Africa, Asia, Latin America, and Oceania grew to exceed the number of cross-cultural missionaries sent from North America and Europe. When first enumerated in 1972, Majority World missionaries totaled 2,951 sent out by 368 agencies and organizations.

---

14. A-WCC/IMC "Joint Committee," box 270006; for more examples see Larson, Pentecost, and Wong, "Perspectives."

15. Latourette, *World Service*, 113; Sundkler, *Church*, 34–35. For the biography of Bishop Azariah see Harper, *Shadow*.

By 1995 their cross-cultural missionaries numbered 88,000 sent out by 1,600 non-Western mission organizations. Panya Baba, respected leader of the Evangelical Church of West Africa, for example, reported in 1990 that under the auspices of the indigenous Evangelical Missionary Society over 700 Nigerian missionaries working among Muslims and animists in northern Nigeria had established over 250 churches. By 2006 the Nigeria Evangelical Missions Association had 95 member bodies with nearly 5,200 missionaries working in 56 countries[16]

Cooperation in mission is a strong quality of many Majority World mission efforts. In Latin America COMIBAM is a movement for mobilization of Latin Americans for mission to unreached peoples. Researchers estimated that there were 1,600 Latin Americans sent by 60 agencies engaged in such a mission in 1987. By 1997 that number had increased to 4,000 workers sent by 300 agencies. The statistics for 2006 showed that Latin America had more than 10,000 missionaries sent outside their home countries by some 400 agencies. COMIBAM conducts research on the multiple social factors affecting mission in Latin America, including urbanization, the world of religious plurality, violence, displaced peoples, refugees, and poverty. As it trains leaders it continues to search for new viable models for cooperation.[17]

National Missions Associations

Mission associations multiplied in Asia, Africa, and Latin America as churches intensified their commitment to spread the gospel to people of different ethnicities within their own countries and beyond. The largest of these is the India Missions Association (IMA). In India there were only four indigenous missions prior to 1965. Thereafter concern for cross-cultural evangelism within India grew rapidly. In 1977 the newly emerged missions gathered under the auspices of the Evangelical Fellowship of India to form the new association. By 1999 more than 100 missions became members eager to connect and deal with cross-cultural mission issues. In the next ten years the IMA grew to represent 210 Indian mission organizations, agencies and church groups that support about 40,000 Christian workers within India and beyond. Think tanks are a regular part of IMA activities. Typical were those held in 2005 on

---

16. *EDWM*, s.v. "Non-Western Mission Boards and Societies"; Keyes and Pate, "Two-Thirds," 191; Olonade, "Nigerian Church"; Keyes, *Last Age*.

17. See their Web site: http://www.comibam.org/indexcomibam.html.

women in mission, emerging church planting, and younger CEOs. The IMA recognized the challenge that although the Christian community is increasing in numbers in India, the Christian percentage of the total population has been decreasing. Of India's 953 ethnic people groups identified in 2009, each with a population of more than 10,000, 204 did not yet have a worshiping Christian fellowship.[18]

CONCLUSION

"The future of missions," missiologist Paul Hiebert wrote, "is based in the formation of international networks rather than 'multinational organizations.' Networks build up people, not programmes; they stress partnership and servanthood, not hierarchy; they help to build up the local church, not undermine it." But probing questions remain: Will the emerging structures for mission in the twenty-first century be centralized, corporate and multinational, modeled after the transnational corporations, or will new patterns develop of decentralized groupings with maximum local control? Will future partnerships include multiple linkages utilizing the latest information technologies? National and regional associations for mission can look forward to future opportunities in which to develop creatively flexibility and innovation to meet new challenges.[19]

---

18. India Missions Association, "Indian Missions."
19. Quoted in Keyes and Pate, "Emerging," 158.

11

Regional and National Councils

THE MOTT VISION

THE YEAR 1907 WAS auspicious for Asian Christianity as two major mission conferences took place. The Centenary Conference of Christian Missions in Shanghai included 1,104 missionaries (500 of them official delegates)—nearly one-third of the 3,445 Protestant missionaries then in China. Only nine Chinese nationals attended, without vote in this missionary-organized event. In the same year the World Student Christian Federation held its Seventh Conference in Tokyo, its first held in Asia. Asian delegates, 500 of the 627 present, came from 25 countries. The Tokyo conference was the realization of John R. Mott's vision. "Never has there been such an assembly of Oriental Christians," Mott announced at a Japanese student rally. For Mott Tokyo was "one of the most notable events in the history of Christianity in the extreme Orient."[1]

It was Mott more than others who had insisted, even in the face of conservative opposition, that younger churches be represented at the Edinburgh Conference in 1910. The contributions there by Asians, notably Cheng Jingyi Cheng of China, T. Harada of Japan, and V. S. Azariah of India, were among the most memorable. A key step was the bringing of K. C. Chatterji, Y. Honda, and other younger church leaders into international decision-making—a responsibility previously reserved for mission executives.[2]

---

1. China Centenary Conf., Shanghai 1907, *Records*, v; Mott, *Addresses and Papers*, 2:433.
2. Mott to Oldham, February 16, 1910, in A-YDSL/Mott, "Correspondence"; Oldham, "John R. Mott," 258; Hopkins, *Mott*, 348; Weber, *Asia*, 132–35.

One of the best measures of what a person truly values is the use they make of discretionary time and money. That was true of John R. Mott in 1912 and 1913. Eagerly he poured his energies into carrying the gospel of ecumenism from Edinburgh to Asia. He led twenty-one area and national conferences on that continent between November 1912 and April 1913, with the entire cost of $101,000 raised by Mott himself from fifty friends in the U.S., including John D. Rockefeller. The countries Mott visited as chairman of the Edinburgh Continuation Committee were "fields embracing over three-quarters of the inhabitants of the non-Christian world."

Mott's tour gave a jump-start to Asian leadership. Although, as a rule, Western mission agencies working in the Majority World appointed missionaries as their delegates to international conferences, Mott was concerned that national church leaders, including women, not be overlooked. The National Conference in China averted "a grave crisis" in relations between Chinese churches and certain traditional missions. For the first time during Mott's visits missionaries and Chinese leaders deliberated together. The nationals were "by far the most able company of Chinese Christian leaders ever assembled," Mott noted in his report. In Japan missionaries met as the "Federated Missions" in 1910 while nationals organized as the "Federation of Churches in Japan" in 1911–12, Mott first held separate conferences for each group and then a combined national conference. At the conclusion all agreed to unite in forming the Continuation Committee of Japan.[3]

In 1922 Mott returned to Asia. The mood and leadership had changed. The meetings were no longer "Mott conferences," but rather national Christian conferences with the chairman of the International Missionary Council as their honored guest. In China C. Y. Cheng, of Edinburgh fame, was in the chair with a brilliance of leadership of which Mott must have been proud. The conference theme was "The Chinese Church." Despite theological tensions between liberal and conservative missionaries the Chinese delegates, more than half of the thousand persons present, gained near-unanimous approval to form the Chinese National Christian Council affiliated with the IMC. China provided the model soon replicated with slight modifications in the launching of na-

---

3. Mott, *Addresses and Papers*, 2:173–76; Hopkins, *Mott*, 387. For more details see Hopkins, *Mott*, 386–404; and Hogg, *Foundations*, 151–56.

tional councils in India, Japan, Korea, and subsequently in other Asian countries.[4]

Twenty-five years later, reflecting back on his labors for international cooperation in missions, the venerable ecumenist said, "My first and my greatest contribution to the International Missionary Council was to bring about the formation of the National Christian Councils."[5]

ASIA

East and South Asia[6]

Initiatives for the coming together of Asian church leaders began in the student movements. As early as the 1922 WSCF world conference in Peking (now Beijing) it was recommended "that an international conference in the Far East be continued regularly as a means to promote co-operation between the Eastern Movements and to make them know and understand one another better."[7]

The IMC's Assembly at Tambaram/Madras, India, in 1938 deeply influenced all who attended. Chinese and Japanese delegates, although their nations were at war, drank deeply of their fellowship there. They brought communications from their respective NCCs proposing that the IMC establish a Far East office. War intervened, but action was finally taken by the IMC Committee in 1946 on a proposal from the Chinese and Indian NCCs. It was their vision that such a body "promote and give expression to the spirit of Christian unity among the churches of East Asia," encourage common witness, deepen unity, and "bring to the life of the world Church the distinctive contribution of the churches in East Asia."[8]

Three years later the first East Asian Christian Conference met in Bangkok, Thailand. Official delegates represented nine Asian NCCs and came from fifteen countries. Rajah B. Manikam of India, chairman of the Joint Commission on Eastern Asia of the IMC and WCC, gave the charge. "Never before in the history of Protestant Christendom has there been held a conference of delegates from non-Roman churches and Christian councils of East Asian countries," he declared. The focus

    4. Weber, *Asia*, 138–42; Hogg, *Foundations*, 211–14.
    5. Hogg, *Foundations*, 156.
    6. For a detailed history see Koshy, *History*, vol. 1.
    7. WSCF, Peking 1922, *Minutes*, 27; quoted in Weber, "Out of All Continents," 68.
    8. IMC, Meetings, *Minutes*, 46; quoted in Weber, "Out of All Continents," 69.

was on "The Christian Task in Changing East Asia," with evangelization among persons of other faiths a central concern.[9]

Delegates meeting at the second EACC conference in Prapat, Indonesia, in 1957 chose a distinct structure by which to affirm their unity. They did not want to be an ecclesiastical replica of the 1955 Bandung conference of the "non-aligned" nations of Asia and Africa. Delegates from Australia and New Zealand moved from observer to full-member status in the EACC. D. T. Niles of Ceylon, U. Kyaw Than of Burma, and Alan Brash of New Zealand became co-secretaries.

In the next decade the EACC unpacked for Asia the call for "partnership in obedience" voiced by the IMC in 1947. "How could the Asian churches be authentic in their obedience and be themselves before Christ, if they had always to be reacting or responding to initiatives from outside and struggling with the consequences of the decades (or even centuries) of missions operations?" U Kyaw Than asked.[10]

Increasingly at EACC-sponsored situation conferences the focus shifted to Christian involvement in struggles for justice for the peoples of Asia. The Fifth Assembly (Singapore 1973) was a watershed as the Conference changed its name to become the Christian Conference of Asia (CCA). Its broadened understanding of mission was best articulated by M. M. Thomas of India in his opening address on the Conference theme, "Christian Action in the Asian Struggle." Thomas urged the church to enter into that struggle on two levels. First is the "level of spirituality" in which the church's central mission is "the mission of presenting Christ as the Saviour of the human spirit." Then, with no sense of contradiction, Thomas called upon the church to enter into "the struggle for social justice, that is, the transformation of existing structures of State, economic order and society so that the poor and the oppressed may become full participants in the total life of society." It is ironic that the CCA headquarters, established in Singapore in 1973, was expelled by that government in 1987 because the Conference vocally identified with the marginalized in its host country and elsewhere. Concerns for mission as "living together with people of other faiths and ideologies," and for "restoration of whole creation" also emerged as key issues in the 1980s.[11]

9. EACC, Bangkok, 1949, *Christian Prospect*, 3.
10. Than, "Ear," 457, 462.
11. M. Thomas, "Action," 7. See Koshy, *History*, 1:199–261, for a detailed history.

Emphasis on people has been a hallmark of Asian ecumenism. Sang Jung Park, the CCA general secretary in 1987, called it "a dynamic understanding of *oikoumene* becoming a new humanity." He continued, "The key to our grasp of the ecumenical issue was whether we enabled people to participate responsibly and creatively in the process of changing the world into one that is truly human and democratic."[12]

The CCA sought also to bridge confessional and national divides in the region. It is an association of sixteen national councils and over one hundred churches in Asia—not a regional council of the WCC. D. T. Niles, one of its first secretaries, encouraged "a growing cordiality between the churches which are conservative-evangelical and those which are not." The CCA has cooperated in many programs and conferences with the Federation of Asian Bishops' Conferences (FABC) since its establishment in 1972 as the official umbrella organization of the Catholic Church in Asia. In the 1970s the two bodies collaborated in development programs at grassroots levels, in advocacy for women workers' rights, and in studies of the negative impact of tourism on peoples and the environment. In the last three decades, in addition to expanded programs on social issues, the two conferences have explored interchurch relationships, including preparation of resources for ecumenical worship and joint program for spiritual formation.[13]

Ahn Jae Woong, general secretary of the CCA in 2002, called Asian Christians to reclaim "the radical meaning of ecumenism." As "*theo-ecumenics*" it has "a theocentric emphasis on God as source and creator, protector, and liberator of the world." As "*eco-ecumenics*" it is "eco-friendly and must involve the whole of God's creation." As "*geo-ecumenics*" it is contextual "where Asia's unique plurality of religions, cultures, races, languages, peoples, creeds, and colours are affirmed and helped to flourish."[14]

Middle East

Defined by the dominance of Islam, the lands from Morocco to Iran and from Turkey to central Sudan have been known collectively as the Near or Middle East. The scars of the Crusades remain not just in ruined fortresses, but in the hearts of the people. Muslim mistrust of Christian

---

12. CCA, *Minutes*.
13. Niles, *Upon the Earth*, 187; Fabella, "RCC."
14. Antone, *Living*, 13.

motives, as well as Orthodox fear of Catholic or Protestant proselytism, have made interreligious cooperation difficult.

The IMC was the first organization to stimulate a common approach by the churches as it convened a conference on missions to Moslems in 1911 at Lucknow, India. Following John R. Mott's series of conferences on Islam in 1924, church leaders formed a regional Christian council in 1927 (since 1929 called the Near East Christian Council).[15] Presenting the need for the Council, C. R. Watson wrote in 1926, "Just because sections of the area seem to be condemned to a separate existence and action because of national separation, there is the greater need for a Council which will unite them and rid them of a narrowing denominationalism and sectarianism."[16] J. H. Nicol believed that its greatest work should be to unite the hearts and minds of Christian workers so that the non-Christians of the Near East might not be further confused by the variety of Christian approaches.[17]

Until 1964 the Council functioned primarily as a means for missionary cooperation in evangelism, education, medical mission, literature, and relations with governments, with the Christian approach to Islam as its focal issue. The participating bodies by 1961, however, were churches rather than missionary societies. All were from the Reformed tradition with the sole exception of the Syrian Orthodox Church.[18] A 1964 change of name to the Near East Council of Churches signaled the Council's desire to bring together the various churches of the region. However, it was the Arab-Israeli wars, and the ensuing persistent refugee problems, that served as the catalyst to bring vision to reality. Having worked together for a decade, sixty-three delegates from twenty churches in the enlarged region formally established the Middle East Council of Churches in 1974. Membership grew to include three families of churches: Eastern Orthodox (four), Oriental Orthodox (three) and Protestant and Anglican (fifteen), with the Roman Catholic Church joining in 1990.[19]

At the Council's Fifth Assembly in 1990 the churches achieved a new recognition that their witness and survival depends on unity. No

15. Weber, "Out of All Continents," 79.
16. "Memorandum on Council for Western Asia and Northern Africa," in A-YDSL/Wilder, "NECC."
17. News bulletin of the Near East Christian Council, December 1930, in A-YDSL/Wilder, "NECC."
18. WCC/DWME, *Survey*, 7.
19. For descriptions of participating bodies see Horner, *Guide*.

separatist ghetto mentality would provide security when facing the challenges from Islamic fundamentalism. Their resolutions included stands on regional conflicts (Palestinian self-determination, Lebanese national unity, Iran/Iraq, and the Sudan civil war). The Council gained confidence that it was no longer marginal in the life of the region's churches and societies. Aware that the first divisions of the Christian church took place in their region, they accepted responsibility to manifest signs of unity, not only for the Middle East, but also for the strengthening of the worldwide ecumenical movement.[20]

AFRICA

Regional Unity

The history of ecumenism in Africa might have been different if William Carey's "pleasing dream" of 1806 to hold world missionary conferences at the Cape of Good Hope had been realized. A century later John R. Mott visited South Africa for the first time, following up on the continent's first interdenominational missionary conference held in Johannesburg in 1904. It was IMC secretary Oldham who organized the first major conference on Christian mission in Africa, held at Le Zoute, Belgium, in 1926. Again it was the indomitable John R. Mott who in 1934 stimulated the formation of Christian councils in several African countries. By 1955 they numbered fourteen, although only three (Belgian Congo, Sierra Leone, and South Africa) affiliated with the IMC.[21]

A distinctly Pan-African vision of unity, however, surfaced initially at the Lutheran World Federation's first All Africa Conference in Tanzania in 1955. Three years later the IMC used the occasion of its assembly in Ghana to initiate the first representative All Africa Church Conference under the auspices of the Christian Council of Nigeria. In his opening speech, Francis Akanu Ibiam articulated what was to become a common vision in the years ahead: "In the process of time we hope by the grace of God to achieve something which will bring all the churches in Africa together in our efforts to build up the great countries of this continent."[22]

20. Reidy, "Watershed," 22.
21. Weber, "Out of All Continents," 73–75.
22. AACC, Ibadan 1958, *Church*, 9–10.

All-Africa Conference of Churches

Ibiam's vision was realized in 1963 as representatives from some 100 churches and 42 countries of Africa met in Kampala, Uganda, to inaugurate the All Africa Conference of Churches (AACC). Although many delegates came from newly independent nations, their churches were not yet autonomous. The delegates sought for a radical change in relationships, including autonomy for all the churches of Africa.[23]

The next two AACC assemblies (Abidjan 1969 and Lusaka 1974) took place during years of growing African frustrations over unrealized social goals. While the World Bank set a target of 3.5 percent growth in per capita income for developing countries, Africa achieved only 0.2 percent in the 1960s. Growing income disparities within and between countries, plus the sheer scale of poverty, assaulted Christian consciences. Liberation, evangelism, self-reliance, and justice—these were the central issues at Lusaka. To facilitate cooperation in mission the AACC increasingly fulfilled a broker role between churches and donor agencies, working closely with the WCC, national councils, and the various African churches.[24] On two fronts the AACC became actively involved in politics as its general secretary, Canon Burgess Carr, mediated peace in the long-standing Sudan civil war, and the AACC backed the WCC's Program to Combat Racism in southern Africa.[25]

Association of Evangelicals of Africa and Madagascar

Not all African Christians supported the AACC's political agenda or applauded its financial dependence on outside donors and large requests for project funds through the WCC.[26] In 1966, 192 representatives of evangelical churches gathered in Limuru, Kenya, to form a separate Association of Evangelicals of Africa and Madagascar (AEAM) with its headquarters in Nairobi. Member fellowships were required to have no connection with the WCC or AACC, but were encouraged to become members of the World Evangelical Fellowship. The AEAM sought to unite Christians in fellowship and service and saw no need for organic church unity. "Political compromise may be in order for Africa, but gloss-

---

23. AACC, Kampala 1963, *Drumbeats*; Oduyoye, "Decade."
24. In Kenya, for example, 30 percent of all health and community development services in 1991 were provided by the churches (Crafford, "Ecumenism," 7).
25. Adegbola, "Christian Responsibility"; Rafransoa, "CETA."
26. Totaling US $726,500 in 1965.

ing over spiritual absolutes is suicidal," declared Byang H. Kato, AEAM's first general secretary.²⁷

Is there a recipe that could mix together such divergent streams? After decrying the scandal of Christian disunity, Aylward Shorter proposed three commitments as the way forward toward authentic Christian unity in Africa: (1) to pluralism and internationalism; (2) to a progressive and optimistic view of the church; and (3) to African culture "as a common basis for mutual discovery and joint contribution to world-church."²⁸

OCEANIA

In 1961 an "ecumenical explosion" shook the churches of the Pacific region. They had been the most isolated of churches scattered as dots of land in the Pacific Ocean. Member awareness of being part of a larger church came almost entirely through missionary societies and denominational families.

The IMC as early as 1938 had proposed that a permanent consultative organization of missions in the Pacific be formed, but it remained a dream until 1957. In that year C. Stuart Craig, general secretary of the London Missionary Society, acted on behalf of the IMC to invite leaders of Protestant churches and missions in the Pacific region "to discuss the opportunities and problems they face in common, especially in regard to their relationship to the environment and the changes taking place within it."²⁹

Enthusiastically the churches responded. The Pacific Conference of Churches (PCC) was born as they met at Malua, Samoa, in April–May 1961 and appointed a regional secretary and continuation committee. The inaugural Assembly (Lifou, New Caledonia, 1966) began the series which was to continue in five-year intervals. Two breakthroughs in women's leadership for Pacific churches took place as the 1971 Assembly selected Fetaui Mata'afa, wife of the then prime minister of Western Samoa, as its chairperson, and in 1977 Lorine Tevi from Fiji as its general secretary.³⁰

27. Kato, *Pitfalls*, 169; a work containing an extended critique of the AACC. By 1991 the AEAM comprised twenty-two national evangelical fellowships claiming to represent fifty million African Christians. See Crafford, "Ecumenism," 4.
28. Shorter, "Factors," 353.
29. Forman, *Voice*, 1–2; IMC Conf., New Delhi 1961, *Report*, 17.
30. For the history of ecumenism in the region see Forman, *Voice*, Forman; "Recent

In 1972 the conference's Executive Committee, looking to the future, considered church unity their top priority. "One can see the scandal of division in almost all the territories of the Pacific," it reported. A widening view of the Christian *oikoumene* was revealed as the Pacific leaders wrote:

> It looks as if there are possibilities of discussing church union in the Pacific. One will be for the main denominations to discuss together the possibility of organic union including the Catholics, and then an attempt should be made to bring in sects to the discussion. Even though actual organic union might not be possible yet, the fact that the churches and sects enter into dialogue may clear up misunderstanding and establish a bridge of fellowship between them, which should lessen the strain of relationship which exists today between the churches and the sects.[31]

Although the PCC was the first regional council actively to pursue membership by Roman Catholics, their formal membership was delayed until the 1976 assembly. Thereafter Catholics became vigorous participants and generous contributors. The appointment of Catholic bishop Patelesio Finau of Tonga to be the PCC's chairperson in 1991 was another important milestone.

The PCC, however, has found it difficult to represent territories on the vast region's periphery. The Hawaiian Islands are part of the U.S.; Micronesians face horrendous travel costs to reach Fiji or Samoa; Australia and New Zealand remain with Asia where they have been for decades. Serving Papua New Guinea has been a challenge as few churches from that island joined the Conference, although their Melanesian Council of Churches became a member in 1981.[32]

Fractures in the Pacific oikoumene deepened as the PCC boldly addressed social injustice in the region. Participants at a PCC seminar with Paulo Freire in 1974 urged "that the churches make a positive effort to grasp every opportunity to cooperate in investigating and denouncing the oppressive elements in society in all areas."[33] In the next two decades the Conference engaged in both education and social action on

---

Developments"; Crocombe, Afeaki, and McLaren, *Cooperation*. See Forman, "Sing," for data on women's leadership.

31. "Minutes of the Executive Committee, 17–21 July 1972," in A-YDSL/PCC, "Records," HR987.2.

32. Forman, "Recent Developments," 30–32; Forman, *Voice*, 44–50.

33. From the Suva 1974 seminar statements, quoted in Forman, *Voice*, 103.

the dangers from militarization of the Pacific, nuclear testing and waste dumping, and destructive aspects of tourism.

"There is no other regional organisation that has such a good structural network as the Pacific Conference of Churches," declared Mrs. Lorine Tevi, the Conference's general secretary, in 1981. Focusing on "serving God's mission in the whole world," she articulated a specific Pacific-region mandate—to help the churches rediscover their Pacific identity, to uphold Pacific solidarity in the light of the gospel, and to be pilgrims with God for a more just world.[34]

LATIN AMERICA

Regional Ecumenism

J. H. Oldham's "gravest issue" as secretary for the Edinburgh Conference of 1910 was the exclusion of participants from Latin America. That exclusion resulted from a judgment by the planning committee that only mission societies working "among non-Christian peoples" would be eligible for membership. This controversial decision drew much attention to the continent by mission leaders.[35]

In 1913 the Foreign Missions Conference of North America appointed a temporary Committee on Latin America with John R. Mott as its secretary. Planning for the first Congress on Christian Work in Latin America to be held in Panama in 1916 was extraordinarily difficult. Latin America lacked united administrative bodies, schools, and publications for the churches. Thus the original goal "to consider the closer unity of the Evangelical forces" was enlarged to include issues both of Protestant/Catholic relationships in Latin America, and of relationships between the U.S. and the Latin American countries. This triad of issues was to remain the central focus of ecumenism in Latin America throughout the century.[36]

The Committee on Cooperation in Latin America (CCLA), established by the Panama Congress in 1916, was for Luis Odell "the true beginning of the ecumenical movement on the Latin American continent." Under its auspices Protestant missions and churches engaged in creative

---

34. "Background Reading Book, 4th PCC Assembly, 1981," 7, in A-YDSL/PCC, "Records."
35. Weber, "Out of All Continents," 85–86.
36. A-YDSL/CCLA, report.

cooperative programs in evangelization, radio evangelism, Christian literature, Christian education, and church and society issues. Inspired in 1959 by the WCC's study of rapid social change, leaders in 1962 organized the Latin American Commission on Church and Society (ISAL). The decades of the 1960s through the 1980s were a period of enormous turmoil in the region, of the emergence of liberation theology, and of polarization both within churches and between traditions. Through continent-wide conferences progressive church leaders reflected on their social responsibilities and became committed to social change in Latin America. Representing that viewpoint, Emilio Castro declared in 1973 that "the goal of ecumenism in Latin America is to prepare the Christian community for full participation in the liberation of our continent."[37]

Barriers to unity included the prevailing anti-modernist and anti-Roman Catholic attitudes of the growing conservative-evangelical and Pentecostal missions, but as Latin Americans developed their own ecumenical conscience these barriers began to break down. The Latin American Protestant Congress of Havana, Cuba, in 1929 was a significant milestone. It was both the first regional ecumenical conference organized by Latin American leadership and the first to call for an Evangelical International Federation. But first the building blocks were put into place as many national councils or federations of churches were established in the 1930s. Seeking broad evangelical participation, most of them worked for cooperation but excluded "faith and order" issues, instead referring to "a spiritual as opposed to organic unity."[38]

CELA and UNELAM

Between 1949 and 1978 four Latin American Protestant conferences stimulated ecumenically-minded evangelicals to think deeper concerning unity and mission.[39] The first was the *Conferencia Evangélica Latinoamericana* ("Latin America Protestant Conference" or I CELA) held in Buenos Aires, Argentina, in 1949. With its two main themes of "The Latin American Reality and the Presence of the Protestant Churches" and "Message and Mission of Protestantism for Latin America," the Conference affirmed the reality of Protestantism as an

---

37. Odell, "Fifty Years," 96; Castro, "Forward," 39. For the history of these developments see Odell, "Fifty Years"; and Miguez-Bonino, "Mirror."

38. Castro, "Evangelism," 348–49; Odell, "Fifty Years," 99–101; Miguez-Bonino, "Mirror," 45–46.

39. Odell, "Fifty Years," 106–10; Miguez-Bonino, "Mirror," 45–51.

integral part of the life of the Latin American people. While advocating "interdenominational cooperation," it did not set up a continuation committee to carry on that work.

The second conference (II CELA) was held in Lima, Peru, in 1961. Under the theme of "Christ, the Hope for Latin America," it adopted a confession of faith and mission related to the human problems of the continent. "Our Latin America appears as a continent restless and eager for its evolution and change of structures, hungering for a total transformation," the delegates declared. In contrast to I CELA in 1949, which had spoken of "spiritual unity," the Lima conference spoke of the "unity of the body" and structural unity needed "in the fulfillment of our task." Due to strong opposition from fundamentalist associations of the U.S. and the International Council of Christian Churches (ICCC), a new cooperative structure to be called the *Comision pro Unidad Evangelica Latinoamericana* (UNELAM) was not established until 1964 at a separate assembly in Montevideo, Uruguay. With national councils or church federations as its members, and with Emilio Castro as its dynamic executive secretary, it sought to reach out to those many Protestants for whom unity was a low priority.[40]

The third conference (III CELA, Buenos Aires 1969) was called by UNELAM after delays over its sponsorship. Organizers sought for an "open ecumenism," including a wide variety of Protestants with Pentecostal and Roman Catholic observers. Like the Medellín 1968 conference of Catholic bishops, III CELA found its focus of mission in commitment to liberty and justice for the poor and oppressed. It declared that "the church needs to promote . . . the process of transformation of the dominant political systems, as well as to work for the replacement of structures of oppression by structures of justice."[41]

The momentum of III CELA led to the fourth conference (Oaxtepec, Mexico, 1978), which was even more representative of Latin American Protestants. Instead of participants from national councils and federations, representatives came from 110 denominations and 10 "ecumenical organisms" (parachurch bodies) in 19 countries. They met under the theme "Unity and Mission in Latin America." Their statement on "The Mission of the Church" concluded with a call to "remember that the task of proclaiming the gospel is integral: evangelize, form the people of God,

---

40. Yoder, "Second."
41. Costas, *Theology of the Crossroads*, 86–126.

and promote the liberty of the oppressed." Delegates voted to establish the Latin American Council of Churches (CLAI) with objectives to promote unity, evangelism, and the mission of the church particularly in relation to the poor and oppressed.[42]

CLAI and CONELA

The Latin American Council of Churches (CLAI), at its first assembly (Huampani, Peru, 1982), brought together more than 300 delegates from 85 member churches and six associated ecumenical bodies—representing about one-fourth of Latin American Protestants. Unity and mission remained a key theme in each of the assemblies to follow. The fourth assembly (Barranquilla, Colombia, 2001), for example, restated the indissoluble link between unity and mission in two aspects: first, "internally, where the will of God is realized in the faith community of love and mutual sharing," and second, "externally, where God acts through the church centrifugally, seeking to reach humanity and the whole cosmos with the message of salvation and reconciliation. That is the mission."[43]

With CLAI's leadership largely drawn from WCC-affiliated denominations, other evangelicals formed their own Latin American Evangelical Confederation (CONELA) in 1982. Claiming to represent the majority of Latin American Protestants, it gained support more from newer denominations that were outgrowths of faith missions. Whereas CLAI promoted mission primarily as social justice, CONELA emphasized evangelism.[44]

The Caribbean

Are language differences to be a major barrier to Christian unity? The Caribbean region is a test case. In 1971 representatives from fifteen church traditions in the English- and Dutch-speaking lands of the Caribbean (with observers from the Spanish- and French-speaking islands) met to draft a constitution for a proposed Caribbean Conference of Churches. They were not meeting as strangers, although there were no national Christian councils in the region. Earlier in 1957 the IMC and the World Council of Christian Education had jointly sponsored a consultation in Puerto Rico that defined five areas of common need: Christian educa-

42. Rooy, "Missions," 117–21.
43. Ibid., 130–35.
44. Ibid., 124.

tion, theological education, home and family life, evangelism (especially among Hindus and Muslims), and special south Caribbean problems. In response the Caribbean churches created two associations for joint action: the Caribbean Committee for Joint Christian Action (CCJCA) in 1959 and Christian Action for Development (CADEC) in 1968, and received major funding for projects through the WCC.[45]

The Caribbean Conference of Churches embraced the work of these two bodies upon its inauguration in 1973. Roman Catholics made ecumenical history as they joined a regional council for the first time with seventeen member dioceses (but not those of Cuba, Haiti and the Dominican Republic). The fourteen member churches included Christians not only in the Caribbean islands, but also in Central America (Belize, Panama, and Costa Rica) and in South America (Guyana and Suriname). With four official languages (Dutch, English, French, and Spanish) the Council aimed to bridge the language barriers between Caribbean Christians.

Delegates to the Inaugural Assembly affirmed their common concerns and destiny as they declared, "We as Christian people of the Caribbean, separated from each other by barriers of history, language, culture, class and distance, because of our common calling to Christ, desire to join together in a regional fellowship of Churches for inspiration, consultation, and co-operation. We are deeply concerned to promote the human liberation of our people, and are committed to the achievement of social justice and the dignity of [all persons]."[46]

Philip Potter, the WCC's general secretary, himself born on the island of Dominica, urged the delegates in his keynote address to join in the struggle for human rights. As Christ came to liberate and reconcile, we are called to be "in solidarity with our fellow Caribbeans and with all peoples in the struggle to make God's rights, his righteousness, his justice their own."[47] Human rights for the region's people became the focal missional issue for the Council. The fifth centennial in 1992 of the arrival of Columbus was the catalyst for affirmation of solidarity with other oppressed peoples—African Americans in North, Central, and South America, Africans in "Mother Africa," indigenous Caribbean and American peoples, "and indeed all oppressed people in the world."[48]

---

45. IMC Conf., New Delhi 1961, *Report*, 16–17; K. Davis, "Story," 134–55.
46. K. Davis, "Story," 136.
47. Albert, "Ecumenism," 824.
48. "Verdun Proclamation," 73.

EUROPE

The cradle of collective mission planning, Europe was the last continent to form a united conference of churches.

National Missionary Conferences

The oldest of national bodies for missionary cooperation was formed in Germany in 1885 by representatives of twelve German societies and named the Committee of the German Evangelical Missions (*Ausschuss der deutschen evangelischen Missionen*). Although absent from the founding meeting of the IMC in 1921, in protest over the barring of German missions from Allied-held areas following World War I, the German societies were to become strong participants and supporters. Soon the IMC counted ten European missionary conferences among its members—all of them distinct from the national councils of churches insofar as they existed.[49]

The Conference of British Missionary Societies (CBMS) was a direct outgrowth of Edinburgh 1910. J. H. Oldham, Edinburgh's organizer, simultaneously worked for the formation of the IMC and the CBMS, served as secretary of both, and combined their offices. During World War I he chose to deal with mission problems of literature, education, medicine, and liaison with the British government through the CBMS, rather than creating parallel organizations, thereby establishing a breadth of mission concerns and actions for the British Conference that would continue.[50]

Archbishop William Temple and others formed the British Council of Churches (BCC) in 1942 in the depths of World War II, bringing together streams of activity concerning international affairs and social questions. After the War its department of interchurch aid mushroomed. Was this not also a form of mission? Although the 1961 IMC-WCC merger combined programs of global mission and interchurch aid, British union of similar bodies was delayed. In 1973, however, the committees on restructuring of the BCC and CBMS declared, "We believe that the total witness of British Christians as they act together must include within it forms of partnership with overseas Churches in mission to the world. The BCC is therefore incomplete without this emphasis. We

---

49. Hogg, *Foundations*, 202–6; Latourette, "Ecumenical Bearings," 373–74; IMC Conf., New Delhi 1961, *Report*, 19.

50. Hogg, *Foundations*, 175–78.

also believe that the co-operative activities of the missionary societies need to be seen as part of the ecumenical movement in this country, reflecting the life and faith of British Christians."[51]

In the next decade a desire for common witness by Catholics and Protestants in Britain and Ireland moved the BCC to dissolve in favor of a more inclusive Council of Churches for Britain and Ireland (CCBI). The new body included a Churches' Commission on Mission, reflecting the change "from mission being seen as an overseas activity to the Churches' commitment to one mission in one world." The Commission included representation by churches, non-denominational mission agencies, and by the four national ecumenical bodies for England, Ireland, Scotland, and Wales, which were strengthened in the new structure. There was, however, a frequent criticism that the new ecumenical arrangement reinforced what divided churches (both denominationalism and regionalism) rather that what united them.[52]

The Conference of European Churches

The rebuilding of Europe after World War II, including vibrant new forms of Christian witness and service through youth organizations, lay academies, worker priests, and industrial missions, will be considered in other chapters. One pressing need remained for reconciliation across the Iron Curtain. That was to become the impulse bringing churches of Eastern and Western Europe together to form the Conference of European Churches (CEC) in 1959 at Nyborg in Denmark. The old Christian symbol of the church as a ship was revived in 1964 as delegates to the second CEC assembly met on a ship in the neutral Baltic Sea. Visser 't Hooft, the WCC's general secretary, challenged the 1968 Assembly: "To reconcile the two halves of the world, to take away the mounting bitterness, is now the primary task. It is up to the European Churches to shout from the rooftops that unless we take this task of service and reconciliation seriously Europe will betray its calling." In response the Conference's message to the churches began with the statement that "The mission of the European churches should be characterised by service and reconciliation." Not everyone shared the WCC secretary's enthusiasm. Cecil Northcott of Britain charged that "confessionalism has already dimmed

---

51. Payne, *Thirty Years*, 5–17; BCC, *Structure*, 29.
52. Davey, "Churches," 194; Meylink and Reardon, "Council."

the vision and frustrated the growth of world churchmanship. Now regionalism appears to add complexity and confusion to the scene."[53]

In 1967, under the chairmanship of Visser 't Hooft, the Conference invited other regional councils to send representatives to a consultation on "The Churches of Europe and the Churches of Other Continents." The first step toward "the increasing integration of churches and missions," the CEC drafters wrote, should be that individual congregations "come to look upon themselves as missionary congregations." They appealed for a basic unity in mission of churches in Europe and other continents as together they tried "to overcome national, ethnic, racial tensions and enmities and to show forth the reconciling love of God."[54]

The smashing of the Berlin Wall in 1989 symbolized a new challenge for the CEC. Could the conference lead amid the ensuing crises over competing national identities? Jean Fisher, the CEC's general secretary, hoped that the Conference would move to a higher degree of communion and fellowship, although theological conservatism, fears of proselytism, and political triumphalism were rife. In the world's most secularized societies, the challenge of the CEC was to become a catalyst for churches needing to recover their sense of mission.[55]

NORTH AMERICA

Foreign Missions Conference of North America (FMC)

Founded in 1893, the FMC by its 25th anniversary in 1918 had grown to represent 178 Protestant mission bodies, including 19 in Canada. Historian James Murch judged it to have been "probably the largest number ever to be associated in American inter-church activity." Concerning the FMC's spirit of unity, R. P. Mackay of Toronto concluded, "It has steadily grown until almost every Board is more or less intimately associated with other Boards in work that could not be as well done if at all without such co-operation. That is true in evangelistic and educational and medical work, in missionary survey, in literary work, amongst Anglo-American communities."[56]

---

53. Weber, "Out of All Continents," 82–85; De-la-Noy, *Task*, 33, 41; Northcott, "Ecumenical," 1358.
54. CEC, *Churches*, 11, 79.
55. Fischer, "Fellowship," 968–71; Williams, "Ecumenism."
56. Hogg, *Foundations*, 77–79; Murch, *Cooperation*, 99; FMC, *Report*, 235.

Nevertheless, the intense fundamentalist/modernist controversies in the churches in the 1920s profoundly limited North American mission cooperation. On the one hand, conservative evangelicals formed separate associations based on "fundamental doctrine," including the National Association of Evangelicals (1943) and the Evangelical Foreign Missions Association (1945). On the other hand, mainline Protestants grew in conviction that emerging needs in mission required ecumenical unity rather than a plurality of cooperative agencies.

In the late 1930s the FMC jointly sponsored with the Federal Council of Churches a number of cooperative efforts. These included China relief, support of missions orphaned by World War II, a major study on religious liberty, and the manifold ministries of relief and reconstruction after World War II. Church World Service became the agency for these combined efforts in 1946. As early as 1941 a study conference at Atlantic City, New Jersey, on "the closer relationships of general interdenominational agencies," had recommended a single corporate structure for eight existing cooperative groups.[57] By 1949 only the FMC among them opposed entry into a new National Council of Churches. It was reluctant to break fellowship with a wider range of mission boards and societies, including Southern Baptists, Assemblies of God, Nazarenes, Advent Christians, and Church of God. "Are foreign missions to be relegated to the care of a minority or are they to become the concern of the entire church?" the *Christian Century* asked in December 1948, urging the FMC to enter the new Council and become "the center of the interchurch missionary planning." This latter view prevailed. In a special session in 1950 the FMC reversed its stand and voted to become the Division of Foreign Missions of the new NCC. The price was the loss of participation by those conservative-evangelical churches unwilling to join the NCC.[58]

National Association of Evangelicals

Although the Federal Council included many evangelicals at its founding in 1905, dissatisfaction increased among them in subsequent years

---

57. The Federal Council of Churches, the International Council of Religious Education, the Home Missions Council, the Foreign Missions Conference, the Missionary Education Movement, the Council of Church Boards of Education, the United Stewardship Council, and the United Council of Church Women. Cavert, *American Churches*, 184–88.

58. Cavert, *Church Cooperation*, 50–51; "Missions: Cult or Crusade?" 1421.

over the Council's social agenda, predominance of theological liberals among its leadership, and openness to cordial relations with both Orthodox churches and the Roman Catholic Church. Plans for a national association of evangelicals, begun in 1941, were consummated in 1943 in Chicago at a constitutional convention attended by a thousand evangelical Protestants representing some fifty denominations. The stated purpose of the National Association of Evangelicals (NAE) was "to provide a medium for voluntary united action among the several groups of Evangelical Christians of America." In addition to denominations, the NAE's membership was open to independent religious organizations, local churches, and groups of churches. The goal, however, was for united evangelical action in evangelism, home and foreign missions, education, welfare, mass media, and social welfare. The Committee on Policy, stating that evangelicals were unwilling to be represented "by organization and agencies unfaithful to the Gospel of Christ," expressed the view that in time "new functioning units in all fields of inter-church cooperation would have to be formed."[59] Consistent with that understanding of the limits of unity, NAE leaders advocated the formation of the World Evangelical Fellowship and national fellowships of evangelicals in many lands. In 1950 the NAE's Commission on International Relations sent a team around the world to visit evangelical leaders. Following these visits evangelical fellowships came into being in some twenty countries, with the Evangelical Fellowship of India emerging as one of the strongest.[60]

National Council of Churches in the USA (NCCUSA)

Founded in 1950, the NCCUSA brought together twelve interdenominational bodies, including the Federal Council of Churches, the Foreign Missions Conference of North America, and the Home Missions Council of North America. Among its stated aims was to "share resources for unity and mission." Its charter membership included twenty-nine denominations with a combined church membership of thirty-three million. Remaining outside were the majority of Christian churches in the U.S., including the Roman Catholic, Southern Baptist, Lutheran Church-Missouri Synod, as well as many Pentecostal, Holiness, evangelical, and fundamentalist churches. Some non-member bodies cooperated in sig-

---

59. Murch, *Cooperation*, 64–68.
60. Cattell, "NEA," 13.

nificant programs of the Council, such as Bible translation, including publication of the Revised Standard Version in 1952.

Church World Service is the Council's most far-reaching ministry, with funding by an annual "One Great Hour of Sharing" offering by churches, and large grants from government for its work of relief, development, and compassion. With commitment "to assist the churches in self-examination of their life and witness," the Council joined with Roman Catholics and Jews in the civil rights movement, and developed significant pioneer bridge-building in Eastern Europe, Vietnam, and China.[61]

PROSPECTS FOR WIDER UNITY

With the WCC

The decision upon its founding to be a council of *churches* did not resolve the issue of how the WCC was to relate to national and regional *councils* of churches. Should the Council cooperate exclusively with member churches, or should it consider regional and national councils also as partners?

The WCC-IMC merger of 1961 reopened that basic issue inasmuch as the missionary body was a council of councils, not of churches. "What is the ecclesiological significance of councils?" Norman Goodall asked in 1960. What should be their place in the ecumenical movement? What, therefore, should be their relationship to the WCC? At that time the world body had eighteen "associated" councils, but only four of them were among the thirty to thirty-five member councils of the IMC. WCC-IMC integration in 1961 was to bring the latter into direct participation in the WCC with authority "to formulate the general lines of policy and program" of a new Commission on World Mission and Evangelism (CWME) within the Council.[62]

The new structure began with great promise. Only two IMC member councils rejected the new status as "affiliate" members—Norway and the Congo, the latter because of pressures by anti-WCC mission agencies in the U.S. The rest hoped that the IMC's purpose "to deepen the sense of

---

61. Bent, *Historical Dictionary*, q.v. "NCCUSA"; Reid, ed., *Dictionary of Christianity in America*, q.v. "NCCUSA."

62. Vischer, "Christian Councils," 100; Goodall, "The Ecumenical Movement and National and Regional Councils," Appendix III in "WCC/IMC Joint Committee Minutes, 9–11 August 1960," A-WCC/IMC, "Joint Committee," box 270005.

missionary obligation in the churches throughout the world" would not only remain the purpose of the WCC's new CWME but also promote the growth of ecumenical and missionary consciousness throughout the world body.[63]

In 1968 Lukas Vischer, director of the WCC's sub-unit on Faith and Order, advocated the vision that the world body would encourage the extension of the national and regional councils in concern for their life, for closer alliances and unions, as well as "for the development of relations between all the Churches."[64]

With World Confessional Families

Chapter 8 contained the sharp critique by Majority World church leaders of the ecclesiology of world confessional bodies like the LWF. Much of the strongest criticism came from leaders of national and regional councils. Gabriel Setiloane of South Africa, former youth secretary of the AACC, judged that world confessional organizations "have hindered the development of ecumenism on the African continent." While they have encouraged unions of churches within one confessional tradition, some churches hesitate to venture in fellowship beyond world confessional families. Asian church leaders concurred at an EACC-sponsored consultation in 1965: "While membership in a confessional family of churches can assist an Asian church to a sense of belonging to a world-wide family in Christ, and so assist in overcoming a possible isolation, we believe that world confessional organizations . . . should not weaken or hinder Asian churches from belonging together in their locality or nation."[65]

With Roman Catholics

In Latin America "the trial by fire of ecumenism for Protestant churches is their relation with the Catholic Church," Emilio Castro declared in 1956. Three years later Fr. Vincent Donovan from Tanzania wrote of the "Protestant-Catholic scandal in Africa" that "in the name of the Christian message of Love, we have brought enmity and strife."[66]

---

63. Short, "National Councils," 103–4.
64. Vischer, "Christian Councils," 108.
65. Setiloane, "Movement," 145–46; "Confessional Families," 205.
66. Castro, "Evangelism," 349; Donovan, "Scandal."

For Roman Catholics the Vatican II "Decree on Ecumenism" opened doors for new ecumenical action for those willing to walk through them. "Cooperation among all Christians vividly expresses that bond which already unites them," the Council declared, and specifically called for its increase "in regions where a social and technical evolution is taking place."[67]

Empowered by this mandate, Catholics and ecumenical Protestants multiplied joint action programs. In Africa these included common medical mission strategies in Ghana and Malawi, joint training of journalists and religious broadcasters in Zambia and Kenya, an agreed religious syllabus, including prayers for use in the public schools of Kenya, joint action against racism in Rhodesia (Zimbabwe), and many others.[68]

In some countries Roman Catholics joined in national bodies for mission cooperation prior to Vatican II. From its formation in 1922 the General Missionary Conference of Northern Rhodesia (present Zambia) included every mission society in the land.[69]

With Others

"How large is your family?" is an issue every conciliar body has to face. Conservatives often oppose wider associations lest they break existing fellowships. For example, the Melanesian Council of Churches in 1977 voted not to join the Pacific Conference of Churches for fear of losing its close and cooperative relationship with the Evangelical Alliance. Others, affirming that the Spirit works outside our institutional channels, are open to wider fellowship. Some Pentecostals, recognizing that their movement originated to reconcile the different Christian denominations, began in the 1960s to participate in the ecumenical movement in Latin America (UNELAM and CLAI).[70]

In the 1990s the Rubicon for councils was their relationship to persons of other faiths. The Christian Conference of Asia pioneered in this area by organizing structured dialogues involving Christians, Hindus, Muslims, and Buddhists. CCA leaders believed that an ongoing "dialogue of life" is an imperative in religiously and culturally pluralistic Asian societies, as well as an opportunity for Christian witness.[71]

---

67. "Decree on Ecumenism," 2, 12, in Vatican Council, *Documents*, 354-55.
68. Bühlmann, "Ecumenism."
69. J. V. Taylor and Lehmann, *Copperbelt*, 18; Beaver, *Ecumenical Beginnings*, 254.
70. Forman, *Voice*, 35; Alvarez, "Pentecostals," 94; Cronje, "Influence," 115.
71. Yuzon, "Perspectives."

CONCLUSION

At the close of this long survey of regional councils three basic questions remain: First, what is the ecclesiological significance of councils? Second, what is their missiological importance? Third, are they in fact "an ecclesiological anomaly which ought not to continue indefinitely in its present form?" The last question reflects the position of those who would deny that a council is partially, and at some moments, a church. Admittedly councils, whenever they tackle urgent issues of mission and service, fill important gaps. How then can the churches leave "empty space" for councils to fill, yet deny them the authority to speak and act on behalf of the churches? Lukas Vischer offered an alternative perspective: councils may become the "true church" whenever they represent Christ as "salt" and "light" in the world (Matt 5:13–14; 25:31–40). Their challenge is to eschew fixed structures, remaining always provisional and mobile. Only by doing so can they lead the people of God in missional, rather than maintenance, ministries, and be open to the fresh winds of the Spirit.[72]

---

72. Vischer, "Christian Councils," 101–8. See also Tsetsis, "Significance."

12

Towards Church Union

THE IMPULSE TO UNION

Bishop Stephen Neill, in his history of plans of union and reunion, judged that the Christian churches made greater progress "towards the recovery of the lost unity of the body of Christ" in the years between 1910 and 1950 than in any period of equal length in the Christian era. He believed that the Edinburgh Missionary Conference of 1910 had much to do with that achievement.[1]

It has already been noted that "Cooperation and the Promotion of Unity" was one of the eight major themes at Edinburgh. Although the study report and discussion focused upon practical issues of missionary cooperation, the promotion of unity was emphasized also. The report surveyed progress toward two alternative plans of union: organic union, or federation including intercommunion. The study commission concluded, "While we may differ from one another in our conception of what unity involves and requires, we agree in believing that our Lord intended that we should be one in a visible fellowship." It recognized that realization of the ideal may be in the distant future with many difficulties to be surmounted. Nevertheless, participants rejoiced in having felt together "the stirring of a hope so rich and so wonderful."[2]

Neill called Edinburgh "one of the first manifestations of that new ecumenism, in which Christians have learned to accept with equal sincerity both the underlying unity of faith in Christ which has never been lost, and the seriousness of the differences by which the Christian communions are kept in separation."[3]

---

1. Neill, "Plans," 445.
2. *World Missionary Conference, 1910*, 8:83–118; Gairdner, *Edinburgh*, 204.
3. Neill, "Plans," 445.

At the inaugural assembly in 1959 of the East Asia Christian Conference D.T. Niles spoke on "A Church and Its 'Selfhood.'" Much of his address concerned new partnerships between younger and older churches, and between missionaries and nationals. Niles closed with a crescendo of affirmations concerning "oneness." We face "two explosive realities," he declared: "a world in travail to find its peace, a church in travail to find its unity." Niles professed his belief that in each the Holy Spirit is the reality controlling the currents of history. In the Spirit's discipline of love and understanding, the churches are enabled both to make their unity more visible and to prosecute with power their mission. "The fellowship of the Holy Spirit," Niles concluded, is "nothing else and nothing less than the churches in their oneness."[4]

By 1960 Christians in several lands, guided by that Spirit, broke the old denominational boundaries to form wider church unions. It is significant that of the eighteen united churches formed before 1960, thirteen were in the Majority World of Africa, Asia, Latin America, and Oceania.[5] To understand the dynamic contribution of the missionary movement to Christian unity, consider three case studies from India, China, and the Congo.

CHURCH OF SOUTH INDIA (CSI)

Exactly forty-three days after India and Pakistan gained their independence from Great Britain on August 15, 1947, more than 3,500 South Indian Christians gathered at St. George's Cathedral in Madras (now Chennai), together with representatives from churches around the world. They came together to inaugurate and consecrate the Church of South India. One by one authorized representatives of the three uniting churches walked forward to the chancel. Each read a resolution accepting the union, and then laid on the altar their church's copy of the Scheme of Union signed by all ministers assenting to it.

---

4. Niles, "Church," 95.
5. The Church of Jesus Christ in Madagascar, the Église du Christ au Congo-Zaire, the United Church of Zambia, the United Congregational Church of Southern Africa, the Church of Bangladesh, the Church of Christ in Thailand, the Church of North India, the Church of Pakistan, the Church of South India, the United Church of Christ in Japan, the United Church of Christ in the Philippines, the United Church in Jamaica and the Cayman Islands, and the United Church in Papua New Guinea and the Solomon Islands.

The preamble contained their affirmation that the new church shall relate unity and mission: "The uniting Churches believe ... that the result of union will be ... renewed eagerness and power for the proclamation of the Gospel of Christ. It is their hope that the Church thus united may be a true leaven of unity in the life of India, and that through it may be a greater release of divine power for the fulfillment of God's purpose for His world."[6]

Lesslie Newbigin, a Church of Scotland missionary consecrated a bishop on that day, recalled, "What struck me over and over again in it was that the two notes which are so often opposed—Catholic and Evangelical—were constantly and completely blended through.... It made one so utterly sure that what we are doing is not patching things together, but being led by the Holy Spirit back to the fullness and simplicity of Gospel truth."[7]

Why did the bold experiment of the Church of South India uniting Anglicans with others succeed, when so many others failed?

Seeds Sown

Impulses to unity can be traced back to the nineteenth century. "Family reunions" and federation were the goals as missionaries met in Madras in 1879. Jacob Chamberlain, respected leader in the Arcot Mission connected with the Reformed Church in America, appealed to various Presbyterian churches to unite. Similarly churches of Anglican heritage would merge, as could various Methodists, and so on. Thereafter, he believed, a federation could be formed in order to have "one self-supporting, self-governing Church of Christ in India." Such a church would not be called American or English or German or Danish but "*of India and suited to India.*"[8]

Home mission boards at times were concerned that mere cooperation among missions would not meet the felt needs of Indian Christians with their growing national consciousness. At the 1888 Missionary Conference in London, C. C. Fenn, the CMS secretary, asked participants to consider the realities of two contiguous districts in India. In one all Christians are Anglicans; in the other they are Presbyterians. If "left to their own decision," he concluded, they would recognize each other as

---

6. Sundkler, *Church*, 342–43.
7. Newbigin, *Unfinished*, 96; Stanley, ed., *World*, 121–30.
8. Sundkler, *Church*, 25.

belonging to the same visible church and be in intercommunion. The ecclesiastical barriers brought from the West would be swept away.[9]

Edinburgh to Tranquebar

V. S. Azariah and Sherwood Eddy were the twin apostles of organic unity for India at the 1910 World Missionary Conference. When delegates extolled the United Church of South India, a 1908 union of 150,000 Congregationalists and Presbyterians, Azariah and Eddy in their addresses probed the barriers to deeper unity. Azariah condemned the prevailing master-servant relationship of missionary to Indian church worker, and called for a true spiritual unity. Meanwhile Eddy, referring to unity already achieved in India, asked, "If we can unite on the foreign field, why can we not also on the home field?" But such an appeal did not shake the Christendom perspective of the church leaders of the North. The report on cooperation and unity, after a review of the South India scheme, contained the comment that "no young native Church could afford at present to be indifferent to the bonds of fellowship which bind it to the foreign Churches which have given it its faith."[10]

Returning to India, Azariah and Eddy, representing respectively the Anglican and United churches, convened a 1919 conference of Indian church leaders to consider the union issue. Tranquebar, the site chosen, had historic significance: it was the site of the first Protestant mission in India in 1706. After much prayer and discussion, the thirty-three participants declared in their Manifesto, "Union is the will of God.... The challenge of the present hour ... calls us to mourn our past divisions and turn to our Lord Jesus Christ to seek in Him the unity of the body expressed in one visible Church. We face together the titanic task of the winning of India for Christ—one-fifth of the human race."

A fourfold common ground for union was proposed: the Holy Scriptures, the historic Apostles' and Nicene Creeds, the two sacraments of baptism and the Lord's Supper, and "the historic Episcopate, locally adapted." While taking a group photo of participating church leaders, Eddy commented, "This will be an historic photo! For the first time in history an episcopal church and a non-episcopal are united." A Joint Committee of the Anglicans and the United Church began to

---

9. Paul, *First*, 18.
10. *World Missionary Conference, 1910*, 9:311, 320; 8:117. For assessments of the life and work of Bishop Azariah see Harper, *Shadow*; and C. Graham, "Azariah."

meet in 1920, and was joined by the Wesleyan Church in Southern India in 1925.[11]

Negotiating in the Fishbowl of World Opinion

The next critical milestone was passed not in India, but in Lausanne, Switzerland, in 1927. At the first World Conference on Faith and Order, the South India scheme of union attracted the most attention. Not only did Azariah and three other Anglican bishops from India advocate the union, but also three key leaders of the South India United Church who were present. It was Azariah who once again gave the clarion call to unity as he declared, "Unity may be theoretically a desirable ideal in Europe and America, but it is vital to the life of the church in the mission field. The divisions of Christendom may be a source of weakness in Christian countries, but in non-Christian lands they are a sin and a scandal."

The final "Call to Unity" of the Lausanne Conference did reflect Azariah's concern. It included the recognition that more than half the world is waiting for the gospel, and that multitudes are turning away because Christians lack unity: "Our missions count that as a necessity which we are inclined to look on as a luxury," Lausanne declared. It recognized the impatience of the "mission field" where, in revolting against Western church divisions, church leaders "make bold adventure for unity in its own right."[12]

Later Edwin James Palmer, the Anglican bishop of Bombay, was to write of Lausanne, "the only insistent note of urgency came from the mission fields, and especially from the countries where Christianity is making its way in the midst of an ancient civilization—India, Japan, China. . . . we represented unity as a matter of life or death for the Church."[13]

Church Union News and Views, published in India beginning in 1930, chronicled the slow but steady progress in unity negotiations. It also revealed that the South Indian church leaders remained both responsive to world ecumenical thought and active agents for a bold experiment in organic unity. It rejoiced in the IMC's 1932 resolution "that the fulfillment of the universal missionary task can only be achieved through the

11. Neill, "Plans," 473; Joint Committee, *Proposed Scheme*, iv–v; Sundkler, *Church*, 100–101; Palmer, "Unity," 283. It is Susan Harper's judgment that "Azariah's greatest contribution to the unity debates may well have been his promotion of an Indian Christian identity that was both national and transnational in character" (*Shadow*, 240).

12. Faith and Order, Lausanne 1927, *Proceedings*, 495, 461.

13. Palmer, "Unity," 255.

life and witness of a united Church." It reported, however, that John R. Mott, at the same meeting, called for missionary cooperation but not for organic union.[14]

Bishop Azariah once again championed the cause of unity at the Second World Conference on Faith and Order (Edinburgh 1937). He reported not only on progress made in the South India church union negotiations, but also on opposition and indifference from both "the extreme Anglican and the extreme Congregationalist." This, he asserted, can only be overcome by the resolute commitment to unity by every church. "When such an atmosphere favourable to union is created in the older churches," he declared, "the union movement will certainly go forward in the younger churches." The Conference report echoed Azariah's appeal: "Experience shows that the injury done to the Christian cause by the multiplicity of separate Churches within a given area is so great that the territorial unity of Churches should normally be regarded as desirable where it can be accomplished without violating the principles of the Churches concerned."[15]

The next development came at the IMC Tambaram/Madras Conference of 1938. The section on "Cooperation and Unity" gave major attention to the South India proposals and Basis of Union. Its report concurred with that of Faith and Order at Lausanne, declaring that the scheme "deserves particular attention and study because in it an attempt is being made to include within a united Church communions holding to the episcopal, the presbyterial, and the congregational principles."[16]

Responding to Dissent

During the 1930s the negotiations focused on the concerns of Anglo-Catholics and Congregationalists. High-church Anglicans stressed the need for continuity with the "historic episcopate" and with the worldwide Anglican Communion. Negotiators, however, rejected all their proposals

---

14. IMC, Meetings, *Minutes* (1932), 29; *Church Union News and Views* 3 (1932) 78, 100. A large opinion poll taken in the USA in 1932 disclosed that 4/5 of 624 church leaders agreed that "while church union may be incidental in Christian countries, it is vitally necessary on mission fields," and that most church members very strongly opposed denominational competition in India (Douglass, *Movements*, 278-83).

15. Faith and Order, Edinburgh 1937, 52-55, 267.

16. IMC Conf., Madras 1938, *"Madras Series"*, 4:382-95; IMC Conf., Madras 1938, *World Mission*, 154; *Church Union News and Views* 9.1-2 (September-October 1938) 34; 9.3 (March 1939) 44.

that non-Anglican ministers be re-consecrated, feeling that for Anglo-Catholics it would constitute re-ordination of those not episcopally ordained. Instead, all existing ministries of a participating church were to be accepted during a thirty-year period after inauguration of the union. Meanwhile, all new ordinations were to take places in services, including bishops in the historic episcopate. Anglicans worldwide debated this compromise and gave varying responses, including the 1951 withdrawal of support by the Anglican Society for the Propagation of the Gospel (SPG).[17]

Some Congregationalists of the South India United Church brought a different concern: could lay pastors administer the sacraments? Such had become the practice in some districts in which rapid church growth among the poor outstripped the church's capacity to supply ordained ministers. Their position, emphasizing the priesthood of all believers, threatened to split the United Church in the 1930s. Reconciling voices prevailed. A coalition of leaders opposed to lay celebration prevailed. The final Union Scheme emphasized the priesthood of all believers, while requiring consecration by ordained clergy of the elements for the Holy Communion.[18]

Why India?

Why did the Church of South India succeed while similar union efforts failed across the world? First, from Tranquebar in 1919 the Indian leaders believed that union is the will of God. Their basic question was not "Ought we to come together?" but "Have we any right to stay apart?" Second, they acknowledged the partial blindness of their respective traditions, and that the Holy Spirit would guide them as they reached agreement on essentials and left many issues for later guidance and development. Third, they believed that only through union could Christianity achieve credibility among the millions in India's mass movements who did not know Christ as Savior. Fourth, in a country in which Hinduism was presented as the unified faith of India, a divided Christianity appeared foreign and divisive. Fifth, the geographic movement of Christians out

---

17. For details of this debate see Sundkler, *Church*, 214–74; Newbigin, *Reunion*, 104–23; and Neill, *Church*, 361–66. Neill disclosed that continued Anglo-Catholic dissatisfaction with the CSI's mutual recognition of ministries contributed to the breakdown of union negotiations both in Nigeria and that between Methodists and Anglicans in England.

18. Newbigin, *Reunion*, 170–80; Sundkler, *Church*, 283–95.

of homogeneous rural districts into cities required denominations either to follow their own members (thereby increasing signs of Christian disunity) or form a united church.[19]

Evaluation

The South India scheme was lauded at the time as "the most important concrete proposal for union now before the churches of the world." When consummated, it was predicted that "it will furnish precedents for the solution of every considerable obstacle to Christian unity among all of the communions of Protestantism." Bengt Sundkler, in his CSI history, finds in the negotiations the whole of church history present and modified in both its vertical and horizontal dimensions. By vertical he referred to the chronological history from the early church to the present. The CSI, in its attempted return to a New Testament understanding of the church as the whole body of Christians in one place, threw a challenge to the very concept of denomination. By horizontal he recognized that issues of church order and mission from North America, Europe, and other continents found a new meeting place in South India.[20]

In 1948 the Lambeth Conference of Anglican bishops, just one year after the inauguration of the CSI, asked for a reconsideration of certain features of the Scheme of Union. In reply the CSI reaffirmed that they shared the Anglican Conference's concerns over the position of bishops, the due administration of sacraments, and the historic faith of the Catholic Church. But then the CSI issued this challenge: "We are united in one Church; our parent Churches are divided. If it is now insisted that we state what our permanent relation with them is to be, we can only say that we can be content with nothing except that they should be united as we are. So long as they remain divided our position must remain anomalous."[21]

Twenty years after union, while calling for a united church continually renewed for mission, Samuel Amirtham of the CSI listed the positive benefits of union. For him they included a greater confidence in bearing witness to the world, a greater credibility for the church as reconciler of

---

19. Joint Committee, *Proposed Scheme*, iv; Sundkler, *Church*, 12; Neill, *Christian Partnership*, 96–99; Chellappa, "Challenge," 8; Newbigin, *Reunion*, 20–21.

20. Van Dusen, *World Christianity*, 104–5; 288–93; Sundkler, *Church*, 14–15; Chellappa, "Challenge," 5.

21. "Church Union," in A/CWM, "Church Union in South India."

divisions, a stronger sharing of resources, and an enhanced service to society and action for justice.[22]

In 1950 Norman Goodall addressed the London Missionary Society on the South India union and said, "I am more than ever convinced that we are all caught up into certain great world movements of the Spirit" that challenge those with more limited insight and loyalties "to refashion themselves as more worthy instruments of one holy, Catholic and missionary Church." Later Cyril Firth, in his introduction to Indian church history, would write, "The Church in India throughout its history has usually been dependent on the churches of the West, and has had little opportunity to play a conspicuous part in general Church History; but in this matter of church union in the twentieth century it has played a leading role and makes a notable contribution to the Christian world."[23]

Others, more recently, have been more critical in their evaluations. In 1997 Stanley Samartha concluded that "after five decades of living together in the united church there is little evidence that the enthusiasm of the church for mission has increased or that any significantly 'new visions' of mission have emerged in its life."[24]

CHINA

At the World Missionary Conference (Edinburgh 1910) Cheng Jingyi of China, the youngest delegate present and one of the few from Asia, gave a memorable speech. While other delegates talked cooperation among denominations, he boldly called for a united church of China.

Cheng began his brief but powerful seven-minute speech by reporting that Chinese leaders have welcomed the Christian federation movement, joining hands in both educational and evangelistic work. But having "enjoyed the sweetness of such a unity," he continued, "they long for more and look for yet greater things." Then he spoke plainly: "We hope to see in the near future a united Christian Church without any denominational distinctions." It is needed, Cheng continued, for three reasons: First, to help the growing movement of self-support and self-government of the Church in China. Second, denominationalism

---

22. Amirtham, "Experience," 36. See Best, "Survey," 11–17, for later developments in union negotiations between the Church of South India, the Church of North India, and the Malankara Mar Thoma Syrian Church.
23. Scopes, "Evaluation," 335; Firth, *Introduction*, 247.
24. Samartha, "Vision," 490.

"has never interested the Chinese mind." Third, only through unity can a small and struggling church combat the powerful forces of heathenism. Cheng called for three unities to complement each other—of nation, family, and church.[25]

Cheng's was an authentic voice of the Chinese church. Considered to be the jewel of Protestant missions, every mission society wanted to enter China. As a result 61 of the larger Protestant societies were at work there by 1900. Their number more than doubled to 130 by 1919.[26]

Much of the early unity efforts in China involved getting churches of the same confessional family to unite. As early as 1862 English Presbyterians and the Reformed Church in America formed a common presbytery in Amoy. Nevertheless, joint action was not a strong imperative as late as the 1890s. The pace quickened, however, in the 1900s. In 1909 Anglican missions from England, Canada, and the U.S. agreed on a constitution for a united church named the *Chung Hua Sheng Kung Hui* or Holy Catholic Church of China. Eight Presbyterian bodies joined in 1907 to form the *Chung Kuo Chi Tu Sheng Chiao Chang Lao Hui* or Presbyterian Church of China.[27]

Such confessional efforts, however, did not eclipse the vision of a wider unity. The Centenary Missionary Conference for Protestant Missions in China (Shanghai 1907) resolved to form "the Christian Federation of China." It was to work "to encourage everything that will demonstrate the existing essential unity of Christians." The formation in 1922 of the National Christian Council of China was a giant step in that direction. In its very first year it resolved, "We believe that there is an essential unity among all Chinese Christians and that we are voicing the sentiment of the whole Chinese Christian body in claiming that we have the desire and the possibility to effect a speedy realization of corporate unity."[28]

Meanwhile plans for a wider organic union proceeded apace. Union talks between Congregationalists and Presbyterians, begun in 1918, included by 1922 a broader call to union. Methodists, Baptists, Reformed, United Brethren in Christ, United Church of Canada, and independents agreed to join. Sixteen missionary societies gave their support. In 1927

25. Gairdner, "Edinburgh," 184–86; Stanley, ed., *World*, 107–11.
26. Latourette, *History of Christian Missions*, 594.
27. *World Missionary Conference, 1910*, 8:91: Latourette, *History of Christian Missions*, 662–65.
28. *World Missionary Conference, 1910*, 8:108; Neill, "Plans," 458–59.

the Church of Christ in China (CCC) was officially inaugurated. Since Anglicans and Lutherans declined participation, tough doctrinal and church policy issues dividing Protestants, including episcopacy, did not have to be faced. Cheng Jingyi, youthful star of Edinburgh 1910 and now secretary of the National Christian Council of China, was elected as moderator. The CCC's statement of purpose reflected Cheng's compelling vision that the new church "should serve as an adequate point of departure for our ultimate goal—*one indigenous Christian Church for China*." Such a church would at one and the same time continue in sympathy and harmony with the churches of the West, yet also be "expressive in worship, fellowship and service to the Chinese Christian in ways suited to Chinese culture and customs."[29]

In the years that followed, the CCC sought to carve out for itself a clear identity as an indigenous Chinese church. Prominent in its pronouncements were the goals of self-support, self-government, and self-propagation. It established three mission fields of its own. Alone among Protestant churches in China it could claim that all its presiding officers were Chinese. These were important qualities and emphases in the twenty years of turmoil that were to follow.[30]

The mood of the CCC in 1949 upon the Communist takeover was well expressed by H. H. Tsui, soon to become its general secretary. Having resisted efforts by the embattled Nationalist government to gain the CCC's endorsement, the Church was open to political change. Tsui declared that the Church of Christ, although but one of the churches of China, "strives to be a united and uniting church, constantly praying for the time when there will be one Church of Christ in China."[31]

Under Communism criticism mounted of the "foreignness" of even the National Christian Council and the CCC. Did not the large relief supplies received from the West denote dependence on foreign elements? Yes, the CCC's officers were Chinese; but nine out of ten dioceses related to Western mission societies were still headed by missionary bishops. The "Christian Manifesto," published in July 1950 in an anti-American campaign during the Korean War, was a confession that Christianity "consciously or unconsciously, directly or indirectly, became related with imperialism." But the Manifesto also set goals for the church in-

---

29. Neill, "Plans," 459; Merwin, *Adventure*, 53–57.
30. Neill, "Plans," 460; Merwin, *Adventure*, 67.
31. Editorial in *The Church* (February 1949), quoted in Merwin, *Adventure*, 213.

cluding "closer fellowship and unity among the various denominations," and the objective of "self-reliance and rejuvenation" for all still relying upon foreign personnel and funding. By 1952 at least 400,000 Protestant Christians had added their names to those of the original 40 prominent signees to the Manifesto.[32]

The cutoff of overseas aid, and the departure of foreign missionaries, set the stage for new forms of national Christian unity. The first was the Three-Self Patriotic Movement (TSPM). Established provisionally in 1951, it was endorsed by 232 representatives from 62 churches and Christian organizations at the First National Christian Conference (Beijing 1954). That meeting represented a broader Christian unity than had been experienced before. Leaders of the indigenous Little Flock met with Anglicans. Preachers from the old China Inland Mission prayed with YMCA secretaries. Although a few Protestant groups were absent (most notably the independent Christian Tabernacle of Beijing led by Wang Mingdao), major breakthroughs had been achieved.

The policy was to be one of "mutual respect" with affirmation of a common goal. In its "Letter to Christians throughout China" the Conference declared, "The purpose of the Three-Self Patriotic Movement is to unite Christians throughout the country in order to promote the thoroughgoing realization of self-government, self-support and self-propagation in the Chinese church.... We should have mutual respect for the differences that exist among the churches in creed, organization and ritual."[33]

Could churches ranging from conservative-fundamentalist to mainline-ecumenical unite? A major catalyst was the Nanjing Union Theological Seminary, which in 1952 combined eleven independent seminaries. The simple four-point statement of faith for entering students affirmed the historic Trinitarian faith and the inspiration of Scripture, while allowing latitude for diverse interpretations.

The next development was the movement in 1958 to unify worship services. Many outsiders attributed this to government pressure. Within China initiatives often began locally, with the encouragement of the TSPM. In Beijing sixty-five places of worship were reduced to four. Cheng Guani, Cheng Jingyi's younger sister, reported a dual motivation—the expression of Chinese Christians' long cherished hope for unity, and a

---

32. Merwin, *Adventure*, 212; NCCUSA, *Documents*, 20.
33. Wickeri, *Seeking*, 146–51.

contribution to the nation through a more economical use of resources. In the years that followed a critical shift took place from dependence upon historic "bricks and mortar" to affirmation of oneness in Christ. This took place during the Cultural Revolution from 1966 to 1976, when persons of every faith suffered persecutions. In house churches believers met together for Bible study, prayer, and mutual support regardless of their former denominations affiliations.[34]

The year 1979 marked the beginning of new life for the Christian community in China. Churches began to reopen to overflow congregations. The first national gathering in more than ten years, an enlarged meeting of the TSPM, took place in Shanghai in March 1980. Its Open Letter, addressed simply to "brothers and sisters in Christ of all China," was a sign that the "post-denominational era" was at hand. Next, delegates to the Third National Christian Conference in Nanjing in October approved a "new national structure" called the China Christian Council (CCC). Bishop K. H. Ting was elected president. It was to give major leadership in pastoral care, training of church workers, publication of the Bible, and production of Christian literature. Chinese Christians created in 1985 the Amity Foundation as an independent organization able to attract funds and personnel both from within and outside China to promote health, education, publishing, and social service projects.[35]

In 1985 sentiment grew in the CCC that the time might be ripe to build on local experiences of unity in forming a united church. Local and provincial Christian councils and TSPM committees were invited to express what kind of church order they would prefer. Meanwhile a national committee representing various church traditions drafted the unity plan. The goal was to embrace various traditions, including the historic episcopate so treasured by former Anglicans. Based on the principle of mutual respect, groups like the Little Flock and the Seventh-Day Adventists would be permitted to maintain their distinctive beliefs and practices. Six years later, however, a new "Church Order" left many issues unresolved. Since there was no church creed, the parameters of affiliation were not clear. The question remained, "Does the CCC claim to be an established church, to speak on behalf of all Chinese Christians, or to be one amongst several organizations of equal status?" Virtually all estimates of Christians in China since 1949 have suggested that there

34. Ibid., 219–27; G. Brown, *Christianity*, 115–34.
35. G. Brown, *Christianity*, 169–72.

are more members of autonomous house churches than TSPM/CCC members. Although historic differences have been eroded between these groups in the last ten years, many Chinese Christians felt that the CCC leadership was too compliant with the government's desire to control all religious groups. These dynamics, however, have not slowed the vigorous and rapid growth of Christianity in China.[36]

Note the common threads in a century of aspirations for church unity in China. The expressed goal since 1910 has been one indigenous Christian church in China. Long before the TSPM, Chinese Christians advocated self-government, self-support, and self-propagation. The prime movers for unity both before and after 1949 have been church rather than government leaders. Organic church union proposals in China were not imitations of plans in other countries. Instead, they represented the authentic desire of Chinese leaders to respond to the felt needs of their own people and to the guidance of the Holy Spirit.[37]

THE CHURCH OF CHRIST OF THE CONGO

A third, and quite different model for church union comes from the Democratic Republic of the Congo.[38] Roman Catholics trace their mission heritage in that country back to Portuguese missions in the Kingdom of the Kongo established in the 1480s. Protestant missions began in 1878 following H. M. Stanley's explorations demonstrating that the Congo River was navigable for one thousand miles above Leopoldville [present Kinshasa]. By 1886 five Protestant missions had been planted from the coast at Matadi to Leopoldville. Close cooperation among missionary societies led by American Baptists characterized upriver expansion.[39]

By 1902 Congo Protestant missionaries felt the need to prevent overlap of work, and also for a common policy in relations with the state. Nine of the ten mission societies formed the General Missionary Conference in that year. Congo was the first mission field in Africa to form an Edinburgh Continuation Committee following the World Conference of 1910. This was "an expression of the belief of the Congo Protestant missions in their essential unity, a unity which could be ob-

36. Wickeri, *Seeking*, 234–40; G. Brown, *Christianity*, 173; Hunter and Chan, *Protestantism*, 261; *WCE* 1:191–98; Han, "Amity."
37. Xu Rulei, interview, December 2, 1990, quoted in Wickeri, *Seeking*, 238–40.
38. Formerly Congo Free State (1885–1908), Belgian Congo (1908–1960), Republic of the Congo (1960–1965), and Republic of Zaire (1966–1997).
39. Groves, *Planting*, 1:127–30; 2:321–25.

scured, but not denied, by their differences of organization and practice." A further step took place in 1924 when the Continuation Committee merged into the new Congo Protestant Council (CPC), which then affiliated with the IMC.[40]

In 1934 John R. Mott visited the Congo, holding three mission consultations. His concern was not only for unity among the missions, but also among the churches. Inspired by his vision, the Leopoldville Consultation recommended that all Protestant churches use a common name, with uniform membership cards, transfer cards, and other documents. From that year the name *Église du Christ au Congo* (Church of Christ of the Congo) came into standard usage.[41]

"*L'Église du Christ au Congo* . . . this name has caught the imagination of the people in Congo," reported Herbert Smith to the Diamond Jubilee conference of 1938. He continued, "One Lord, one church, one redeeming message for all people is an inspiring thought for all of us." He reported that the name of the one church was beginning to appear in newspapers and elsewhere. The idea of unity was growing. The delegates concluded "that those missions that are acting in harmonious fellowship through the Congo Protestant Council are fostering and encouraging one Church of Christ in Congo."[42]

Congo delegates to the IMC Tambaram Conference of 1938 felt affirmed by others. They experienced a "well-nigh universal support and appreciation of the Congo Protestant Council" for its use of a common name, mutual acceptance of members by transfer, and general observance of comity agreements.[43]

World War II stimulated the next surge toward unity. With normal means of communication and support disrupted, especially for the German "orphaned missions," the churches in the Congo considered closer unity. In 1941 the CPC's Commission on Church Policy raised anew the question of organic union. The following year it was agreed that every church that became a member of the Congo Protestant Council would also be a member of the Church of Christ in Congo. This was important in the years following World War II as a flood of more "sectarian" missions began work in the Congo. Although smaller in

---

40. Slade, *English-Speaking*, 236; Groves, *Planting*, 4:132.
41. "Findings," in A-YDSL/Mott, "Conferences"; E. Ross, *Out of Africa*, 206.
42. Congo Protestant Council, *Sixty Years*, 48, 57.
43. A-NCC, "CPC Minutes, 1940," 16.

membership, the new entrants were given equal voice and vote with the older missions in the CPC. This proved pivotal in 1958 when the CPC resigned its historic membership in the IMC because of the proposed IMC-WCC merger.[44]

Is the *Église du Christ au Congo* a missionary dream or a national reality? That was the key issue during the 1950s. The CPC's transition came rapidly from being a mission council to becoming a council of churches. Congolese became voting members for the first time in 1956. By 1960 all CPC leaders were to be Congolese, with foreigners serving only as technical aides. In its inaugural assembly in 1958, the All-Africa Conference of Churches urged the CPC rapidly to transfer responsibility to Africans and to realize "one church."[45]

On the eve of Zaire's troubled independence in 1960 Hank Crane, a Presbyterian missionary, expressed his conviction that God requires a unity that goes beyond the mere cooperation of comity. "If we are to be used of God to make real the idea of the Church in Africa as the new Tribe of Christ," he continued, "then we must face the necessity for regarding our separate denominational traditions as nothing more or less than charismatic gifts which we bring into the 'one New Tribe', for the enrichment of the whole Household of God."[46]

Political chaos swept over the newly independent Congo like a firestorm in the seven years following independence in 1960. Mutinies, civil war, economic collapse, and anarchy destroyed old institutions, leaving little opportunity to build new ones in their place. The churches were the exceptions. Although most missionaries were evacuated (and some martyred), national leaders stood up to take their places. Out of the chaos grew the yearning for a new united Congolese nation.

It was Jean Bokeleale, elected general secretary of the CPC in 1968, who articulated the challenge of the new era. "The unity of our country and the reconciliation of all Congolese," he declared, is "the will and love of God for the Congo nation which has suffered so much because of divisions and troubles." He reminded delegates to the CPC's General Assembly in 1969 that Protestants had used a common membership card since 1935. He challenged the churches to unite so as to bring strong

---

44. Bokeleale, "Case for Unity," 11; Crawford, *Protestant Missions*, 10–11; Howell, "Ecumenical Background," 8–9.
45. Howell, "Ecumenical Background," 12.
46. Crane, "Revolution."

Christian influence to bear on the nation and its people. In response, the General Assembly voted "to solidify the organic unity of the Church of Christ in Congo." They authorized the National Executive Committee to draft a constitution to be presented at the 1970 assembly.[47]

Can a united church be voted into existence without long negotiations? Many older mission leaders in other countries who had followed the long process in South India questioned the Congo way. Certain former members of the Protestant Council of the Congo, who opposed the new structure fearing a loss of autonomy, formed an alternative alliance known as the Council of Protestant Churches in Zaire (CPCZ). Some feared that the ECZ would join the WCC.[48]

"We just want to be free to determine our own future, to form our own church." With these words Pierre Shaumba, the first general secretary of the CPC, supported the proposed constitution. Noah Kabeya spoke as an active Presbyterian layman: "The old mission structures must go and the daughter Church of Congo must take the place of the mission." Then he spoke directly to missionaries present: "Instead of being sad, the missionaries should be proud of the new Church. It is the magnificent work of missionaries." To allay certain fears, it was agreed that the new church would adopt a policy of neutrality toward both the WCC and the World Evangelical Alliance.

On March 8, 1970, delegates voted thirty-two to fourteen, with two abstentions, in favor of the new constitution that transformed the Protestant Council of the Congo into the Church of Christ in the Congo. All former members of the CPC automatically became members of the new Church. The text introducing the constitution of the new Church began with the conviction that "To perpetuate divisions is disobedience pure and simple to the Word of God." "As of today," the enabling resolution began, "all the mission associations cease to exist as autonomous institutions, either through merger with the national Christian community to which they gave birth, or else through the transfer of their legal charter." The Zaire government assisted the unity effort by granting legal recognition to only three churches: the *Église du Christ au Zaire* (ECZ), the Roman Catholic Church, and the Kimbanguists, a large Zairois African-initiated church.[49]

47. Bokeleale, "Bokeleale," 7; Bokeleale, "Case for Unity," 13; Howell, "Ecumenical Background," 13.
48. "Survey of Church Union Negotiations," *ER* 26 (1974) 307.
49. Niklaus, "New," 4–7; Makanzu, *L'Histoire*, 18–30. For the structure of the ECZ see "Survey of Church Union Negotiations," *ER* 24 (1972) 357–58; 26 (1974) 306–8.

The Congo model of organic union will be misunderstood, however, if it is interpreted as autocratic centralism. Instead, it represents a federal approach to church union similar to that advocated a generation earlier by E. Stanley Jones. Jean Bokeleale, its general secretary, declared in 1971 that "with the help of the Holy Spirit we are able to unite while preserving our diversity and to present ourselves as a single Church, as one family, with each member or branch of the Church retaining internal autonomy, to the glory of God in our country." Each member body remained a distinct community with its own constitution. Each had its own structure, agencies, functions, and doctrinal basis. Each continued under law its own *personnalité civile* (civil personality or legal status).[50]

In the years that followed Congo's political turmoil and autocracy put severe strains on the union. The Church of Christ was widely perceived to be controlled by President Mobutu in the 1980s and 90s. The ruler's attempt in 1989 to handpick and appoint for life the leaders of all member families, however, was opposed vigorously by Presbyterians, Baptists, Methodists, and Mennonites. Although member denominations were free to leave the ECZ upon the end of Mobutu's rule in 1997, there was no guarantee of protection from government interference in the practice of the Christian faith.[51]

Why did the Congo union succeed while others in Africa failed? Ogbu Kalu suggests that a key factor was the absence of an Anglican presence. He traced the abortive attempts to unite Anglicans with non-Anglicans in Ghana, Nigeria, Kenya, and Zambia. In Zambia many years of negotiation among leaders of the Methodist, Congregational, and Reformed traditions resulted in the formation of the United Church of Zambia in 1974. Thereafter, the attempt for a wider union with Anglicans and the African Reformed Church came to naught.[52]

Unity efforts in Africa display two competing impulses. On the one hand, most Christian groups believe firmly that their churches must remain faithful to traditions passed on by the missionaries and first generation of believers. On the other hand, faced with new national challenges for unity (as in the Congo and Zambia), leaders may be open to an "outpouring of the Spirit" that is able to move persons off their old

50. E. Jones, *Reconstruction*, 199–208; Bokeleale, "Church," 215; Church of Christ in Congo, "Constitution"; Irvine, *Church of Christ*, xix.
51. *WCE* 1:214; "Zairian Church."
52. Kalu, "Church Unity," 172; Kalu, *Divided People*, 84–86; Bolink, *Church Union*, 408–10; Howell, "Ecumenical Background," 15–18.

denominational securities "towards the realization of Christ's promise of a new heaven and a new earth."[53]

MISSION—THE ESSENTIAL COMPONENT

What is the importance of the imperative of mission for church union? As instructive as the above case studies are, the cumulative evidence is that without a compelling sense of mission church union efforts fail. Consider four case studies supporting this argument from Japan, India, Nigeria, and Rhodesia (now Zimbabwe).

The Church of Christ in Japan

For many years Protestant leaders, both Japanese and missionaries, had dreamed of a united church embracing all Protestants. Ken Ishihara, a Japanese church historian, argued "that from the beginning the Japanese churches tended to accept Christianity as one church regardless of their individual affiliations with different sending churches." In 1940, under the cloud of war, they agreed to unite as the Church of Christ in Japan (*Nihom Kirisito Kyodan*, often in use shortened to *Kyodan*). The original structure was a kind of federation, with denominations retaining much autonomy under a "bloc" system. In 1942 the Japanese government forced the *Kyodan* into a monolithic structure, although the church resisted government pressure to change its Creed, and a great deal of informal autonomy continued under eleven bloc leaders. Following the war Japan welcomed a huge influx of Protestant missionaries who had not shared the earlier struggle for authentic unity. From 1947 to 1950 several confessional groups left the *Kyodan* to form separate denominations, including the Southern Baptists, Lutherans, the Church of the Nazarene, and conservative pastors of the Reformed tradition who founded a separate denomination called the Japan Reformed Church. They did not share the impulse to unity in mission of those who remained in the *Kyodan*, who "firmly believe that it is God's will that this unity be maintained."[54]

Church of North India

For forty years leaders of the Anglican, Baptist, Brethren, and Disciples of Christ churches in North India, together with Methodists related to

---

53. Kalu, "Church Unity," 175.
54. Latourette, *Revolutionary Age*, 5:432–36; Iglehart, *Century*, 229–35, 291–92; Rhee, "Quest," 207, 208.

conferences in Great Britain, Australia, and the U.S., worked and prayed for a United Church of North India. Seeking to avoid certain delays experienced in South India negotiations, they worked on a plan to unify ministries as the first act of the United Church.

The year 1970 was a tumultuous one for the union efforts. Methodists, who were part of the church in the U.S., and expected to provide half the membership of the United Church, abruptly withdrew at the last minute, although they had earlier approved the union by large majorities at each level of decision making. Institutional maintenance concerns by leaders won the day over the urgency of unity for more effective mission. The Church of North India was formally inaugurated in November 1970, In neighboring Pakistan, however, Methodists of U.S. origin felt a greater urgency to unite for mission. In that majority Muslim nation, they joined the Church of Pakistan in 1970 on the same Plan of Union as that offered them in North India.[55]

Nigeria

The original impulses for church unity began in the various regions of Nigeria about 1905 as missionaries addressed common problems and sought cooperation instead of undignified competition. National union negotiations began in 1947, inspired by the Church of South India. Negotiations between the Anglican, Methodist, and Presbyterians churches were on the verge of success in 1965 when negotiations broke down.

Ogbu Kalu, a respected Nigerian historian, did not think the collapse was due to the deepening political unrest of the period. He judged that "there was so much time spent on organizational matters, especially polity, that little was done on mission." He cited the Inauguration Committee's own radical self-criticism in 1965 that persons "needed to be convinced that this was a Church with a mission, and that renewal and reunion went hand in hand." Church representatives had met "determined to ensure the preservation" of each denomination's tradition, rather than seeking union "as a means of rooting the church in, while transforming, the culture."[56]

---

55. Moede, "Methodist Participation," 376–77; "Survey of Church Union Negotiations," *ER* 22 (1970) 259; 24 (1972) 359. See United Methodist Church, "Decision no. 410," for a digest of the legal appeals made to the Judicial Council on this case.

56. Kalu, "Shattered Cross," 353; Church of Nigeria, *Way Forward*; Kalu, *Divided People*, 46, 86, 87.

Rhodesia/Zimbabwe

During years of increasing political unrest in the 1960s, Anglican, Presbyterian, Methodist, and Congregational church representatives began church union negotiations. Impetus came more from a desire to be in step with organic church union negotiations by their respective denominations in England and Southern Africa than out of urgency for unity in mission in Rhodesia. Despite completion in 1968 of draft statements on common belief, ministry, and oversight by bishops, and wording of a Solemn Covenant, political and racial tensions caused postponement of covenant services planned for 1970, and a suspension of negotiations in 1972.[57]

In each of these case studies the loss of mission as the motivation for unity contributed to the failure of union negotiations.

CONCLUSION

In 1982 two program units of the WCC issued their "Magna Cartas"— Faith and Order's *Baptism, Eucharist and Ministry* (*BEM*), and the CWME's theology of mission, entitled "Mission and Evangelism: An Ecumenical Affirmation." Both included the conviction that unity and the missionary calling of the church are inseparable. *BEM* reads, "The Holy Spirit unites in a single body those who follow Jesus Christ and sends them as witnesses into the world." It was supported initially by more than one hundred Catholic, Orthodox, and Protestant theologians at the Lima conference. The WCC's mission statement opens with the dual convictions that "the divisions of Christians is a scandal and an impediment to the witness of the church," and that there are "inextricable relationships between Christian unity and missionary calling."[58]

In this chapter we have traced the development of this conviction out of the missionary movement, with case studies from India, China, and the Congo. Seeds sown in the nineteenth century that God's will for unity demanded a coming together of Christian churches grew and bore fruit in the twentieth century, most conspicuously in the union churches of Asia and Africa.

In 1952 thirteen prominent South Asian church leaders, including D. T. Niles, J. R. Chandran, R. B. Manikam, and P. D. Devanandan, attend-

---

57. "Survey of Church Union Negotiations," *ER* 16 (1964) 416; 20 (1968) 269-70; 22 (1970) 256; 24 (1972) 356.

58. WCC/CFO, *Baptism*, 20; WCC, *Mission and Evangelism*, 4.

ed the Third World Conference on Faith and Order in Lund, Sweden. As representatives of the "younger churches," they desired "to say a word in love" to those who had been used of God to bring the gospel and the church to South Asia. "Will our church unions, which we believe are the will of God, remain anomalies in the world church?" they asked. Will you use your influence "to encourage similar schemes of union amongst yourselves and your kindred overseas?"[59]

The union churches of Asia and Africa for forty years have waited for the reply. The silence of the WCC's 1982 documents concerning organic church union, while affirming in principle the link between unity and mission, speaks volumes concerning the changed priorities. Is the tide of world confessionalism so strong that it threatens to engulf those remaining islands of Christian unity of "all in each place"? Or are the united churches of India, China, and the Congo witnesses to the unity others will seek in the twenty-first century? Answers remain speculative, but to the missionary movement and the leaders of those churches belongs the credit for raising the key questions.

"Are united and uniting churches sent by God with a special vocation in mission and service?" This was a central question at the Sixth International Consultation of United and Uniting Churches in 1995. What is the test by which their "success" will be judged? Mission is the mother of unity, but unity has not yet proved to be the mother of mission. Out of the experience of eight united churches on five continents that are part of the Council of World Mission, Roderick Hewitt answered that renewal in ministry and mission is the litmus test. "People will not embrace united and uniting churches simply because of their non-confessional name," he wrote. "On the contrary, people generally prefer the certainty that denominational identities offer.... United and uniting churches have no choice but to demonstrate their credibility through concrete mission action in their respective communities.... They can only be truly effective if they are missionary, reaching out beyond themselves."[60]

---

59. WCC/CFO, "Communication," 70.
60. Hewitt, "Vocation," 462.

13

"All in Each Place": Local Unity

THE NEW TESTAMENT MODEL
AND THE TWENTY-FIRST-CENTURY VISION

They devoted themselves to the apostles' teaching and fellowship, to the breaking of bread and the prayers. . . . All who believed were together[1]

THIS HAS BEEN THE model for the church since Pentecost—a church uniting all Christians in each place for worship, study, fellowship, and mission. Delegates to the WCC's Third Assembly (New Delhi 1961) renewed their commitment to local unity as they declared, "We believe that the unity which is both God's will and his gift to his Church is being made visible as *all in each place* who are baptized into Jesus Christ and confess him as Lord and Savior are brought by the Holy Spirit into one fully committed fellowship, holding the one apostolic faith, preaching the one Gospel, breaking the one bread, joining in common prayer, and having a corporate life reaching out in witness and service to all." Simultaneously they linked the local with the global. The "all in each place" are those who "at the same time are united with the whole Christian fellowship in all places and all ages."[2]

Fulfilling the apostolic model, New Delhi interpreted "place" not as a church building, but rather as both a local neighborhood and as other areas (schools, factories, offices, etc.) where Christians need to express unity in Christ. The "all in each place" refers to "all Christian people . . . regardless of race and class." Building on that understanding, others have

---

1. Acts 2:42, 44–45.
2. WCC/A, New Delhi 1961, *Report*, 116.

conceived of "place" not in terms of geographic location, but of place in the "fabric of human society."[3]

Peter Kasenene of Swaziland spoke to the churches in Africa of the need to rediscover the African value of community "as the basis of ecumenical activity." In African cultures mutuality assures survival of the society. It is healthy only when the weak and ostracized and disadvantaged (the poor, the orphans, the sick, and the aged) are cared for. "It is not enough," Kasenene wrote, "to think of ecumenical activity in terms of dialogue and co-operation initiated by churches and church organizations, but more in terms of human needs." When one rediscovers the African ethos of human solidarity, he concluded, "any situation or activity which promotes friendship, happiness, mutual support and mutual trust in the community, is ecumenical." In addition to ecclesial, spiritual and social ecumenicity initiated by churches, Christians can support and often partner with "secular initiatives which promote fellowship and the well-being of the community."[4]

"Ecumenism began as a local affair," Stephen Petersen relates, and "good ecumenism is always at least local ecumenism, that which takes place in specific places in time and space." Admittedly, "local" and "local church" are terms with a variety of meanings in various confessional traditions and in different languages. In one tradition, the term "local church" includes both parishes and the diocese under a bishop's leadership. In another, it is the gathered community of faith that may be found in a rural village or urban neighborhood.[5]

UNITED PARISHES AND UNION CHURCHES

Fifty-two years after the bold experiment of uniting Protestant and Anglican churches to form the Church of South India, one of its talented sons asked, "Is full church unity possible or desirable?" In the first St. Thomas of India Unity Lecture in Great Britain, Thomas Thangaraj argued that "full church unity begins with the local." He continued, "Each town and village is the place where full church unity has to take flesh ... At the local level, the members of the Church of South India need to be dreaming of unity with the Lutherans, Baptists and Roman Catholics."[6]

3. Ibid., 118.
4. Kasenene, "Secular," 45, 58.
5. Petersen, "Local Ecumenism," 219; WCC, *In Each Place*, 3–12.
6. Thangaraj, "Unity," 97.

In 1966 and 1967 large numbers of Indonesians made inquiries about the Christian faith during a period of political turmoil. In response, churches worked together in evangelistic outreach. Each day services were held in the Bandung marketplace in Java. Pastors and evangelists of different churches shared in leadership. Meanwhile, a breakthrough in joint baptism followed similar evangelistic outreach among the Karobatak people of North Sumatra. No denomination had worked there previously. On June 19, 1966, in a village called Tigalinga, nearly 2,000 new Christians were baptized by fifteen pastors belonging to six different denominations. Together they formed one united church called the Karobatak Church.[7]

In 1975 pastors of union churches in Latin America declared their conviction "that Union Churches overseas—as international, interracial, intercultural, interdenominational congregations—are a prototype of the church of the future." Case studies can be found on six continents. In a large housing estate outside Auckland, New Zealand, a former rural community church was upstaged as each denomination rushed in to serve its own members, even though these small congregations would not grow to be self-supporting. In 1975 Anglicans and Methodists covenanted to become a cooperating parish. "Perhaps the most positive outcome," leaders report, "has been a new sense of mission in the local community." They shifted from survival to mission as their priority concern. A new Social Service Center provided counseling services, citizens' advice, and marriage guidance. Local youths flocked to a "drop-in center," and a caring ministry team reached the homebound where they lived.[8]

Union churches have been a vital overseas ministry of the National Council of Churches in the USA. The Council provides ministers in congregations serving North Americans, and others living and working overseas, from Hong Kong to Helsinki, and from Beirut to Bombay. Their ecumenical witness is non-sectarian. In some congregations Unitarians and Pentecostals share the same communion table. At other local union churches Buddhist diplomats and Mulsim shopkeepers bow in respect before the same Christian pulpit. While predominately of the liberal wing of Protestantism, members share common belief in the Lordship of Jesus Christ. Rather than being secure islands for expatriates, these

---

7. Margull, "Parish Level," 370.
8. MacHarg, "Union Churches," 417; WCC, *In Each Place*, 64–66. See Linn, *Hear*, 17–58, for additional case studies from Europe.

parishes tended to provide "the point of contact, dialogue, and involvement with the 'host' culture."[9]

LOCAL COUNCILS OF CHURCHES

Following Edinburgh 1910 a team led by John R. Mott encouraged formation of regional, national, *and* local councils of churches. Often the latter were supplemented by ministers' fraternals, many of which included a broader range of denominational participation by clergy than the local councils. In Southern Africa local councils of churches flourished from 1960 onwards. As in other countries, they identified felt needs that could best be addressed on a cooperative basis. These ranged from evangelistic efforts, to addressing needs of the poor, to being a prophetic voice on social issues. They achieved what Diane C. Kessler, in the U.S. context, called the vitality resulting by combined clergy and lay leadership, including participation by young people.[10]

A NEW WAY OF BEING CHURCH

Writing out of a dangerous situation in El Salvador, Pablo Galdámez (a pseudonym) expressed the joy of sharing and caring that is at the heart of a new way of being church shared globally by millions of Christians. He wrote, "Now we were a people. We were like a big family. We were friends. The community meetings bound us closer and closer together. The doors were open. We said hello to one another, we went to one another's houses. For the first time, this scattered people was united. Gone were fear and embarrassment. We shared everything, a cup of coffee, a glass of water—and the quest. We'd learned to share the solutions to our problems together."[11]

Such groups in the predominately Roman Catholic countries of Latin America are called basic Christian communities (BCCs) or base ecclesial communities (BECs). Begun in the 1960s in Brazil, they spread in the 1980s throughout Latin America and to other continents as they embraced liberation theologies that taught God's "preferential option for the poor" and the mission of liberation from injustice. In 1978 I visited one such community in Cuernavaca, Mexico. When forced to leave their

---

9. McConkey, "Union Churches," 918; Outterson, "Overseas," 606.
10. D. Kessler, "Future"; N. Thomas, "Cooperation."
11. Galdámez, *Faith*, 21.

favella on railroad property, about forty families "occupied" one night a vacant hillside outside the city. There they built as a BEC not only their homes, but also a shelter that housed a primary school during the weekday, and was their meeting place for Bible study with discussion on Sundays. Responding to what the gospel said to them for their life together, they added a grinding machine to turn maize into flour for tortillas, and a clinic.[12]

The arrival of the vision of BCCs in Tanzania in East Africa in the 1970s coincided with the advocacy of *ujamaa* (familyhood) by Julius Nyerere, the nation's first president. *Ujamaa* had three facets: a resolve to use one's powers not for personal advantage but for the good of the entire community, a readiness to recognize others as persons of worth opposing all exploitation of others, and reliance on local resources. The BCCs formed in villages and included two to twelve families each. Each was ecumenical in basis since not all persons in a village were Roman Catholics. Religion was never to be a cause of discrimination or separation. The bond of union was not the Eucharist, but rather the reading of the Bible together and meditation upon it, applying its message to one's personal life and their life together in community. It was felt that "from this life in *ujamaa* is born a Church which, far more than in previous times, is profoundly Tanzanian and fundamentally Christian."[13]

In other contexts the BCCs are called "small Christian communities" or "small faith communities" or "Christian popular communities." Where the body of Christ is divided among several denominations, such grass roots movements can be vibrant forms of local ecumenism. BCC teams, led by Father José Marins, held workshops in Birmingham, England, beginning in 1979 on "A New Way of Being Church." Concerned that the poor of the Ladywood District of Birmingham were unrepresented in development planning, Christians associated with different local congregations formed a BCC with the aim of being "a visible loving Christian community of openness, reflection and celebration."[14]

Australia, like the U.S., has a great mixture of Christian traditions. It has been described as a "fertile and inviting soil in which to grow vital, real praying/caring Christian community." Initial efforts to form BCCs in the 1980s largely failed, however, because each community tried to go

---

12. For an extensive bibliography on BECs see W. Cook, *Expectation*, 283–306.
13. "Basic Christian Communities," 271–73.
14. Hinton, *Walking*, 32–34.

it alone. The "building community" project grew only as volunteers of the Anglican, Catholic, Church of Christ, Baptist, and Uniting Church worked together. From Europe came a similar report that the BCCs increasingly are ecumenical, and hold in common the aim of building a church in solidarity with the poor. "There is no 'official' Catholic or Protestant character to the Dutch BCC," one participant declared. "It is a movement church.... I never knew who was Catholic and who was Protestant. I once again believe in the ecumenical movement."[15]

Christians in China, witnessing to a postdenominational Christianity, have found in the house church movement their new way of being church. In retelling the stories of fourteen house churches during the Cultural Revolution, Raymond Fung found this commonality: "Confessional and denominational claims have lost their binding power in China. The factors that divide Protestant churches elsewhere have little significance. In this sense, we can speak legitimately of the *Church in China*."[16]

INTENTIONAL COMMUNITIES

Ralph Winter's distinction between *modalities* and *sodalities*, presented in chapter 9, applies also to local structures for ministry and mission. A distinction can be made between two structures of local ecumenism. Often sodalities form among Christians concerned to take cooperative action to meet critical human needs such as disaster relief, food distribution to the hungry, and shelter for the homeless.[17]

Sometimes persons in mission locally form intentional communities for mutual support and creative ministry. Ruth Bottoms, a Baptist minister, joined the Pilston Community in the English county of Dorset in 2004. Although Anglican in foundation, it became ecumenical in membership the following year as Ruth and a "house church evangelical" became its fourth and fifth members. Supported financially by outside earnings of its members, and undergirded by the daily rhythm of prayer, the Pilston Community's ministry was to "guests" who were alcohol or drug users, or mentally ill, or homeless. Most meals were served to twenty-five to thirty "wayfarers" who became part of this healing community. "Those who are guests are treated as persons of worth," Bottoms related.

15. Ibid., 40–42, 48–52.
16. Fung, *Households*, ix.
17. Winter, "Two Structures," 227; Petersen, "Local Ecumenism," 219–31.

Guests felt safe in the community's rural setting. Some found their first meaningful relationships there with the cows and sheep they cared for, and later became open to human sharing.[18]

Some communities begun with an intention to meet a local felt need gained national or international significance. Roger Schutz, a Reformed theologian, came in 1940 to the half-abandoned village of Taizé in central France. In a donated house Brother Roger began to care for war refugees. After flight from persecution to his native Switzerland, he returned in 1948 with the nucleus of an intentional community in which seven "brothers" took life vows. Initially the community was a sign of Christian care for the world's needy. It focused its mission first on agricultural development, promoting agricultural cooperatives in France and Latin America. Later it welcomed thousands of students and other young people—Catholics and Protestants, from East and West—for ecumenical worship and renewal.[19]

In 1971 seven seminarians at Trinity Evangelical Divinity School near Chicago shared radical, evangelical, and activist interests. Together they began the next year to publish a magazine for Christians and to live in intentional community in inner-city Chicago. They sought "mutual respect and trust between those in the radical evangelical movement and those in the charismatic renewal." In 1975 the community, which had grown to twenty in number, moved to Washington D.C. and renamed their journal *Sojourners*, with Jim Wallis as editor.

In that same year the Sojourners Fellowship joined with twelve other intentional local groups to form "The Community of Communities." Bob Sabath, a Sojourner member, reported in 1980:

> A genuinely ecumenical fellowship is taking place among us. While respecting the integrity of each local community, we are striving to be accountable to more than just ourselves or our own ecclesiastical traditions. This fellowship is forming us into a circle of church communities based on a unity not dependent on a covenant or formal rule of life. We do not seek to create a new denomination; rather, we are committed to rebuilding the church both within and without traditional church structures and calling it to be an agent of change in the world. This community of communities has strengthened us all in our common ministry to the church.[20]

18. Ruth Bottoms, interview. For other case studies of European congregations "meeting Christ in the wounded" see Linn, *Hear*, 59–79.
19. D. Edwards, "Signs," 378–81.
20. Sabath, "Community," 17, 19.

The Sojourners Community has always been small, never numbering more than fifty people. They lived, together with interns, in six houses owned cooperatively in the Columbia Heights neighborhood of inner-city Washington. The seventh, a former drug house, became their Neighborhood Center, which focused on a year-round "Freedom School" for at-risk young people. Members understood "community" broadly to include not only those in residence, but also those who are involved in Sojourner ministries, or who have participated in them in the past thirty-five years. "Now we are like a dispersed community," wrote Wallis, "a Diaspora, scattered across the country and around the world [that] probably numbers in the hundreds of thousands by now."[21]

UNITED SEEKING JUSTICE

Joint action in mission often overflows the boundaries of established ecumenical bodies. In Indonesia, local cooperation often includes both Protestants and Roman Catholics. Women often initiate joint efforts. In Jakarta their joint life developed out of the experience of worshiping together on the World Day of Prayer. Next, they responded to felt needs—for example in South Jakarta where the Ecumenical Cooperation of Christian Women for many years sold healthy yet inexpensive food to low-income families.[22]

Indian leaders report that "in case of national catastrophes people join together to help each other—regardless of religion, caste or denomination." Together they build houses, provide clothes for the homeless, and meet other needs.[23]

In São Paulo, Brazil, Roman Catholic, Methodist, and Lutheran churches as well as individual Presbyterian, Reformed, and Pentecostal pastors formed after Vatican II the Movement for Fellowship and Reconciliation between the Christian churches. It stimulated the formation of four centers on evangelism and popular education for people in situations of deprivation and injustice. Catholic Archbishop Arns, a key leader, wrote that "ecumenism finds expression in practical projects with specific aims, such as the struggle for land, the campaign for housing, and other popular [responses to] to the cry of the poor."[24]

21. Wallis, "Celebrating"; Wallis, "One Constant."
22. Hutabarat-Lebang, "Journeying," 288.
23. Birmelé, *Local Ecumenism*, 2.
24. Arns, "Example," 432.

The West Side Cooperative Ministry in Fort Wayne, Indiana, is part of a "community-ministries movement" that proliferated in the U.S. beginning in the 1960s. Eight center-city churches provided a wide range of social services for poor children, adults, and seniors in an economically depressed section of the city. Reflecting on such ministries after twenty years of deep involvement, David Bos judged them to be "the wild card in ecumenical relations." Those that focus on charity, rather than justice and empowerment of the poor, may become anti-ecumenical and even detached from parishes largely engaged in maintenance ministries. Those that "aspire to an image of cooperation, service, and advocacy on behalf of a local community where justice and peace were hallmarks," and have close ties to local congregations and communities, deepen understandings of mission and unity, engage in public policy issues, and contribute to a vital and vibrant local ecumenism.[25]

CONCLUSION

Is "all in each place" just a New Testament utopian vision of the local Christian community, or an impractical option in the fragmented twenty-first-century church? Some would argue that "the local church, in order to be authentically related to the place, needs to be one fully committed fellowship." They contend that the existence of "church row"—of several churches on the same street divided along confessional lines, is "a denial of the nature and the calling of the local church." They regard that reality as "an anomaly."[26]

What is the antidote for "exclusive preoccupation with limited interests and sectional loyalties?" the IMC delegates to the Willingen 1952 conference asked. They found their answer in "a sense of partnership in obedience and mutual help among all the churches which compose the Universal Church." What would make this possible? "Only a rediscovery of the purpose of Christ for His Church," they responded, "can redirect the Church towards unity."[27]

An Indonesian leader expressed well the imperative as he wrote, "The manifestation of fellowship in faith, life and witness which is the core of any ecumenical endeavour should be at the heart of the life of the

---

25. Bos, "Community."
26. WCC, *In Each Place*, 10.
27. IMC Conf., Willingen 1952, *Missions*, 200.

local churches.... Ecumenism is not one agenda among other agendas of the local church, but rather it is the way of being the church."[28]

The reality, however, is that ecumenical witness and service in most local communities remains the concern of a very few individuals, or of very small groups, rather than a priority for parishes and local churches. That individual Christians are participating in local ecumenical initiatives can become a kind of "ecumenical alibi" that allows local churches to continue to exist unchanged. "Ecumenical indifference" is strengthened in many places by "a certain fear of the loss of individual identity."[29]

On the other hand, local ecumenism may be vibrant where institutionalized ecumenism is weak and ineffective. In Latin America Julio de Santa Ana found that unity in service and worship seemed to be more easily achieved among the poor. "It is an ecumenism of the people . . . which does not care about the formal aspects of Christian unity or inter-religious/inter-ideological dialogues," he wrote. "Be alert," he advised, "to what lay men, women and young people are trying to practice and communicate about Christian unity." It is to be understood as a community of ministries that seek "to be obedient to Jesus Christ in serving all beings and, in particular, the poorest."[30]

Dionne Crafford wrote from the African reality that "for far too long ecumenism was practiced on the leadership level of churches." At the local level very few people knew the meaning of the word. Her conviction was that "if the church really wants to make its influence felt in a future Africa, it will have to develop a local ecumenism." Evangelism, mission, relief work, community development, and witness to authorities all "can best be done jointly in a local situation between churches that face a common challenge."[31]

---

28. Hutabarat-Lebang, "Journeying," 285.
29. Birmelé, *Local Ecumenism*, 6, 33.
30. Santa Ana, ed., *Towards*, 175–76.
31. Crafford, "Ecumenism," 8.

PART THREE
Wider Ecumenism

14

One World: The Secular Vision

On April 25, 1945, representatives of forty-six nations met at San Francisco in the historic conference to form the United Nations. It was "the first major international conference for two millennia not dominated by Europe." Although proposals for the new world body had been formulated at the Dumbarton Oaks Conference the previous year, the provisions of the charter were to be drafted. The structure of the body also was to be negotiated.[1]

The U.S. government decided to invite forty-two national organizations to send consultants. Secretary of State Edward Stettinius, in his official report to President Truman, called this arrangement "not only an innovation in the conduct of international affairs by this Government, but also, as events proved, an important contribution to the Conference itself." The consultants represented labor, law, agriculture, business, education, women, veterans, and the churches. They chose as their chairperson a church leader, O. Frederick Nolde of Philadelphia. He was at San Francisco representing both the Federal Council of the Churches of Christ in America (FCC) and the Foreign Missions Conference of North America (FMC). His major concern was human rights.[2]

Negotiations reached a critical stage on May 1st. Confidential remarks of delegates revealed that "prompt and virtually drastic action was needed" if substantial provisions for human rights were to be inserted in the U.N. Charter. Hastily, Nolde convened a drafting committee of key consultants. By morning Secretary of State Stettinius had on his desk a letter containing their urgent appeal. Nolde's group proposed four key

---

1. *Encyclopedia Britannica*, s.v. "United Nations."
2. "Charter of the United Nations: Report to the President on the Results of the San Francisco Conference by the Chairman of the United States Delegation, The Secretary of State, Edward R. Stettinius, Jr.," quoted in Nolde, *Free*, 20. Nurser, *Peoples* contains detailed analysis of the historic events presented in this chapter, and the texts of key source documents.

amendments to the Dumbarton Oaks Proposals: (1) that the words "to promote respect for human rights and fundamental freedom" be added to the stated purpose of the U.N., (2) that the Charter contain the principle that religious freedom shall be defended alongside other freedoms, (3) that the function and powers of the U.N. Economic and Social Council include "developing and safeguarding human rights and fundamental freedoms," and (4) that the U.N. set up a human rights commission. The Secretary of State received the suggestions with appreciation, promising to forward them immediately to President Truman for approval.[3] Anxious days followed as the consultants lobbied informally and U.N. delegates proposed amendments. On June 26, 1945, the Charter as signed contained the essential four points that Nolde had submitted to Stettinius. Concerning the consultants the Secretary of State wrote to President Truman, "In no part of the deliberations of the Conference was greater interest displayed than by the group of American consultants representing forty-two leading American organizations and groups concerned with the enjoyment of human rights and basic freedoms to all peoples. A direct outgrowth ... was the proposal ... that the Charter (Article 68) be amended to provide for a Commission on Human Rights."[4]

At his address to the closing session of the U.N. Conference, President Truman expressed gratification that the Charter was dedicated "to the achievement and observance of human rights and fundamental freedoms." He declared that "Unless we can attain those objectives for all men and women everywhere—without regard to race, language or religion—we cannot have permanent peace and security." He looked forward to the framing of an international bill of rights.[5]

DEVELOPMENT OF THE SECULAR VISION

What impact did the missionary movement have upon the secular vision of unity and efforts to achieve it? This chapter focuses upon that question. Often missions appeared in the past to be preoccupied with institutional concerns and remote from the political decision-making process. In the case of the drafting of the U.N. Charter, however, the churches and their missionary agencies played a pivotal role.

The Dumbarton Oaks Proposals for the U.N. Charter had contained only one brief and subordinate reference to human rights and

---

3. Nolde, *Free*, 21–24; A-WCC/CCIA, "CCIA NY."
4. Quoted in Nolde, *Free*, 25; A-WCC/CCIA, "CCIA NY."
5. Truman, *Public Papers*, 142.

fundamental freedoms. Between their publication in October 1944 and the San Francisco Conference in 1945, Christians in several countries became aroused to an awareness of this defect. Church leaders in at least four countries petitioned their representatives to support at the San Francisco founding conference the establishment of a commission on human rights. Nolde judged that "an international Christian influence played a determining part in achieving the more extensive provisions for human rights and fundamental freedoms which ultimately found their way into the Charter."[6]

The Legacy of Human Rights Concerns

For missions and the churches, human rights were not a new concern in 1945. "Missions and Government" had been one of the eight commissions of the World Missionary Conference in Edinburgh in 1910. Its mandate, in addition to issues of missions, missionaries, and government, included both the social and political aspirations of colonial peoples and religious liberty.[7]

Church leaders, following the tragedies of World War I, felt a new urgency to focus Christian thought and action upon widespread injustices. They held a major Conference on Christian Politics, Economics and Citizenship (COPEC) in Birmingham, England, in 1924. The resulting twelve volumes of reports were a major effort to relate the Christian faith to politics and economics. J. H. Oldham, in a closing address on the relation of COPEC to the missionary enterprise, contrasted the Edinburgh and Birmingham conferences. Whereas the missionary movement at Edinburgh believed in the gospel for every person in the whole world, COPEC emphasized "the new continents of human life which were not but must be brought to be under the redeeming sway of the Kingdom of God." He continued, "As with the missionary revival in the nineteenth century, so here we may be on the verge of another great revival of religious life."[8]

Such idealism continued at the next IMC World Missionary Conference (Jerusalem 1928). There T. C. Chao of China expressed hope that the universal humanity realized in the person of Jesus Christ would

---

6. Nolde, "Freedom," 151. See also E. Duff, *Social Thought*, 277, for an independent support of this assessment by Senator Vandenburg.

7. *World Missionary Conference, 1910*, 7:88–121; Stanley, ed., *World*, 248–76. See also D. Hudson, *World Council* and Teinonen, *Missio* for analyses of the thought of ecumenical conferences concerning international politics.

8. CEC, Conf., Birmingham, 1924, *Proceedings*, 262.

become a kingdom which "will extend its boundaries to include all humanity, and to be consummated in the final triumph of the good and true and beautiful." The Conference pioneered in concern for race relations. Delegates declared in their concluding statement that the principles and ideals of worldwide interracial unity for which they stood applied also to "the equal rights of men and women in and between all races."[9]

During the 1930s staff members of the IMC provided major leadership in conferences sponsored by the parallel ecumenical streams of Life and Work and Faith and Order. Oldham chaired the massive research project preparing for the Oxford Conference on Church, Community and State of 1937. To John R. Mott he wrote, "If, through the cooperation of the best Christian minds which the Church has at its command, a new vision of the significance of Christianity for the present situation were really to take shape, more would have been done for the missionary cause than could be done by any other means."[10]

The Oxford Conference, however, met at a time of international uncertainty. Fascism was on the rise. Already Japan had invaded China. Europeans feared war would result from Hitler's territorial ambitions. The League of Nations seemed impotent to resolve international conflicts. "Perplexity," "fear," "conflict"—these were the opening notes of the Conference message to the churches.

Delegates, acutely aware of the churches' divisions, resolved to work for greater unity. In the face of their own divisions, could church leaders challenge political leaders to seek for a new world order?

At Oxford an effort was made to analyze the key issues. Philip Henry Kerr Lothian spoke on the "Demonic Influence of National Sovereignty." He found no ultimate remedy except the creation of a world body representing all persons and nations. In it states would pool their authority in matters of supranational interest. They would legislate, judge, and tax everybody for the good of the whole. Wilhelm Menn, in his paper on "The Church and the International Order," added that international law would require new premises and new leadership. World justice, he declared, cannot be achieved so long as national interest is the motivation for international relations. He suggested that persons influenced by the church, because of their higher loyalty, may have "that sensitiveness to

---

9. IMC Conf., Jerusalem 1928, *Meeting*, 1:293–94; 4:201–2.
10. Oldham to Mott, November 14, 1934, in A-YDSL/Mott, "Correspondence," box 66.

One World: The Secular Vision

the needs of others which is the necessary condition of all international understanding."[11]

The Conference in its report made a fundamental distinction between *international* and *ecumenical*. The term *international* necessarily accepts the human division into separate nations "as a natural if not a final state of affairs." *Ecumenical*, by contrast, refers to the fact of unity in Christ. Where disruptive nationalism and aggressive imperialism make brotherhood and sisterhood seem unreal, the church is to offer not just the ideal but the living reality of a community of persons united by the love of God. In its message the Conference challenged the church to be a fellowship that binds persons together in a common dependence on God so that it "overleaps all barriers of social status, race or nationality." Then the church as a true community could "call the nations to order their lives as members of the one family of God."[12]

The next conference of the IMC was held at Tambaram near Madras, India, in 1938. Its deliberations on the church and the international order continued concerns raised at Oxford. The threat of war was on the increase, but the delegates were convinced that Christians could still make a special contribution to worldwide cooperation.

T. Z. Koo of China, secretary of the World Student Christian Federation, contrasted world politics and the church. The *international order*, he began, starts from the fact of division of the world into separate states. So long as every nation state is a sovereign unit, a law unto itself, there is a constant threat of rivalry and violence. There is no international law. By contrast the church, although international, is also *ecumenical*. As such it starts from the fact of unity—the unity founded in Christ. To a world of "disruptive nationalism, brutal militarism and aggressive imperialism," Koo continued, the ecumenical church offers not only an ideal of one family, but the fact of its realization by the love of God.

Then Koo spoke passionately of his personal struggle amidst the Sino-Japanese war. He reminded the listeners of the "wanton murder of civilians and the wild orgy of lust" committed by the Japanese army in Nanking and other Chinese cities. At first he thought of the Japanese

---

11. Menn, "Church," 235–36. In that year William Paton, secretary of the IMC, wrote: "If the Churches have done much to popularize the idea of the League of Nations ever since its formation, ought they not . . . to teach that one absolute condition of a better international world order is that separate nations should be willing to make some surrender of their individual sovereignty?" (Paton, *World Community*, 157).

12. World Conf., Oxford 1937, *Universal Church*, 152–53, 47.

only as the opponents, as the enemy. But then God spoke to him out of the Bible, as he read in 1 John 3:14, "He that loveth not his brother abideth in death ... [but] we know that we have passed from death unto life, because we love the brethren." "Only those who have caught the meaning of God's suffering love," Koo concluded, "can render this help to an age living in fear and trembling."[13]

In their report the Tambaram delegates declared that "in the missionary enterprise the Christian movement makes an indispensable contribution to the international order." Through the ever-widening fellowship of the ecumenical church the walls of partition between nations and races are broken down. Worldwide conflict and stress may intensify the problems of missionaries, but they also bring to each one opportunities for healing and reconciliation. The storm clouds of war did not discourage the delegates, who concluded, "We are profoundly convinced that the Church has a unique opportunity and responsibility to bring its Gospel to the world of nations at this tragic time, looking humbly to God to bless that witness to His gracious purpose."[14]

Wartime Proposals for Peace

As the tide of World War II engulfed the nations, church leaders deepened their commitment to seek for post-war arrangements that could eliminate, or certainly minimize, the prospects of future wars.

It was William Paton, the IMC secretary, who convened a Peace Aims Group in 1940 to help bring international Christian thinking to bear upon the problems of war and peace. Archbishop William Temple was an active participant, as were John Foster Dulles and his brother Alan from the U.S. The goal was to stimulate thinking by Christian leaders, and ultimately by national political leaders, on alternatives for a new international order. Some influential members had intimate connections with key leaders of the British government.[15]

Meanwhile a parallel group, called the Commission to Study the Bases of a Just and Durable Peace, met in North America. In 1941 the

13. Koo, "Church," 73–74, 78, 84–85.
14. IMC Conf., Madras 1938, *World Mission*, 119–21.
15. A-WCC/IMC, "William Paton," box 261141 ; Jackson, *Red Tape*, 266–67. Paton also attempted to convene a meeting in Stockholm, Sweden, in 1943 of church representatives from as many countries as possible, including Germany, but transportation to Sweden proved impossible (Nolde, "Christian Action in International Affairs—War Years," in A-WCC/CCIA, "O. Frederick Nolde."

One World: The Secular Vision

FCC gave it a major task: "to clarify the mind of our churches regarding the moral, political and economic foundations of an enduring peace," and "to prepare the people of our churches and of our nation for assuming their appropriate responsibility for the establishment of such a peace."[16]

The Commission soon launched a nationwide program that including distribution of 45,000 copies to churches of the study book entitled *A Just and Durable Peace*. After receiving proposals from many church leaders, the Commission early in 1943 took a next step to stimulate thinking on prospects for a new world order. Their "Six Pillars for Peace" contained the following proposals on international collaboration, economic cooperation, peaceful change, autonomy of peoples, armament control, and religious liberty:

1. The peace must provide the political framework for a continuing collaboration of the United Nations and, in due course, of neutral and enemy nations.
2. The peace must make provision for bringing within the scope of international . . . agreement those economic and financial acts of national governments which have widespread international repercussions.
3. The peace must make provision for an organization to adapt the treaty structure of the world to changing underlying conditions.
4. The peace must proclaim the goal of autonomy for subject peoples, and it must establish international organization to assure and to supervise the realization of that end.
5. The peace must establish procedures for controlling military establishments everywhere.
6. The peace must establish in principle, and seek to achieve in practice, the right of individuals everywhere to religious and intellectual liberty.[17]

The Six Pillars sparked the interest of newspaper editors, columnists, and radio commentators. The resulting public discussion "placed the churches in the forefront of thinking about the post-war world." Meanwhile church mission agencies cooperated with the FCC in spon-

---

16. FCC, *Annual Report* (1941), 93–94. The blue-ribbon commission, chaired by John Foster Dulles, included noted Christian ethicists John Bennett and Georgia Harkness, philosopher William E. Hocking, and church leaders Bishop Bromley Oxnam and Henry P. van Dusen. The Foreign Missions Conference of North America and the Home Missions Councils each designated two representatives.
17. Ibid. (1941), 52; (1943), 62.

soring a Christian Mission on World Order. This reached residents of one hundred cities during the month of November of 1943. Mission speakers shared the Pillars with churches, universities, high schools, women, clergy, and leaders of business and labor. They set up study groups to continue the peace education efforts.[18]

National and world attention focused on an International Round Table of Christian Leaders convened at Princeton University in July 1943. The sixty-one participants represented twelve different countries, including not only England, Canada, and the U.S., but also Poland, the Netherlands, Germany, China, Japan, Norway, and Russia. John Foster Dulles served as chairman and Nolde as secretary.

Could a political union evolve out of those nations united in war against totalitarianism? The Princeton Round Table said "yes" as it agreed in principle to the "Six Pillars for Peace." It favored a new political framework that would include not only wartime allies, but also neutral and enemy nations. Such a "United Nations" should be concerned about international economic agreements, support of peoples struggling for autonomy, and control of military establishments. Furthermore, "the peace must establish in principle, and seek to achieve in practice, the right of individuals everywhere to religious and intellectual liberty."

The Round Table heightened worldwide discussion of the Pillars. In the months before his untimely death in August 1943, William Paton, the IMC secretary, devoted much energy to promoting discussion through the Peace Aims Group. Official responses came both from Moscow and the U.S. Senate. Dulles and Nolde collaborated with Catholic and Jewish leaders in the formulation of a "Declaration on World Peace." Considered "essential to peace" were individual rights, rights of minorities, and international institutions to maintain peace with justice.

Twenty-five years later Nolde wrote concerning this formative period, "The Round Table stimulated an international Christian impact upon the deliberations of the Conference on International Organization at San Francisco in 1945, where the Charter of the United Nations was drafted. It also gave impetus to an organized ecumenical approach to problems of peace, justice, and freedom."[19]

18. Ibid. (1943), 65. The sponsoring groups included the Foreign Missions Conference of North America, the Home Missions Council of North America, and the Missionary Education Movement.

19. Jackson, *Red Tape*, 322; FCC, *Annual Report* (1943), 63–64, 157–60; A-WCC/CCIA, "O. Frederick Nolde"; Nolde, "Ecumenical Action," 263.

A parallel initiative came from the IMC. It proposed to the FCC and the FMC that they set up a Joint Committee on Religious Liberty. A. L. Warnshuis was the key mover. Co-secretary of the IMC since 1921, and head of its New York office when it was established in 1946, Warnshuis provided an unexcelled maturity of staff leadership. His interest in issues of religious liberty and world order went back to his years as a missionary in China and staff member of China's national Christian council from 1900 to 1920. While the New York secretary for the IMC, he also served the FMC, with offices in the same building, as organizer for many of its field committees and secretary of its committee on missions and government.[20] Under Warnshuis' leadership the concerns of mission leaders for religious liberty predominated in the work of the FCC-FMC Joint Committee on Religious Liberty.[21]

Warnhuis proposed that the Joint Committee promote the serious study of issues of religious liberty begun both by the IMC and by North American university scholars and mission board executives. The Committee had the advantage of collaboration with Roman Catholic clergy, international lawyers, and outstanding Protestant historians and theologians. The result was the monumental work *Religious Liberty: An Inquiry*, by M. Searle Bates published in February 1945. The IMC edition of 5,000 copies was quickly exhausted. A commercial edition of 3,000 copies followed. The IMC distributed 500 of its copies to the members of India's first Constituent Assembly as well as to key government officials. This timely output undoubtedly influenced the liberal provisions for religious liberty finally adopted by the U.N. Later the IMC and Church World Service arranged for translations of *Religious Liberty* into Chinese, French, German, Italian, Japanese, Portuguese, and Spanish.[22]

Founding the United Nations

The term *United Nations* achieved worldwide prominence when twenty-six wartime allies on January 1, 1942, signed the "Declaration of the United Nations," setting forth their war aims. The first major step in the planning for a permanent body for world order took place at the Dumbarton Oaks Conference in early autumn 1944. On an estate out-

20. Hogg, *Foundations*, 200, 222–23; Goodall, *Christian Ambassador*, 79–121.
21. Nurser, *Peoples*, 81.
22. "Minutes, Joint Committee on Religious Liberty, 6 May 1942," in A-WCC/IMC, "Religious Liberty"; FMC, *Report* (1944), 247; (1950), 82–83.

side Washington D.C. diplomatic experts of the Big Four powers (U.S., U.K., U.S.S.R., and China) drafted the proposals for the mandate and structure of the new body.[23]

Recognizing that the key hour for church influence was at the UNO's formative stage, the Commission on a Just and Durable Peace called for a second National Study Conference in Cleveland, Ohio, in January 1945. The 481 delegates who attended came from 34 communions, 18 allied religious bodies, and 70 city and state councils of churches. Dulles chaired the Conference, Methodist bishop G. Bromley Oxnam headed the Message Committee, and Nolde served as conference secretary.

Although the participants were from North America, the Cleveland Conference was strongly influenced by previous ecumenical deliberations, especially the Princeton International Round Table. In its "Message to the Churches" the Conference recommended that the churches support the Dumbarton Oaks proposals "as an important step in the direction of world cooperation." Nine specific changes, however, were proposed. The conference called for a preamble reaffirming the purposes of justice and human welfare of the Atlantic Charter, a clear statement that the U.N. Charter would operate under international law, the required abstention of nations from vote in cases involving themselves, and liberal provisions for amending the Charter. Special concern was expressed for the progress of colonial and dependent areas to autonomy, and for establishing a special commission on human rights and fundamental freedoms. The Conference proposed that all nations be eligible for membership, that armaments be limited, and that small nations be defended against the arbitrary power of the great.[24]

The clear intention of the Conference and its organizers was to impact decision makers and mobilize public opinion. Denominational agencies distributed 700,000 pieces of Commission literature related to the Conference, including its Message. Copies of the Message were placed in the hands of the U.S. President, Secretary of State, members of Congress, and the delegates to the San Francisco Conference.

23. *Encyclopedia Britannica*, s.v. "United Nations."
24. "Cleveland Conference." The Conference built also on the work of a first National Study Conference on the Churches and a Just and Durable Peace held at Ohio Wesleyan University, Delaware, Ohio, March 1942. Its message included guiding principles, general statements on political, economic, and social bases for peace, and an affirmation that the church's mission required its involvement in peace issues. No specific proposals concerning human rights or world order were given (National Study Conf., *Message*).

As the San Francisco Conference ended in June 1945, Nolde reflected on the impact of the churches upon its deliberations. The Charter had been liberalized, placing the world body clearly under international law with responsibility for the defense of human rights. Comparing the Charter with the Dumbarton Oaks proposals, the improvements both in concepts and in specific wording reflected closely the impact of the churches.[25]

THE MISSION TO BUILD A LASTING PEACE

On June 26, 1945, the Executive Committee of the FCC expressed satisfaction that the U.N. Charter embodied "many of the changes recommended by thoughtful Christians." And to the churches it issued this statement and challenge:

> To establish a strong core of world-minded Christians at the center of international life is the inescapable duty of the ecumenical Church. To this end we need to intensify our efforts for Christian reconstruction and missions. We must increase our educational programs for training Christian citizens in their obligations in an interdependent world. We ought to help build the World Council of Churches into the living expression of God's will for the Christian community. Let Christian fellowship pioneer in international understanding and reconciliation, so that all of the family of nations may work together in harmony![26]

In 1946 Nolde completed for the Commission on a Just and Durable Peace a survey of the opinions of heads of church agencies in forty-four countries. This told of "an unprecedented eagerness to apply Christian principles to international relations" during the Second World War. However, with the cessation of hostilities, cooperation between Roman Catholics and Protestants dropped off and became once again "spotty and inconsistent." Nolde in his conclusions judged as exemplary the prophetic witness by church leaders at the San Francisco Conference. In contrast churches "generally have not succeeded in establishing effective

---

25. FCC, *Annual Report* (1945), 52. A chapter of Nolde's unpublished manuscript entitled "Christian Action in International Affairs—War Years" (in A-WCC/CCIA, "O. Frederick Nolde") contains a detailed comparison of the Dumbarton Oaks proposals, the U.N. Charter, and the churches' proposals.
26. FCC, *Churches and the Charter*, 3.

procedures through which their witness is made articulate among the masses of our secular society."[27]

Could the momentum of San Francisco be maintained? This was a major concern at the inaugural meeting of the Joint Committee of the WCC and IMC. The venerable John R. Mott chaired its first session in Geneva, Switzerland, in February 1946. Those present agreed to set up a common department for international affairs. Furthermore, they determined that religious liberty should be a problem to receive special attention. However, they resolved that "the existence of such a common department should not curtail the freedom of each body to make its own approaches to governments or its own utterances with regard to questions which it considers as its own specific concern." Later the Commission on a Just and Durable Peace, under Nolde's able direction, was asked to convene on behalf of the Joint Committee an international conference of church leaders to consider the problems of peace and war.[28]

Forming the Commission of the Churches on International Affairs (CCIA)

The first project of the Joint Committee was an International Conference of Christian Leaders on the Problem of World Order held at Cambridge University in August 1946. The sixty distinguished participants were a veritable "who's who" of First World ecumenical leaders. Dulles, later to become the U.S. Secretary of State under President Eisenhower, was in the chair, with Walter W. Van Kirk of the FCC and Visser 't Hooft of the WCC as secretaries of the Conference. Reinhold Niebuhr and Emil Brunner were there—respected theologians from both sides of the Atlantic.

Dulles recalled for the group what had happened at the close of the First World War. "The Paris Peace Conference was a shocking affair," he declared. He judged that there had been a "complete absence of any Christian influence whatsoever" on the working of that Conference, although almost all present would have declared themselves to be Christians. None of the church groups "attempted to exer-

27. Nolde, "Comment on Replies to Questionnaire on the Churches and World Order," in A-WCC/CCIA, "Survey."
28. Nolde, "Ecumenical Action," 264. The record of proposals for a separate WCC or joint IMC/WCC committee are found in WCC Provisional Committee, *WCC*, 24, 43–44, 99–102, 128–30; A-WCC/IMC, "Joint Committee," box 270001. See also WCC/A, Evanston 1954, *Report*, 181–82.

cise the slightest influence on the outcome," naively trusting that their members "would automatically carry the Christian tradition into the affairs of the world."[29]

The Conference responded by supporting the IMC-WCC proposal to establish a joint Commission of the Churches on International Affairs (CCIA). It recognized that "the nations are faced with the necessity of political action of unprecedented gravity." Enormous challenges lay ahead to overcome the chaos of war, reshape the world's economic and political life, and achieve peace. It recognized the formidable task of interpreting the will of God in relation to "the tangled problems of world politics and economics." Accurate information and prudent judgment would be needed.

Much attention was given to the mandate and future work of the CCIA. Its primary responsibility should be to serve the churches and ecumenical agencies "as a source of stimulus and knowledge in their approach to international problems, as a medium of common counsel and action, and as their organ in formulating the Christian mind on world issues and in bringing that mind effectively to bear upon such issues." The Conference proposed that the CCIA study selected international problems, and encourage the formation of parallel national bodies. In addition it should represent the WCC and IMC at the U.N. and with related agencies. Article 71 of the U.N. Charter, for example, provided for international NGOs to have such a relationship to it.[30]

CCIA Leadership

For its first twenty-three years the CCIA was led by two remarkable pioneers—Kenneth Grubb as chair, and O. Frederick Nolde as director.

An Anglo-Irishman and Anglican, Grubb headed the Latin American section of the British Ministry of Information and later controlled its overseas publicity during the Second World War. Coeditor of the *World Christian Handbook*, president of the CMS, and officer of numerous church and mission agencies, Grubb brought to his CCIA leadership a wealth of insights and personal contacts. Deftly he fielded the charges in church circles that the Commission was meddling in politics. Chairing the CCIA placed him as its spokesperson at the WCC Central Committee and its assemblies. But Sir Kenneth was not to be cloistered

29. A-WCC/CCIA, "Early History," box 428.0.01.
30. IMC, *Conference of Church Leaders*.

in church councils. Instead, he brought the CCIA staff into active negotiations with political leaders on human rights issues. As African states achieved independence he appealed to their leaders to include human rights guarantees in their new constitutions. Building on his Latin American experience he became the chief representative of the churches to Latin American governments on religious liberty concerns.[31]

Nolde was the unanimous choice as first director of the CCIA. As a professor and the dean of the Graduate School of the Lutheran Theological Seminary in Philadelphia, he had a long-standing concern for the church's leadership in global affairs. He was a member of his denomination's Department of International Justice and Goodwill, and of the Commission to Study Origins of Peace. He also was a member of the Executive Committee of the Board of Trustees of the Carnegie Endowment for International Peace. Through his leadership as part-time executive secretary of the Joint Committee on Religious Liberty, Nolde maintained close links both with the FCC and the FMC. He kept that connection when he became the director of the CCIA in 1946 in order to have a base from which to speak directly to U.S. political leaders on international issues.[32]

ADVOCATING UNIVERSAL HUMAN RIGHTS

In its decision to act as a champion of human rights, the CCIA not only built upon a primary interest of its executive director, but also carried on a long tradition of involvement by the missionary movement. Following World War I, John R. Mott and Charles R. Watson represented an Emergency Committee of Co-operating Missions in seeking through the peace settlement not only missionary freedom, but also religious freedom in the former German colonies to be placed under League of Nations mandate. From its inception the IMC lifted up religious liberty as a paramount concern. It stimulated formation of national committees sharing this concern, such as the Joint Committee in the U.S. organized in 1942, and a similar group in Britain yoking the Conference of British

---

31. Bent, *Christian Response*, 74. See also Grubb, *Crypts*, 163–200, on his CCIA and WCC involvements.

32. Bent, *Christian Response*, 74–75; FMC, *Report* 54 (1948), 54–55; 55 (1949), 93–94; 57 (1950), 82–84. Nolde resigned as executive secretary of the Joint Committee in 1949. In the ensuing transfer from a Federal Council to a National Council of Churches, with changes of staff, momentum was lost and no concerted church effort was made to gain ratification by the U.S. Congress of the Universal Declaration of Human Rights.

One World: The Secular Vision

Missionary Societies and the British Council of Churches.[33] Truly, "much of the impulse for the protection of religious freedom had originally come from the Protestant missionary movement."[34]

A unique opportunity to influence world order emerged in 1946. In that year the U.N. established its Human Rights Commission. It was given primary responsibility for "promoting and encouraging respect for human rights and for fundamental freedoms." It needed to be a major actor if the U.N. Charter was to be fulfilled "to achieve international cooperation . . . in promoting and encouraging respect for human rights and for fundamental freedoms for all without distinction as to race, sex, language, or religion." Eighteen nations appointed members. They elected Eleanor Roosevelt of the U.S. as their first chairperson and Charles Malik of Lebanon as secretary.[35]

Nolde had close friendships with both Roosevelt and Malik and poured his energies into a unique partnership. He was present at most of the eighty-five major sessions of the Commission, as well as those of many of its subcommittees. So great was his knowledge and commitment that language in his "Draft Statement on Article 16" on religious liberty became incorporated in the Declaration as adopted by the U.N.[36]

As the drafting process continued the CCIA's concerns broadened. They began with a focus on issues of religious freedom. This included freedom for public expression of belief, freedom of thought and conscience, and the right to change one's religious affiliation or beliefs. The latter was included only after strenuous debate and lobbying. Fortunately, the First Assembly of the WCC met in Amsterdam prior to the U.N.'s session in Paris in 1948. The CCIA helped to draft an influential WCC report which stated, "Churches should support every endeavour to secure within an international bill of rights adequate safeguards for freedom of religion and conscience, including rights of all persons to hold and change their

---

33. Hogg, *Foundations*, 183–90, 327; A-WCC/CCIA, "Mailings."
34. Little, "Foreword," x.
35. A-WCC/CCIA, "CCIA NY"; Nolde, "Possible Functions," 144.
36. Of his participation Mrs. Roosevelt was later to write: "Dr. Nolde has attended almost every session of the Commission on Human Rights. He is one of the few observers representing non-governmental organizations who attends as constantly as the delegates do. Because he is such a careful observer he sometimes gauges the mood of the members more accurately than we ourselves do." (Roosevelt, "Introduction," 3). See also Nurser, *Peoples*, 160–71, for a detailed history of the deliberations and Nolde's contribution.

faith, to express it in worship and practice, to teach and persuade others, and to decide on the religious education of their children."[37]

Other rights of particular concern to the CCIA included freedoms of opinion and expression across all frontiers, of assembly, of association, of education including the prior right of parents in the education of their children, and freedom from the retroactive application of penal law. At the 1948 Paris U.N. Assembly Nolde also devoted much time to lobbying for the Convention on Genocide, and to preserving the clause in the Universal Declaration granting "freedom to change one's religion or belief," as it was under attack by several predominantly Muslim nations.[38] The narrow concern of the missionary societies had been to secure "freedom for missionaries (including foreign nationals) to preach at will anywhere in the postwar world, and for their hearers to be free to convert to Christianity without penalty."[39] Under Nolde's leadership the CCIA broadened its human rights concerns. Religious freedom was placed firmly in the context of other human rights, with a campaign for their adoption as a total package. Nevertheless, the right to change one's religion or belief was included only after strenuous debate and lobbying.

On December 10, 1948, the U.N. General Assembly formally adopted the Universal Declaration of Human Rights by a vote of forty-eight in favor, none against, and eight abstentions. The preamble included the fundamental "recognition of the inherent dignity and of the equal and inalienable rights of all members of the human family."

Ten years later Malik, then president of the U.N. General Assembly, gave his judgment that "never has organized humanity spoken with one voice so emphatically on the nature of man." He continued, "The message comes from the combined and considered views of all religions, all cultures and all outlooks."[40]

Such concerns did not end with the passage of the U.N. Declaration on Human Rights. In 1950, for example, NGOs met with Eleanor Roosevelt to consider next steps. They stressed the importance of completing the Covenant on Human Rights "as adding to the body of international law on human rights and definitely making human rights

---

37. Nolde, *Free*, 38–41; WCC/A, Amsterdam 1948, *First Assembly*, 93–94.
38. Nolde, *Free*, 39–46.
39. Nurser, *Peoples*, 174.
40. A-WCC/CCIA, "Mailings."

the subject of international concern." Even that would not constitute a completed bill of rights, in their judgment, for "the battle for human freedom is never-ending." They expressed deep concern for enforcement and establishing rights for individual and group petition.[41]

In the years that followed the CCIA continued in human rights advocacy. In the 1950s it gave particular emphasis to four aspects: provisions for religious liberty, rights of parents in the education of their children, threats to religious liberty from national suspension of human rights during states of emergency, and rights of individuals and NGOs to petition under the U.N.'s human rights covenants and protocols.[42]

How shall we assess the contribution of the CCIA, representing as it did both the IMC and the WCC? Consider the judgment of insider Malik of Lebanon. To Nolde he wrote on June 29, 1949, "The text on freedom of thought and conscience is your own contribution. Other representatives of the churches contributed other texts, particularly in relation to the family. You have also helped considerably in preparing the atmosphere and contacting delegates." Malik, the Christian statesman, continued, "Equally important with these direct material fruits is your sheer presence with us. To those of us who believe in Christ and His Church nothing heartens us more in our arduous and at times frustrated endeavors than the presence of church representatives. Through this presence we realize that He cares. I assure you in dark moments this mere realization is enough."

Later he would add that Nolde "acquired such a reputation for fairness and objectivity that when the non-governmental organizations sought someone to represent them as a group, almost always they asked him to speak in their name." Nolde's personal assessment was that "at no previous time have the non-Roman churches attempted [so] to coordinate their resources for effective testimony in the world of nations." That this was achieved, with the Declaration accepted as the view on humanity of all religions, made this the churches' finest hour in their advocacy for human rights.[43]

---

41. Ibid.
42. WCC/A, Evanston 1954, *Report*, 136.
43. A-WCC/CCIA, "CCIA: WCC Gen. Sec."; Malik, "Universal," 10; Nolde, "Amsterdam," 412.

THE CCIA'S LATER CONCERNS AND INVOLVEMENTS

Having concentrated first on issues of human rights, the Commission expanded its concerns in later years. It gave increasing attention to the promotion of peace with justice and freedom, and to self-determination of peoples under colonial or alien domination.[44]

The CCIA's style at the U.N. has been one of "quiet diplomacy." Its observers attend the annual sessions of the Commission on Human Rights and report on its activities to their network of concerned church leaders around the world. Informal contacts with members of various U.N. commissions, and submission of position papers, are added ways of influence. The Commission grew in its monitoring function on behalf of the churches, and sometimes became an active participant in conflict resolution, such as the 1971 negotiation to end seventeen years of civil war in Sudan.

Since 1968 the CCIA has been authorized to negotiate directly in its own name and that of the WCC with the U.N. and other international bodies. It is formally registered as an NGO with the U.N. Economic and Social Council and its commissions, the Food and Agriculture Organization (FAO), and UNESCO. Contacts are kept with most agencies of the U.N.[45]

The forty-person Commission enables creative politicians, academics, and church leaders to focus their energies as committed Christians upon major international issues. Dulles served as a CCIA commissioner until he was appointed U.S. Secretary of State. On the tenth anniversary of the CCIA he recalled its accomplishment, adding, "I am confident that, if the religious resources throughout the world are effectively utilized, the dynamic action which is an indispensable requisite for a creative and curative peace will be assured." Malik also served as a commissioner while also his country's U.N. delegate, president of the UNO's Economic and Social Council, and secretary of its Human Rights Commission.

---

44. See Nolde, *Churches*; and the special issue *ER* 19 (1967) 113–238 on the first twenty years (1947–67) of the CCIA. For the later significance of the Universal Declaration of Human Rights see Heideman, "Significance."

45. See Bent, *Christian Response*, for a brief history of the Commission and its work, and A-WCC/CCIA, "Mailings," for documents. Potter, in "On Coming-of-Age," questions whether the CCIA has "come of age" if it is "predominately Western in its orientation" and not representative of the problems and crises in Asia, Africa, Latin America, and the Near East.

Such linkages have given CCIA commissioners and staff ready access to decision makers in the world body.[46]

ONE GOSPEL—ONE WORLD

In 1973 Philip Potter, in his report as general secretary to the WCC's Central Committee, reported on the Council's phenomenal growth in its first twenty-five years. Membership increased to include 263 churches in over 90 countries. Most Orthodox, Protestant, and Anglican churches had become members. Some Pentecostal and independent churches had also joined. Close working relationships had been established with the Roman Catholic Church.

The West Indian general secretary next gave a broadened understanding of unity. He returned to the original Greek meaning of *oikoumene*. Potter reminded the church leaders that "ecumenical" refers "not only to the coming and being together of churches, but more biblically to 'the whole inhabited earth' of men and women struggling to become what they were intended to be in the purpose of God." He continued, "The ecumenical movement is thus seen to be wherever Christians and others are one way or another seeking to work for the unity of [humanity]." Behind this understanding is the faith that the whole earth belongs to God, and that God is actively at work for the redemption of all humankind and all creation. "Thus the search for the unity of the Church," he concluded, "is inextricably bound up with the struggle for the unity of [humanity]."[47]

The IMC pioneered in actions representative of this understanding of unity. Its joint action with the WCC through the CCIA is a clear example of its acceptance of the political mission of the churches. In moving in this direction the churches lived out together a dynamic understanding of the church. The body of Christ, from this perspective, is neither an aggregate of buildings nor of church hierarchies. It is the people of God in action—throbbing like a human heart. At one time they gather together for worship and study and feel Christ's living presence through the Eucharist. At another they join their living Savior in mission and service in a needy world. This may include political action as the church fulfills its mission to be "the salt of the earth and the light of the world."[48]

---

46. J. Dulles, "Measures," 389.
47. Potter, "Report," 415–17.
48. Teinonen, *Missio*, 36, 66.

Nolde, in "Religion and the United Nations," stressed the importance of this approach for political leaders. Those who would build for humankind a world of peace, with order and justice, need religious leaders as their allies. Religion has a particular stake and distinctive contribution to offer wherever human factors dominate in decision-making. He reminded his readers that leading politicians and scientists declare that the fundamental issues of our day are spiritual and moral. Finally, "one conclusion seems unavoidable. The power of religion must be brought to bear more directly upon our human problems if there is to be *peace on earth, goodwill among [all persons]*."[49]

---

49. A-WCC/CCIA, "O. Frederick Nolde ." The noted church historian Kenneth Scott Latourette concurred on the importance of the religious factor: "The Christian faith has been of great importance in the creation of the League of Nations and of its successor, the United Nations.... The chief architect of the League of Nations, Woodrow Wilson, was inspired and sustained in his effort by a profound Christian faith ... the churches as churches had a much greater share in preparing the way for the United Nations" (Latourette, *Christian Outlook*, 76).

15

Christianity and Other Faiths

"ONE OF THE MOST encouraging phenomena of our times is a worldwide and sincere desire for mutual understanding and a real thirst for universality." With these words Raymond Panikkar in 1964 continued to develop a newer Christian approach to unity. It is not one of seeking the minimum that we have in common, the young Indian theologian argued. Instead, it is a striving "to reach a deeper and more real Christian unity." He commended those Christian churches which had engaged in dialogue and encounter in this way.

Then Panikkar proposed a search for a wider unity. He called it an "ecumenical ecumenism." In it participants would engage "not only in the dialogue and encounter between Christian confessions, but also between religions." Returning more recently to the same theme, Panikkar described it as a common search for truth through dialogue rather than debate. In it persons are not only open to one another, but also to new understandings of divine immanence and transcendence.[1]

What has the missionary movement contributed in the twentieth century to a vision of a wider human unity which includes persons of other faiths? That question is the focus of this chapter.

MISSIONS, UNITY, AND THE RELIGIONS

Edinburgh 1910

In preparation for the 1910 World Missionary Conference, John R. Mott wrote to individuals and missionary organizations around the world. He asked, "Do you consider that we now have on the home field a type of

---

1. Panikkar, *Unknown Christ*, 62–66; idem, "Editorial," 782.

Christianity which should be propagated all over the world? And does this type possess world propagating and world conquering power?"[2]

Commission 1 on "Carrying the Gospel to all the Non-Christian World" reflected the triumphalism prevailing among the respondents. It concluded that the church was at the critical time to make Christ known to all the non-Christian world. Delegates judged that ancient faiths were in demise, either weakened or abandoned. Meanwhile nations in the East were awakening and looking both for enlightenment and liberty. They believed that only Christianity, with its roots in an ethic of self-sacrifice and love, had the potential to satisfy these aspirations.[3]

Commission 4 on "The Missionary Message in Relation to Non-Christian Religions" based its report on more than 200 answers to a questionnaire sent to missionaries (and some nationals) on their experience in preaching the gospel to people of other faith traditions. The report emphasized the "points of contact" between the religious life of the people of Asia and the gospel message. It also highlighted what scholars of world religions later judged to be the highpoint of the Conference—the growing conviction that the gospel fulfills other religions that are of worth in themselves.[4]

Jerusalem 1928

The world had inalterably changed by the time of the next world missionary conference at Jerusalem. Confidence that Western Christendom would provide the model for all emerging peoples died in the trenches at Verdun and the Somme together with the flower of Europe's youth. The awakening of Majority World peoples was an unquestioned social reality, together with the resurgence of their historic faiths.

The central issue for the conference was how Christian missions were to respond to this reality. Concerning the Christian life and message in relation to non-Christian systems of life and thought, a study commission asked, "What are the various elements of good and evil in the non-Christian religions and what should be our attitude toward them? How far are individuals to be won from the non-Christian reli-

---

2. Reprinted in Kähler, *Schriften*, 257–58.
3. *World Missionary Conference, 1910*, 1:362; 9:145.
4. See Cracknell, *Justice* for Protestant attitudes towards other faiths from 1846 to 1914, and Stanley, ed., *World*, 205–47, for a fuller analysis of the Edinburgh debate and documents.

gions to Christ, and how far are the religions themselves convertible or absorbable by Christianity?"⁵

The Jerusalem debate was lively. Participants from Western Europe emphasized the uniqueness of the Christian gospel. From this perspective the convert was to renounce completely his or her old system of religious belief and practices. Voices from North America appealed to insights from the comparative study of religions. They recognized elements of value in non-Christian religions, believing that Christianity could be presented as the fulfillment of other historic faiths. Pandipeddi Chenchiah from India argued that non-Christian religions are no longer in opposition to Christianity "but like secular sciences have become the competitors of Christianity." Francis Wei and T. C. Chao of China saw Christianity as the religion that "fulfills" the best in Confucian culture.⁶

The official statement of the Council from Jerusalem sought to meld these viewpoints. On the one hand, Christ was affirmed as the one in whom we find God incarnate, "the final, yet ever-unfolding, revelation of the God in whom we live and move and have our being." On the other hand, the call to non-Christians contains the belief that God who sent Christ "has nowhere left Himself without witness." Rays of the light of Christ were believed to be present in the noble qualities of non-Christians even where Christ remains unknown or is rejected. These were potential seeds for a theology of religions.⁷

In the 1930s alternative Christian responses to other faiths became known as "the Hocking-Kraemer debate." William Ernest Hocking, professor of philosophy at Harvard University, represented that continuing liberal openness to other faiths that had inspired the 1893 World Parliament of Religions. He regarded secularism as the decisive missionary problem, with an alliance of world religions the best antidote. Hocking proposed a Christian attitude of openness. "Christianity must speak the language and use the conceptions of other religions, in order to be understood," he argued at the Jerusalem missionary conference in 1928. Rather than the goal of "conquest of the world by Christianity," he favored strengthening the best or "whatever is genuine in the non-Christian religions."⁸

5. A-WCC/IMC, "Joint Committee," box 261003.
6. Hogg, *Foundations*, 247; Hallencreutz, "Tambaram," 351; IMC Conf., Jerusalem 1928, *Meeting*, 1:17, 358–59.
7. IMC Conf., Jerusalem 1928, *Meeting*, 1:402, 410.
8. Ibid., 1:302; Laymen's Inquiry, *Rethinking*, 35, 38.

Hendrik Kraemer sharply disagreed. He was at that time both a missionary to Indonesia and secretary of the Netherlands Bible Society. Kraemer voiced at Jerusalem the concerns of Dutch and German delegates as he declared, "However great our appreciation of the religious values and forces in other religions may be, we simply may not and cannot move from the fundamental base and nerve of all real missionary activity; that God revealed Himself by His saving acts towards mankind in history and in an absolutely unique and unsurpassable way in Jesus Christ, who is the way to come to the Father, the divine token of mercy and reconciliation."[9]

The Laymen's Report

The Hocking position received a controversial presentation in *Rethinking Mission*, the report of the Laymen's Foreign Mission Inquiry published in 1932. The report included a call for Christian missions to join with other religions in a common search for truth: "Look not at what is weak or corrupt in those faiths, but at what is strong and sound in them. That offers the best hearing for whatever Christianity may have to say. Within the piety of the common people of every land," it continues, encrusted though it may be with superstition, there is "the inalienable religious intuition of the human soul." Critics leading several mission societies responded in fear that this more positive evaluation of other faiths would cut at the very nerve of the missionary endeavor.[10]

Tambaram/Madras 1938

In preparation for the next world mission conference, the IMC asked Hendrik Kraemer "to write a book on evangelism in the modern world, with especial reference to the non-Christian religions." The purpose was "to state the fundamental position of the Christian Church as a witness-bearing body in the modern world, relating this to different conflicting views of the attitude to be taken by Christians towards other faiths."[11]

Kraemer's magnum opus, *The Christian Message in a Non-Christian World*, became the preparatory volume for the conference. He rejected all natural theologies which would draw values from various religions.

---

9. IMC Conf., Jerusalem 1928, *Meeting*, 1: 346.

10. Laymen's Inquiry, *Rethinking*, 37; Hogg, *Foundations*, 282; Hutchison, *Errand*, 158–75.

11. IMC, Meetings, *Minutes* (1936), 15.

Instead of seeking points of contact in other faiths for communicating the Christian message, he found in "biblical realism" the only grounds for normative truth. For Kraemer "evangelization, proselytism and conversion, then, belong to the core of the missionary enterprise."[12]

The Dutch scholar's theology of radical discontinuity between Christianity and other living religions, however, did not go unchallenged. A. G. Hogg, the distinguished principal of Madras Christian College, responded with an alternative form of biblical realism. It include belief in the revelation of an Almighty God "who longs to make of His human children little comrades, and is ever taking the initiative toward that end." The paradox is that where Christ has not yet been spiritually apprehended, persons by other ways come to trust in God. Hogg believed that such faith "enables our Heavenly Father to bestow on a [person] some measure of communion with Himself." The best-known critic of Kraemer's approach was E. Stanley Jones, the world evangelist, who through ashrams shared spiritual experiences with Hindus. He preferred an emphasis on the kingdom of God, which he judged to be more inclusive and socially radical than Kraemer's emphasis on the church.[13]

In the final Madras statement a contrast was drawn between Jerusalem and Madras. Whereas Jerusalem faced the challenge from a godless secularism, Madras met the challenge of a "new paganism" represented by resurgent nationalism, Marxist communism, and scientific skepticism. As for non-Christian religions, in them were to be found "values of deep religious experiences and great moral achievements." God has not been left without witnesses in any age, although that seeking and longing has often been misdirected. There are, however, "glimpses of God's light in the world of religions, showing that His yearning after His erring children has not been without response." Furthermore, each church should be rooted in the soil of its own country as an authentic indigenous form of Christianity. But each church and believing Christian also must be rooted in the Christian heritage and fellowship of the church universal, with faith in God as revealed fully in Jesus Christ, His Son, our Lord.[14]

---

12. Kraemer, *Message*, 296. IMC Conf., Madras 1938, *Papers*, 1:172-199, contains the Conference findings. See also Hallencreutz, *Kraemer*; Jongeneel, "Christianity"; Mulder, "Dialogue"; and Potter, "WCC" for later assessments of Kraemer's contribution.

13. IMC Conf., Madras 1938, *Papers*, 1:114; Hallencreutz, *New Approaches*, 30-31.

14. Ibid., 178-86. Hallencreutz notes that this report of Section I, in which D. T. Niles served as secretary, "does not reflect a forthright Kraemerian takeover of the discussion" and is open to different interpretations (Hallencreutz, "Tambaram," 356).

UNITY AND DIALOGUE

New Delhi to Uppsala

The next major ecumenical conference held in Asia was the WCC's Third Assembly (New Delhi 1961). Paul D. Devanandan of the Church of South India presented the keynote address on "Called to Witness." He declared that the witness of the church begins with the congregation as the "community of the New Age," but it also must be a witness in a world of other faiths. He challenged Christians so to engage in serious conversation with persons of other faiths that they would become "instruments of interpretation of the Gospel." The report on witness picked up this idea in the affirmation that dialogue is "a form of evangelism which is often effective today."[15]

Dialogue was not a new concern for the World Council or its member churches in their life and work. The Division of World Mission and Evangelism linked Christian study centers engaged in dialogue. Jewish-Christian dialogue was a major interest of the Committee on the Church and the Jewish People. Meanwhile the Ecumenical Institute at Bossey sponsored programs involving people of different faiths and ideologies.[16]

As early as 1956 the WCC's Central Committee approved a study project on "The Word of God and the Living Faiths of Men." With the merger of the IMC and WCC in 1961 this became part of the mission division's concern. In the consultations that it sponsored in the next nine years an important shift took place. From the study of religions as systems of thought and ritual the conversations shifted to dialogue between people of living faiths as they shared in the lives of their communities. Protestant, Orthodox, and Roman Catholic participants in the 1967 consultation at Kandy, Sri Lanka, declared, "True dialogue is a progressive and cumulative process, which takes place not only through verbal communication, but through the dynamic contact of life with life. . . . Nothing less than living in dialogue is the responsibility and privilege to which we are called."[17]

---

15. WCC/A, New Delhi 1961, *Report*, 1, 12, 84.
16. Samartha, "Christian Study Centres"; idem, "WCC," 193.
17. Samartha, "Dialogue with Men of Living Faiths and Ideologies: A Brief Report," in A-WCC/DWG, "Departmental"; "Christians in Dialogue," 340. See also Sheard, *Dialogue*, 135–270, for the development of the WCC's thought concerning dialogue to 1979.

The WCC's Faith and Order Commission in 1967 raised the question, "What is the function of the church in relation to the unifying purpose of God for the world?" A year later Bishop Lesslie Newbigin spoke to that question at the WCC's Fourth Assembly (Uppsala 1968). He sharpened the debate as he asked, "Is the restoration of the visible unity of the Church something of really primary importance for the Christian today? Is it not far more important to be concerned with the unity of the whole human family?" The Assembly report included the affirmation that "The Church is bold in speaking of itself as the sign of the coming unity of mankind."[18]

Uppsala outlined as no assembly before it the task of working towards a viable form of world community. There was a sharp awareness of the growing interdependence of humankind, yet of the inevitable problems that would arise as nations and peoples became more involved with each other. The report adopted on "Renewal in Mission" included dialogue concerns. Assuaging the fears of some, the Council declared that "a Christian's dialogue with another implies neither a denial of the uniqueness of Christ, nor any loss of his own commitment to Christ." The genuinely Christian approach to others is to be "human, personal, relevant and humble." The report continued, "In dialogue we share our common humanity, its dignity and fallenness, and express our common concern for that humanity. Dialogue includes sharing of common concerns. It may result in common service to meet human needs. We recognize a mutual challenge when each party shares deeply in word and in action."[19]

Stanley J. Samartha

Two months after Uppsala, Stanley J. Samartha joined the World Council staff as director of its program of studies on Mission and Evangelism. Former principal of Serampore College and professor at the United Theological College in Bangalore, India, Samartha came to Geneva with solid credentials as a pioneer in interreligious dialogue.[20]

Samartha's proposals found a responsive chord. The Central Committee welcomed the increased emphasis on dialogue, and encouraged his department to "study further the relation between dialogue and mis-

---

18. WCC/CFO Conf., Bristol 1967, *New Directions*, 131-32; Newbigin, "Which Way," 128; WCC/A, Uppsala 1968, *Report*, 17.
19. WCC/A, Uppsala 1968, *Report*, 29.
20. See Samartha, *Between Two Cultures* for his later reflections on his lifetime of involvement in interreligious dialogue.

sion" as well as the relation between our common humanity with other persons and our new humanity in Christ.[21]

Dialogue with Living Faiths and Ideologies

The Ajaltoun (Beirut) Consultation in 1970 was Samartha's giant step forward. There for the first time the WCC brought together leaders of four major faiths: Hinduism, Buddhism, Christianity, and Islam. The goal was to move dialogue from polite bilateral conversations to become a more global forum. It was to be an engagement in dialogue itself, not another consultation *about* dialogue. Christian participants came away with a new appreciation of what sharing one's particular witness can mean in building world community. Dialogue was understood as response to God's call to the whole church to work for the unity and the building up of "the truly universal community of mankind."[22]

Recognizing the need to develop a theology of dialogue, twenty-three scholars from fifteen countries, including four Orthodox Christians and three Roman Catholics, met in Zurich, Switzerland in 1970. They began with the understanding that dialogue is an integral part of an open and authentic human existence. For Christians it begins with God's activity for the salvation of the whole world. They declared that it is "the grace of God that draws us out of our isolation into genuine dialogue." Therefore, dialogue is neither a *betrayal* of mission, nor a *new tool for mission*. Instead, it is an integral part of faithful mission "which neither betrays the commitment of the Christian nor exploits the confidence and the reality" of the partners in dialogue of other faiths.[23]

Dialogue took off like a rocket in 1971. In the new structure of the WCC for Faith and Witness, the dialogue program became a subunit alongside the historic big three: Faith and Order, Mission and Evangelism, and Church and Society. Intentionally, the dialogue program was placed within the larger unit on Faith and Witness "because without its being anchored in faith dialogue is liable to become pleasant conversation, and without the challenge to witness it can easily slip into the shallow waters of relativism." The goal was to advance "an authentic ecumenical understanding of the faith of the Church in our world." The stated goals of the

---

21. WCC/CC, *Minutes* (1969), 29.
22. Potter, "Christians," 384, 389. See also Samartha, "More"; and idem, *Between Two Cultures*, 49–62, for his interpretation of the Ajaltoun Consultation.
23. Potter, "Christians," 382, 384–85.

Dialogue program were "to promote dialogue with [persons] of living faiths including secular ideologies, and to help the churches discern its implications for their life and for the understanding and communication of the Gospel in different situations."[24]

"Dialogue has become a permanent Christian obligation." This was the judgment in 1971 of Carl Hallencreutz, the mission specialist from Uppsala, Sweden. No longer is it confined to the particular sphere of "foreign mission," he continued. The interest in various religions has increased as Asian peoples have migrated to every continent. Just as the term "foreign mission" has been superseded by "mission in six continents," so interest in interreligious dialogue has spread from Asia to other continents. What is at stake, he concluded, is nothing less than "a new grasp of God's purpose" for humanity as a whole.[25]

Nairobi 1975

The WCC's Fifth Assembly (Nairobi 1975) had global community as a central theme. Section 3 was titled "Seeking Community: The Common Search of People of Various Faiths, Cultures and Ideologies." Discussion focused on three questions:

1. What kind of community are Christians committed to seek?
2. In what ways can dialogue help or hinder people of living faiths in their search for community?
3. What are the ideological dimensions in the search for community?

More specifically, concerning mission and dialogue these questions were raised: "What is the *nature* of Christian witness and what are its *forms* in the context of dialogue? Are 'dialogue' and 'mission' really valid alternatives? Does openness in dialogue betray Christ-centeredness? Is dialogue a tool for mission or a betrayal of it? To what extent and by what criteria could we recognize any validity in the truth claims and even the 'missions' of other faiths and ideologies?"[26]

Sharp differences emerged as the Assembly debated the draft report. While some delegates characterized it as too cautious, the majority of speakers believed it would be understood as spiritual compromise.

---

24. WCC/CC, *Minutes* (1971), 18–22, 130–35, 162; (1973), 69.
25. Hallencreutz, "Long-Standing Concern," 71.
26. WCC/A, Nairobi 1975, *Workbook*, 33, 37–38; Samartha, *Between Two Cultures*, 103–10.

Particularly objectionable were paragraphs stating that Christians should not allow their faith to add to the divisions of humanity "because, as fellow-creatures of God, we are linked together." To this Bishop Lesslie Newbigin responded, "The one holy reason we have for seeking community is that God has become man and reconciled man to God. What separates us is our sin. It is on this basis that we have to seek for community for all."

The revised preamble opened with the affirmation that belief in Jesus Christ will always be a *skandalon* (stumbling block) and the cause of tension. It continued, "Dialogue is both a matter of hearing and understanding the faith of others, and also of witnessing to the gospel of Jesus Christ." Several delegates from Asia would have preferred a stronger endorsement of the dialogue approach. Russell Chandran of the Church of South India spoke for them in suggesting that those who preach Christ to people of other faiths can in the witness of others expect "to learn about the fullness of the reality of Christ."[27]

A first for a WCC Assembly was the presence at Nairobi of five guests belonging to other faiths. Two reactions on their part to the debate on dialogue may be revealing. One said, "From the Assembly I have learned that there is a Christian Church, and not just churches." Another responded, "We seem to get along fine talking with Christians. But can you Christians talk with one another?"[28]

Chiang Mai 1977

Returning from Nairobi, leaders in the WCC's Dialogue subunit realized that many ecumenical leaders still questioned the compatibility of dialogue and mission, and feared that dialogue would lead to religious syncretism. The succeeding consultations addressed these concerns, most notably that held at Chiang Mai, Thailand, in April 1977 with the theme, "Dialogue in Community."[29]

A first concern was the nature of the community Christians were called upon to seek. The vision from Chiang Mai was of a worldwide "community of communities"—not of homogeneous unity or totalitarian uniformity, but one in which each faith community would retain its distinctiveness yet contribute to the good of all.

27. WCC/A, Nairobi 1975, *Breaking Barriers*, 70–73.
28. R. Edwards, *Nairobi*, 29.
29. WCC/CC, *Nairobi*, 110–12.

Second, the consultation reaffirmed that dialogue was part of the Christian ministry in a pluralistic world. It was understood to be "a means of living out our faith in Christ in service of community with our neighbors." Such service includes "giving witness," without witness and dialogue being in any contradiction to each other.

Third, the Chiang Mai participants considered whether or not God was at work among people of other faiths and ideologies. They felt that no agreement could be reached on the salvific activity of other religions. Left for further theological attention was the question whether the WCC should speak of "God's self-disclosure to people of living faiths." They also assigned for further study the biblical foundation for dialogue and openness to peoples of other faiths.

Every effort was made at Chiang Mai to be in continuity with the WCC consensus reached at the Nairobi Assembly in 1975. Although by intention the words "mission" and "evangelism" were not often used in the Consultation's documents, the desire was to explore other ways of affirming the Nairobi theme, "Confess Christ Today." As a result the new "Guidelines on Dialogue," as approved in 1979 by the WCC Central Committee in Kingston, Jamaica, repeat almost word for word the Chiang Mai declaration.[30]

Melbourne 1980 to Vancouver 1983

The Chiang Mai consultation and the "Guidelines" were the high water mark for the Dialogue unit of the WCC. Its pioneer director, Stanley Samartha, left in 1980, with Wesley Ariarajah of Sri Lanka, his replacement, not appointed as program director until 1983. It was the tide of Latin American concerns that swept in as Emilio Castro succeeded Philip Potter first as head of Mission and Evangelism for the WCC, and then as its general secretary.

The mission arm of the Council considered dialogue to be the concern of another program unit. It was scarcely mentioned at the next world mission conference at Melbourne in 1980. There the focus was on participation in God's mission among the poor. The agenda of liberation theologians from Latin America was in the ascendancy. Emphasizing the theme "Your Kingdom Come," Melbourne delegates affirmed that

---

30. Samartha, ed., *Faith*, 134–49; idem, *Between Two Cultures*, 111–30; Sheard, *Dialogue*, 238–70. WCC, *Guidelines on Dialogue* was revised as *Ecumenical Considerations* in 2003.

God is present in human struggles for dignity and human rights. "Is God at work in the revivals of religions which are one dimension of that struggle?" they asked. But they did not give a simple "yes" or "no" answer. Yes, God may be seen to be at work wherever religious revival enhances human dignity. But negative elements not of God are present, as they are also in the life of Christian churches. As for any salvific value of other faiths, no opinion was given.

This last position did not please those in Asia immersed in dialogue concerns. "The focus of Melbourne was not on Asia," a Christian Conference of Asia correspondent concluded. "Our captivities include the captivity of the traditional Christian understanding of other religions." The writer called for "liberation into dialogue" because the resurgence of religions is a reality of Asian existence. His assessment was that Melbourne "had little to offer to Asian Christians in their predicament of religious pluralism."[31]

Vancouver 1983 to San Antonio 1989

Dialogue received a mixed reception once again at the World Council's Sixth Assembly (Vancouver 1983). Again persons of other faiths were present at a WCC Assembly, and this time permitted to address the delegates in plenary session. But there was sharp opposition to the first wording of the report on "Witnessing in a Divided World" that "we recognize God's creative work in the religious experience of people of other faiths." The amendment, as approved later by the WCC's Central Committee, sounded like Tambaram 1938. Prefaced by the reaffirmation of "the uniqueness of the birth, life, death and resurrection of Jesus," it read, "we recognize God's creative work in the *seeking for religious truth* among people of other faiths." The theological outcome, in Wesley Ariarajah's view, was that the WCC allowed for *seeking* within other faiths but discounted the possibility of *finding*. Clearly it was a mistake to expect a world ecumenical assembly to develop a new theology of the religions.[32]

Recognizing that the WCC appeared to speak with two discordant voices, its leaders in mission, evangelism, and dialogue covenanted in 1988–89 to reconsider the interrelation between mission and dialogue.[33]

31. WCC/CWME Conf., Melbourne 1980, *Kingdom*, xiv, 187; "Melbourne 1980," 6.
32. WCC/A, Vancouver 1983, *Gathered*, 40; Ariarajah, "San Antonio," 7.
33. Duraisingh, "Issues," 398.

Christianity and Other Faiths

Fifty years after the 1938 IMC Conference at Tambaram, where the issues of mission and dialogue had been so vigorously discussed, an international team of scholars updated the debate at the same location. Stanley Samartha, former director of the WCC's Dialogue program, called for a breakthrough in the present "confusion" over the relation between mission and dialogue. He would have based it upon two premises: the acceptance of the plurality of religions, and the re-examination of all exclusivist claims. But the outcome was thirty-five questions on seven issues for further study, with no suggested answers. They included:

1. In what ways is plurality, including religious plurality, within God's purpose?
2. What do we say about the saving work of God through other religious traditions?
3. How do the confessions in other religious traditions of decisiveness/ uniqueness/ universality challenge and clarify Christian convictions about the uniqueness of Jesus Christ?[34]

This set the stage for a full debate on mission and dialogue at the WCC's World Conference on Mission and Evangelism (San Antonio 1989). What Ariarajah described as "an almost forgotten agenda for fifty years" regained its prominence. The theology of religions was back on to the world mission agenda. Eugene Stockwell, in his opening address as director of the WCC's Commission on World Mission and Evangelism (CWME), chose to make this one of the four main issues for the Conference. For the first time at a world mission conference persons of other faiths became consultants and active discussion participants.[35]

Most of the work at San Antonio was done in section meetings rather than in plenary sessions. Section 1, entitled "Witness among People of Other Living Faiths," included leaders and staff representing both the dialogue and the evangelism units of the WCC. It was their joint desire to avoid polarization and achieve a new synthesis between witness, proclamation, and mission concerns on the one hand, and dialogue concerns on the other.

As the participants witnessed to each other about how each had received God's grace through Jesus Christ, a strong consensus emerged that San Antonio must reaffirm the ecumenical movement's evangelis-

---

34. Samartha, "Mission," 320; Stromberg, "Witness," 414, 421.
35. Ariarajah, "San Antonio," 4; WCC/CWME Conf. San Antonio, 1989, *Report*, 124–26.

tic mandate. They agreed that "the proclamation of the gospel includes an invitation to recognize and accept in a personal decision the saving lordship of Christ." Furthermore, they declared that "Christians owe the message of God's salvation in Jesus Christ to every person and to every people." The statement continued, "We cannot point to any other way of salvation than Jesus Christ."[36]

Next, the Section considered the mystery that "the Spirit of God is constantly at work in ways that pass human understanding." They understood that we cannot set limits to the saving power of God. Therefore, "in dialogue we are invited to listen, in openness, to the possibility that the God we know in Jesus Christ may encounter us also in the lives of our neighbours of other faiths." The mood was one of honest sharing of religious experiences rather than of Christian triumphalism. "In entering into a relationship of dialogue with others," they declared, "Christians seek to discern the unsearchable riches of God and the way he deals with humanity." For some persons the attempt at San Antonio to affirm simultaneously God's saving grace through Jesus Christ, and God's Spirit at work in other faiths, is contradictory. For others it is living in creative tension.

Concerning the relation between *witness* and *dialogue*, the delegates concluded that "dialogue has its own place and integrity and is neither opposed to nor incompatible with witness or proclamation." They continued, "We do not water down our own commitment if we engage in dialogue; as a matter of fact, dialogue between people of different faiths is spurious unless it proceeds from the acceptance and expression of faith commitment." With confidence the delegates affirmed "that witness does not preclude dialogue with people of other living faiths, but that dialogue extends and deepens our witness."[37]

The Continuing Debate, 1990–2010

During the past two decades, 1990–2010, the WCC has wrestled with the placement of interfaith concerns within its structure. In 1992 the former subunit on Dialogue became the Office on Inter-Religious Relations attached to the General Secretariat, with a mandate to enable churches in their relationships to people of other faiths, and to respond to specific issues including concrete situations of conflict where religions play a role.

---

36. *ME*, ¶¶ 10, 41; quoted in WCC/CWME Conf., San Antonio 1989, *Report*, 32.
37. WCC/CWME Conf., San Antonio 1989, *Report*, 31–32, 36.

To provide a renewed emphasis on dialogue the office in 1999 became the team on Interreligious Relations and Dialogue.

The Seventh Assembly (Canberra 1991) gave a high profile to interfaith issues. A dramatic presentation by theologian Chung Hyun Kyung of Korea provoked controversy as she invoked spirits of her Korean ancestors in presenting the Canberra theme, "Come, Holy Spirit—Renew the Whole Creation." Fifteen official guests of other faiths spoke at special events and in section plenaries. One subsection was devoted to "Dialogue with Peoples of Other Faiths." Seeking to give a scriptural basis for dialogue, the report read, "We recognize God's covenant with Abraham and Israel. In the history of this covenant we are granted to come to know God through Jesus Christ. We also recognize that other people testify to knowing God through other ways. We witness to the truth that salvation is in Christ and we also remain open to other people's witness to truth as they have experienced it."[38]

The Eighth Assembly (Harare 1998) closed with a recommitment service in which delegates reaffirmed their ecumenical vision, saying, "We open ourselves for a culture of dialogue and solidarity, sharing life with strangers and seeking encounter with those of other faiths." Reaffirming the work of interfaith dialogue, the Assembly amended the WCC Constitution and for the first time identified relations with communities of peoples of other faiths as one of the functions of the fellowship of churches within the Council.[39]

THE ORTHODOX CONTRIBUTION

Since they became members of the WCC in 1961, Orthodox churches have contributed greatly to the deliberations and programs of that body concerning peoples of other faiths and ideologies. Metropolitan Georges Khodr of Lebanon gave one of two key speeches to the WCC Central Committee at Addis Ababa in 1971, along with that of Stanley Samartha, as that body deliberated on creating the WCC's subunit on Dialogue. Representatives of the Orthodox churches have been active leaders in the WCC's advisory groups on dialogue. Bishop Anastasios of Tirana and All Albania has provided major leadership.[40]

---

38. See WCC/A, Canberra 1991, *Signs*, 202–34.

39. Selvanayagam, "Interfaith Dialogue," 160–61; see 149–74 for further details of 1968–2000 developments.

40. Archbishop Anastasios [Yannoulatos] was elected president of the WCC in 2006,

Christians in the West, having lived for many centuries in a more homogenous religious world, often face religious pluralism as a new threat or challenge. By contrast, Christians in the East have long lived in societies having cultural, linguistic and religious pluralism. They honor the patristic fathers who engaged in active dialogue with the Greco-Roman religious and philosophical thinkers of their day. Many have lived under Islamic political domination for more than ten centuries, with important precedents for fruitful dialogue with Muslim scholars. Most have developed attitudes of respect, tolerance, and understanding toward persons of other faiths.[41]

In contrast to most Christianity in the West that centers debate concerning a theology of religions on Christology, the Orthodox approach in general is more anthropological and always based on a Trinitarian perspective. Divine grace is understood "not only as the source of human justification (as in the typical Western outlook), but also as undergirding a process of radical ontological transformation (*theosis*) of God's spiritual and rational creatures." Archbishop Anastasios believed that "dialogue can contribute to transplanting new seeds from one culture to another and to bringing into maturity existing dormant seeds in the field of old religions."[42]

At the first Pan-Orthodox Conference (Chambésy, Geneva, 1976), the Orthodox participants unanimously declared their desire "to contribute to interreligious understanding and cooperation, and in this way to eliminate fanaticism in all aspects, and in every way contribute to the reconciliation of peoples." At the third conference in 1986 the proposals were renewed and developed more systematically. It stated that local Orthodox churches had a duty to work for peace and "brotherly relations between people . . . in close collaboration with all the peace-loving adherents of other religions." However, in spite of occasional efforts to hold unofficial talks with representatives of other faiths, the Orthodox churches have eschewed official theological dialogues.[43]

---

having served as a member of its Central Committee (1998–2006) and as moderator of its Commission on World Mission and Evangelism (1984–1991).

41. Yannoulatos, "Emerging Perspectives," 332; Yannoulatos, "Facing People," 139.
42. Rivera-Pagán, "Porto Alegre," 12; Yannoulatos, "Emerging Perspectives," 343.
43. Selvanayagam, "Interfaith Dialogue," 161–62; Pan-Orthodox Conf., "Decisions," ¶ A.5; Lemopoulos, "Prophetic Mission," 370.

EVANGELICAL PROTESTANT CONCERNS

Evangelical Protestant opposition to conciliar Protestant and Roman Catholic thought on world religions swelled in the 1960s. We have already considered in chapter 9 the factors that contributed to this anti-ecumenical tide, especially in missions associations.

Syncretism and universalism were the two devils to be cast out in the opinion of 938 delegates from 71 countries who attended the 1966 Congress on the Church's Worldwide Mission in Wheaton, Illinois. They criticized many Catholic theologians for displaying great interest in "speculative universalism and existentialism." Their greatest concern was with contemporary Protestant movements "that propagate a neo-universalism denying eternal condemnation." There are deviant and heretical views within Christianity, they declared, which advocate "a depersonalized theism acceptable to religions of East and West" and deny the uniqueness and finality of Christian truth. Repudiating universalism, they felt a great urgency to preach the gospel to all persons "before they die in their sins."[44]

Four years later professor Peter Beyerhaus of the University of Tübingen, Germany, convened a small group of German professors of mission who shared the same concerns. Their Frankfurt Declaration represented a parallel response by evangelicals in Western Europe. They charged that since 1961 the ecumenical movement had spread false teaching "that Christ is anonymously so evident in world religions, historical changes, and revolutions that man can encounter him and find salvation in him without the direct news of the Gospel." Beyerhaus intended the Declaration to be "an all-out attack on the ecumenical program of humanization," but was disappointed when the WCC gave no response.[45]

For evangelicals the 1974 International Congress on World Evangelization (Lausanne I) was the heir to the vision of mission of Edinburgh 1910. However, concerning Christian approaches to other faiths the Congress broke no new ground. Representative was the presentation by Lit-sen Chang on "Evangelization among Buddhists and Confucianists." He found the root cause of the "suicide of missions" is a failure to differentiate general from special revelation. Yes, God does reveal himself to all creatures, but general revelation is "absolutely insuf-

---

44. Congress, Wheaton 1966, *Mission*, 222–26. See also Lindsell, "Missionary Imperatives," 57–65.
45. Beyerhaus, *Missions*, 115; idem, *Shaken*, 68–73.

ficient" for persons to know the way of salvation and the only Savior of humanity.[46]

The Lausanne Covenant became the new litmus test of evangelical faithfulness in missions and evangelism in the years that followed. While recognizing that all "have some knowledge of God through general revelation in nature," the Covenant signers denied that this can save. They rejected as "derogatory to Christ and the Gospel every kind of syncretism and dialogue which implies that Christ speaks equally through all religions and ideologies."[47]

Lausanne II (Manila 1989) continued the traditional evangelical position in its Manifesto: "We affirm that other religions and ideologies are not alternative paths to God, and that human spirituality, if unredeemed by Christ, leads not to God but to judgment, for Christ is the only way." The statement went on to reject "both the relativism which regards all religions and spiritualities as equally valid approaches to God, and the syncretism which tries to mix faith in Christ with other faiths."[48]

Ralph Covell summarized well in 1993 the dominant evangelical position on other faiths and yet the dilemma of Christians in witness to persons of other faiths: "Evangelicals as a group have long neglected to analyze these issues (of Christian attitudes toward other religions). They are clear on the uniqueness of Christ and on God's will to save all humanity, but they face the dilemma that most of the people of the world are comfortable in the religion in which they were born."[49]

ROMAN CATHOLICS AND THE THEOLOGY OF RELIGIONS

"All peoples comprise a single community." With this affirmation the Catholic bishops opened their Vatican II "Declaration on the Relationship of the Church to Non-Christian Religions" (*Nostra Aetate*). They insisted on the essential unity of the human race—a unity based on the fact that all persons have God both as their creator and as their final goal.[50]

Walbert Bühlman found in Vatican II a giant leap forward from the earlier attitudes toward other faiths shared by missionaries and popes alike. Benedict XV, in his 1919 encyclical *Maximum Illud*, subtitled *On*

46. LCWE, Lausanne I, *Let the Earth*, 829.
47. Ibid., 3–4.
48. LCWE, Lausanne II, *Proclaim Christ*, 111, 114–15.
49. Covell, "Jesus Christ," 162–63. See also Netland, *Pluralism*; and Stackhouse, *No Other Gods* for a variety of perspectives by evangelicals.
50. See also Hallencreutz, *Dialogue*, 35–48.

Spreading the Catholic Faith throughout the World, wrote of the urgency of saving an enormous number of souls from the proud tyranny of Satan, for nonbelievers "do not know God at all." Pius XI in *Rerum Eccelsiae* (1926) considered "one of the greatest and most wonderful signs of love for one's neighbor is when, by our loving care, the pagans are led out of their murky superstitions and are filled with the true faith in Christ." Pius XII, in his encyclical on missions (*Evangelii praecones*, 1951), still spoke of pagans, and in 1957 in *Fidei Donum* stated that "still about 85 million black Africans worship their heathen gods." Only with Pope John XXIII does the attitude and terminology change from traditional usage.[51]

Article 16 of the Dogmatic Constitution of the Church (*Lumen Gentium*) of Vatican II dealt with the people of God. Concerning those who have not yet found faith in Jesus Christ it reads:

> Nor is God Himself far distant from those who in shadows and images seek the unknown God, for it is He who gives to all men life and breath and every other gift (cf. Acts 17:25–28), and who as Saviour wills that all men be saved (cf. 1 Tim 2.4). Those also can attain to everlasting salvation who through no fault of their own do not know the gospel of Christ or His Church, yet sincerely seek God and, moved by grace, strive by their deeds to do His will as it is known to them through the dictates of conscience.[52]

"The Declaration on the Relationship of the Church to Non-Christian Religions" (*Nostra Aetate*) was the shortest, yet most controversial, of Vatican II documents. The first draft limited the discussion to Catholic relations with Jews. Only the preface contained a brief mention of "conversing and cooperating with Non-Christians who nevertheless worship God, or at least with good will, try to follow their conscience in carrying out the moral law situated in human nature." This dissatisfied many of the bishops from Africa, Asia, and Oceania, who represented one-third of the total bishops in attendance. Just two lines for two-thirds of the world! Fortunately Vatican II was not a hurried seven-day event. It took place over seven years, allowing time for considered rethinking and redrafting. The bishops agreed to expand the document.[53]

The Declaration, as adopted, opens with the observation that the human family is "being drawn closer together." "All peoples comprise a

---

51. Bühlmann, *Search*, 26–27.
52. *Lumen Gentium*, no. 16, in Vatican Council, *Documents*, 35.
53. Ibid., 656–59; Stransky, "Church," 155; Bühlmann, *Search*, 29–31.

single community," it continued, picking up the theme of the solidarity of humanity which had been one of Pope John XXIII's operating principles. Concerning other faiths it read, "The Catholic Church rejects nothing which is true and holy in these religions." This reaffirmed a traditional viewpoint. But it went on to declare that those religions "often reflect a ray of that Truth which enlightens all." Robert Graham, in notes on the official text, commented that this marked an "authoritative change in approach. Now, for the first time, there is recognition of other religions as entities with which the Church can and should enter into dialogue."[54]

Although the Vatican II documents contained no systematically developed theology of the religions, concerned theologians welcomed the new openness. Meeting one week after the bishops' adoption of *Nostra Aetate*, Hans Küng, Raymond Panikkar and others proposed that the old church-centered view of "outside the church no salvation" be replaced by a theocentric view that the whole of humanity "is embraced by the one salvific plan of God which includes all the world religions." Küng, in the debate, consented to change his assertion that the non-Christian religions were roads to salvation to read that "for the person who is not confronted with the gospel of Jesus Christ in an existentialist way, these religions *can be a channel* for the grace of the salvation of Christ." The declarations of the International Theological Conference at Bombay also contained these words: "Christian faith represents radical universalism. Every human being and every world religion is under God's grace. But Christian universalism is grounded and centred in Christ."[55]

Concerning the Church's missionary task the theologians declared, "The Church will not conquer but serve the world religions ... rooted in her primary mission, to witness to Christ and his Gospel before the world and its religions." Coming as it did during a large eucharistic congress attended by Pope Paul VI, and so soon after *Nostra Aetate*, the Küng/Panikkar debate both awakened and polarized Roman Catholics on the issues.[56]

Since Vatican II Catholic popes have maintained a continual tension between two aspects of mission entrusted by Jesus to his followers. On the one hand, they continue to teach the intent of bringing the gospel of salvation through Jesus Christ to the whole world, teaching and bap-

---

54. Vatican Council, *Documents*, 661–62. See also Hallencreutz, *Dialogue*, 35–48.
55. Neuner, ed., *Christian Revelation*, 21–22.
56. Bühlmann, *Search*, 40–55.

tizing in Christ's name. On the other hand, they support the continuing search for truth wherever it may be found, and learning from it.

Pope John Paul II, in his 1990 encyclical *Redemptoris Missio* (*RM*), sought to rekindle Catholic enthusiasm to proclaim the gospel "as the permanent priority of mission" (*RM* 44), converting as many as possible to the Christian faith. While interreligious dialogue is an essential part of missionary activity, it should "be conducted and implemented with the conviction that *the Church is the ordinary means of* salvation and that *she* alone possesses the fullness of the meaning of salvation" (*RM* 55). In 1991 the Pontifical Council for Interreligious Dialogue and the Congregation for the Evangelization of Peoples jointly published the official document *Dialogue and Proclamation* (*DP*). It gave a more nuanced view with both proclamation and dialogue seen "as component elements and authentic forms of the one evangelizing mission of the Church" (*DP* 2). The dialogue of religious experience, of mutual enrichment through sharing and common prayer with those of other spiritualities and religions, was one kind of dialogue commended in the document. Pope John Paul II modeled this kind of dialogue as he met and prayed with Buddhists, Muslims, Jews, and Hindus in 1986 and again in 2000 at the shrine of St. Francis in Assisi, Italy.[57]

Cardinal Joseph Ratzinger (later Pope Benedict XVI), director of the Congregation for the Declaration of the Faith, sought to clarify the teaching of the Catholic Church "On the Unicity and Salvific Universality of Jesus Christ and the Church" in the declaration *Dominus Iesus* published in 2000. Jesus in this document is "the 'exclusive, universal, and absolute' source of salvation for the world" (*DI* 15). Its condemnation of "relativistic theories which seek to justify religious pluralism" (*DI* 4) seemed like a regression. The declaration, however, needs to be balanced with that of Ratzinger in 1998 as he wrote, "mission and dialogue should no longer be opposites but should mutually interpenetrate. Dialogue is not aimless conversation; it aims at conviction, at finding the truth; otherwise it is worthless."[58]

---

57. Bevans and Schroeder, *Constants*, 323–25, 358–59; see also Burrows, *Redemption*, 3–90 for text and commentary of *RM*, and 93–158 for text and commentary of *DP*.

58. See Pope and Hefling, eds., *Sic et Non*, 3–26 for text of *DI*, and 27–178 for commentary; also Ratzinger, *Many Religions*, 110–12.

UNITY: THE CONTINUING IMPERATIVE

In 1989 Bishop Lesslie Newbigin, an active participant for more than four decades in the debate on missions and other faiths, published *The Gospel in a Pluralist Society*. In it Newbigin called the paramount need for human unity "one of the genuinely new facts of our time" insofar as it now embraces the whole globe. "How are we to regard other commitments, faiths, worldviews to which the people around us and with whom we live and move adhere?" he asked. One approach Newbigin identified is to filter out all particularities in religion and affirm only universals. Belief in a ultimate Being, or affirmation of the values of justice and love, or common experience of the Transcendent, would be that type of response. But the Christian faith, Newbigin argued, is "personal, concrete, historical." It is faith that God reconciled the world in the man Jesus Christ. While acknowledging "the gracious work of God in the lives of all human beings," including those not members of the Christian church, he rejected an inclusivism that regards other religions as "vehicles of salvation."[59]

Paul Knitter, on the other hand, claimed that a pluralistic theology of religions "can offer even greater missionary inspiration than traditional, conservative views that deny any salvific role to other faiths." He argued that the earlier theory of "anonymous Christianity," proposed by the Roman Catholic theologian Karl Rahner, weakened the Christian's motivation to witness since Christ was believed already to be known by persons of other faiths. Knitter affirmed what he called the "universal and relational uniqueness" of Jesus. Holding to such a theology, Christians are motivated to share what they have experienced and known in Jesus Christ, for that message "must be related to the possible message God gives to others." He concluded that missionary work from this perspective is essential to Christianity "not just that the church may bring about the conversion of others, but also to bring about its own conversion--and thus to remain the authentic church of Jesus Christ."[60]

Rather than despairing over the disagreement between Lesslie Newbigin and Paul Knitter, or earlier between William Hocking and Hendrik Kraemer, Raymond Panikkar considered such a struggle to be essential in the ongoing search for a wider unity. "Dialogue does not exclude controversy; encounter does not mean agreement," he wrote.

---

59. Newbigin, *Gospel*, 157, 170, 176, 182–83.
60. Knitter, "Author's Reply," 179.

"Ecumenism does not aim directly at unity but at understanding; it does not dream of uniformity but the closest possible harmony." The goal is a better understanding, corrective criticism, and eventually mutual re-creation among the religious traditions of the world—a bold attempt to extend openness to the entire human family.[61]

Will the search for a wider ecumenism in the twenty-first century become a mission imperative? Stephen Bevans and Roger Schroeder believe that in coming decades "the church's promotion of interreligious dialogue may be one of its greatest missionary services" in a world in which confrontation and violence is on the increase. It will be an engaged dialogue of persons who witness to truth as they understand and experience it. It will be a "prophetic dialogue" demanding "honesty, conviction, courage and faith." It will be a "dialogue of action" of persons engaged both in theological exchange and in joint action for peace, justice and the integrity of creation.[62]

---

61. Panikkar, "Editorial," 785, 781.
62. Bevans and Schroeder, *Constants*, 383–85.

Conclusion

THIS STUDY BEGAN WITH two questions: What did the modern missionary movement contribute to understandings and work for Christian unity? How did it help persons to understand and accept their unity as part of one human family which includes persons of various faiths and ideologies?

Much of the earlier literature in the field took a normative approach asking "How *should* Christians be united in mission?" That method of study, in this author's judgment, is too restrictive and tends to exclude much relevant and important data. The alternative approach chosen was to begin with the empirical question "How *have* Christians worked together in mission?" That question opened up for inclusion various responses from across the wide spectrum of Christian churches and organizations. That approach brought to light rich data that confirmed the validity of the ten models of unity in Christian mission posited from a preliminary literature review.[1]

MAJOR FINDINGS

This study has sought to elucidate the great variety of ways in which Christians have united in mission. Persons in every era have sought to respond to the founder's prayer "that they may be one" (John 17:21), and to his dual commissioning of his disciples: to "go and make disciples of all nations" (Matt 28:19), and to continue his ministry of healing and liberation (Luke 4: 18).

Responses by Christians to this calling for unity in mission are both varied and in dynamic flux. Both idealism and pragmatism motivate efforts toward unity, from the local to the global. Relationships are not fixed; over time there is continuing development. Momentous events such as Vatican II can overturn centuries of practice. For Protestants the failure of the largest mission conference in history, the Ecumenical

---

1. See the table on "Models of Christian Unity" in the Introduction for this typology.

Missionary Conference (New York 1900), to produce any lasting result led to a new style of international conference participation, organization, and staffing ten years' later at the World Missionary Conference (Edinburgh 1910), which became a lasting model for Christians desiring greater unity in mission.

The task of any historian is to provide an interpretive framework enabling the enquirer to gain understanding of what at first approach seems to be a bewildering variety of historical events, and to select from among innumerable facts and case studies what is to be presented and elucidated. The historian then must: (1) select an inclusive framework of interpretation, and (2) select supporting data representative of the total data as he or she perceives it. That selection process is the historian's bias.

This study has employed a sociological explanatory framework. The ten models of unity are components of a two-dimensional grid. One is organizational, including voluntary/informal groupings, those that are cooperative or conciliar, and those that are institutional and formal. The second dimension is spatial, from purely local groupings for mission, to those organized on a national or regional basis, to those engaged in mission globally. The phenomena, however, suggest a third dimension, namely time. Adding the historical dimension helps us to recognize that responses of Christians to the call for unity in mission are never static and unchanging, but rather dynamic and in flux.

Consider the findings on the organizational dimension of the grid. Catholic theologian Avery Dulles, in his chapter on "Ecumenical Strategies for a Pluralistic Age," argued that Christians committed to expressing visibly their commitment to unity have been divided "not so much about the ultimate goal of the movement as about the strategies for attaining that goal." [2] In the findings of this study I follow that argument, grouping the mission groups by four organizational strategies: (1) Covenantal/Voluntary, (2) Cooperative Interchurch, (3) Conciliar, and (4) Organic Unity.

Covenantal/Voluntary Unity

Each Christian needs to experience both the intimacy of the small, caring and witnessing fellowship, and the joy of oneness in Christ in larger gatherings of Christians of different backgrounds. Engaged in mission, they need both hands-on involvement and opportunities to celebrate

2. Dulles, *Resilient Church*, 174–76.

oneness in mission. This study includes illustrative examples of both types from modern church history.

Ralph Winter, in his influential article on "The Two Structures of God's Redemptive Mission," marshaled evidence from the apostolic church to the modern era of both church structures for mission (*modalities*) and of the missionary bands (*sodalites*). The former are the church judicatories seeking to be inclusive of all who profess that allegiance. The latter are persons engaged in mission with some measure of autonomy, from Paul's missionary team, to Catholic monastic orders, to the parachurch organizations of today.[3]

History is replete with both types of structures in mission on a sectarian, denominational, or confessional basis. Of particular interest in this study were those groups that bridged the sectarian divisions of their day. The Church Missionary Society, formed in 1799 in England, initially sent out as missionaries more Lutherans from Germany than Anglicans from England, and numbered those from the Continent as among their most noted pioneers. Seminarians of different denominations, but from the same school, went out at missionaries on the U.S. western frontier in the 1820s and 30s under the auspices of a united Protestant agency, the American Home Missionary Society.

Important later for both motivation for missions and celebration of Christian unity were the gatherings of Christians across denominational lines. In 1846 the international and interchurch gathering of 800 Christian leaders in London that founded the Evangelical Alliance was the prototype of even larger conferences and assemblies to promote unity in mission. Open for participation by all interested persons, they celebrated oneness in Christ and inspired hundred of thousands to greater commitment for missions. Examples include the Ecumenical Missionary Conference (New York 1900), the Lausanne congresses on world evangelization and those of the AD2000 Movement, and the triennial conventions of the InterVarsity Christian Fellowship.

Baptist historian Kenneth Scott Latourette did not find in the early church unity and agreement on doctrine so much as "the unity which it seems to me the New Testament stresses, namely of love." He continued, "to identify Christian unity with inclusion in one organizational pattern or conformity to a particular formulation of words even in the great historic creeds seems to me to be untrue to the New Testament and to be one of the rocks on which earlier efforts at Christian unity have

---

3. See Winter, "Two Structures" and my discussion of these structures in ch. 9.

foundered." He found "some of the greatest breaches of Christian unity of love" in the first century and today to be "within ecclesiastical bodies which present to the outward world a unity of organizational structure and of creed."[4] I found this to be true. The resistances to proposals for greater structural unity were greater where mission was not central as a motivation for greater unity.

Cooperative/Interchurch Unity

Of the varied types of Christian unity in mission, that of cooperation by autonomous Christian organizations was found to be most common. In 1935 John R. Mott expressed well its rationale: "The magnitude, complexity, and difficulty of the world missionary program are so great, and the available resources are relatively so meager, that it is an idle dream to assume that the overwhelming waiting task can be performed with divided ranks. Nothing will suffice but the statesmanlike cooperation of the Christians of all communions, achieved through sharing counsel, blending experiences, uniting in planning and action, and liberating and massing latent energies." Mott contended that cooperation "adds enormously to the power of appeal of the world-wide mission, makes for higher efficiency and abler leadership, greatly facilitates entering doors of opportunity, affords enlargement," and "helps greatly to emphasize and illustrate the truly catholic and ecumenical nature of the Christian Church."[5]

Competing Models of Institutional Unity

Most mission histories record from 1792 to 1910 the growing awareness of the need for unity in missions under missionary leaders. Muted are the stories of Majority World missionaries during this period, such as the more than 1,000 Pacific islanders in cross-cultural mission in the nineteenth and early twentieth century.

Would the urgency of unity in mission wane as leadership of Majority World churches passed from expatriate missionaries to nationals? This fear by mission agencies in Europe and North America was dispelled as Christian leaders in country after country in Asia, Africa, Latin America, and the Pacific became passionate and committed to unified efforts in mission. Majority World churches became advocates for all the ten models of unity in mission analyzed in this study.

---

4. Latourette to Ruth Rouse, April 28, 1949, in A-YDSL/Lat, "Correspondence."
5. Mott, *Cooperation*, 69–74.

Four divergent, and sometimes competing, institutional models have been analyzed: the global church, conciliar unity, confessional unity, and organic unity. Each has had its strong advocates in both the global North and South. The approach in this presentation is designed to enhance understanding of each model, exposing the tensions that have developed between advocates of each. Relevant in this context are the debates over whether the World Council of Churches should change its structure, and whether reconciled diversity as proposed by world confessional bodies shall be embraced alongside the conciliar approach.

Organic Unity and Unity in Mission

In chapter 12 were told the stories of consummated organic union by churches of different confessional backgrounds in India, China, and the Congo. Equally instructive are the cases of aborted attempts at such unions. The drag of institutional maintenance concerns has been overcome only when Christians have become convicted that God's mission impels organic unity.

Mission historian Stephen Neill argued "that co-operation and unity are both good things, but that they are strictly incommensurables, since they belong to different dimensions of existence." Cooperation, he believed, "is best served by not raising untimely questions of principle. Co-operation thrives on compromise. Co-operation leaves undisturbed the sovereignty of all the contracting parties." Out of his experience of negotiating for the Church of South India, Neill described the transition from cooperation to union as being "of the nature of what Kierkegaard called an existential leap." Those who attained union described it as "a gift from God" not achieved without loss as well as gain, and achieved only at the price of death of old structures and institutions.[6] Neill put forward the same "high church" conception of unity in his introduction to *A History of the Ecumenical Movement*.[7]

Speaking thirty-five years later in 1990, out of the struggles of the Church of South India in which he was ordained, Thomas Thangaraj expressed the same passion for full church unity as Neill, but with a nuanced and self-critical reflection. "Church unity is a missiological task," Thangaraj declared, if "mission is not an appendix to the life of the church" but rather "the very life breath of the church." Then he got to the essence of the issue: "if the church exists because of its mission then

---

6. Neill, "Co-operation," 439–44.
7. Latourette, "Introduction," 1–24.

it ceases to be church when it is divided, because division violates its very being and denies its very essence." He was emphatic, however, that by "full church unity" he did not mean "uniformity." For him "full unity means a unity which is spiritual and structural, visible and invisible, and related to faith, practice and structure."[8]

Thangaraj went on to emphasize that "church unity is an eschatological task." It is oriented towards the goal and end. In reality, however, "full church unity is further and further from us as we keep moving towards it." He likened it to the stars in the sky that elude us even as we make our moves towards them. That, he confessed, has been very true of the first forty-three years of the Church of South India. Its inauguration in 1947 marked only the beginning of what full unity requires. He related that "denominational labels were soon given up, but then caste labels arose to haunt us and divide us." His aspiration was that "the scandal and tragedy of these caste divisions, and the pain of this division, will hopefully turn into the birth pangs for a more fully united church in South India" that would include not just ordaining women to the full ministry, but becoming a "united church of men *and* women."[9]

The flowering of organic union in India as a fruit of mission, however, did not transplant well to many younger churches or to the older churches in the north. To Oscar Cullmann, the noted New Testament scholar, that came as no surprise for he had found that "there was no uniformity even in earliest Christianity." He argued that an "ecumenism of unity" based on New Testament principles would be one of "charismatic diversity." Cullmann judged the goal of merger of confessional bodies in one great church to be "unrealistic and utopian." Instead he proposed "a real community of completely independent churches that remain Catholic, Protestant, and Orthodox, that preserve their spiritual gifts, not for the purpose of excluding each other, but for the purpose of forming a *community of all those churches that call on the name of our Lord Jesus Christ*."[10]

Wider Ecumenism

The Secular Vision

Jesus did not call his followers to be the salt of the *koinonia*, the gathered community of the faithful, but of the earth. They were to be the light not of the religious sanctuary, but of the world (Matt 5:13).

---

8. Thangaraj, "Unity," 93–95.
9. Ibid., 95.
10. Cullmann, *Unity*, 29, 32–33.

In his first report as general secretary of the World Council of Churches, Philip Potter in 1973 emphasized as more important than the coming together of churches the struggle of men and women in "the whole inhabited earth . . . to become what they were intended to be in the purpose of God." Potter was convinced that the search for the unity of the church is inextricably bound up with the struggle for the unity of humankind. In that struggle Christians can experience that oneness that overarches differences of nation, social class, ideology, and faith perspective.[11]

Chapter 14 focuses upon how the conciliar model of Christian unity responded to the challenge to create a new structure for world order after World War II and a Universal Declaration of Human Rights. Rarely are the churches able to move from concern to education to advocacy on issues and legislation affecting nations. This extended case study has been documented to show that the churches can move from prophetic resolutions to constructive action if they see it as part of their mission and act together.

There are possibilities for similar creative actions by Christian groups representative of each of the ten models for mission. Case studies have been given in chapters 9 and 13 on world associations and local unity. Many creative examples are worthy of inclusion in another book. New histories deserve to be written of Christians who worked actively for social, economic, and political change on a nonsectarian basis at all levels from the local to the global.[12]

In the Netherlands ten Christian leaders met in 1970 to form the Kairos workgroup. Each individually had been concerned about the absence of a firm stand by their government against apartheid in South Africa. In close contact with Beyers Naudé and others of the Christian Institute of South Africa, they covenanted to fill the need for a Christian anti-apartheid organization in the Netherlands. Their first political action was to publish a booklet titled "What the Government Has Said about Apartheid in South Africa." All cabinet ministers and members of the Dutch Parliament opened copies to find just blank pages after the cover picture of the prime minister. It symbolized the absence of their government's stand on this issue. Shamed into action by the committed few, Parliament took action to condemn apartheid in South Africa. In 1971 Queen Juliana gave a donation to the Anti-Racism fund of the

---

11. Potter, "Report," 416–17.
12. For a model see J. Findlay, *Church People*.

Conclusion

WCC, to be followed in the next five years with direct aid to liberation movements in Southern Africa. The initial catalyst was creative action for change by just ten committed Christians.[13]

WIDER UNITY

The variety of Christian responses to issues of unity in mission is starkly evident in the varied Christian approaches to other faiths enumerated in chapter 15. The most controversial debate among mission theologians since the 1990s has been over the question, "Can God's salvific action be found in faiths other than Christianity?"

In 1998 S. Wesley Ariarajah called for a "new ecumenism" that accepts the interreligious realities of Asia. Does the "ecumenical household," he asked, have "room in it for the 92.5 percent of the people of my country [Sri Lanka] who live by other faith traditions?" He continued, "Unless what is 'ecumenical' is not simply *about,* but in some measure *constitutes,* the whole inhabited earth, it has too little to say to, and much less to do with, the majority of the world's population." He would base this "wider ecumenism" on the WCC's own statement that "it is committed to the search for visible unity, not as an end in itself but in order to give credible witness 'so that the world may believe' and to serve the healing of the human community and the wholeness of God's entire creation."[14] In 2004, early into a new century in which confrontation and violence were on the increase, and leaders proclaimed a war against terrorism, Stephen Bevans and Roger Schroeder concluded that "the church's promotion of interreligious dialogue may be one of its greatest missionary services."[15]

FUTURE EXPECTATIONS

Can we expect multiple expressions of unity in the church's mission in coming years? Yes. Astute Christian leaders predict that "the era that is now emerging will likely be marked not by a single new paradigm but by multiple centers of energy, multiple methodologies, multiple priority concerns."[16]

Catholic theologian Avery Dulles in 1995 pointed to an important anomaly in "classical ecumenism." On the one hand, it sought to promote organic unions of churches but "did not accomplish many signifi-

---

13. Klein, "Nederland tegen apartheid?"
14. Ariarajah, "Wider Ecumenism," 328; WCC/CC, "Common Understanding," 103.
15. Bevans and Schroeder, *Constants,* 385.
16. Kinnamon and Cope, eds., *Ecumenical,* 8.

cant mergers." On the other hand, it "stimulated contact with new and unfamiliar styles of Christianity" and by doing so helped "to overcome the excessive inbreeding of churches and to bring the benefits of heterogeneous community." Christians of widely divergent traditions "can join in their fundamental witness to Christ and the gospel." They "can labor side by side" for justice and by doing so "can savor and deepen the unity that is already theirs in Christ."[17]

Nigerian Catholic missiologist Francis Anekwe Oborji wrote in 2006 of "the intimate link between mission and Christian unity" and judged it to be "nonnegotiable." His reasoning was that "it is not simply derived from the Third World experience of mission or from changing realities, but from God's gift of unity in the one body of Christ and the mission of the same Christ for the unification of all things in him." Oborji began with the conviction that "God's people is one: Christ's body is one." Nevertheless, he recognized genuine differences among Christians. "The relation between mission and Christian unity does not presume uniformity and reductionism or denying the differences," he wrote. Overcoming those differences requires a self-critical attitude and repentance. He firmly believed that "ecumenism is possible where people accept one another despite their differences." The big challenge ahead, Oborji concluded, is "how Christians and, indeed, the whole human family are to live their unity in diversity and diversity in unity."[18]

Those who are searching for a "right" way to be united in mission, with clarification of the "wrong" ways to do mission with unity, will be disappointed with this study. Conversely, those who are open to the dynamic working of the Spirit in the variety of Christian approaches to unity in mission will welcome the approach taken here. They will find diversity to be a trend to welcome rather than to abhor. When they find omissions by the author they will not be surprised. This book will have achieved its purpose if readers achieve greater awareness of the diverse ways in which Christians unite in mission. If they become engaged in new and challenging united actions in mission, and reflect critically on those involvements, they will become the living witnesses to the ideals presented in this study.

---

17. A. Dulles, "Unity," 143–44.
18. Oborji, *Concepts*, 17.

Bibliography

PUBLISHED SOURCES

AACC, Kampala 1963. *Drumbeats from Kampala: Report of the First Assembly of the All Africa Conference of Churches.* London: Lutterworth, 1963.

Abbott, Walter M. "Interconfessional Cooperation in Bible Work." In *Word in the World: Essays in Honor of Frederick L. Moriarty, S.J.*, edited by Richard J. Clifford and George W. MacRae, 193–208. Cambridge, MA: Weston College Press, 1973.

ABCFM. *Annual Report* . . . Boston: ABCFM, 1836.

Achútegui, Pedro S. de. "Missions and the Ecumenical Dimension." In *Missions and the Ecumenical Dimension*, edited by P. Achútegui, 117–46. Manila: Loyola School of Theology, Manila University, 1972.

Adegbola, Adeolu. "Christian Responsibility in the Political Economy of Africa." *ER* 37 (1985) 86–97.

―――. "Ecumenism for All People." In *Faith and Faithfulness: Essays on Contemporary Ecumenical Themes: A Tribute to Philip A. Potter*, edited by Pauline Webb, 52–60. Geneva: WCC, 1984.

Ahlstrom, Sydney E. *A Religious History of the American People.* New Haven, CT: Yale University Press, 1972.

Albert, Richard J. "Ecumenism in the Caribbean." *JES* 15 (1978) 823–25.

All Africa Church Conference, Ibadan 1958. *The Church in Changing Africa: Report.* New York: IMC, 1958.

Alvarez, Carmelo E. "Latin American Pentecostals: Ecumenicals and Evangelicals." *One in Christ* 23 (1987) 93–97.

Amirtham, Samuel. "The Experience in and towards Unity." *M-S* 18 (1979) 35–39.

Anderson, Allan. "Global Pentecostalism in the New Millennium." In *Pentecostals after a Century: Global Perspectives on a Movement in Transition*, edited by Allan H. Anderson and Walter J. Hollenweger, 209–223. JPTSup 15. Sheffield, UK: Sheffield Academic, 1999.

―――. "Introduction: World Pentecostalism at a Crossroads." In *Pentecostals after a Century: Global Perspectives on a Movement in Transition*, edited by Allan H. Anderson and Walter J. Hollenweger, 19–31. JPTSup 15. Sheffield, UK: Sheffield Academic, 1999.

Anderson, Gerald H. "American Protestants in Pursuit of Mission: 1886–1986." *IBMR* 12 (1988) 104–18.

―――, editor. *Biographical Dictionary of Christian Missions.* New York: Macmillan, 1998.

Anderson, Gerald H., James M. Phillips, and Robert T. Coote, editors. *Mission in the Nineteen 90s.* Grand Rapids: Eerdmans, 1991.

Anderson, Gerald H., Robert T. Coote, Norman A. Horner, and James M. Phillips, editors. *Mission Legacies: Biographical Studies of Leaders of the Modern Missionary Movement.* ASMS 19. Maryknoll, NY: Orbis, 1994.

Anderson, Gerald H., and Thomas F. Stransky. *Third World Theologies.* Mission Trends 3. New York: Paulist; Grand Rapids: Eerdmans, 1976.

Anderson, Rufus. *To Advance the Gospel: Selections from the Writings of Rufus Anderson.* Edited by R. Pierce Beaver. Grand Rapids: Eerdmans, 1967.
Andrews, Loretta Kreider, and Herbert D. Andrews. "The Church and the Birth of a Nation: The Mindolo Ecumenical Foundation and Zambia." *JC&S* 17 (1975) 191–216.
Antone, Hope S., editor. *Living in Oikoumene.* Hong Kong: CCA, 2003.
Ariarajah, S. Wesley. "San Antonio and Other Faiths," *Current Dialogue* 16 (August 1989) 3–8.
———. "Wider Ecumenism: A Threat or a Promise?" *ER* 50 (1998) 321–29.
Arias, Mortimer. "That the World May Believe." *IRM* 65 (1976) 13–26.
Arns, Paulo Evaristo. "An Example of Local Ecumenism—São Paulo." *ER* 40 (1988) 431–33.
Askew, Thomas A. "The New York 1900 Ecumenical Missionary Conference: A Centennial Reflection." *IBMR* 24 (2000) 146–54.
———. "The 1888 London Centenary Missions Conference: Ecumenical Disappointment or American Missions Coming of Age?" *IBMR* 18 (1994) 113–18.
Assemblies of God General Council. *Minutes. . . . The Forty-Second General Council, August 6–11, 1987.*
Austin, Alvyn J. "Blessed Adversity: Henry W. Frost and the China Inland Mission." In *Earthen Vessels: American Evangelicals and Foreign Missions, 1880–1980*, edited by Carpenter and Shenk, 47–70. Grand Rapids, Eerdmans, 1990.
———. "Only Connect: The China Inland Mission and Transatlantic Evangelicalism." In *North American Foreign Missions, 1810–1914: Theology, Theory and Policy*, edited by Wilbert R. Shenk, 281–313. SHCM. Grand Rapids: Eerdmans, 2004.
Barrett, David B. *Seven Hundred Plans to Evangelize the World: The Rise of a Global Evangelization Movement.* The AD 2000 Series. Birmingham, AL: New Hope, 1988.
———. "Signs, Wonders, and Statistics in the World of Today." In *Pentecost, Mission and Ecumenism: Essays on Intercultural Theology*, edited by Jan A. B. Jongeneel, 189–96. Studies in the Intercultural History of Christianity 75. Frankfurt: Lang, 1992.
———. "The Twentieth-Century Pentecostal/Charismatic Renewal in the Holy Spirit, with Its Goal of World Evangelization." *IBMR* 12 (1988) 119–29.
———, editor. *World Christian Encyclopedia: A Comparative Study of Churches and Religions in the Modern World, AD 1900–2000.* New York: Oxford University Press, 1982.
Barrett, David B., and Todd M. Johnson. "Annual Statistical Table on Global Mission: 2001." *IBMR* 25 (2001) 24–25.
———, editors. *World Christian Trends, AD 30–AD 2200: Interpreting the Annual Christian Megacensus.* Pasadena, CA: William Carey Library, 2001.
Barrett, David B., Todd M. Johnson, and Peter F. Crossing. "Missiometrics 2008: Reality Checks for Christian World Communions." *IBMR* 33 (2009) 27–32.
Barrett, David B., Todd M. Johnson, and George T. Kurian, editors. *World Christian Encyclopedia: A Comparative Survey of Churches and Religions in the Modern World.* 2 vols. 2nd ed. New York: Oxford University Press, 2001.
"Basic Christian Communities in Africa." *AFER* 19 (1977) 268–79.
Bassham, Rodger C. *Mission Theology, 1948–1975: Years of Worldwide Creative Tension— Ecumenical, Evangelical, and Roman Catholic.* Pasadena, CA: William Carey Library, 1979.
Bates, M. Searle. *Religious Liberty: An Inquiry.* New York: IMC, Harper, 1945.
BCC. *Structure Report to the B.C.C.* London: BCC, 1973.
Beahm, William M. "Factors in Development of the Student Volunteer Movement for Foreign Missions." PhD diss., University of Chicago, 1941.
Beaver, R. Pierce. *American Protestant Women in World Mission: A History of the First Feminist Movement in North America.* Rev. ed. Grand Rapids: Eerdmans, 1980.

———. "The Concert for Prayer for Missions: An Early Venture in Ecumenical Action." *ER* 10 (1958) 420–27.

———. *Ecumenical Beginnings in Protestant World Mission: A History of Comity*. New York: Nelson, 1962.

Beek, Huibert van, editor. *Revisioning Christian Unity: The Global Christian Forum*. Regnum Studies in Global Christianity. Oxford: Regnum, 2009.

Béguin, Olivier. "The Weakness and Strength of the Bible Societies Today." *IRM* 43 (1954) 413

Benjamin, P. V. "A New Outlook in Christian Medical Work." *IRM* 28 (1939) 562–68.

Bent, Ans J. van der. *Christian Response in a World of Crisis: A Brief History of the WCC's Commission of the Churches on International Affairs*. Geneva: WCC, 1986.

———. *Historical Dictionary of Ecumenical Christianity*. Historical Dictionaries of Religions, Philosophies, and Movements 3. Metuchen, NJ: Scarecrow, 1994.

———, editor. *Voices of Unity: Essays in Honour of Willem Adolf Visser 't Hooft on the Occasion of His 80th Birthday*. Geneva: WCC, 1981.

Berg, Johannes van den. *Constrained by Jesus' Love: An Inquiry into the Motives of the Missionary Awakening in Great Britain in the Period between 1698 and 1815*. Kampen: Kok, 1956.

Best, Thomas F. "Survey of Church Negotiations, 1996–1999." *ER* (2000) 3–45.

Bevans, Stephen B., and Roger P Schroeder. *Constants in Context: A Theology of Mission for Today*. ASMS 30. Maryknoll, NY: Orbis, 2004.

Beyerhaus, Peter. "Evangelicals, Evangelism and Theology: A Missiological Assessment of the Lausanne Movement." *ERT* 11 (1987) 169–85.

———. *Missions: Which Way?: Humanization or Redemption*. Contemporary Evangelical Perspectives. Grand Rapids: Zondervan, 1971.

———. *Shaken Foundations: Theological Foundations for Mission*. Contemporary Evangelical Perspectives. Grand Rapids: Zondervan, 1972.

Birmelé, André, editor. *Local Ecumenism: How Church Unity Is Seen and Practiced by Congregations*. Geneva: WCC, 1984.

Blanc, René. "An Original Ecumenical Experiment: CEVAA." *LW* 22 (1975) 107–12.

Bokeleale, Jean. "Bokeleale and the Press." *CMN* 223 (April–June 1969) 6–7.

———. "The Case for Unity." *CMN* 227 (April–June 1970) 10–13.

———. "Church of Christ in Zaire." *IRM* 24.2 (April 1972) 214–16.

Bolink, Peter. *Towards Church Union in Zambia: A Study of Missionary Co-operation and Church-Union Efforts in Central Africa*. Franeker: Wever, [1967].

Bonk, Jon, editor. *Between Past and Future: Evangelical Mission Entering the Twenty-First Century*. Evangelical Missiological Society Series 10. Pasadena, CA: William Carey Library, 2003.

Bos, A. David. "Community Ministries: The Wild Card in Ecumenical Relations and Social Ministry." *JES* 25 (1988) 592–98.

Bosch, David. "'Ecumenicals' and 'Evangelicals': A Growing Relationship." *ER* 40 (1988) 458–72.

———. "In Search of Mission: Reflections on 'Melbourne' and 'Pattaya.'" *Missionalia* 9 (1981) 3–18.

———. *Transforming Mission: Paradigm Shifts in Theology of Mission*. ASMS 16. Maryknoll, NY: Orbis, 1991.

Bridston, Keith R. "Is Ecumenism a Hindrance to Evangelism?" *SW* 50 (1957) 347–60.

Brown, Arthur J. *Unity and Missions: Can a Divided Church Save the World?* New York: Revell, 1915.

Brown, G. Thompson. *Christianity in the People's Republic of China*. Atlanta: John Knox, 1983.

Brown, Raymond M. *The Ecumenical Revolution: An Interpretation of the Catholic-Protestant Dialogue*. New York: Doubleday, 1967.

Browne, Stanley G. "Medical Missions at the Crossroads." *IRM* 45 (1956) 278–88.
Brunner, Daniel L. *Halle Pietists in England: Anthony William Boehm and the Society for Promoting Christian Knowledge*. Arbeiten zur Geschichte des Pietismus 29. Göttingen: Vandenhoeck & Ruprecht, 1993.
Bühlmann, Walbert. "Ecumenism in Africa." *AFER* 13 (1971) 234–55.
———. *The Search for God: An Encounter with the Peoples and Religions of Asia*. Translated by B. Krokosz. Maryknoll, NY: Orbis, 1980.
Burrows, William R. *Redemption and Dialogue: Reading* Redemptoris Missio *and Dialogue and Proclamation*. Maryknoll, NY: Orbis, 1993.
Burton, Ernest D. "The Findings of the Continuation Committee Conferences in Asia on Education." *IRM* 3 (1914) 670–82.
Bush, Luis. "The AD2000 Movement as a Great Commission Catalyst." In *Between Past and Future: Evangelical Mission Entering the Twenty-First Century*, edited by Jon Bonk, 17–36. Evangelical Missiological Society Series 10. Pasadena, CA: William Carey Library, 2003.
Butselaar, Jan van. "Thinking Locally, Acting Globally: The Ecumenical Movement in the New Era." *IRM* 81 (1992) 363–73.
Carey, S. Pearce. *William Carey, D.D., Fellow of Linnaean Society*. 6th ed. London: Hodder & Stoughton, 1925.
Carey, William. *An Enquiry into the Obligations of Christians to Use Means for the Conversion of the Heathens*. Facsimile of 1792 ed. London: Kingsgate, 1961.
Caribbean Conference of Churches. "Statement of the General Secretary on the Occurrence of the January 12, 2010 Earthquake in Haiti." Press release, January 15, 2010, Online: http://www.ccc-caribe.org/eng/releases/jan2010_haitiquake.htm.
Carpenter, Joel A., and Wilbert R. Shenk, editors. *Earthen Vessels: American Evangelicals and Foreign Missions, 1880–1980*. Grand Rapids, Eerdmans, 1990.
Carr, Burgess. "The Relation of Union to Mission." In *Third World Theologies*, edited by Gerald H. Anderson and Thomas F. Stransky, 158–68. Mission Trends 3. New York: Paulist; Grand Rapids: Eerdmans, 1976.
Cassidy, Michael, and Gottfried Osei-Mensah. *Together in One Place: The Story of PACLA*. Kisumu, Kenya: Evangel, 1978.
Castro, Emilio. "Editorial." *IRM* 70 (1981) 233–39.
———. "Evangelism and Ecumenism in Latin America." *SW* 49 (1956) 343–52.
———. "Forward in Ecumenism." In *Christian Action in the Asian Struggle*, edited by K. Than, 38–46. Singapore: CCA, [1973].
———. "New Perspectives in Mission." In *The Vision of Christian Unity: A Life Given to the Ecumenical Quest; Essays in Honor of Paul A. Crow, Jr.*, edited by Thomas Best and Theodore Nottingham, 71–88. Indianapolis: Oikoumene, 1997.
———. *Sent Free: Mission and Unity in the Perspective of the Kingdom*. Risk Book Series 23. Geneva: WCC, 1985.
Catholic Church, Pope John Paul II. *The Encyclicals in Everyday Language*, edited by Joseph G. Donders. Maryknoll, NY: Orbis, 1996.
———, Pope Paul VI. *On Evangelization in the Modern World: Apostolic Exhortation* Evangelii nuntiandi, *Dec. 8, 1975*. Washington, DC: United States Catholic Conference, 1976.
Cattan, Louise Armstrong. *Lamps Are for Lighting: The Story of Helen Barrett Montgomery and Lucy Waterbury Peabody*. Christian World Mission Books. Grand Rapids: Eerdmans, 1972.
Cattell, Everett L. "National Association of Evangelicals and World Evangelical Fellowship." *CT* 9 (January 29, 1965) 12–14.
Cavert, Samuel McCrea. *The American Churches in the Ecumenical Movement, 1900–1968*. New York: Association, 1968.

---. *Church Cooperation and Unity in America: A Historical Review, 1900–1970.* New York: Association, 1970.
CCA. *Christian Action in the Asian Struggle.* Edited by U. Kwaw Than. Singapore: CCA, 1973.
---. *Minutes of the General Committee and Executive Committee.* Hong Kong: 1987.
CEC. *The Churches of Europe and the Churches of the Other Continents: A Report of a Consultation Held at Basle, Switzerland, 27th–30th November 1967.* CEC Occasional Papers 1. Geneva: CEC, 1968.
---, COPEC, Birmingham 1924. *Proceedings of C.O.P.E.C; Being a Report of the Meetings of the Conference on Christian Politics, Economics and Citizenship.* London: Longmans, Green, 1924.
Centenary Conference, London 1888. *Report of the Centenary Conference on the Protestant Missions of the World, Held in Exeter Hall (June 9th–19th), London, 1888.* Edited by James Johnston. 2 vols. London: Nisbet, 1889.
Champion, L. G. "William Carey, a Pioneer of the Ecumenical Movement." *Indian Journal of Theology* 11 (1962) 54–59.
Chandran, J. Russell. "IMC-WCC Merger, BEM; an Ecumenical Council?" *ER* 40 (1988) 424–31.
Chapman, Alister. "Evangelical International Relations in the Post-Colonial World: The Lausanne Movement and the Challenge of Diversity, 1974–89." *Missiology* 37 (2009) 355–68.
Chapman, H. Owen. "Christian Medical Co-operation in China." *IRM* 37 (1948) 163–71.
Chellappa, David. "The Challenge of the Church of South India to Other Churches and to the Ecumenical Movement." *Indian Journal of Theology* 6.2 (November 1952) 5–11.
China Book International. "Official pledges support for publication of Bible." Publishing News. Online: http://www.cbi.gov.cn/wisework/content/13620.html.
China Centenary Missionary Conference, Shanghai 1907. *China Centenary Missionary Conference Records: Held at Shanghai, April 25 to May 8, 1907.* New York: American Tract Society, 1907.
Christensen, Torben, and William R. Hutchison, editors. *Missionary Ideologies in the Imperialist Era, 1880–1920: Papers from the Durham Consultation, 1981.* 2nd ed. Copenhagen: Aros, 1982.
Christian Beacon 54–55 (1989–90).
"Christians in Dialogue with Men of Other Faiths, the Statement of the Kandy Consultation." *Study-Encounter* 3 (1967) 52–56.
Church of Christ in Congo. "Constitution." *CMN* 227 (Apri–June 1970) 14–15.
Church of Nigeria. *The Way Forward.* Ibadan: Church of Nigeria Inauguration Com-mittee, [1965].
Church of the Nazarene. *Journal of the 22nd General Assembly.* Kansas City, MO: Nazarene Pub., 1989.
---. *Manual: 2005–2009.* Kansas City, MO: Nazarene Pub., 2005.
"The Church of the Nazarene." *ER* 23 (1971) 303–16.
Church Union News and Views 1–18 (July 1930—November 1947).
"Cleveland Conference on a Just and Durable Peace." *Federal Council Bulletin* 28.2 (February 1945) 6–8.
Coggins, Wade T., and E. L. Frizen Jr., editors. *Evangelical Missions Tomorrow.* Pasadena, CA: William Carey Library, 1977.
"Confessional Families and the Churches in Asia: Report of the Kandy Consultation, December 1965." *LW* 13 (1966) 196–205.
Congo Protestant Council. *After Sixty Years, 1878–1938: Report and Findings of Conference Held at Léopoldville, Congo Belge, to Celebrate the Diamond Jubilee of the Foundation of Congo Protestant Missions.* Léopoldville: Conseil Protestant du Congo, [1938].

Congress on the Church's Worldwide Mission, Wheaton, IL, 1966. *The Church's Worldwide Mission: An Analysis of the Current State of Evangelical Missions, and a Strategy for Future Activity.* Edited by Harold Lindsell. Waco, TX: Word, 1966.

Cook, William (Guillermo). *The Expectation of the Poor: Latin American Base Ecclesial Communities in Protestant Perspective.* ASMS 9. Maryknoll, NY: Orbis, 1985.

Coote, Robert T. "'AD 2000' and the '10/40 Window': A Preliminary Assessment." *IBMR* 24 (2000) 160–66.

———. "Lausanne II and World Evangelization." *IBMR* 14 (1990) 10–17.

Costas, Orlando E. "A Strategy for Third-World Missions." In *The Church in New Frontiers for Missions*, edited by David A. Fraser, 225–34. Monrovia, CA: MARC, 1983.

———. *Theology of the Crossroads in Contemporary Latin America: Missiology in Mainline Protestantism, 1969–1974.* Amsterdam: Rodopi, 1976.

Covell, Ralph R. "Jesus Christ and World Religions: Current Evangelical Viewpoints." In *The Good News of the Kingdom: Missiology for the Third Millenium*, edited by Charles van Engen, Dean Gilliland, and Paul Pierson, 162–80. Maryknoll, NY: Orbis, 1993.

Cracknell, Kenneth. *Justice, Courtesy and Love: Theologians and Missionaries Encountering World Religions, 1846–1914.* London: Epworth, 1995.

Crafford, Dionne. "Ecumenism in Africa and the Future of the Continent." *Scriptura* 39 (September 1991) 1–8.

Crane, William H. "Dropping the S: Editorial." *IRM* 58 (1969) 141–44.

———. "Revolution and the New Tribe in Africa." Paper presented at the Africa Committee of the NCCUSA Division of Foreign Mission, September 16, 1959. YDSL/Pam, box 254.

Crawford, John R. *Protestant Missions in Congo: 1878–1969.* Kinshasa: [1970].

Crocombe, Ronald G., Emilaina Afeaki, and John McLaren. *Religious Cooperation in the Pacific Islands.* Suva, Fiji: University of the South Pacific, 1983.

Cronje, F. H. J. "The Influence of Pentecostalism on Church Unity and Diversity." In *Church Unity and Diversity in the Southern African Context: Proceedings of the Third Symposium of the Institute for Theological Research (UNISA) . . .* , edited by Willem S. Vorster, 110–40. Pretoria: University of South Africa, 1980.

Crow, Paul A., Jr. "Ecumenics as Reflections on Models of Christian Unity." *ER* 39 (1987) 389–403.

———. "Impulses toward Christian Unity in Nineteenth Century America." *M-S* 22 (1983) 419–40.

———. "The Legacy of Four World Conferences on Faith and Order." *ER* 45 (1993) 13–26.

———. "Reflections on Models of Christian Unity." In *Living towards Visible Unity: The Fifth International Consultation of United and Uniting Churches*, edited by Thomas F. Best, 21–38. FOP 142. Geneva: WCC, 1988.

Cryderman, Lyn. "Global Camp Meeting." *CT* 33 (August 18, 1989) 39–41.

Cullmann, Oscar. *Unity through Diversity: Its Foundation, and a Contribution to the Discussion Concerning the Possibilities of Its Actualization.* Translated by M. Eugene Boring. Philadelphia: Fortress, 1988.

Daneel, Marthinus L. *African Earthkeepers: Wholistic Interfaith Mission.* Maryknoll, NY: Orbis, 2001.

———. "African Initiated Churches in Southern Africa: Protest Movements or Mission Churches?" In *Christianity Reborn: The Global Expansion of Evangelicalism in the Twentieth Century*, edited by Donald M. Lewis, 181–218. Grand Rapids: Eerdmans, 2004.

———. *Fambidzano: Ecumenical Movement of Zimbabwean Independent Churches.* Gweru, Zimbabwe: Mambo, 1989.

Davey, Colin. "Churches Together in Pilgrimage: The Interchurch Process in the British Isles." *One in Christ* 25 (1989) 180–96.

Davies, Ronald E. "Jonathan Edwards: Missionary Biographer, Theologian, Strategist, Administrator, Advocate—and Missionary." *IBMR* 21 (1997) 60–67.

Davis, J. Merle. *Modern Industry and the African: An Enquiry into the Effect of the Copper Mines of Central Africa upon Native Society and the Work of Christian Missions.* New York: Macmillan, 1933.

Davis, Kortright. "The Story of the Caribbean Conference of Churches." In *New Mission for a New People: Voices from the Caribbean*, edited by D. I. Mitchell. New York: Friendship, 1977.

Dawson, David G. "Funding Mission in the Early Twentieth Century." *IBMR* 24 (2000) 155–59.

De-la-Noy, Michael. *A Task for the Churches in Europe, to Serve and Reconcile: A Report of the "Nyborg V" Assembly of the Conference of European Churches in Pörtschach 1967.* Geneva: CEC, 1968.

Deichmann Edwards, Wendy J. "Forging an Ideology for American Missions: Josiah Strong and Manifest Destiny." In *North American Foreign Missions, 1810–1914: Theology, Theory and Policy*, edited by Wilbert R. Shenk, 163–91. SHCM. Grand Rapids: Eerdmans, 2004.

Delaney, Joan. "The Relationship of the Roman Catholic Church to the Commission on World Mission and Evangelism of the World Council of Churches." *Verbum SVD* 28 (1987) 82–88.

Derr, Thomas Sieger. *Barriers to Ecumenism: The Holy See and the World Council of Churches on Social Questions.* Maryknoll, NY: Orbis, 1983.

Dickinson, Richard D. N. "Diakonia in the Ecumenical Movement." In *HEM* 3:403–31.

Donovan, V. J. "The Protestant-Catholic Scandal in Africa." *AFER* 1 (1959) 169–77.

Douglass, H. Paul. *Church Unity Movements in the United States.* New York: Institute of Social and Religious Research, 1934.

Drewery, Mary. *William Carey: Shoemaker and Missionary.* London: Hodder & Stoughton, 1978.

Dries, Angelyn. *The Missionary Movement in American Catholic History.* ASMS 26. Maryknoll, NY: Orbis, 1998.

———. "U.S. Catholic Women and Mission: Integral or Auxiliary?" *Missiology* 33 (2005) 301–11.

Drummond, Richard Henry. *A History of Christianity in Japan.* Grand Rapids: Eerdmans, 1971.

Duchrow, Ulrich. *Conflict over the Ecumenical Movement: Confessing Christ Today in the Universal Church.* Translated by David Lewis. Geneva: WCC, 1981. Originally published as *Konflikt um die Ökumeme. Christusbekenntnis—in welcher Gestalt der ökumenischen Bewegung.* Munich: Kaiser, 1980.

Duff, Edward. *The Social Thought of the World Council of Churches.* New York: Association Press, 1956.

Dulles, Avery. *The Resilient Church: The Necessity and Limitations of Adaptation.* Garden City, NY: Doubleday, 1977.

———. "The Unity for Which We Hope." In *Evangelicals and Catholics Together: Toward a Common Mission*, edited by Charles Colson and Richard John Neuhaus, 115–46. Dallas: Word, 1995.

Dulles, John Foster. "Positive Measures for Peace." *ER* 8 (1956) 387–89.

Duraisingh, Christopher. "Issues in Mission and Dialogue: Some Reflections." *IRM* 77 (1988) 398–411.

Dwight, Henry O., H. Allen Tupper, and Edwin Munsell, editors. *The Encyclopedia of Missions.* 2nd ed. New York: Funk & Wagnalls, 1904.

EACC. *Confessional Families and the Churches in Asia: Report from the Consultation Convened by the East Asia Christian Conference and Held at Kandy, Ceylon, December 6–8, 1965.* Redfern, Australia: Epworth, 1967.

———. *A Decisive Hour for the Christian Mission: The Eastern Asia Christian Conference, 1959, and the John R. Mott Memorial Lectures*. London: SCM, 1960.

———. "Issues on Confessional Families and the Churches in Asia." *ER* 16 (1964) 553–57.

———, Bangkok 1949. *The Christian Prospect in Eastern Asia: Papers and Minutes of the Eastern Asia Christian Conference, Bangkok, December 3–11, 1949*. New York: Friendship, 1950.

EATWOT, International Conference, New Dehli 1981 (5th). *Irruption of the Third World: Challenge to Theology; Papers from the International Conference of the Ecumenical Association of Third World Theologians, August 17–29, 1981, New Delhi, India*, edited by Virginia Fabella and Sergio Torres. Maryknoll, NY: Orbis, 1983.

———. "Message of Hope: Statement of *the* Fifth General Assembly of EATWOT." *Voices from the Third World* 24.2 (December 2001) 38–44.

Ecumenical Dialogue of Third World Theologians, Dar es Salaam 1976. *The Emergent Gospel: Theology from the Underside of History; Papers from the Ecumenical Dialogue of Third World Theologians, Dar es Salaam, August 5–12, 1976*, edited by Sergio Torres and Virginia Fabella. Maryknoll, NY: Orbis, 1978.

Ecumenical Missionary Conference, New York 1900. *Report of the Ecumenical Conference on Foreign Missions, Held in Carnegie Hall and Neighboring Churches, April 21 to May 1*. 2 vols. New York: American Tract Society, 1900.

"Ecumenical Romance: The WEF Courts the Lausanne Committee." *CT* 24 (May 2, 1980) 54.

Ecumenical Study Conference for East Asia, Lucknow 1952. *Christ—the Hope of Asia: Papers and Minutes of the Ecumenical Study Conference for East Asia, Lucknow, India, December 27–30, 1952*. Madras: CLS for the Study Department of the WCC, 1953.

Edwards, David L. "Signs of Radicalism in the Ecumenical Movement." In *HEM* 2:373–409.

Edwards, Jonathan. *Apocalyptic Writings*. Edited by Stephen J. Stein. WJE 5. New Haven: Yale University Press, 1977.

Edwards, Robert L. *Nairobi Notebook: Impressions and Reflections from the Fifth Assembly of the World Council of Churches, Nairobi, Kenya, November 23—December 10, 1975*. Hartford, CT: R. L. Edwards, [1976].

Ehrenström, Nils. "Movements for International Friendship and Life and Work, 1925–1948." In *HEM* 1:545–96.

The Encyclopedia of Christianity. 5 vols. Grand Rapids: Eerdmans; Leiden: Brill, 1999–2008.

Engen, Charles van, Dean Gilliland, and Paul Pierson, editors. *The Good News of the Kingdom: Mission Theology for the Third Millennium*. Maryknoll, NY: Orbis, 1993.

Ernst, Eldon G. *Moment of Truth for Protestant America: Interchurch Campaigns Following World War One*. AAR Dissertation Series 3. Missoula, MT: Scholars, 1974.

Escobar, Samuel. "Missionary Dynamism in Search of Missiological Discernment: An Evangelical Perspective on Mission." *ERT* 23 (1999) 70–91.

———. "Recruitment of Students for Mission." *Missiology* 15 (1887) 529–45.

Ewing, John W. *Goodly Fellowship: A Centenary Tribute to the Life and Work of the World's Evangelical Alliance, 1846–1946*. London: Marshall, Morgan & Scott; Grand Rapids: Eerdmans, 1946.

Fabella, Virginia. *Beyond Bonding: A Third World Women's Theological Journey*. Manila: EATWOT and the Institute of Women's Studies, 1993.

———. "The Roman Catholic Church in the Asian Ecumenical Movement." In *A History of the Ecumenical Movement in Asia*, edited by Ninian Koshy, 2:115–38. Hong Kong: CCA, WSCF Asia-Pacific Region, and Asia and Pacific Alliance of YMCAs, 2004.

Fahs, Charles Harvey, and Helen E. Davis. *Conspectus of Cooperative Missionary Enterprises*. New York: IMC, 1935.

Fairbank, John King. "Assignment for the '70s." *American Historical Review* 74 (1969) 861–79.

Faith and Order (World Conference), Lausanne 1927. *Faith and Order: Proceedings of the World Conference, Lausanne, August 3-21, 1927.* Edited by H. N. Bate. 2nd ed. Garden City, NY: Doubleday, Doran, 1928.

———, Edinburgh 1937. *The Second World Conference on Faith and Order: Held at Edinburgh, August 3-18, 1937.* Edited by Leonard Hodgson. New York: Macmillan, 1938.

FCC. *Annual Report of the Federal Council of Churches of Christ in America.* 1941-47. New York: FCC.

———. *The Churches and the Charter of the United Nations: A Statement Adopted by the Executive Committee of The Federal Council of The Churches of Christ in America, June 26, 1945.* New York: FCC, 1945.

Fey, Harold. "Confessional Families and the Ecumenical Movement." In *HEM* 2:115-42.

Findlay, G. G., and W. W. Holdsworth. *The History of the Wesleyan Methodist Missionary Society.* 5 vols. London: Epworth, 1921.

Findlay, James F., Jr. *Church People in the Struggle: The National Council of Churches and the Black Freedom Movement, 1950-1970.* Religion in America. New York: Oxford University Press, 1993.

Firth, Cyril Bruce. *An Introduction to Indian Church History.* Rev. ed. Madras: CLS for the Senate of Serampore College, 1976.

Fischer, Jean E. "Fellowship amid Turmoil: An Interview with Jean Fischer." *CC* 109 (1992) 968-71.

———. "Inter-Church Aid and the Future." In *Hope in the Desert: The Churches' United Response to Human Need, 1944-1984: Essays to Mark the Fortieth Anniversary of the World Council of Churches' Commission on Inter-Church Aid, Refugee and World Service,* edited by Kenneth Slack, 119-32. Geneva: WCC, 1986.

Fisher, Galen M. *John R. Mott: Architect of Co-operation and Unity.* New York: Association, 1952.

FMC. *Report of the Meeting of the Conference of Foreign Mission Boards in Canada and in the United States.* 57 vols. New York: FMC, 1893-1950.

Forman, Charles W. "Recent Developments in Pacific Island Christianity." *MS* 9 (1992) 24-39.

———. "Sing to the Lord a New Song: Women in the Churches of Oceania." In *Rethinking Women's Roles: Perspectives from the Pacific,* edited by Denise O'Brien and Sharon W. Tiffany, 153-72. Berkeley: University of California Press, 1984.

———. *The Voice of Many Waters: The Story of the Life and Ministry of the Pacific Conference of Churches in the Last 25 Years.* Suva, Fiji: Lutu Pacifika, 1986.

Frizen, E. L. *75 Years of IFMA, 1917-1992: The Nondenominational Missions Movement.* Pasadena, CA: William Carey Library, 1992.

Fuller, W. Harold. "From the Evangelical Alliance to the World Evangelical Fellowship: 150 Years of Unity with a Mission." *IBMR* 20 (1996) 160-62.

———. *People of the Mandate: The Story of the World Evangelical Fellowship.* Grand Rapids: Baker, 1996.

Fung, Raymond, compiler and translator. *Households of God on China's Soil.* WCC Mission Series 2. Geneva: WCC, 1982.

Funkschmidt, Kai Michael. "New Models of Mission Relationship and Partnership." *IRM* 91 (2002) 558-76.

Gairdner, W. H. T. *Edinburgh 1910: An Account and Interpretation of the World Missionary Conference.* Edinburgh: Oliphant, Anderson and Ferrier, 1910.

Galdámez, Pablo. *Faith of a People: The Story of a Christian Community in El Salvador, 1970-1980.* Maryknoll, NY: Orbis, 1986.

Gensichen, Hans-Werner. "German Protestant Missions." In *Missionary Ideologies in the Imperialist Era: 1880–1920: Papers from the Durham Consultation, 1981*, edited by Christensen and Hutchison, 181–90. 2nd ed. Copenhagen: Aros, 1982.

George, Timothy. *Faithful Witness: The Life and Mission of William Carey*. Birmingham, AL: New Hope, 1991.

Glasser, Arthur. "The Evangelicals: Unwavering Commitment, Troublesome Divisions." In *Mission in the Nineteen '90s*, edited by Gerald H. Anderson, James M. Phillips, and Robert T. Coote, 6–13. Grand Rapids: Eerdmans, 1991.

Glasswell, M. E., and E. W. Fasholé-Luke, editors. *New Testament Christianity for Africa and the World: Essays in Honour of Harry Sawyerr*. London: SPCK, 1974.

Global Christian Forum. "Proposals for the Future of the Forum." Nairobi 2007: Documents. Online: http://www.globalchristianforum.org/documents/index.php.

"The Global Christian Forum: Special Issue." *Transformation* 27 (2010) 3–64.

Goheen, Michael W. "Mission and Unity: The Theological Dynamic of Comity." In *That the World May Believe: Essays on Mission and Unity in Honour of George Vandervelde*, edited by Michael W. Goheen and Margaret O'Gara, 83–91. Lanham, MD: University Press of America, 2006.

Goodall, Norman. *Christian Ambassador: A Life of A. Livingston Warnhuis*. Manhasset, NY: Channel, 1963.

———. *The Ecumenical Movement: What It Is and What It Does*. London: Oxford University Press, 1964.

———. "The Limits of Co-operation." *IRM* 44 (1955) 447–54.

———. *Second Fiddle: Recollections and Reflections*. London: SPCK, 1979.

———. "WCC and IMC Relationships: Some Underlying Issues." *ER* (1957) 395–401.

———. "World Confessionalism and the Ecumenical Movement." *LW* 10 (1963) 53–57.

Goodykoontz, Colin Brummitt. *Home Missions on the American Frontier, with Particular Reference to the American Home Missionary Society*. Caldwell, ID: Caxton, 1939.

Gowing, Peter G. "Frank Charles Laubach, 1894–1970: Apostle to the Silent Billion." In *Mission Legacies: Biographical Studies of Leaders of the Modern Missionary Movement*, edited by Gerald H. Anderson et al., 500–507. ASMS 19. Maryknoll, NY: Orbis, 1994.

Goyau, Georges. *La femme dans les Missions*. [Paris]: Flammarion, 1933.

Graham, Carol. "V. S. Azariah 1875–1945." In *Mission Legacies: Biographical Studies of Leaders of the Modern Missionary Movement*, edited by Gerald H. Anderson et al., 324–29. ASMS 19. Maryknoll, NY: Orbis, 1994.

Grootaers, Jan. "An Unfinished Agenda: The Question of Roman Catholic Membership of the World Council of Churches, 1968–1975." *ER* 49 (1997) 305–47.

Groscurth, Reinhard, editor. *What Unity Implies; Six Essays after Uppsala*. WCC Studies 7. Geneva: WCC, 1969.

Groves, C. P. *The Planting of Christianity in Africa*. 4 vols. Mission Research Series 12. London: Lutterworth, 1948–58.

Grubb, Kenneth. *Crypts of Power: An Autobiography*. London: Hodder & Stoughton, 1971.

Grundmann, Christoffer. *Sent to Heal!: Emergence and Development of Medical Missions*. Lanham, MD: University Press of America, 2005.

———. "The Role of Medical Missions in the Missionary Enterprise: A Historical and Missiological Survey." *MS* II-2 (1985) 39–48.

Halévy, Élie. *The Birth of Methodism in England*. Translated and edited by Bernard Semmel. Chicago: University of Chicago Press, 1971.

Hallencreutz, Carl F. *Dialogue and Community: Ecumenical Issues in Inter-religious Relationships*. Studia Missionalia Upsaliensia 31. Uppsala: Swedish Institute of Missionary Research, 1977.

———. *Kraemer towards Tambaram: A Study in Hendrik Kraemer's Missionary Approach*. Studia Missionalia Upsaliensia 7. Uppsala: Gleerup, 1966.

———. "A Long-Standing Concern: Dialogue in Ecumenical History 1910–1971." In *Living Faiths and the Ecumenical Movement*, edited by S. J. Samartha, 57–71. Geneva: WCC, 1971.

———. *New Approaches to Men of Other Faiths, 1938–1968: A Theological Discussion*. WCC Research Pamphlet 18. Geneva: WCC, 1970.

———. "Tambaram Revisited." *IRM* 78 (1988) 347–59.

Han, Wenzao. "The Amity Foundation: An Ecumenical Venture Becomes Official." *Missiology* 13 (1985) 373–74.

Harder, Ben. "The Student Volunteer Movement for Foreign Missions and Its Contribution to 20th Century Missions." *Missiology* 8 (1980) 142–54.

Harding, Alan. *The Countess of Huntington's Connexion: A Sect in Action in Eighteenth-Century England*. Oxford: Oxford University Press, 2003.

Harper, Susan Billington. *In the Shadow of the Mahatma: Bishop V. S. Azariah and the Travails of Christianity in British India*. SHCM. Grand Rapids: Eerdmans, 2000.

Harrell, David Edwin. *A Social History of the Disciples of Christ*. 2 vols. Nashville: Disciples of Christ Historical Society, 1966–1973.

Harvey, Charles E. "John D. Rockefeller, Jr., and the Interchurch World Movement of 1919–1920: A Different Angle on the Ecumenical Movement." *Church History* 51 (1982) 198–209.

Hastings, Adrian. *Robert Runcie*. Philadelphia: Trinity, 1991.

Haug, Del. "The Cooperative Church of Nepal." *CC* 108 (1991) 435–37.

Hawkins, Chauncey J. *Samuel Billings Capen: His Life and Work*. Boston: Pilgrim, 1914.

Heideman, Eugene. "The Missiological Significance of the Universal Declaration of Human Rights." *Missiology* 28 (2000) 163–76.

Henry, Carl "Toward a Brighter Day" *CT* 20 (Aug 6, 1976) 1140.

Hewitt, Roderick R. "A Present Vocation in Mission and Service: The Challenge to United and Uniting Churches." *ER* (1995) 451–63.

Hinson, E. Glenn. "William Carey and Ecumenical Pragmatism." *JES* 17 (1980) 73–83.

Hinton, Jeanne. *Walking in the Same Direction: A New Way of Being Church*. Risk Book Series 67. Geneva: WCC Pub., 1995.

A History of the Ecumenical Movement. Vol. 1: *1517–1948*, edited by Ruth Rouse and Stephen C. Neill. 3rd ed. 1986. Vol. 2: *The Ecumenical Advance: 1948–1968*, edited by Harold E. Fey. 3rd ed. 1993. Vol. 3: *1968–2000*, edited by John Briggs, Mercy Amba Oduyoye, and Georges Tsetsis. 2004. Geneva: WCC.

Hoekema, Alle G. *Dutch Mennonite Mission in Indonesia: Historical Essays*. Occasional Papers 22. Elkhart, IN: Institute of Mennonite Studies, 2001.

Hoekstra, Harvey T. *The World Council of Churches and the Demise of Evangelism*. Wheaton, IL: Tyndale, 1979.

Hogg, William Richey. *Ecumenical Foundations: A History of the International Missionary Council and Its Nineteenth-Century Background*. New York: Harper, 1952.

Hollenweger, Walter J. *Pentecostalism: Origins and Developments Worldwide*. Peabody, MA: Hendrickson, 1997.

Hopkins, C. Howard. *John R. Mott: A Biography*. Grand Rapids: Eerdmans, 1979.

Horner, Norman A. *A Guide to Christian Churches in the Middle East: Present-Day Christianity in the Middle East and North Africa*. Elkhart, IN: Mission Focus, 1989.

———, editior. *Protestant Crosscurrents in Mission: The Ecumenical-Conservative Encounter.* Nashville: Abingdon, 1968.
Houtepen, Anton. "Towards Conciliar Collaboration: The WCC and the Roman Catholic Communion of Churches." *ER* 40 (1988) 473–87.
Howard, David M. *The Elusive Dream: The Eventful Story of the World Evangelical Fellowship.* Grand Rapids: Baker, 1989.
Howell, John R. "The Ecumenical Background of the Church of Christ of Zaire." Department of Religious Studies, School of Oriental and African Studies, University of London [1974].
Hudson, Darril. *The World Council of Churches in International Affairs.* Leighton Buzzard: Faith Press for the Royal Institute of International Affairs, 1977.
Hughes, Richard T. *Reviving the Ancient Faith: The Story of the Churches of Christ in America.* Grand Rapids: Eerdmans, 1996.
Hunter, Alan, and Kim-Kwong Chan. *Protestantism in Contemporary China.* Cambridge Studies in Ideology and Religion. Cambridge: Cambridge University Press, 1993.
Hutabarat-Lebang, Henriette T. "Journeying Together: The WCC's Common Understanding and Vision, the Local Church and Local Ecumenism." *ER* (1998) 285–91.
Hutchison, William R. *Errand to the World: American Protestant Thought and Foreign Missions.* Chicago: University of Chicago, 1987.
———. "A Moral Equivalent for Imperialism: Americans and the Promotion of 'Christian Civilization,' 1880–1910." In *Missionary Ideologies in the Imperialist Era: 1880–1920: Papers from the Durham Consultation, 1981*, edited by Christensen and Hutchison, 167–77. 2nd ed. Copenhagen: Aros, 1982.
———. "Preface: From Protestant to Pluralist America." In *Between the Times: The Travail of the Protestant Establishment in America, 1900–1960*, edited by William R. Hutchison, vii–xv. Cambridge Studies in Religion and American Public Life. Cambridge, Cambridge University Press, 1989.
Hutton, James. *A Letter to a Friend in Which Some Account Is Given of the Brethren's Society for the Furtherance of the Gospel among the Heathen.* London: 1769.
Iglehart, Charles W. *A Century of Protestant Christianity in Japan.* Rutland, VT: Tuttle, 1954.
IMC. *Conference of Church Leaders on International Affairs, Cambridge, England, 4–7 August 1946.* New York: IMC, 1946.
———. *Minutes of the International Missionary Council, Including Minutes of the Ad Interim Committee, 1921–1961.* London: IMC, 1962.
———. Conference, Ghana 1957–88. *The Ghana Assembly of the International Mis-sionary Council, 28 December, 1957 to 8 January, 1958; Selected Papers, with an Essay on the Role of the I.M.C.* Edited by Ronald Kenneth Orchard. London: Edinburgh House, 1958.
———. Conference, Jerusalem 1928. *The Jerusalem Meeting of the International Mis-sionary Council, March 24th—April 8th, 1928.* 8 vols. New York: IMC, 1928.
———. Conference, Madras 1938. *"The Madras Series": Presenting Papers Based upon the Meeting of the International Missionary Council, at Tambaram, Madras, India, December 12th to 29th, 1938.* 7 vols. New York: IMC, 1939.
———. Conference, Madras 1938. *The World Mission of the Church: Findings and Recommendations of the International Missionary Council, Tambaram, Madras, India, December 12th to 29th, 1938.* London: IMC, 1939.
———. Conference, New Delhi 1961. *Report to the Final Assembly of the International Missionary Council and the Third Assembly of the World Council of Churches, New Delhi, 1961.* Lausanne: La Concorde, 1961.
———. Conference, Whitby 1947. *Minutes of the Enlarged Meeting of the International Missionary Council and of the Committee of the Council, Whitby, Ontario, July 5-24, 1947.* London: IMC, 1947.

———. Conference, Whitby 1947. *Renewal and Advance: Christian Witness in a Revolutionary World*. Edited by C. W. Ranson. London: Edinburgh House, 1948.

———. Conference, Willingen 1952. *Missions under the Cross: Addresses Delivered at the Enlarged Meeting of the Committee of the International Missionary Council at Willingen, in Germany, 1952; with Statements Issued by the Meeting*. Edited by Norman Goodall. London: Edinburgh House, 1953.

India Missions Association. "Indian Missions Challenges Today." Online: http://www.imaindia.org/challenges/main.htm.

International Consultation of United and Uniting Churches, Potsdam 1987 (5th). *Living towards Visible Unity: The Fifth International Consultation of United and Uniting Churches*, edited by Thomas F. Best. FOP 142. Geneva: WCC, 1988.

Irvine, Cecilia. *The Church of Christ in Zaïre: A Handbook of Protestant Churches, Missions, and Communities, 1878–1978*. Indianapolis: Dept. of Africa, Division of Overseas Ministries, Christian Church, 1978.

Jackson, Eleanor M. *Red Tape and the Gospel: A Study of the Significance of the Ecumenical Missionary Struggle of William Paton (1886–1943)*. Birmingham, AL: Phlogiston, 1980.

Jaffarian, Michael. "The Statistical State of the North American Protestant Missions Movement from the *Mission Handbook*, 20th edition." *IBMR* 32 (2008) 35–38.

James, J. A., et al. *Essays on Christian Union*. London: Hamilton, Adams, 1845.

Jenkins, Paul. "The Church Missionary Society and the Basel Mission: An Early Experiment in Inter-European Cooperation." In *The Church Missionary Society and World Christianity, 1799–1999*, edited by Kevin Ward and Brian Stanley, 43–65. SHCM. Grand Rapids: Eerdmans, 2000.

Johnson, Philip A. "Communication and Kairos." *IRM* 60 (1971) 490–504.

Joint Committee of the Church of India, Burma and Ceylon. *Proposed Scheme of Union*. 7th ed. Madras: CLS, 1947.

Jones, E. Stanley. *The Reconstruction of the Church—on What Pattern?* Nashville: Abingdon, 1970.

Jones, Tracey K., Jr. "Mission, Unity, World Methodism and a Board of Missions." *IRM* 55 (1966) 171–81.

Jongeneel, Jan A. B. "Christianity and the Isms: A Description, Analysis, and Rethinking of Kraemer's Theology of Missions." *Bangalore Theological Forum* 20 (1988) 17–41.

———, editor. *Pentecost, Mission and Ecumenism: Essays on Intercultural Theology; Festschrift in Honour of Professor Walter J. Hollenweger*. Studien zur interkulturellen Geschichte des Christentums 75. Frankfurt: Lang, 1992.

Jordan, Philip D. *The Evangelical Alliance for the United States of America, 1847–1900: Ecumenism, Identity, and the Religion of the Republic*. Studies in American Religion 7. New York: Mellen, 1982.

Kähler, Martin. *Schriften zur Christologie und Mission*. Theologische Bücherei 42. Munich: Kaiser, 1971.

Kalu, Ogbu U. "Church Unity and Religious Change in Africa." In *Christianity in Independent Africa*, edited by Edward Fasholé-Luke et al., 164–75. Ibadan: Ibadan University, 1978.

———. *Divided People of God: Church Union Movement in Nigeria, 1875–1966*. New York: NOK, 1978.

———, editor. *The History of Christianity in West Africa*. London: Longman, 1980.

———. "The Shattered Cross: The Church Union Movement in Nigeria 1905–66." In *The History of Christianity in West Africa*, edited by O. U. Kalu, 340–64.

Kalu, Ogbu U., and Alain M. Low, editors. *Interpreting Contemporary Christianity: Global Processes and Local Identities*. SHCM. Grand Rapids: Eerdmans, 2008.

Kane, J. Herbert. "J. Hudson Taylor 1832-1905: Founder of the China Inland Mission." In *Mission Legacies: Biographical Studies of Leaders of the Modern Missionary Movement*, edited by Gerald H. Anderson et al., 197-204. ASMS 19. Maryknoll, NY: Orbis, 1994.

Kärkkäinen, Veli-Matti. "Pentecostal Missiology in Ecumenical Perspective: Contribu-tions, Challenges, Controversies." *IRM* 88 (1999) 207-25.

Kasenene, Peter. "Secular Ecumenicity: A Challenge to the Church in Africa." *AFER* 34.1 (February 1992) 44-59.

Kato, Byang. *Theological Pitfalls in Africa*. Kisumu, Kenya: Evangel, 1975.

Kerr, David A., and Kenneth R. Ross. *Edinburgh 2010: Mission Then and Now*. Oxford: Regnum; Pasadena, CA: William Carey International University Press, 2009.

Kessler, Diane. "The Future of Local Councils of Churches: Some Practical Observations." *ER* 43 (1991) 50-56.

Kessler, J. B. A. *A Study of the Evangelical Alliance in Great Britain*. Goes, Netherlands: Oosterbaan & Le Cointre, 1968.

Keyes, Lawrence. *The Last Age of Missions: A Study of Third World Missionary Societies*. Pasadena, CA: William Carey Library, 1983.

Keyes, Lawrence E., and Larry D. Pate. "Emerging Missions in a Global Church." *IBMR* 10 (1986) 156-61.

———. "Two-Thirds World Missions: The Next 100 Years." *Missiology* 21 (1993) 187-206.

Kinnamon, Michael, and Brian E. Cope, editors. *The Ecumenical Movement: An Anthology of Key Texts and Voices*. Geneva: WCC Publications; Grand Rapids: Eerdmans, 1997.

Kiplagat, Bethuel. "Ecumenism in Africa Today." In *Facing the New Challenge: The Message of PACLA* [Pan African Christian Leadership Assembly], *December 9-19, 1976*, by Michael Cassidy and Luc Verlinden, 240-43. Kisumu, Kenya: Evangel, 1978.

Klein, Genevieve. "Nederland tegen apartheid?" Online: http://www.anc.org.za/ancdocs/history/aam/nederland.html.

Knight, George R. *A Brief History of Seventh-Day Adventists*. Hagerstown, MD: Review and Herald, 1999.

Knitter, Paul. "Author's Reply." *IBMR* 14 (1990) 178-79.

Koo, T. Z. "The Church and the International Order." In *"The Madras Series"...*, 7:73-94. New York: IMC, 1939.

Koshy, Ninian, editor. *A History of the Ecumenical Movement in Asia*. 2 vols. Hong Kong: CCA, WSCF Asia-Pacific Region, and Asia and Pacific Alliance of YMCAs, 2004.

Kraemer, Hendrik. *The Christian Message in a Non-Christian World*. London: Edinburgh House, 1938.

Lacy, Creighton. *The Word-Carrying Giant: The Growth of the American Bible Society (1816-1966)*. Pasadena, CA: William Carey Library, 1977.

Lambuth, Walter. *Medical Missions: The Twofold Task*. New York: SVM, 1920.

Land, Gary. *Historical Dictionary of Seventh-Day Adventists*. Historical Dictionaries of Religions, Philosophies and Movements 56. Lanham, MD: Scarecrow, 2005.

Larson, Peter, Edward Pentecost, and James Wong. "Historical Perspectives." In *Readings in Third World Missions: A Collection of Essential Documents*, edited by Marlin I. Nelson, 82-101. Pasadena, CA: William Carey Library, 1976.

Larsson, Birgitta, and Emilio Castro. "From Missions to Mission." In *HEM* 3:125-45.

Latham, Robert O. "London Missionary Society." In *Concise Dictionary of the Christian World Mission*, edited by Neill, Anderson, and Goodwin, 355-56. Nashville: Abingdon, 1971.

Latourette, Kenneth Scott. *The Christian Outlook*. New York: Harper, 1948.

———. *Christianity in a Revolutionary Age: A History of Christianity in the Nineteenth and Twentieth Centuries*. 5 vols. New York: Greenwood, 1973.

———. *Christianity through the Ages*. New York: Harper, 1965.

———. "Colonialism and Missions: Progressive Separation." *JC&S* 7 (1965) 330–49.
———. "Distinctive Features of the Protestant Missionary Methods of the Nineteenth and Twentieth Centuries." *IRM* 26 (1937) 441–52.
———. "Ecumenical Bearings of the Missionary Movement and the International Missionary Council." In *HEM* 1:353–402.
———. *A History of Christian Missions in China*. New York: Macmillan, 1929.
———. *A History of Christianity*. New York: Harper, 1953.
———. *A History of the Expansion of Christianity*. 7 vols. Grand Rapids: Zondervan, 1970.
———. "Introduction." In *HEM* 1:1–24.
———. "Missions and Wars." *IRM* 31 (1942) 394–99.
———. *Missions Tomorrow*. New York: Harper, 1936.
———. *World Service: A History of the Foreign Work and World Service of the Young Men's Christian Associations of the United States and Canada*. New York: Association, 1957.
Lausanne Movement. "About the Lausanne Movement." Online: http://www.lausanne.org/about.html.
Laymen's Foreign Missions Inquiry. *Re-thinking Missions: A Laymen's Inquiry after One Hundred Years*. New York: Harper, 1932.
LCWE, Consultation on World Evangelization, Pattaya 1980. Lausanne Occasional Papers 5–19, 22–23. Online: http://www.lausanne.org/pattaya-1980/pattaya-1980-documents.html.
———, Consultation on World Evangelization, Pattaya 1980. "The Thailand Statement 1980," *IBMR* 5 (1981) 29–31.
———, Forum for World Evangelization, Pattaya 2004. *A New Vision, A New Heart, A Renewed Call*. Edited by David Claydon. 3 vols. Lausanne Occasional Papers 30–60. Pasadena, CA: William Carey Library, 2005.
———, Lausanne I, Lausanne 1974. *Let the Earth Hear His Voice: International Congress on World Evangelization, Lausanne, Switzerland: Official Reference Volume Papers, and Responses*, edited by J. D. Douglas. Minneapolis: World Wide Pub., 1975.
———, Lausanne II, Manila 1989. *Proclaim Christ Until He Comes: Calling the Whole Church to Take the Whole Gospel to the Whole World*. Edited by J. D. Douglas. Minneapolis: World Wide Pub., 1990.
Le Guillou, M.-J. *Mission et Unité: Les Exigences de la Communion*. 2 vols. Paris: Cerf, 1960.
Lemopoulos, George. "The Prophetic Mission of Orthodoxy: Witness to Love in Service: Reflections on a Text of the Third Preconciliar Pan-Orthodox Conference." *GOTR* 32 (1987) 359–72.
Leonard, D. L. *A Hundred Years of Missions: The Story of Progress Since Carey's Beginning*. New York: Funk & Wagnalls, 1895.
Lienemann-Perrin, Christine. *Training for a Relevant Ministry: A Study of the Contribution of the Theological Education Fund*. Madras: CLS in association with the Programme on Theological Education of the WCC, 1981.
Lindell, Jonathan. *Nepal and the Gospel of God*. New Delhi: United Mission to Nepal, 1979.
Lindgren, Juhani. *Unity of all Christians in Love and Mission: The Ecumenical Method of Kenneth Scott Latourette*. Annales Academiae Scientiarum Fennicae, Dissertationes humanarum litterarum 54. Helsinki: Suomalainen Tiedeakatemia, 1990.
Lindsell, Harold. "Lausanne 74: An Appraisal." *CT* 18 (1974) 1327–32.
———. "Missionary Imperatives: A Conservative Evangelical Exposition." In *Protestant Crosscurrents in Mission: The Ecumenical-Conservative Encounter*, edited by Norman A. Horner, 50–77. Nashville: Abingdon, 1968.
Linn, Gerhard, editor. *Hear What the Spirit Says to the Churches: Towards Missionary Congregations in Europe*. WCC Mission Series, new series, 2. Geneva: WCC, 1994.

Littell, Frankin H., editor. *The Growth of Interreligious Dialogue, 1939-1989: Enlarging the Circle.* Toronto Studies in Theology 46. Lewiston, NY: Mellen, 1989.

Little, David. "Forward." In *For All Peoples and All Nations: The Ecumenical Church and Human Rights*, by John S. Nurser, ix–xii. Advancing Human Rights. Washington, DC: Georgetown University Press, 2005.

Lovett, Richard. *The History of the London Missionary Society, 1795-1895.* 2 vols. London: H. Frowde, 1899.

LWF. *The Identity of the Church and Its Service to the Whole Human Being: Final Reports of a Study Process in Lutheran Churches.* Vol. 1. Geneva: LWF, 1977.

———. "Together in God's Mission: An LWF Contribution to the Understanding of Mission." *LWF Documentation* 26 (November 1988) 1–31.

———. Assembly, Curitiba 1990. *I Have Heard the Cry of My People: Proceedings of the Eighth Assembly Lutheran World Federation, Curitiba, Brazil, January 29—February 8, 1990.* Edited by Norman A. Hjelm. LWF Report 28/29. Geneva: LWF, 1990.

———. Assembly, Evian 1970. *Sent Into the World: The Proceedings of the Fifth Assembly of the Lutheran World Federation, Evian, France, July 14–24, 1970.* Edited by LaVern K. Grosc. Minneapolis: Augsburg, 1971

———. Assembly, Lund 1947. *Proceedings of the Lutheran World Federation Assembly, Lund, Sweden, June 30—July 6, 1947.* Philadelphia: United Lutheran Publishing House, 1948.

———, Department for Mission and Development. *Mission in Context: Transformation, Reconciliation, Empowerment; An LWF Contribution to the Understanding and Practice of Mission.* Geneva: LWF, 2004.

MacHarg, Kenneth D. "Union Churches in Latin America." *CC* 93 (1976) 417.

Mackay, John A. "John R. Mott: Apostle of the Oecumenical Era." *IRM* 44 (1955) 331–38.

———. "Let the Church Live on the Frontier." *Theology Today* 1 (1944) 145–52; 40 (1983) 39–43.

———. "The Missionary Legacy to the Church Universal." *IRM* 37 (1948) 369–74.

———. "A Theological Foreword to Ecumenical Gatherings." *Theology Today* 5 (1948) 145–50.

Maclennan, Kenneth. *The Laymen's Missionary Movement.* Edinburgh: LMM in Scotland, 1911.

Makanzu, Mavumilusa. *L'Histoire de l'Église du Christ au Zaïre: Nous n'avons pas trahi l'évangile de Jesus-Christ.* Kinshasa: CEDI, 1973.

Malik, Charles Habib. "The Universal Declaration of Human Rights." In Nolde, *Free and Equal: Human Rights in Ecumenical Perspective*, 7–13. Geneva: WCC, 1968.

Manikam, Rajah Bhushanam. "New Era in the World Mission of the Church." *Union Seminary Quarterly Review* 13.1 (1957) 31–39.

Margull, Hans Jochen. "The Ecumenical Movement in the Churches and at the Parish Level." In *HEM* 2:353–72.

Martensen, Daniel F. "The Federation and the World Council of Churches." *LWF Report* 3 (December 1978) 1–87.

Marty, Martin E. *Pilgrims in Their Own Land: 500 Years of Religion in America.* Boston: Little, Brown, 1984.

Martyn, Henry. *Journals and Letters of the Rev. Henry Martyn, B.D., Late Fellow of St. John's College, Cambridge; and Chaplain to the Honourable East India Company.* Edited by S. Wilberforce. London: Seeley & Burnside, 1837.

Matthey, Jacques. "Evangelism, Still the Enduring Text of Our Ecumenical—and Missionary—Calling." *IRM* 96 (2007) 355–67.

———. "Milestones in Ecumenical Missionary Thinking from the 1970s to the 1990s." *IRM* 88 (1999) 291–303.

———. "Missiology in the WCC: Update." *IRM* 90 (2001) 427–43.

McConkey, Clarence. "Union Churches: A Vital Overseas Ministry." *CC* 90 (1973) 918.
McDonnell, John J. *The World Council of Churches and the Catholic Church*. Toronto Studies in Theology 21. Lewiston, NY: Mellon, 1985.
McGavran, Donald, editor. *The Conciliar-Evangelical Debate: The Crucial Documents, 1964–1976*. Pasadena, CA: William Carey Library, 1977.
———. "Will Uppsala Betray the Two Billion?" In *The Conciliar-Evangelical Debate: The Crucial Documents, 1964–1976*, edited by Donald McGavran, 233–41. Pasadena, CA: William Carey Library, 1977.
McGee, Gary B. *Miracles, Missions, and American Pentecostalism*. ASMS 45. Maryknoll, NY: Orbis, 2010.
McGilvray, J. C. "The Union Christian Medical College, Vellore." *IRM* 34 (1945) 315–21.
McIntire, Carl. "A Critique of the WCC by the ICCC." *The Reformation Review* 28 (1983) 197–209.
———. *Servants of Apostasy*. Collingswood, NJ: Christian Beacon, 1955.
McLeod, Hugh. *Religion and the People of Western Europe, 1789–1970*. 2nd ed. New York: Oxford University Press, 1997.
McNeill, John T. *Unitive Protestantism: The Ecumenical Spirit and Its Persistent Expression*. Richmond: John Knox, 1964.
Meeking, Basil. "After Vatican II." *IRM* 73 (1984) 57–65.
Meeking, Basil, and John Stott, editors. *The Evangelical-Roman Catholic Dialogue on Mission, 1977–1984: A Report*. Grand Rapids: Eerdmans, 1986.
"Melbourne 1980: An Asian Comment." *CCA News* 15:6 (June 15, 1980) 6.
Menn, Wilhelm. "The Church of Christ and the International Order." In *The Universal Church and the World of Nations*, by Marquess of Lothian et al., 201–38. Church, Community, and State 7. London: Allen & Unwin, 1938.
Merwin, Wallace C. *Adventure in Unity: The Church of Christ in China*. Grand Rapids: Eerdmans, 1974.
Meyer, Harding H. "Christian World Communions." In *HEM* 3:103–22.
———. "Christian World Communions: Identity and Ecumenical Calling." *ER* 46 (1994) 383–93.
———. "Relations between United Churches and World Confessional Families." *M-S* 9 (1969) 101–20.
Meylink, Placid, and John Reardon. "Council of Churches for Britain and Ireland Assembly, Swanwick, 1992)." *One in Christ* 28 (1992) 183–35.
Miguez-Bonino, José. "A Mirror for the Ecumenical Movement? Ecumenism in Latin America." In *Voices of Unity: Essays in Honour of Willem Adolf Visser 't Hooft on the Occasion of His 80th Birthday*, edited by Ans J. van der Bent, 41–56. Geneva: WCC, 1981.
———. "A 'Third World' Perspective on the Ecumenical Movement." *ER* 34 (1982) 115–24.
"Missions: Cult or Crusade?" *CC* 65 (1948) 1421–22.
Moede, Gerald F. "Methodist Participation in Church Union Negotiations and United Churches: Possible Implications for Methodist-Roman Catholic Dialogue." *JES* 12 (1975) 367–88.
Montgomery, Helen B. *Western Women in Eastern Lands: An Outline Study of Fifty Years of Women's Work in Foreign Missions*. New York: Macmillan, 1910.
Moomaw, I. W. *Crusade against Hunger: The Dramatic Story of the World-wide Antipoverty Crusades of the Churches*. New York: Harper, 1966.
Mooneyham, W. Stanley. "World Vision: A Different Opinion." *CC* 96 (1979) 707–8.
Moorshead, R. Fletcher. "The Church in the Mission Field and Medical Missions." *IRM* 5 (1916) 277–89.

Moreau, A. Scott, general editor. *Evangelical Dictionary of World Missions*. Baker Reference Library. Grand Rapids: Baker, 2000.
Mott, John R. *Addresses and Papers of John R. Mott*. 6 vols. New York: Association, 1946–47.
———. *Cooperation and the World Mission*. New York: IMC, 1935.
———. *The Decisive Hour of Christian Missions*. New York: SVM, 1910.
———. *The Evangelization of the World in This Generation*. New York: SVM, 1901.
———. *Five Decades and a Forward View*. New York: Harper, 1939.
———. "Gains Made In Fifty Years." In *Report of the Annual Meeting of the Conference of Foreign Missions Boards of North America*, 51:26–41. New York, FMC, [1945].
M'Passou, Denis. *Mindolo: A Story of the Ecumenical Movement in Africa*. Lusaka, Zambia: Mindolo Ecumenical Foundation, 1983.
Mulder, D. C. "The Dialogue between Cultures and Religions: Kraemer's Contribution." *ER* 41 (1989) 13–19.
Mumper, Sharon E. "Assembly Installs First Non-western Director." *CT* 36 (August 17, 1992) 54.
Mundt, William F. *Sinners Directed to the Saviour: The Religious Tract Society Movement in Germany (1811–1848)*. Serie MISSION 14. Zoetemeer: Boekencentrum, 1996.
Murch, James Deforest. *Cooperation without Compromise: A History of the National Association of Evangelicals*. Grand Rapids: Eerdmans, 1956.
Murray, Geoffrey. "Joint Service as an Instrument of Renewal." In *HEM* 2:199–231.
Murray, Jocelyn. "The Role of Women in the Church Missionary Society, 1799–1917." In *Church Mission Society and World Christianity, 1799–1999*, edited by Kevin Ward and Brian Stanley, 66–90. SHCM. Grand Rapids: Eerdmans, 2000.
National Study Conference on the Churches and a Just and Durable Peace. *A Message from the [NSCCJDP]: Convened at Ohio Wesleyan University, Delaware, Ohio, March 3–5, 1942*. New York: Commission to Study the Bases of a Just and Durable Peace, 1942.
NCCUSA, Division of Foreign Missions, Far Eastern Office. *Documents of the Three-Self Movement: Source Materials for the Study of the Protestant Church in Communist China*. New York: NCCUSA, 1963.
Neill, Stephen. *Christian Partnership*. London: SCM, 1952.
———. *The Church and Christian Union*. The Bampton Lectures, 1964. London: Oxford University Press, 1968.
———. *Colonialism and Christian Missions*. New York: McGraw-Hill, 1966.
———. "Co-operation and Unity." *IRM* 44 (1955) 439–46.
———. "Epilogue." In *HEM* 1:725–31.
———. *A History of Christian Missions*. Pelican History of the Church 6. Rev. ed. New York: Penguin, 1986.
———. *Men of Unity*. London: SCM, 1960.
———. "The Missionary Movement and the Ecumenical Movement." *SW* 53 (1960) 242–51.
———. "Plans of Union and Reunion, 1910–1948." In *HEM* 1:445–505.
Neill, Stephen, Gerald H. Anderson, and John Goodwin, editors. *Concise Dictionary of the Christian World Mission*. Nashville: Abingdon, 1971.
Nelson, Marlin I, editor. *Readings in Third World Missions: A Collection of Essential Documents*. Pasadena, CA: William Carey Library, 1976.
Netland, Harold. *Encountering Religious Pluralism: The Challenge to Christian Faith and Mission*. Downers Grove, IL: InterVarsity, 2001.
Neuner, Joseph, editor. *Christian Revelation and World Religions*. London: Burns & Oates, 1967.

Newbigin, Lesslie. "All in One Place or All of One Sort." In *Creation, Christ and Culture: Studies in Honour of T. F. Torrance*, edited by Richard W. A. McKinney, 288–306. Edinburgh: T. & T. Clark, 1976.

———. "Ecumenical Amnesia." *IBMR* 18 (1994) 2–5.

———. *The Gospel in a Pluralist Society*. Grand Rapids: Eerdmans, 1989.

———. "Mission to Six Continents." In *HEM* 2:171–97.

———. "The Missionary Dimension of the Ecumenical Movement." *IRM* 70 (1981) 240–46.

———. "The Pattern of Partnership." In *A Decisive Hour for the Christian Mission: The Eastern Asia Christian Conference, 1959 and the John R. Mott Memorial Lectures*, 34–45. London: SCM, 1960.

———. *The Reunion of the Church: A Defense of the South India Scheme*. London: SCM, 1948.

———. *Unfinished Agenda: An Autobiography*. Grand Rapids, Eerdmans, 1985.

———. "Which Way for 'Faith and Order'?" In *What Unity Implies: Six Essays After Uppsala*, edited by Reinhard Groscurth, 115–32. Geneva: WCC, 1969.

Nicholas, Daniel J. "IFMA and EFMA Announce Name Change." *IBMR* 32 (2008) 43.

Nicholls, Bruce. "The WEF Theological Commission 1969–1986: A Ministry on the Frontiers of Global Evangelical Christianity." *ERT* 26 (2002) 4–22.

Niklaus, Robert L. "All Things New." *CMN* 227 (April–June 1970) 4–9.

Niles, D. T. "A Church and Its 'Selfhood.'" In *A Decisive Hour for the Christian Mission: The Eastern Asia Christian Conference, 1959 and the John R. Mott Memorial Lectures*, 72–96. London: SCM, 1960.

———. *Upon the Earth: The Mission of God and the Missionary Enterprise of the Church*. London: Lutterworth, 1962.

———. *The World Mission Looks Ahead: Groundwork for the Future*. New York: SVM, 1939.

Nolde, O. Frederick. "Amsterdam International." *CC* 65 (1948) 411–13.

———. *The Churches and the Nations*. Philadelphia: Fortress, 1970.

———. "Ecumenical Action in International Affairs." In *HEM* 2:261–85.

———. *Free and Equal: Human Rights in Ecumenical Perspective*. Geneva: WCC, 1968.

———. "Freedom of Religion and Related Human Rights." In *The Church and the International Disorder*, vol. 4 of *Man's Disorder and God's Design*, WCC Assembly, Amersterdam 1948, 143–89. New York: Harper, 1949.

———. *Freedom's Charter: The Universal Declaration of Human Rights*. New York: Foreign Policy Association, 1949.

———. "Human Rights and the United Nations: Appraisal and Next Steps." *Proceedings of the Academy of Political Science* 25 (1953) 39–48.

———. "Possible Functions of the Commission on Human Rights." *Annals of the Academy of Political and Social Science* 243 (1946) 144–49.

Northcott, Cecil. "Ecumenical or Regional?" *CC* 81 (1964) 1358.

Nurser, John S. *For All Peoples and All Nations: The Ecumenical Church and Human Rights*. Advancing Human Rights. Washington, DC: Georgetown University Press, 2005.

Oborji, Francis Anekwe. *Concepts of Mission: The Evolution of Contemporary Missiology*. Maryknoll, NY: Orbis, 2006.

Odell, Luis. "Fifty Years of Ecumenism in Latin America." In *The Growth of Interreligious Dialogue, 1939–1989: Enlarging the Circle*, edited by Franklin H. Littell, 95–111. Toronto Studies in Theology 46. Lewiston, NY: Mellen, 1989.

Oduyoye, Mercy Amba. "A Decade and a Half of Ecumenism in Africa: Problems, Programs, Hopes." In *Voices of Unity: Essays in Honour of Willem Adolf Visser 't Hooft on the Occasion of His 80th Birthday*, edited by Ans J. van der Bent, 70–77. Geneva: WCC, 1981.

———. "Reflections on Geneva 1966 and Liberation Theology from the South." *ER* 59 (2007) 60–67.

Oldham, J. H. "John R. Mott." *ER* 7 (1955) 256–59.

———. "Reflections on Edinburgh, 1910." *Religion and Life* 29 (1960) 329–38.

Oliver, Barry David. *SDA Organizational Structure: Past, Present and Future*. Andrews University Seminary Doctoral Dissertation Series 15. Berrien Springs, MI: Andrews University Press, 1989.

Oliver, Roland. *The Missionary Factor in East Africa*. London: Longmans, Green, 1952.

Olonade, Timothy. "Nigerian Church Takes the Gospel Back to Jerusalem with Vision 50:15." *Lausanne World Pulse*, June 2006, n.p. Online: http://www.lausanneworldpulse.com/themedarticles.php/361/06-2006?pg=all.

Outterson, Hugh. "Overseas Union Churches." *CC* 78 (1961) 606.

Palmer, Edwin James, "Towards Unity." In *The Christian Task in India*, edited by John McKenzie, 255–91. London: Macmillan, 1929.

Panikkar, Raimundo. "Editorial: Toward an Ecumenical Ecumenism." *JES* 19 (1982) 781–86.

———. *The Unknown Christ of Hinduism: Towards an Ecumenical Christophany*. Rev. ed. Maryknoll, NY: Orbis, 1981.

Pan-Orthodox Preconciliar Conference, Chambésy, Geneva, 1986. "Decisions de la 3ème Conference préconciliare." *Episkepsis* 366 (November 1986) 1–23.

Parker, Michael. *The Kingdom of Character: The Student Volunteer Movement for Foreign Missions, 1886–1926*. Lanham, MD: University Press of America, 1998.

Pate, Larry D. "Pentecostal Missions from the Two-Thirds World." In *Called & Empowered: Global Mission in Pentecostal Perspective*, edited by Murray A. Dempster, Byron D. Klaus, and Douglas Peterson, 242–58. Peabody, MA: Hendrickson, 1991.

Paton, William. *World Community*. London: SCM, 1938.

Paul, Rajaiah D. *Ecumenism in Action: A Historical Survey of the Church of South India*. Madras: CLS, 1972.

———. *The First Decade: An Account of the Church of South India*. Madras: CLS, 1958.

Payne, Ernest A. *The Church Awakes: The Story of the Modern Missionary Movement*. London: Edinburgh House, 1942.

———. *Thirty Years of the British Council of Churches, 1942–1972*. London: BCC, 1972.

Peabody, Lucy W. "Woman's Place in Missions Fifty years Ago and Now." *Missionary Review of the World* 1 (1927) 910

Petersen, Rodney L. "Local Ecumenism and the Neo-Patristic Synthesis of Father Georges Florovsky." *GOTR* 41 (1996) 217–42.

Petty, Orville A., editor. *Laymen's Foreign Missions Inquiry: Fact Finders' Report*. 7 vols. New York: Harper, 1933.

Phiri, Isaac. "Mindolo Ecumenical Foundation: A Unique Family." *One World* 148 (August/September 1989) 21–22.

Pierard, Richard V. "John R. Mott and the Rift in the Ecumenical Movement during World War I." *JES* 23 (1986) 601–20.

Pierson, Arthur T. *Forward Movements of the Last Half Century*. New York: Funk & Wagnalls, 1905. Reprint, New York: Garland, 1984.

Piggin, Stuart. *Making Evangelical Missionaries 1789–1858: The Social Background, Motives and Training of British Protestant Missionaries to India*. Evangelicals & Society from 1750, 2. Abingdon, UK: Courtenay, 1984.

Pope, Stephen J., and Charles C. Hefling, editors. *Sic et Non: Encountering Dominus Iesus*. Maryknoll, NY: Orbis, 2002.

Pope-Levison, Priscilla. "Evangelism in the WCC: Part One: From New Delhi to Vancouver." *IRM* 80 (1991) 231–43.

———. "Evangelism in the WCC: Part Two: From Vancouver to Canberra." *IRM* 81 (1992) 119–25.

———. "Evangelism in the World Council of Churches: Part Three: The First Decade." *IRM* 87 (1998) 95–111.
Potter, Philip A. "Christians in Dialogue with Men of Other Faiths." *IRM* 59 (1970) 382–91.
———. "Christ's Mission and Ours in Today's World: Director's Report." In *Bangkok Assembly 1973*, Report. In *WCC/CWME*, 51–63. Bangkok Assembly 1973.
———. "Evangelization in the Modern World." In *Evangelization*, edited by G. Anderson and T. Stransky, 162–75. Mission Trends 2. New York: Paulist, 1975.
———. "On Coming-of-Age." *ER* 19 (1967) 205–6.
———. "Report of the General Secretary." *ER* 25 (1973) 414–29.
———. "The Third World in the Ecumenical Movement." *ER* 24 (1972) 55–71.
———. "WCC and the World of Religions and Cultures." *ER* 41 (1989) 4–12.
Potts, E. Daniel. *British Baptist Missionaries in India, 1793–1837: The History of Serampore and Its Missions.* Cambridge: Cambridge University Press, 1967.
Rafransoa, M. "La CETA et la Liberation de toute l'Afrique." *Bulletin de Theologie Africaine* 6 (1984) 239–46.
Raiser, Konrad. *Ecumenism in Transition: A Paradigm Shift in the Ecumenical Movement?* Translated by Tony Coates. Geneva: WCC, 1991.
———. "Thirty Years in the Service of the Ecumenical Movement: The Joint Working Group between the Roman Catholic Church and the WCC." *ER* 47 (1995) 430–38.
Rakotoarimanana, Victor. "CEVAA, a Response to the Gospel's Demands." *IRM* 62 (1973) 407–14.
Randall, Ian, and David Hilborn. *One Body in Christ: The History and Significance of the Evangelical Alliance.* Carlisle, UK: Paternoster, 2001.
Ranson, Charles W. *That the World May Know.* New York: Friendship, 1953.
Ratzinger, Joseph. *Many Religions, One Covenant: Israel, the Church, and the World.* Translated by Graham Harrison. San Francisco: Ignatius, 1999.
Reid, Daniel G., editor. *Dictionary of Christianity in America.* Downer's Grove, IL: InterVarsity, 1990.
Reid, John R. "The Voluntary Missionary Association." *IRM* 70 (1981) 276–79.
Reidy, Miriam. "A Watershed Assembly." *One World* 154 (April 1990) 20–22.
The Reformation Review 12–29 (1965–84).
Rhee, Jong Sung. "The Quest for Unity in Asia." *IRM* 59 (1970) 206–14.
Rhoades, J. Benton. "Agricultural Missions Today and Yesterday." *IRM* 64 (1975) 346–53.
Rivera-Pagán, Luis N. "Porto Alegre 2006: A Polycentric World Christianity." In *God in Your Grace: Official Report of the Ninth Assembly of the World Council of Churches*, WCC Assembly, Porto Alegre 2006, 5–50. Geneva: WCC, 2007.
Robbins, Bruce W. *A World Parish?: Hopes and Challenges of the United Methodist Church in a Global Setting.* Nashville: Abingdon, 2004.
Robeck, Cecil M. "A Pentecostal Looks at the World Council of Churches." *ER* 47 (1995) 60–69.
———. "Pentecostals and Ecumenism in a Pluralistic World." In *The Globalization of Pentecostalism: A Religion Made to Travel*, edited by Murray W. Dempster, Byron D. Klaus, and Douglas Petersen, 338–62. Oxford: Regnum, 1999.
Robert, Dana L. *American Women in Mission: A Social History of Their Thought and Practice.* The Modern Mission Era, 1792–1992. Mercer, GA: Mercer University Press, 1996.
———. "'The Crisis of Missions': Premillennial Mission Theory and the Origins of Independent Evangelical Missions." In *Earthen Vessels: American Evangelicals and Foreign Missions, 1880–1980*, edited by Joel A. Carpenter and Wilbert R. Shenk, 29–46. Grand Rapids, Eerdmans, 1990.

---. "Introduction: Historical Themes and Current Issues." In *Gospel Bearers, Gender Barriers: Missionary Women in the Twentieth Century*, edited by Dana L. Robert, 1–28. ASMS 32. Maryknoll, NY: Orbis, 2002.

---. "The Origin of the Student Volunteer Watchword: 'The Evangelization of the World in This Generation.'" *IBMR* 10 (1986) 146–49.

Robertson, Edwin H. *Taking the Word to the World: 50 Years of the United Bible Societies*. Nashville: Nelson, 1996.

Roosevelt, Eleanor. "Introduction." In *Freedom's Charter: The Universal Declaration of Human Rights*, by O. Frederick Nolde, 3–4. New York: Foreign Policy Association, 1949.

Rooy, Sidney H. "The Latin American Council of Churches and Missions: An Historical Approach." *MS* 20 (2003) 112–39.

Ross, Emory. *Out of Africa*. New York: Friendship Press, 1936.

Rouse, Ruth. "Voluntary Movements and the Changing Ecumenical Climate." In *HEM* 1:309–49.

---. "William Carey's 'Pleasing Dream.'" *IRM* 38 (1949) 181–92.

---. *The World's Student Christian Federation: A History of the First Thirty Years*. London: SCM, 1948.

Roy, Ralph Lord. *Apostles of Discord: A Study of Organized Bigotry and Disruption on the Fringes of Protestantism*. Beacon Studies in Church and State. Boston: Beacon, 1953.

Russell, C. Allyn. *Voices of American Fundamentalism: Seven Biographical Studies*. Philadelphia: Westminster, 1976.

Saayman, Willem A. *Unity and Mission: A Study of the Concept of Unity in Ecumenical Discussions since 1961 and Its Influence on the World Mission of the Church*. Manualia/UNISA 28. Pretoria: University of South Africa, 1984.

Sabath, Bob. "A Communities of Communities." *Sojourners* 9.1 (1980) 17–19.

Samartha, Stanley J. *Between Two Cultures: Ecumenical Ministry in a Pluralist World*. Geneva: WCC, 1996.

---. "Christian Study Centres and Asian Churches." *IRM* 59 (1970) 173–79.

---, editor. *Faith in the Midst of Faiths: Reflections on Dialogue in Community, Consultation at Chiang Mai, 1977*. Geneva: WCC, 1977.

---, editor. *Living Faiths and the Ecumenical Movement*. Geneva: WCC, 1971.

---. "Mission in a Religiously Plural World: Looking beyond Tambaram 1938." *IRM* 78 (1988) 311–24.

---. "More than an Encounter of Commitments." *IRM* 59 (1970) 392–403.

---. "Vision and Reality: Personal Reflections on the Church of South India, 1947–1997." *ER* 49 (1997) 483–92.

---. "The World Council of Churches and Men of Other Faiths and Ideologies." *ER* 22 (1970) 190–98.

Samuel, Vinay. "Pentecostalism as a Global Culture: A Response." In *The Globalization of Pentecostalism: A Religion Made to Travel*, edited by Murray W. Dempster, Byron D. Klaus, and Douglas Petersen, 254–58. Oxford: Regnum, 1999.

Sandidge, J. L. "World Council of Churches." In *Dictionary of Pentecostal and Charismatic Movements*, edited by Stanley M. Burgess and Gary B. McGee, 901–3. Grand Rapids: Zondervan, 1988.

Santa Ana, Julio de. "Evaluation of EATWOT." *Voices from the Third World* 22 (1999) 189–98.

---, editor. *Towards a Church of the Poor: The Work of an Ecumenical Group on the Church and the Poor*. Geneva: WCC, 1979.

Scherer, James A. *Mission and Unity in Lutheranism: A Study in Confession and Ecumenicity*. Philadelphia: Fortress, 1969.

Schlatter, Wilhelm. *Geschichte der Basler Mission, 1815–1915.* 3 vols. Basel: Basel Mission, 1916.
Schmidt, Martin. "Ecumenical Activity on the Continent of Europe in the Seventeenth and Eighteenth Centuries." In *HEM* 1:73–120.
Schmidt-Clausen, Kurt. "Launching a Worldwide Venture: History of the Lutheran World Convention 1923–1947." *LW* 23 (1976) 274–84.
———. "The World Confessional Families and the Ecumenical Movement." *LW* 10 (1963) 35–44.
Schwager, F. "Missionary Methods from a Roman Catholic Standpoint." *IRM* 3 (1914) 488–505.
Scopes, Wilfred. "Church of South India: An Evaluation." *Congregational Quarterly* 29 (1951) 328–35.
Scott, Waldron. "Evangelical Cooperation." In *Evangelical Missions Tomorrow*, edited by Wade T. Coggins and E. L. Frizen Jr., 61–73. Pasadena, CA: William Carey Library, 1977.
———. "The Significance of Pattaya." *Missiology* 9 (1981) 57–76.
Selvanayagam, Israel. "Interfaith Dialogue." In *HEM* 3:149–74.
Semmel, Bernard. "Introduction: Élie Halévy, Methodism, and Revolution." In *The Birth of Methodism in England*, by Élie Halévy, translated and edited by Bernard Semmel, 1–29. Chicago: University of Chicago Press, 1971.
———. *The Methodist Revolution.* New York: Basic Books, 1973.
Setiloane, Gabriel. "The Ecumenical Movement in Africa: From Mission Church to Moratorium." In *Resistance and Hope: South African Essays in Honour of Beyers Naudé*, edited by Charles Villa-Vicencio and John W. De Gruchy, 137–47. Grand Rapids: Eerdmans, 1985.
Seventh-Day Adventist Church. "Seventh-Day Adventist World Church Statistics." Facts and Figures. Online: http://www.adventist.org/world_church/facts_and_figures/index.html.en.
Seventh-Day Adventist Encyclopedia. 2nd rev. ed. 2 vols. Commentary Reference Series 10–11. Hagerstown, MD: Review and Herald, 1996.
Sharpe, Eric J. "The Legacy of Nathan Söderblom." *IBMR* 12 (1988) 65–70.
Sheard, Robert B. *Interreligious Dialogue in the Catholic Church since Vatican II: An Historical and Theological Study.* Toronto Studies in Theology 31. Lewiston, NY: Mellen, 1987.
Shedd, Clarence Prouty. *Two Centuries of Student Christian Movements: Their Origin and Intercollegiate Life.* New York: Association, 1934.
Shenk, Wilbert R. *By Faith They Went Out: Mennonite Missions, 1850–1999.* IMS Occasional Papers 20. Elkhart, IN: Institute of Mennonite Studies, 2000.
———, editor. *North American Foreign Missions, 1810–1914: Theology, Theory, and Policy.* SHCM. Grand Rapids: Eerdmans, 2004.
Short, Frank. "National Councils of Churches." In *HEM* 2:93–113.
Shorter, Aylward. "Factors in African Ecumenism." *AFER* 24 (1982) 347–53.
Sider, Ronald J., editor. *Lifestyle in the Eighties: An Evangelical Commitment to Simple Lifestyle.* Contemporary Issues in Social Ethics 1. Philadelphia: Westminster, 1982.
Slade, Ruth M. *English-Speaking Missions in the Congo Independent State (1878–1908).* Académie royale des sciences coloniales, Classe des sciences morales et politiques, mémoires in-8, new series, 16/2. Brussels: 1959.
Smalley, William A. *Translation as Mission: Bible Translation in the Modern Missionary Movement.* The Modern Mission Era, 1792–1992. Macon, GA: Mercer, 1991.
Smith, Gary Scott. "The Men and Religion Forward Movement of 1911–12: New Perspectives on Evangelical Social Concern and the Relationship between Christianity and Progressivism." *Westminster Theological Journal* 49 (1987) 91–118.
Smith, Timothy. "An Historical Perspective on Evangelicalism and Ecumenism." *M-S* 22 (1983) 308–25.

Stackhouse, John G., Jr., editor. *No Other Gods before Me?: Evangelicals and the Challenge of World Religions.* Grand Rapids: Baker Academic, 2001.

Stafford, Tim. "The Colossus of Care: World Vision Has Become an International Force and a Partner with the Poor." *CT* 49 (March 2005) 50–56.

Stanley, Brian. *The History of the Baptist Missionary Society, 1792–1992.* Edinburgh: T. & T. Clark, 1992.

———. *The World Missionary Conference, Edinburgh 1910.* SHCM. Grand Rapids: Eerdmans, 2009.

"Statement of a Joint Consultation Concerning Confessional Movements and Mission and Unity." *LW* 13 (1966) 192–96.

Stott, John R. W. "The Rise and Fall of Missionary Concern in the Ecumenical Movement." In *Vocation and Victory: An International Symposium Presented in Honour of Erik Wickberg, LL.D.*, edited by J. W. Winterhager and Arnold Brown, 53–65. Basel: Brunnen, 1974.

———. "Twenty Years after Lausanne: Some Personal Reflections." *IBMR* 19 (1995) 50–55.

Stransky, Thomas F. "The Church and Other Religions." *IBMR* 9 (1985) 154–58.

———. "Roman Catholic Membership in the World Council of Churches?" *ER* 22 (1968) 203–24.

———. "A Roman Catholic Reflection." *Missiology* 9 (1981) 41–51.

Stromberg, Jean. "Christian Witness in a Pluralistic World: Report on a Mission/Dialogue Consultation." *IRM* 78 (1988) 412–36.

Sundkler, Bengt. *Church of South India: The Movement towards Union, 1900–1947.* Rev. ed. London: United Society for Christian Literature, 1965.

———. *Nathan Söderblom: His Life and Work.* London: Lutterworth, 1968.

"Survey of Church Union Negotiations." *ER Occasional Feature* 16 (1964) 406–43; 20 (1968) 263–92; 22 (1970) 251–82; 24 (1972) 353–70; 52 (2000) 3–45.

"A Survey of the Effect of the War upon Missions." *IRM* 8 (1919) 433–90.

SVM. *The Achievements of the Student Volunteer Movement for Foreign Missions during the First Generation of Its History, 1886–1919.* New York: SVM, 1920.

———, Convention, Indianapolis 1936. *Students and the Christian World Mission: Report of the Twelfth Quadrennial Convention of the Movement.* Edited by Jesse R. Wilson. New York: SVM, 1936.

Sykes, Norman. "Ecumenical Movements in Great Britain in the Seventeenth and Eighteenth Centuries." In *HEM* 1:123–67.

Tatlow, Tissington. "The World Conference on Faith and Order." In *HEM* 1:405–41.

Taylor, Carl E. "A Christian Medical Commission's Role in Health Planning." *IRM* 58 (1969) 181–94.

Taylor, John V., and Dorothea Lehmann. *Christians of the Copperbelt: The Growth of the Church in Northern Rhodesia.* London: SCM, 1961.

Teinonen, Seppo A. *Missio Politica Oecumenica: A Contribution to the Study of the Theology of Ecumenical Work in International Politics.* Suomen Lähetystieteellisen Seuran Julkaisuja 4. Helsinki: Finnish Society for Missionary Research, 1961.

Temple, William. *The Church Looks Forward.* New York: Macmillan, 1944.

Than, U. Kwaw. "Ear, the Eye and the Head." *IRM* 62 (1973) 457–63.

Thangaraj, M. Thomas. "Is Full Church Unity Possible or Desirable?" *ER* 44 (1992) 91–99.

Thomas, M. M. "Christian Action in the Asian Struggle." In *What Asian Christians Are Thinking: A Theological Source Book*, edited by Douglas J. Elwood, 438–53. Quezon City, Philippines: New Day, 1976.

Thomas, Norman E. "Inter-Church Cooperation in Rhodesia's Towns, 1962–1972." In *Themes in the Christian History of Central Africa*, edited by T. O. Ranger and J. K. Weller, 238–55. London: Heinemann, 1975.

Thompson, E. P. *The Making of the English Working Class*. New York: Vintage, 1963.
Thorogood, Bernard G. "Sharing Resources in Mission." *IRM* 76 (1987) 440–51.
———. "Towards Mutuality in Mission: The Council for World Mission." *IRM* 66 (1977) 163–68.
———. "Whom God May Call." In *Gales of Change: Responding to a Shifting Missionary Context; The Story of the London Missionary Society, 1945–1977*, edited by Bernard Thorogood, 238–56. Geneva: WCC, 1994.
Tigert, John James. "The Bible Society and Missions." *Methodist Quarterly Review* 53 (1904) 397–402.
Tillard, J. M. R. "The Roman Catholic Church and Ecumenism." In *The Vision of Christian Unity: A Life Given to the Ecumenical Quest; Essays in Honor of Paul A. Crow, Jr.*, edited by Thomas F. Best and Theodore J. Nottingham, 179–97. Indianapolis: Oikoumene, 1997.
Tomkins, Oliver Stratford. "The Roman Catholic Church and the Ecumenical Movement, 1910–1948." In *HEM* 1:677–93.
Truman, Harry S. *Public Papers of the Presidents of the United States: Harry S. Truman . . . April 12 to December 31, 1945*. Washington, DC: US Government Printing Office, 1961.
Tsetsis, Georges. "The Significance of Regional Ecumenism." In *HEM* 3:461–68.
Twaddell, Elizabeth. "The American Tract Society, 1814–1860." *Church History* 15 (1946) 116–32.
Union Missionary Convention. *Proceedings of the Union Missionary Convention, Held in New York, May 4th and 5th, 1854*. New York: Taylor & Hogg, 1854.
United Methodist Church. "Decision no. 410." Judicial Council Decisions. Online: http://archives.umc.org/interior_judicial.asp?mid=263&JDID=452&JDMOD=VWD&SN=401&EN=500.
United Nations. "Decolonization." Global Issues. Online: http://www.un.org/en/globalissues/decolonization/.
Universal Christian Conference on Life and Work, Stockholm 1925. *The Stockholm Conference, 1925: The Official Report . . .* Edited by G. K. A. Bell. London: Oxford University Press, 1926.
Ury, Ruth. *The Highway of Print, a World-Wide Study of the Production and Distribution of Christian Literature*. Studies in the World Misison of Christianity 7. New York: Friendship Press for the Committee on World Literacy and Christian Literature of the FMC, 1946.
Vallée, Gérard. *Mouvement Oecuménique et Religions non Chrétiennes: Un Débat Oecuménique sur la Rencontre Interreligiouse de Tambaram à Uppsala (1938–1968)*. Théologie 14. Tournai: Desclée, 1975.
Van Doorn, C. L., and W. S. F. Van Doorn-Snijders. *The Churches and Social Change in the Copperbelt of Northern Rhodesia*. Geneva: WCC, 1962.
Van Dusen, Henry Pitney. "Amsterdam: 1948." *Christianity and Crisis* 8.7 (April 26, 1948) 49–50.
———. "Christian Missions and Christian Unity." *Theology Today* 16 (1959) 319–28.
———. *One Great Ground of Hope: Christian Missions and Christian Unity*. Philadelphia: Westminster, 1961.
———. "United Strategy in Christian Missions: The Next Step." *Theology Today* 6 (1949) 217–23.
———. *World Christianity: Yesterday, Today, Tomorrow*. Nashville: Abingdon-Cokesbury, 1947.
Vatican Council (2nd, 1962–65). *The Documents of Vatican II*. Edited by Walter M. Abbott. New York: Herder & Herder, 1966.
"The Verdun Proclamation: A Statement from the CAAD/CCA." *IRM* 82 (1993) 63–73.
Vischer, Lukas. "Christian Councils: Their Future as Instruments of the Ecumenical Movement." *Study Encounter* 4 (1968) 97–108.

———. "The Ecumenical Movement and the Roman Catholic Church." In *HEM* 2:311–52.

———. "World Communions, the WCC and the Ecumenical Movement." *ER* 54 (2002) 142–61.

Visser 't Hooft, Willem Adolf. "Inter-Church Aid: How It All Began." In *Hope in the Desert: The Churches' United Response to Human Need, 1944–1984: Essays to Mark the Fortieth Anniversary of the World Council of Churches' Commission on Inter-Church Aid, Refugee and World Service*, edited by Kenneth Slack, 1–11. Geneva: WCC, 1986.

———. "John R. Mott." *SW* 58 (1965) 284–90.

———. "WCC-Roman Catholic Relations: Some Personal Reflections." *ER* 37 (1985) 336–44.

———. "The Word 'Ecumenical'—Its History and Use." In *HEM* 1:735–40.

Voskuil, Dennis N. "Reaching Out: Mainline Protestantism and the Media." In *Between the Times: The Travail of the Protestant Establishment in America, 1900–1960*, edited by William R. Hutchison, 72–92. Cambridge Studies in Religion and American Public Life. Cambridge, Cambridge University Press, 1989.

WACC. "About WACC." Online: http://www.waccglobal.org/en/about-wacc.html.

Wagner, C. Peter. "Lausanne Twelve Months Later." *CT* 19 (1975) 961–63.

Wallis, James. "Celebrating 15 Years." *Sojourners* 15.10 (November 1986) 5–6

———. "The One Constant Is Change." *Sojourners* 27.4 (July–August 1998) 9–10.

Walls, Andrew F. "British Missions." In *Missionary Ideologies in the Imperialist Era: 1880–1920: Papers from the Durham Consultation, 1981*, edited by Torben Christensen and William R. Hutchison, 159–66. 2nd ed. Copenhagen: Aros, 1982.

———. *The Missionary Movement in Christian History: Studies in Transmission of Faith*. Maryknoll, NY: Orbis, 1996.

———. "Missionary Societies and the Fortunate Subversion of the Church." *Evangelical Quarterly* 88 (1988) 141–55.

———. "Missionary Vocation and the Ministry: The First Generation." In *New Testament Christianity for Africa and the World: Essays in Honour of Harry Sawyer*, edited by M. E. Glasswell and E. W. Fasholé-Luke, 141–56. London: SPCK, 1974.

Ward, W. Reginald. *The Protestant Evangelical Awakening*. Cambridge: Cambridge University Press, 1992.

Warneck, Gustav. *Outline of a History of Protestant Missions from the Reformation to the Present Time*. 7th ed. London: Oliphant, 1901.

Warnshuis, A. L. "The Story of the Orphaned Missions." *SW* 37 (1944) 23–31.

Warren, Max. "The Fusion of IMC and WCC at New Delhi: Retrospective Thoughts after a Decade and a Half." *Occasional Bulletin of Missionary Research* 3 (1979) 104–8.

———. *Partnership: The Study of an Idea*. London: SCM, 1956.

WCC. *Guidelines on Dialogue with People of Living Faiths and Ideologies*. Geneva: WCC, 1979.

———. *In Each Place: Towards a Fellowship of Local Churches Truly United*. Geneva: WCC, 1977.

———. *Mission and Evangelism: An Ecumenical Affirmation; A Study Guide*. Compiled by Jean Stromberg. WCC Mission Series 4. Geneva: WCC, 1983.

———. "Report of the Joint Committee of the WCC and the IMC: A Draft Plan of Integration." *ER* 10 (1957) 72–81.

———. *A Theological Reflection on the Work of Evangelism*. WCC Division of Studies Bulletin 5. Geneva: WCC, 1959.

WCC/A, Amsterdam 1948 (1st). *The First Assembly of the World Council of Churches: Held at Amsterdam August 22nd to September 4th, 1948*. Edited by W. A. Visser 't Hooft. The Amsterdam Assembly Series 5. London: SCM, 1949.

———, Amsterdam 1948 (1st). *Man's Disorder and God's Design*. 4 vols. 1: *The Universal Church in God's Design*. 2: *The Church's Witness to God's Design*. 3: *The Church and the Disorder of Society*. 4: *The Church and the International Disorder*. The Amsterdam Assembly Series 1–4. New York: Harper, 1948–49.

———, Canberra 1991 (7th). *Signs of the Spirit: Official Report, Seventh Assembly, Canberra, Australia, 7–20 February 1991*. Edited by Michael Kinnamon. Grand Rapids: Eerdmans, 1991.

———, Evanston 1954 (2nd). *The Evanston Report: The Second Assembly of the World Council of Churches, 1954*. Edited by W. A. Visser 't Hooft. London: SCM, 1955.

———, Harare 1998 (8th). *Together on the Way: Official Report of the Eighth Assembly of the World Council of Churches*. Edited by Diane Kessler. Geneva: WCC, 1999.

———, Nairobi 1975 (5th). *Breaking Barriers, Nairobi 1975: The Official Report of the Fifth Assembly of the World Council of Churches, Nairobi, 23 November—10 December, 1975*. Edited by David M. Paton. London: SPCK, 1976.

———, Nairobi 1975 (5th). *Workbook for the Fifth Assembly of the World Council of Churches, Nairobi, Kenya, 23 November—10 December, 1975*. Geneva: WCC, 1975.

———, New Delhi 1961 (3rd). *The New Delhi Report: The Third Assembly of the World Council of Churches, 1961*. London: SCM, 1962.

———, Porto Alegre 2006 (9th). *God in Your Grace: Official Report of the Ninth Assembly of the World Council of Churches*, edited by Luis N. Rivera-Pagán. Geneva: WCC, 2007.

———, Uppsala 1968 (4th). *The Uppsala Report 1968: Official Report of the Fourth Assembly of the World Council of Churches, Uppsala July 4–20, 1968*. Edited by Norman Goodall. Geneva: WCC, 1969.

———, Vancouver 1983 (6th). *Gathered for Life: Official Report, Sixth Assembly of the World Council of Churches, Vancouver, Canada, 24 July—10 August 1983*. Edited by David Gill. Geneva: WCC; Grand Rapids: Eerdmans, 1983.

WCC/CC. "The Calling of the Church to Mission and to Unity" [Rolle 1951]. *Theology Today* 9 (1952) 13–19.

———. *Nairobi to Vancouver, 1975–1983: Report of the Central Committee to the Sixth Assembly of the World Council of Churches*. Geneva: WCC, 1983.

———. "Report of the Joint Committee of the WCC and the IMC: A Draft Plan of Integration." *ER* 10 (1957) 72–81.

———. *The Ten Formative Years, 1938–1948: Report on the Activities of the World Council of Churches during Its Period of Formation*. Geneva: WCC, 1948.

———. *Uppsala to Nairobi, 1968–1975: Report of the Central Committee to the Fifth Assembly of the World Council of Churches*. Edited by David Enderton Johnson. New York: Friendship Press, 1975.

———. *Vancouver to Canberra, 1983–1990: Report of the Central Committee to the Seventh Assembly of the World Council of Churches*. Edited by Thomas F. Best. Geneva: WCC, 1990.

WCC/CFO. *Baptism, Eucharist and Ministry*. FOP 111. Geneva: WCC, 1982.

———. *Church and World: The Unity of the Church and the Renewal of Human Community*. FOP 151. Geneva: WCC, 1990.

———. "A Communication to the Members of the Lund Conference on Faith and Order from some Representatives of the Younger Churches." *ER* 5 (1952) 70–71.

———. *Documentary History of Faith and Order 1963–1993*. Edited by Günther Gassmann. FOP 159. Geneva: WCC, 1993.

———. *Institutionalism and Church Unity: A Symposium*. Edited by Walter G. Muelder and Nils Ehrenström. New York: Association Press, 1963.

———. Conference, Bristol 1967. *New Directions in Faith and Order, Bristol 1967: Reports, Minutes, Documents*. FOP 50. Geneva: WCC, 1968.

———. Conference, Budapest 1989. *Faith and Order 1985-1989: The Commission Meeting at Budapest 1989*. Edited by Thomas F. Best. FOP 148. Geneva: WCC, 1990.

———. Conference, Lund 1952. *Report of the Third World Conference on Faith and Order, Lund, Sweden, August 15-28, 1952*. Edited by Oliver S. Tomkins. London: SCM, 1953.

———. Conference, Montreal 1963. *The Fourth World Conference on Faith and Order, Montreal 1963*. Edited by Patrick C. Rodger and Lukas Vischer. FOP 42. New York: Association Press, 1964.

———. Conference, Santiago de Compostela 1993. *On the Way to Fuller Koinonia: Official Report of the Fifth World Conference on Faith and Order*. Edited by Thomas F. Best and Günther Gassmann. FOP 166. Geneva: WCC, 1994.

WCC/CWME. "Mission and Evangelism: An Ecumenical Affirmation." In *"You Are the Light of the World": Statements on Mission by the World Council of Churches, 1980-2005*, 1-38. Geneva: WCC, 2005.

———. "Mission and Evangelism in Unity Today." In *"You Are the Light of the World": Statements on Mission by the World Council of Churches, 1980-2005*, 59-89. Geneva: WCC, 2005.

———. "Statement of the Stuttgart Consultation on Evangelism." In *Proclaiming Christ in Christ's Way: Studies in Integral Evangelism; Essays Presented to Walter Arnold on the Occasion of His 60th Birthday*, edited by Vinay K. Samuel and Albrecht Hauser, 212-24. Oxford: Regnum, 1989.

———. *"You Are the Light of the World": Statements on Mission by the World Council of Churches, 1980-2000*. Geneva, WCC, 2005

———. Conference, Athens 2005. *Come Holy Spirit, Heal and Reconcile!: Called in Christ to Be Reconciling and Healing Communities; Report of the WCC Conference on World Mission and Evangelism, Athens, Greece, May 9-16, 2005*. Edited by Jacques Matthey. Geneva: WCC, 2008.

———. Conference, Bangkok 1973. *Bangkok Assembly 1973: Minutes and Report of the Assembly of the Commission on World Mission and Evangelism of the World Council of Churches, December 3, 1972 and January 9-12, 1973*. Geneva: WCC, 1973.

———. Conference, Melbourne 1980. *Your Kingdom Come: Mission Perspectives; Report on the World Conference on Mission and Evangelism, Melbourne, Australia, 12-25 May, 1980*. Geneva: WCC, 1980.

———. Conference, Salvador 1996. *Called to One Hope: The Gospel in Diverse Cultures*. Edited by Christopher Duraisingh. Geneva: WCC, 1998.

———. Conference, San Antonio 1989. *The San Antonio Report: Your Will be Done; Mission in Christ's Way*. Edited by Frederick R. Wilson. Geneva: WCC, 1990.

WCC Department on Church and Society. *Dilemmas and Opportunities: Christian Action in Rapid Social Change; Report of an International Ecumenical Study Conference, Thessalonica, Greece, 25 July—2 August 1959*. Geneva: WCC, 1959.

WCC Division of Studies. "A Theological Reflection on the Work of Evangelism." *Division of Studies Bulletin* 5 (1959).

WCC/DWME. *Survey of the Training of the Ministry in the Middle East: Report of Theological Education in Iran, the Arabian-Persian Gulf, Jordan, Lebanon and Syria, and Egypt*. By Douglas Webster and K. L. Nasir. Geneva: WCC, 1962.

———. Conference, Mexico City 1963. *Witness in Six Continents: Records of the Meeting of the Commission on World Mission and Evangelism of the World Council of Churches, Held in Mexico City, December 8th to 19th, 1963*. Edited by Ronald K. Orchard. London: Edinburgh House, 1964.

WCC Provisional Committee. *The World Council of Churches: Its Process of Formation*. Geneva: WCC, 1946.
WCC Theological Education Fund. *Ministry in Context: The Third Mandate Programme of the Theological Education Fund*. Bromley, Kent, UK: Theological Education Fund, 1972.
Weber, Hans-Ruedi. *Asia and the Ecumenical Movement, 1895–1961*. London: SCM, 1966.
———. "Out of All Continents and Nations." In *HEM* 2:63–92.
"WEF: Is There a Future?" *CT* 18 (August 16, 1974) 37.
WEF, Missions Commission Consultation, Foz de Iguassu, Brazil, October 10–15, 1999. "Iguassu Affirmation." *ERT* 24 (2000) 200–206.
Werner, Dietrich. "Evangelism from a WCC Perspective: A Recollection of an Important Ecumenical Memory, and the Unfolding of a Holistic Vision." *IRM* 96 (2007) 183–203.
Westmeier, Karl-Wilhelm. "Becoming All Things to All People: Early Moravian Missions to Native North Americans." *IBMR* 21 (1997) 172–76.
———. *The Evacuation of Shekomeko and the Early Moravian Missions to Native North Americans*. SHCM 12. Lewiston, NY: Mellen, 1995.
Wickeri, Philip Lauri. *Seeking the Common Ground: Protestant Christianity, the Three-Self Movement, and China's United Front*. Maryknoll, NY: Orbis, 1988.
Williams, Glen Garfield. "Is Ecumenism Still Possible in Europe Today?" *Austin Seminary Bulletin: Faculty Edition* 103 (1987) 53–65.
Winter, Ralph D. "Ghana: Preparation for Marriage." *IRM* 67 (1978) 338–53.
———. "The New Missions and the Mission of the Church." *IRM* 50 (1971) 89–100.
———. "Protestant Mission Societies and the 'Other Protestant Schism.'" In *American Denominational Organization: A Sociological View*, edited by Ross P. Scherer, 194–224. Pasadena, CA: William Carey Library, 1980.
———. *The Twenty-Five Unbelievable Years, 1945 to 1969*. Pasadena, CA: William Carey Library, 1970.
———. "The Two Structures of God's Redemptive Mission." In *Perspectives on the World Christian Movement: A Reader*, edited by Ralph Winter and Steven C. Hawthorne, 220–30. 3rd ed. Pasadena, CA: William Carey Library, 1999.
Wood, Rick. "Passing the Baton." *Mission Frontiers* 23 (2001) 132–35.
World Conference on Church, Community and State, Oxford 1937. *The Oxford Conference: Official Report*. By J. H. Oldham. Chicago: Willett, Clark, 1937.
———. *The Universal Church and the World of Nations*. Church, Community, and State 7. London: Allen & Unwin, 1937.
World Congress on Evangelism, Berlin 1966. *One Race, One Gospel, One Task: Official Reference Volumes: Papers and Reports*. Edited by Carl F. H. Henry and W. Stanley Mooneyham. 2 vols. Minneapolis: World Wide Pub., 1967.
World Missionary Conference, 1910. 9 vols. New York: Revell, 1910.
World Vision. "World Vision's History." Online: http://www.worldvision.org/content.nsf/about/history.
Wright, J. Robert. "Mission and Ecumenism: Together Not Apart." In *Beyond the Horizon: Frontiers for Mission*, edited by Charles R. Henery, 97–116. Cincinnati: Forward Movement, 1986.
WSCF General Committee, Peking 1922. *Minutes of the Meeting of the General Committee of the World's Student Christian Federation, Peking, China, March 29 to April 2 and April 11 to 12, 1922*. N.p.: WSCF, 1922.
Yannoulatos, Anastasios, Apb. "Emerging Perspectives on the Relationships of Christians to People of Other Faiths: An Eastern Orthodox Contribution." *IRM* 77 (1988) 332–46.

———. "Facing People of Other Faiths from an Orthodox Point of View." *GOTR* 38 (1993) 131–52.
Yoder, Don Herbert. "Christian Unity in Nineteenth-Century America." In *HEM* 1:221–59.
Yoder, Howard W. "The Second Latin American Evangelical Conference." *IRM* 51 (1962) 75–78.
Yuzon, Lourdino A. "Ecumenical Perspectives in Inter-faith Dialogue." *Asia Journal of Theology* 1 (1987) 531–44.
"Zairian Church in Thick of Conflict." *CC* 114 (May 7, 1997) 444–45.

ARCHIVAL SOURCES

Basel Mission, Basel, Switzerland

A-Basel (Basel Mission Archives)
  "IMC" on orphaned missions. Box QK 4.9–10.

Presbyterian Historical Society, Philadelphia

A-NCC (National Council of Churches Archives)
  "CPC Minutes 1930–1941." NCC8, ser. 2, box 8.

School of Oriental and African Studies, University of London, England

A-CBMS (IMC/Conference of British Missionary Societies Archives), 1912–54
  "Church Union in South India." Box 410.
A-CWM (Archives of the Council for World Mission), incorporating the A-LMS (Archives of the London Missionary Society)
  "Church Union in South India." Box IN/48.
  "London Missionary Society: Board Minutes." Boxes 1, 3, 5, 7.

University of Birmingham Library, England

A-CMS (Archives of the Church Missionary Society)
  W. Summer to Mr. Elliott, September 25, 1795. C7/14.

World Council of Churches Library and Archives, Geneva, Switzerland

A-WCC/CCIA (Commission of the Churches on International Affairs)
  "CCIA New York Office."
  "CCIA: WCC Gen. Sec. Files."
  "Early History." Box 428.0.01–02.
  "Mailings, 1953–56." Box 428.3.25.
  "O. Frederick Nolde Papers."
  "Staff and Commissioners Personal Files."
  "Survey." Box 428.0.0.0.
A-WCC/DWG (WCC Dialogue Working Group)
  "Departmental Committee." DFI-box VI.
A-WCC/GS (WCC General Secretariat)
  "Gen. Sec., World Confess. Meetings, 1958–1968."

"IMC Correspondence: 1931–57."
"A Working Paper on the Basis of Cooperation with the Roman Catholic Church." Box 1.2.
"World Confessional Bodies, 1963–" Box 2.
"World Confessional Families/Bodies."
A-WCC/IMC (WCC International Missionary Council Archives)
"IMC General: Early History & Policy." Box 260001.
"Joint Committee of the WCC and IMC." Boxes 270001–16.
"Letters." Box 26113.
"Religious Liberty, North America." Box 261605.
"William Paton Papers." Boxes 261141–49.

Yale Divinity School Library, Special Collections, New Haven, Connecticut

A-YDSL/CCLA (Committee on Cooperation in Latin America)
Report [1936?]. HR841.
A-YDSL/ICCC (International Council of Christian Churches)
"East Africa Christian Alliance" A094.10.
A-YDSL/Lat (Kenneth Scott Latourette Papers), Record Group 3.
"Correspondence, Rouse, Ruth." Box 104.
A-YDSL/Mott (J. R. Mott Papers), Record Group 45
"Conferences, visits—Africa" (including conference reports). Box 159.
"Correspondence, Oldham, Joseph H." Boxes 63–66.
A-YDSL/Pam (Missions Pamphlet Collection), Record Group 31.
"NCCUSA: Committee on Research in Foreign Missions, 1952–1956." Series I, box 176.
A-YDSL/PCC (Pacific Conference of Churches)
"Records, 1961–1989." HR987.
A-YDSL/SVM (Student Volunteer Movement Archives), 1886–1964, Record Group 42.
"SVM History." Box 449.
"SVM Publications." Box 554.
A-YDSL/Wilder (Robert Parmelee Wilder Papers), Record Group 38.
"Near East Christian Council." Box 21, folder 204.
A-YDSL/WSCF (World Student Christian Federation Archives), 1895–1972, Record Group 46.
"Nybourg Strand 1926." Box 39.

INTERVIEWS

Bottoms, Ruth. Marathon, Greece, May 11, 2005.
Reuver, Marc. Geneva, Switzerland, September 21, 1990.
Tsu, Rulei. New Haven, Connecticut, December 2, 1990.

Subject Index

AACC, 151, 170, 184, 202
ABCFM, 13, **19**, 28–29, 32, 70
ABS, 23, 146
AEAM, 170–71
AICs, 80–82, 109
A.D. 2000 and Beyond Movement, **143–45**, 266
Addis Ababa, 149
Advent Christian Church, 181
Africa, 54, 66, 71, **169–71**; Central, 66; Christianity in, 76, 78; church unity in, 220; East, 15, 66, 124; missions, 62, 160; Southern, 116; Sub-Saharan, 78; West, 66, 131
Africa Inland Mission, 35, 52
Africa Literature Committee, 69
African Independent Church Conference, 81
African Reformed Church, 204
Agricultural Missions, 68–69
All-Africa Church Conference, 169
All-Asia Mission Consultation, 136
Alliance of Reformed Churches, 44
American Baptist Convention, 200
American Council of Christian Churches, 117
American Friends Service Committee, 51
American Home Missionary Society, 22
American Tract Society, 25,
Amity Foundation, 147, 199
Andover Theological Seminary, 22
Anglican Consultative Council, 131
Anglicans, 77, 123, 130, 168; High Church, 45, 49, 192
Angola, 74
Antigua, 9
Arcot Mission, 189
Argentina, 116, 145, 174

Asia, 54, 71; Christianity in, 76, 78, 96, 102; East, **165–67**; missions, 62, 160; South, **165–67**; Southeast, 78
Assemblies of God, 7, 181
Association of African Earthkeeping Churches, 81
Ausschuss, 28, 44, 45, 53, 178
Australasia, 30, 39, 40, 59
Australia, 142, 149, 153, 156, 157, 166, 172, 206; churches in, 35, 116
Awakening, evangelical, **12–13**

BBC, 71
BCC, 178–79, 235
Bangalore, 65
Bangkok, 127, 165
Bangladesh, 131
Baptist: churches, 29, 102, 122, 132; missions, 24
Baptist Missionary Society, 17
Baptist World Alliance, 122
Barclays Bank, 157
Basel Mission, 15, 16, 29, 71
Batak Church of Indonesia, 127
Beijing (Peking), 66, 165, 198
Beirut, 149
Belguim, 71, 169
Belize, 177
Berlin, 14, 71, 180
Bhutan, 99
Biafra, 74, 116
Bible: authority of, 76; New Testament models in, 209; translation of, 24, 146–47, 183
Bible societies, **146–47**; Roman Catholic participation in, 147
Billy Graham Center, 155
Bolivia, 112; Christianity in, 112
Bosnia, 75

Brazil, 151; Christianity in, 78, 116, 212, 216
Bremen Mission, 44
British and Foreign Bible Society, 16, 23, 26, 146
Buddhism, 185
Bulgaria, 60
Burma (Myanmar), 63, 166

CADEC, 177
CARE, 148
CBMS, 66, 69, 178, 235
CCA, 166, 167, 185
CCBI, 179
CCC, 197, 199
CCIA, **232-39**
CCJCA, 177
CCLA, 173
CEC, **179-80**
CELA, **174-75**
CELAM, 175
CLAI, **176**, 185
CMS, x, **15-16**, 17, 25, 87, 102, 154, 160, 189, 233
COMIBAM, 161
CONELA, **176**
COPEC, 223
CROP, 68
CSI, 125, 131, **188-95**, 206, 210, 246, 250, 268, 269
CWC, 77, **130**, 184
CWM, **132-33**
Calcutta, 32, 160
Cameroon, 131
Canada, 61, 149
Cane Ridge Revival, 23
Canstein Bible Institution, 23
Cape Verde, 95, 96
Caribbean, the, **176-77**
Caribbean Conference of Churches, 152, 177
Carnegie Endowment for International Peace, 234
Centenary Conference (London 1888), 32, 34, 43, **45**, 189
Centennial Conference of Christian Missions in China, 40, 163
Central Christian Council, 118

Central Committee for the United Study of Foreign Missions, 43
Charismatics, 78, 143
Chennai (Madras), 188
Chicago, 215
Chicago World's Fair, 43
Children, 70
China, 28, 72; Christianity in, 40, 50, 57, 64, 76, 80, 95, 116, 121, 147, 183, **195-200**, 214; missions in, 28, 34, 40, 63, 95; People's Republic of, 67
China Continuation Committee, 51
China Inland Mission, 32, 35-36, 52, 53, 54, 198. See also Overseas Missionary Fellowship
China Medical Association, 67
China Medical Board, 67
China National Christian Conference, 164
Christian, marginal, 80
Christian and Missionary Alliance, 35
Christian Church in Nepal, 156
Christian Council of Nigeria, 169
Christian Institute of South Africa, 270
Christian literature and media, **69-71**
Christian Manifesto, 197
Christian Medical Commission, 68
Christian Tabernacle of Beijing, 198
Church of Bangladesh, 188
Church of Christ in Japan (*Nihom Kirisito Kyodan*), 188, **205**
Church of Christ in Thailand, 188
Church of England, 5, 8, 10
Church of God, 181
Church of Jesus Christ in Madagascar, 188
Church of North India, 131, 188, 195, **205-6**
Church of Pakistan, 188, 206
Church of Scotland, 56; missions of, 155, 160, 189
Church of the Nazarene, **95-96**, 181, 205
Church planting, 144
Church union, 21, **187-208**; mission and, 205; union churches, 21
Church Women United, 64
Church World Service, 69, 181, 183, 229
Columbia, 176
Colonialism, 6, 74, 76; and missions, **27-29**
Comity, **32-33**

Subject Index

Commission to Study the Bases of a Just and Durable Peace, 226–27, 230, 231, 232, 234
Committee of Christian Literature for Women and Children in Mission Fields, 70
Communauté Évangélique d'Action Apostolique (CEVAA), **131–32**
Communities, base Christian/ecclesial, **212–14**
Conference of Church Leaders on International Affairs, 232, 233
Conference of Swedish Missionary Societies, 51
Conference on the Christian Mission in Africa, 169
Congo (Zaire), 74, 169, 183; church union in, 188, **200–204**, 207, 208, 268
Congo Protestant Council, 201
Congregational churches, 19, 21, 29, 122
Congress on the Church's Worldwide Mission, 139–40, 158, 163, 257
Consultation of United and Uniting Churches, 208
Continental Missions Conference, 44
Continuation Committee of Japan, 164
Copperbelt Christian Service Council, 157
Costa Rica, 177
Council of Church Boards of Education, 181
Councils of churches, local, 77, **212**
Council of Protestant Churches in Zaire, 203
CrossGlobal Link, 159. See also IFMA
Cuba, 174, 177

DP, 261
Dag Hammarskjold Memorial Library, 158
Dahomey, 131
Dalits, 56
Danske Missionsselskab, 18
Dar es Salaam, 150
Darfur, 75
Darwinism, social, 27
Denmark, 44, 179
Deutsche Christentumsgesellschaft, 15, 16, 25
Development, economic, 150

Dialogue: evangelical Protestants and, 257–58; interfaith, 185, **246–55**; Jewish-Christian, 246; Orthodox understandings of, **255–56**
Disciples of Christ, 23
Diversity, reconciled, **129–30**, 135
Doctors without Borders (*Médecins sans Frontières*), 152
Dominica, 177
Dominican Republic, 177
Doshisha College, 39
Dunbarton Oaks Conference, 221, 231
Dutch Reformed, 29, 144

EA, **30–31**, 137, 185
EACC, 103, 126, 127, **165**, 187
EATWOT, **150–52**; Women's Commission, 151
EFMA, 139, **158–59**, 181
East Africa Christian Alliance, 118
Ebionites, 82
Ecology: climate change, 85; ecotheology, 167
Ecuador, 70
Ecumenical Institute (Bossey), 157, 246
Ecumenical Missionary Conference (1900), 32, 33, 34, 43, **46**, 266
Ecumenical Research Institute, 130
Ecumenical Study Conference for East Asia, 125, 126
Ecumenism/ecumenical: ecumenical movement, xxiii; meanings, xxi; secular, 75; wider, xxi
Edinburgh Medical Missionary Society, 34
Education: missions and, **64–66**, 156
Église du Christ au Congo, **200–205**
Encyclopedia of Missions, 27, 137
England, 27, 29, 35, 36, 61, 133, 179; Christianity in, 24
Ethiopia, 15
Eucharist, 81
Europe, 48, 56, 59, 62, 97, 116, **178–80**; Eastern, 119, 155, 183; Western, 76
Evangelical Alliance Mission, 35
Evangelical Church of the Cameroon, 131
Evangelical Church of West Africa, 161
Evangelical Fellowship of India, 161, 182
Evangelical Missionary Society, 161

Evangelical Missions Information Service, 158
Evangelical United Brethren, 97
Evangelicalism, world, **137–45**
Evangelicals, 76–77, 111, 120; Great Commission Christians, 77
Evangelii nuntiandi, 93, 112
Evangelisch-lutherische mission zu Leipzig, 17
Evangelism: unity in, 100, **109–13**, 152–53

FCC, 71, 181, 182, 221, 227, 228, 229, 231, 232, 234
FMC, **44–45**, 49, 66, 70, 79, 173, **180–81**, 182, 221, 229, 234
Faith and Order, **56–57**, 129; Edinburgh 1937, 56–57, 192; Lausanne 1927, 56, 191; unity in, **113–15**
Faith missions, **35–36**
Faith Theological Seminary, 118
Far Eastern Broadcasting Company, 70, 149
Far Eastern Council of Christian Churches, 118
FEBA Radio, 150
Federation of Asian Bishops' Conference, 167
Federation of Churches in Japan, 164
Federation of Women's Boards of Foreign Missions in North America, 64
Fiji, 32, 171, 172
Finland: missions, 18, 35
France, 27, 29, 44, 71, 131; missions, 18
Franciscans, 131
Frankfurt Declaration, 111, 257
Frontier Mission Fellowship, 136
Fukien Christian College, 65
Fullness/Praise Network of Churches, 80

GCOWE, 144
General Missionary Conference of Northern Rhodesia, 185
General Missionary Conference of the Congo, 200
Georgia, 8
Germany, 14, 27, 28, 48, 123, 128; missions, 17, 51–52, 71, 178, 185

Ghana (Gold Coast): church union in, 204; missions, 51
Global Christian Forum, 109, 120
Great Britain, 27, 149; Christianity in, 38; missionary societies in, **13–16**, 35, 49, 51, 62
Great Commission, 9, 101, 159
Greece, 60
Guatemala, 95; Christianity in, 78, 95
Guyana, 177

HCJB, 70, 149
Hague Principle, 53
Haiti, 152, 177
Halle, 17
Hawaiian Islands, 172
Health, 75
Heifer Project, 69
Herrnhut, 17
Hilfswerk, 51
Hinduism, 57, 193, 248
Holy Spirit, 105
Home Missions Council of North America, 181, 182, 227, 228
Hong Kong, 127, 132

ICCC, **117–19**, 175
IFMA, 52, 139, 158–59
IMC, xix, 50, **53–56**, 64, 69, 71, 72, 79, 98, 99, 118, 160, 164, 165, 168, 169, 171, 176, 178, 229, 239; integration with WCC, **101–5**, 139, 140, 183, 202, 246
IMC conferences: Delhi 1961, 177, 178; Ghana 1957–58, 103, 169; Jerusalem 1928, **54–55**, 65, 66, 69; Madras/Tambaram 1938, 54, 55, 66, 68, 69, 165, 192, 225, 226, **244–45**; Whitby 1947, 55, 56, 154; Willingen 1952, 100, 217
ISAL, 174
IVCF, **60**, 266
IWM, **62–63**
Iglesia Pentecostal de Chile, 79
Independency, religious, 78, **80–82**
India, 70, 74; Christianity in, 39, 40, 56, 57, 60, 63, 64, 68, 95, 101, 132, 133, 134, **160–62**; missions in, 7, 15, 33, 34, 56; North India, 33, 131; South India, 124, 131, 160

Subject Index 309

India Missions Association, 161–62
Indonesia, 154, 166; church in, 127, 211, 244; church unity in, 216, 217
Inland South America Missionary Union, 52
Institute of Social and Religious Research, 63
Interchurch World Movement, 62–63
Interdenominational Committee on Christian Literature for Oriental Women, 70
International Christian Media Commission, 149
International Committee for Christian Literature in Africa, 69, 71
International Congregational Council, 122
International Consultation of United and Uniting Churches, xx
International Council of Religious Education, 181
International Review of Missions, 50
International Roundtable of Christian Leaders, 228
Interseminary Missionary Alliance, 38
Iran, 148, 169
Iraq, 75
Ireland, 38, 61, 179
Islam, 87, 167, 185
Israel, 144
Italy, 27, 48

Jakarta, 216
Japan: 40, 57, 64, 65; Christianity in, 39, 70, 224, 225; missions in, 63, 95
Japan Reformed Church, 205
Jews: messianic, 144
Johannesburg, 169
Joint Committee on Christian Liberty, 229, 234
Joint Committee on Society, Development and Peace (SODEPAX), **91–92**
Justice, social: local united action, **216–17**

Kampala, 170
Karobatak Church, 211
Kenya, 120, 170, 185; church union in, 204
Kinshasa (Leopoldville), 200
Kitwe, 156

Korea, 70, 146; missions from, 78; missions in, 136
Korean War, 147, 197
Kuala Lumpur, 138

LCWE, 121, **139–45**; Lausanne Covenant, 93, 112, 141, 142, 152, 258; Manila Manifesto, 143
LCWE conferences: Lausanne I, 1974, **140–41**; Lausanne II, 1989, **142–43**; Lausanne III, 2010, **145**; Pattaya Consultation 1980, 142; Pattaya Forum 2004, 145
LMS, x, 8, **13–15**, 19, 32, 171, 195
LWF, 71, **122–25**, 128, 169; Broadcast Service, 149
LWF assemblies: Curitiba 1990, 125; Evian 1970, 124; Helsinki 1963, 123
Lambeth Conference, 85, 121, 130–31, 194
Latin America: Christianity in, 41, 54, 76, 78, 96, 97, 160, **173–77**; church unity in, 211, 218; missions in, 49, 80, 87
Latin American Alliance of Christian Churches, 118
Latin American Protestant Congress, 174
Lay academies, 157
Laymen United for Missions, 61
Laymen's Foreign Missions Inquiry, **63–64, 244–45**
Laymen's Missionary Movement, 61
League of Nations, 62, 224, 225, 234, 240
Lebanon, 146, 169
Liberia, 74
Liberty, religious, 4, 31, 92, 115, 139, 181, 223, 227–29, 232, 234, 235, 237
Life and Work, 124
Life and Work conferences: Oxford 1937, 58, 224–25; Stockholm 1925, 57
Little Flock, 198, 199
London, 43, 45, 49, 72, 189, 266
London Missionary Conference (1888), 43, **45**, 49
London Secretaries Association, **43**
Lutheran Church-Missouri Synod, 182
Lutheran churches, 121, **139–45**; Germany, 29, 44, 128, 132; Japan, 205
Lutheran Theological Seminary (Philadelphia), 234

ME, 106–7, 112, 207
Madagascar, 131
Madras Christian College, 65, 245
Majority World: missions, 143, **160–62**
Malankara Mar Thomas Syrian Church, 195
Malawi (Nyasaland), 28, 185
Manila, 70, 142–43, 258
Media: and mission, **149–50**
Medical Missionary Association, 34
Medical Missionary Society, 34
Medical missions, **34**, **66–68**
Melanesian Council of Churches, 172, 185
Men and Religion Forward Movement, **61–62**
Mennonites, 17
Methodist churches, 5, 29, 121, 132; in North India, 206; in Pakistan, 206; in Southern Asia, 155
Methodist Episcopal Church, 43
Mexico, 19, 20, 212
Micronesia, 172
Middle East, 56, 69, 149, **167–69**
Middle East Council of Churches, **168–69**
Migration, 74, 78
Mindolo Ecumenical Foundation, **156–58**
Misión Iglesia Pentecostal, 79
Mission: and unity, 49, 99–100; definition, xxi; partnership, **130–32**, **155–58**
Mission Exchange, 159. See also EFMA
Missionaries: Majority World, 161–62; statistics, 27, 42, 77
Missionary Education Movement, 181, 228
Missionary movement: definition, xxiii
Missionary Register, **25–26**
Missions: coordination of, **43–45**; definition, xxi; orphaned, 51, **71–72**, 201; supernationality of, 55
Modalities and sodalities, 136–37, 152, 214
Mohawk Native Americans, 146
Mongolia, 99
Monophysitism, 82
Montevideo, 175
Moravians, ix–x, **7–8**, 17, 18, 44
Mozambique, 148

Nairobi, 106, 109, 134, 151, 170, 249–50

National Association of Evangelicals, 96, 137, 158, **181–82**
National Broadcasting Corporation (NBC), 70–71
National Christian Conference (China), 164, 198, 199
National Christian Council of China, 52, 164, 198, 199
National Council of the Churches of Christ in the USA, 69, 71, 181, **182–83**, 198; Division of Overseas Ministries, 71, 181; United Council of Church Women, 64
National Missionary Council of India, 51
National Missionary Society of India, 160
National Study Conference on the Churches and a Just and Durable Peace, 230
Nationalism, 74; nation states, 74
Native Evangelistic Society, 160
Near East Christian Council, 168–69
Near East Relief, 51
Nepal, 99, 155–56
Nepal Christian Fellowship, 156
Netherlands, the (Holland), 228; churches in, 13, 29, 44, 71, 120, 137, 149, 270
Netherlands Bible Society, 23
Netherlands Missionary Society, 17
Neuendettelsau Mission, 128
New Zealand, 116, 166, 172; union churches in, 211
Nicaragua: Christianity in, 78
Niedersächsische Gesellschaft zur Verbreitung christlicher Erbauungsschriften, 25
Nigeria, 116, 161, 169; church union in, 193, 204, 205, **206**; missions, 15
Nigeria Evangelical Missions Association, 161
Nihom Kirisito Kyodan. See Church of Christ in Japan
Nobel Peace Prize, 57
Norddeutsche Missionsgesellschaft, 17
Norske Missionsselskab, Det, 18
North America, 49, 62, 70, 155; church cooperation in, **180–83**
North China Education Union, 65

Subject Index

Norway, 29, 44, 71, 72, 149, 183; churches in, 35
Nova Scotia, 9

Oceania, xi, 40, 72, 77, 123, 138, 160, 171-73
Old Believers, 116
One Great Hour of Sharing, 118
Orphans, 210
Orthodoxy, 80, 86, 87, 105, 111, 116; Coptic, 60; Eastern, 60, 86, 168; Maronite, 60; missions, 27; Oriental, 60, 168; Syrian, 60, 168; Syrian Orthodox of India, 60
Overseas Missionary Fellowship, 52. See also China Inland Mission

PCC, **171-73**, 185
Pakistan, 74, 131
Palestine, 144, 169
Panama, 173, 177
Pan-Orthodox Preconciliar Conference, 256
Papua New Guinea, 132, 172
Parachurch, 136-37; mission organizations, **146-50**
Partnership, **154-55**
Peace, united Christian action for, **226-33**
Peace Aims Group, 226
Pentecostalism, 36, **78-80**, 102, 109, 182, 185
Peru, 175, 176
Phelps-Stokes Fund, 66
Philadelphia, 118, 221, 234
Philippines, the, 56, 70, 133, 138
Pluralism, religious, **76-77**
Plymouth Brethren, 29
Portugal, 27
Poverty, 75, 150-51, 161, 170
Prayer, 144-45; concert of, 10, 21
Presbyterian churches, 121, 123; England, 196; New School, 29; Scotland, 30; USA, 34, 155
Princeton Theological Seminary, 118
Protestants, 80, 87, 136, 175
Puerto Rico, 176

RCC, 30, 41, 44, 80, **86-93**, 109, 111, 120, 123, 134, 149, 168; and councils of churches, 177, 182, **184-85**; and other religions, **258-61**; and Protestant evangelicals, **93-94**, 143; and WCC, **89-93**; Congregation for the Declaration of the Faith, 261; Congregation for the Evangelization of Peoples, 261; missions, 200; Pontifical Council for Interreligious Dialogue, 261; Secretariat for the Promotion of Christian Unity, 90, 93; Synod of Bishops (1974), 92, 109, 112
Race, churches' concern for, 54-55, 225
Radio Voice of the Gospel, 149
Reconciliation, racial, 144
Red Cross, 37; International, 51
Reformed Church in America, 19, 189, 196
Reformed churches, 29, 44
Regions Beyond Missionary Union, 155
Religious Tract Society, 24, 25
Revolution: American, 5; French, 4
Rheinishe Missionsgesellscaft, 172
Rockefeller Foundation, 67
Rumania, 60
Rural development, **68-69**
Russia, 27, 48, 60
Russian Orthodox Church, 116
Rwanda, 75

SCM, 30, 39, 40
SODEPAX, **91-92**
SPCK, 7, 15, 23
SPG, 7, 15, 86
SVM, 36, **37-38**, **59**, 87
Salvation Army, 45
Samoa, 32, 160, 171, 172
San Francisco, 221
São Paulo, 151, 216
Scotland, 29, 35, 61, 179
Sectarianism, 29
Seoul, 136, 144
Serampore College, 11, 247
Serbia, 60
Service, unity in, **115-17**
Seventh-day Adventist Church, **94-95**, 199
Shanghai, 35, 67, 70, 163, 199
Shantung Christian University, 65

Sierra Leone, 74, 169
Singapore, 144, 166
Social Change, rapid, 75, 157, 174
Société des missions évangélique de Paris, 131
Society of Friends (Quakers), 86
Society of Jesus (Jesuits), 12
Sojourners Fellowship, 215
South Africa, 14, 40, 65, 66, 79, 141, 144, 145, 169
South Africa General Mission, 52
Southern Baptists, 181, 182, 205
Soviet Union, evangelical Christians in, 143
Spain, 27
Spirituality, charismatic, 79
Sri Lanka (Ceylon), 55, 133, 166; Christianity in, 40, 246, 251, 271
Student Foreign Missionary Fellowship, 60
Sudan, 74, 169, 170
Sudan Interior Mission, 35, 149–50
Surinam, 177
Svenska Missionsförbundet, 18
Swaziland, 210
Sweden, 158; churches in, 35, 39, 44
Swedish Baptist Mission, 155
Switzerland, 29, 71, 131
Syrian Protestant College, Beirut, 34

TSPM, 198–200
Tahiti, 160
Taiwan, 127
Taizé community, 215
Tanzania, 124, 150, 169, 184, 213; churches in, 124
Terrorism, 75
Thailand, 14, 127, 151, 166, 169, 189, 212, 274
Theological Education Fund, 66, 150
Thirty Years' War, 6
Togo, 51
Tokyo, 40, 41, 163
Tonga, 32, 172
Tranquebar, 7
Trans World Radio, 149
Trinity Evangelical Divinity School, 215
Tübingen, 111, 257
Turkey, 60, 167
Twinning, **130–31**

UBS, 146, 147
UDHR, **234–37**, 238, 270
UN, 74, 75, 116, 148, 150, **221–22**, 229–32, 240; Economic and Social Council, 222, 238; Food and Agriculture Organization, 238; High Commissioner for Refugees, 116; Human Rights Commission, 222, 235, 238; UNESCO, 238
UNELAM, **174–75**, 185
Uganda, 28, 87, 170
Union Christian College, Vellore, 67
Union Medical College, Peking, 66
Union Missionary Convention, 32, 33
Union Missionary Society, 43
Union Theological Seminary, Nanjing, 198
Union Theological Seminary, New York, 122
United Brethren in Christ, 196
United Christian Missionary Society, 155
United Church in Jamaica and the Cayman Islands, 188
United Church in Papua New Guinea and the Solomon Islands, 188
United Church of Canada, 196
United Church of Christ in the Philippines, 188
United Church of North India, 206
United Church of South India, 190, 191, 193
United Church of Zambia, 132, 188, 204
United Congregational Church of Southern Africa, 188
United Council of Church Women, 181
United Domestic Missionary Society, 22
United Foreign Missionary Society, 19
United Free Church of Scotland, 65
United Methodist Church, **96–97**; Judicial Council, 206
United Mission to Nepal, **155–56**
United Mission to the Copperbelt, 156–57
United Missionary Training College for Women, 65
United parishes/union churches, **210–12**
United States of America (USA), 38, 51; churches in, 35, 76
United Stewardship Council, 181
United Theological College, Bangalore, 65, 247

Subject Index 313

United War Work Campaign, 62
Unity, xxi, 77; competing models of, 267–68; cooperative/interchurch, 267; covenantal/voluntary, 265–67; for social justice, 216–17; future expectations of, 271–72; local, 209–18; organic union, xxii, 170, 172, 268–69; secular, 221–40; 269–71; spiritual, 32, 140; wider, 119–20; 262–63; 271
Universal Christian Council for Life and Work, 57, 58
Universal Week of Prayer, 137
Uruguay, 175
U.S. Center for World Mission, 136

Vanuatu (New Caledonia), 171
Vatican Council II, 87–89, 97, 129, 147, 258–60; *Ad gentes*, 88; *Lumen gentium*, 88, 259; *Nostra aetate*, 258, 259, 260; *Unitatis redintegratio*, 88, 97, 185
Vietnam, 183

WACC, 149
WARC, 121
WCC, xxiii, 40, 75, 89–93, 113, 117, 118, 122, 128–30, 133, 137, 170, 183–84, 203, 246
WCC/Assemblies: Amsterdam 1948, 98, 99, 110, 111, 122, 235, 236; Canberra 1991, 107–8, 255; Evanston 1954, 100, 114, 125, 232, 237; Harare 1998, 108, 255; Nairobi 1975, 90, 106, 109, 110, 112, 135, 249–50, 251; New Delhi 1961, 103, 105, 111, 116, 126, 128, 177, 178, 209, 246, 247; Porto Alegre 2006, 108–9, 120; Uppsala 1968, 90, 106, 111, 116, 129, 246, 247; Vancouver 1983, 119, 252
WCC/CC, 106, 113, 233, 251, 255; Rolle 1951, 99, 100, 107, 113
WCC/CFO, 112, 113–15, 119, 184, 247; Bristol 1967, 247; Budapest 1989, 45; Lund 1952, 77, 113–14, 208; Montreal 1963, 114; Santiago de Compostela 1993, 115
WCC/CWME, 92, 104, 106, 107, 112, 184; Melbourne 1980, 106, 142, 251–52; Salvador 1996, 112; San Antonio 1989, 107, 253–54

WCC/DWME: Mexico City 1963, 75, 104
WCC agencies: Commission on Inter-Church Aid, Refugee and World Service, 116; Department of Evangelism, 110; Dialogue with People of Living Faiths and Ideologies, 248–51; Division of Inter-Church Aid, 101, 116; Division of Studies, 101, 125; Office of Inter-Religious Relations, 254; Programme on Unity, Mission, Evangelism and Spirituality, 113; Programme to Combat Racism, 116, 170
WCE, xxii, 77, 80
WEA, 137–39, 170, 203
WEF, 137–38, 141, 182
WMC, 96, 122
WSCF, 36, 38, 39–40, 60–61, 113, 121, 163, 165, 225
Wales, 146, 179
Washington, DC, 61, 215, 216, 230
Week of Prayer for Christian Unity, 86
Wesleyan Church in Southern India, 191
Wesleyan Methodist, 32
West Indies, 9
West Side Cooperative Ministry (Fort Wayne, IN), 217
Westminster Seminary, 118
White Fathers, 87
Women: education of, 65, 157–58; in mission, 41, 42–43
Women United for Mission, 64
Women's Congress of Missions, 43
Women's Missionary Jubilee (1910), 64
Women's Union Missionary Society, 42, 52
World Bank, 148, 170
World by Radio (Words of Hope), 150
World Christian Trends, 27, 80, 130
World Christian Youth Commission, 113
World confessional families, 128, 184
World Congress on Evangelism (Berlin 1966), 140
World Council of Christian Education and Sunday Schools Association, 113
World Council on Christian Education, 113, 176
World Day of Prayer, 64, 70, 216
World Literacy Committee, 70
World Mission Prayer League, 155

World Missionary Conference (1910), 33, 47, **49-50**, 56, 57, 64, 65, 66, 109, 140, 141, 163, 173, 178, 187, 190, 195, 196, 223, **241-42**, 265; Continuation Committee, 36, 50, 51, 52, 57, 164

World Parliament of Religions, 243

World Radio Missionary Fellowship, 149

World Relief, 148

World Trade Organization (WTO), 148

World Vision International, **147-49**

World War I, **51-52**, 57, 123, 178; Paris Peace Conference, 52, 232

World War II, 51, 67, 74, 98, 116, 117, 133, 146, 154, 178

World's Missionary Committee of Christian Women, 43, 43

YMCA, **36-37**, 39, 51, 62, 113, 160; China, 198

YWCA, **36-37**, 38, 113

Yale Divinity School, 22

Yoruba, 15

Zambia, 74, 132, 156-57, 185; church union in, 204

Zanana Bible and Medical Mission, 155

Zimbabwe (Rhodesia), 81, 185; church union in, **207**

Name Index

Achútegui, Pedro S. de, 87, 92
Addams, Jane, 62
Adegbola, Adeolu, 131, 170
Afeaki, Emilaina, 172
Ahlstrom, Sydney E., 20
Albert, Richard J., 177
Alvarez, Carmelo E., 185
Amirtham, Samuel, 194
Anderson, Allan, 78, 79
Anderson, Gerald H., 29, 35, 50, 52, 60
Anderson, Rufus, 13
Andrews, Herbert D., 157
Andrews, Loretta Kreider, 157
Antone, Hope S., 167
Ariarajah, S. Wesley, 251, 252, 253, 271
Arias, Mortimer, 109–10, 112
Arns, Paulo Evaristo, Archbp., 216
Askew, Thomas A., 45, 46
Austin, Alvyn J., 36, 37, 53
Azariah, V. S., Bp., 56–57, 160, 163, 190, 191, 192

Baba, Panya, 161
Barf, Charles, 32
Barrett, David B., 76, 77, 78, 79, 80–81, 130, 144
Bashford, James, Bp., 64
Bassham, Rodger C., 99, 103, 106, 111, 139
Bates, M. Searle, 229
Beahm, William M., 59
Beaver, R. Pierce, 10, 32, 33, 42, 43, 64, 70, 87, 133, 185
Beek, Huibert van, 120
Béguin, Olivier, 146, 147
Benedict XV, Pope, 258
Benedict XVI, Pope (Cardinal Joseph Ratzinger), 261
Benjamin, P. V., 68
Bennett, John, 227
Bent, Ans Joachim van der, 183, 234, 238
Berg, Johannes van den, 15
Bevans, Stephen B., 261, 263, 271

Beyerhaus, Peter, 111, 143, 257
Birmelé, André, 216, 218
Bismarck, Otto von, 28
Blanc, René, 132
Bogue, David, 14
Bokeleale, Jean, 202, 203, 204
Bolink, Peter, 204
Bos, A. David, 217
Bosch, David, 84, 142
Bottoms, Ruth, 214, 215
Brainerd, David, 10
Brash, Alan, 166
Brauer, Hartwig, 44
Brent, Charles Henry, Bp., 56
Bridston, Keith R., 112–13
Briggs, John, xxi
Brown, Arthur J., 30, 66–67
Brown, G. Thompson, 199
Brown, Raymond M., 89
Browne, Stanley G., 65, 67
Brunner, Daniel L., ix, 7
Brunner, Emil, 232
Bryan, William Jennings, 62
Bühlmann, Walbert, 185, 259, 260
Bunyan, John, 5
Burrows, William R., 261
Burton, Ernest D., 65
Bush, Luis, 144, 145
Butselaar, Jan van, 47, 120

Campbell, Alexander, 23
Campbell, Thomas, 23
Capen, Samuel B., 61
Capon, John, 141
Carey, Luther H., 61
Carey, S. Pearce, 4
Carey, William, x, 3–11, 13, 24, 169
Carr, Burgess, 151, 170
Castro, Emilio, xx, 104, 107, 174, 175, 184, 251
Cattan, Louise Armstrong, 43
Cattell, Everett L., 182

Cavert, Samuel McCrea, 181
Chamberlain, Jacob, 189
Champion, L. G., 11
Chan, Kim-Kwong, 200
Chandran, J. Russell, 104, 207, 250
Chang, Lit-sen, 257
Chao, T. C., 223, 243
Chapman, H. Owen, 67
Chatterji, K. C., 163
Chellappa, David, 194
Chenchiah, Pandipeddi, 243
Cheng Guani, 198
Cheng Jingyi (Ch'eng Ching-yi), 50, 163, 164, 195, 197, 198
Chung, Hyun Kyung, 255
Clement XIV, Pope, 12
Coe, Shoki (C. H. Hwang), 127
Coke, Thomas, 8–9
Cook, James, 6
Cook, William/Guillermo, 214
Coote, Robert T., 143, 145
Cope, Brian E., 85, 271
Costas, Orlando, 175
Covell, Ralph R., 258
Cracknell, Kenneth, 242
Crafford, Dionne, 170, 171, 218
Craig, C. Stuart, 171
Crane, William H., xxii, 202, 226
Crawford, John R., 202
Crocombe, Ronald G., 172
Cronje, F. H. J., 185
Cross, William, 32
Crossing, Peter F., 76, 77
Crow, Paul A., Jr., xx, 21, 23, 30, 114
Cryderman, Lyn, 143
Cullmann, Oscar, 269
Cust, R. M., 87

Daneel, Marthinus L., 81, 82
Davey, Colin, 179
Davies, Ronald E., 10
Davis, Helen E., 66
Davis, J. Merle, 156, 157
Davis, Kortright, 177
Dawson, David G., 61
De-la-noy, Michael, 180
De Plessis, David J., 79
Delaney, Joan, 93

Derr, Thomas Sieger, 92
Devanandan, Paul D., 133, 207, 246
Dickinson, Richard D. N., 117
Dodge, D. Stuart, 34
Donovan, V. J., 184
Douglass, H. Paul, 192
Drewery, Mary, 4, 6, 7
Dries, Angelyn, 87, 131
Duarte, Eugénio R., 95
Duchrow, Ulrich, 122, 123, 124, 130, 134–35
Duff, Alexander, 32, 160
Duff, Edward, 223
Dulles, Alan, 226
Dulles, Avery, xx, 97, 265, 271
Dulles, John Foster, 226, 227, 228, 230, 232, 238, 239
Dunant, Henri, 37
Duraisingh, Christopher, 252

Eddy, Sherwood, 160, 190
Edwards, David L., 215
Edwards, Jonathan, 10
Edwards, Robert L., 250
Ehrenström, Nils, 57, 58
Ellinwood, F. F., 33
Ernst, Eldon G., 63
Escobar, Samuel, 60
Ewing, John W., 31

Fabella, Virginia, 150, 151, 167
Fahs, Charles Harvey, 66
Fairbank, John King, ix
Faucett, John, 94
Fenn, C. C., 189
Fey, Harold E., xxi, 122, 127
Finau, Patelesio, Bp., 172
Findlay, G. G., 9, 121
Findlay, James F., Jr., 270
Firth, Cyril Bruce, 195
Fischer, Jean E., 117, 180
Fisher, Galen M., 36
Fleming, Robert, 155
Forman, Charles W., 171, 172, 185
Forman, John N., 37
Francke, August Hermann, 7
Federick IV, King, 7
Freire, Paulo, 172

Name Index

Frizen, E. L., Jr., 52
Frost, Henry T., 35, 36, 53
Fuller, Andrew, 3, 5, 10
Fuller, W. Harold, 138
Fung, Raymond, 214
Funkschmidt, Kai Michael, 132

Gairdner, W. H. T., 49, 187, 196
Galdámez, Pablo, 212
Gee, Donald, 79
Gensichen, Hans-Werner, 28
George, Timothy, 10
Glasser, Arthur, 141
Gobat, Samuel, Bp., 15
Goheen, Michael W., 33
Goodall, Norman, 52, 71, 101, 102, 122, 130, 138, 160, 183, 195
Goodykoontz, Colin Brummitt, 20, 22
Gowing, Peter G., 70
Goyau, Georges, 43
Graham, Billy, 140, 141, 144
Graham, Carol, 190
Graham, Robert, 260
Granado, Gerald, 152
Grootaers, Jan, 91
Groves, C. P., 200, 201
Grubb, Kenneth, 233, 234
Grundmann, Christoffer, 34
Guansing, Benjamin I., 133
Gützlaff, Karl, 34

Halévy, Élie, 5
Hallencreutz, Carl F., 243, 245, 249, 258, 260
Hamer, Jerome, 90
Han, Wenzao, 200
Harada, T., 163
Harder, Ben, 38
Harding, Alan, 8
Harkness, Georgia, 227
Harper, Susan Billington, 160, 190, 191
Harrell, David Edwin, 23
Hartenstein, Karl, 71
Harvey, Charles E., 63
Hastings, Adrian, 131
Hastings, Celina (Countess of Huntington), 8
Haug, Del, 156

Haweis, Thomas, 8
Hawkins, Chauncey J., 61
Hefling, Charles C., 261
Heideman, Eugene, 238
Henry, Carl F. H., 140, 159
Hewitt, Roderick, 208
Hiebert, Paul, 162
Hilborn, David, 30, 31, 138
Hinderer, David, 15
Hinson, E. Glenn, 10
Hinton, Jeanne, 213
Hirsch, Dean, 148
Hitler, Adolf, 128, 224
Hobart, John Henry, Bp., 24
Hocking, William Ernest, 227, 243, 244, 262
Hoekema, Alle, 17
Hoekstra, Harvey T., 103, 105, 110
Hogg, A. G., 245
Hogg, William Richey, 3, 18, 19, 28, 31, 33, 41, 43, 44, 45, 46, 49, 51, 52, 53, 54, 55, 58, 66, 70, 71, 72, 164, 165, 178, 180, 229, 235, 243, 244
Holdsworth, W. W., 9, 121
Hollenweger, Walter J., 79
Honda, Y., 163
Hopkins, C. Howard, 38, 40, 41, 63, 163, 164
Horne, Melville, 13
Horner, Norman A., 168
Houtepen, Anton, 91
Howard, David M., 138
Howell, John R., 202, 203, 204
Hudson, Darril, 223
Hughes, Richard T., 23
Hunter, Alan, 200
Hutabarat-Lebang, Henriette T., 216, 218
Hutchison, William R., 29, 63, 76, 111, 244
Hutton, James, 8

Ibiam, Francis Akanu, 169, 170
Iglehart, Charles W., 205
Irvine, Cecilia, 204
Ishihara, Ken, 205

Jackson, Eleanor M., 226, 228
Jaffarian, Michael, 77
James, J. A., 30
Jänicke, Johann, 17

Jenkins, Paul, 15, 16
John XXIII, Pope, 87, 259, 260
John Paul II, Pope, 85, 144, 261
Johnson, Philip A., 149
Johnson, Todd M., 76, 77
Jones, E. Stanley, 204, 245
Jones, Tracey K., Jr., 96–97
Jongeneel, Jan A. B., 245
Jordan, Philip D., 31

Kabeya, Noah, 203
Kähler, Martin, 242
Kalu, Ogbu U., 204, 205, 206
Kane, J. Herbert, 35
Kärkkäinen, Veli-Matti, 78, 79
Kasenene, Peter, 210
Kato, Byang, 171
Kaunda, Betty, 157
Kerr, David A., 50, 109
Keshishian, Aram, 108–9, 115
Kessler, Diane, 212
Kessler, J. B. A., 31, 137
Keyes, Lawrence, 155, 161, 162
Khodr, Georges, 255
Kinnamon, Michael, 85, 271
Kiplagat, Bethuel, 120
Kirby, Gilbert, 138
Knight, George R., 95
Knitter, Paul, 262
Koechlin, A., 71
Koo, T. Z., 225–26
Koshy, Ninian, 165, 166
Kotto, Jean, 131
Kraemer, Hendrik, 133, 243–45, 262
Krapf, Johann Ludwig, 15
Krause, W., von, 128–29
Küng, Hans, 260

Lacy, Creighton, 24
Lambuth, Walter, 67
Land, Gary, 95
Larson, Peter, 160
Latham, Robert O., x
Latourette, Kenneth Scott, 3, 6, 9, 12, 18,
   19, 22, 28, 46, 48, 50, 51, 54, 73, 76, 85,
   86, 87, 134, 160, 178, 196, 205, 240, 266,
   267, 268
Laubach, Frank Charles, 70

Lavigerie, Charles-Martial Allemand, 87
Le Guillou, M.-J., 46, 87
Lehmann, Dorothea, 157, 185
Leiper, Henry Smith, 113
Lemopoulos, George, 256
Lienemann-Perrin, Christine, 66
Lindell, Jonathan, 155, 156
Lindgren, Juhani, 86
Lindsell, Harold, 141
Linn, Gerhard, 211, 215
Little, David, 235
Lothian, Philip Henry Kerr, 224
Lovett, Richard, 14

MacHarg, Kenneth D., 211
Machen, J. Gresham, 118
Mackay, John A., 41, 98, 99
Mackay, R. P., 180
Maclennan, Kenneth, 61
Makanzu, Mavumilusa, 203
Malik, Charles Habib, 235, 236, 237, 238
Manikam, Rajah Bhushanam, 74, 165, 207
Margull, Hans Jochen, 211
Maris, José, 213
Martensen, Daniel F., 128
Marty, Martin E., 42
Martyn, Henry, 3
Marx, Karl, 119
Mason, Lowell, 94
Mata'afa, Fetaui, 171
Mathews, E. J. Peter, 157
Matthey, Jacques, 108, 113, 143
McConkey, Clarence, 2121
McDonnell, John J., 89
McGavran, Donald, 111
McGee, Gary B., 78
McGilvray, J. C., 67
McIntire, Carl, 117–18
McLaren, John, 172
McLeod, Hugh, 26, 29, 76
Meeking, Basil, 93
Menn, Wilhelm, 224, 225
Merwin, Wallace C., 197, 198
Meyer, Harding H., 130, 131
Meylink, Placid, 179
Miguez-Bonino, José, 119, 174
Miller, Francis F., 59
Mills, Samuel J., 18

Mobutu Seko Sese, 204
Moede, Gerald F., 206
Montgomery, Helen Barrett, 43, 64
Moody, Dwight L, 35, 37
Moomaw, I. W., 68
Mooneyham, W. Stanley, 148
Moore, Steve, 159
Moorshead, R. Fletcher, 67
Moses, David G., 125–26
Mott, John R., 35, 37, 38–42, 43, 44, 50, 53, 54, 55, 58, 59, 60, 61, 62, 63, 68, 71, 87, 163–65, 168, 169, 173, 192, 201, 212, 224, 232, 234, 241, 267
M'Passou, Denis, 157, 158
Mulder, D. C., 245
Mundt, William F., 24, 25
Murch, James Deforest, 137, 180, 182
Murray, Geoffrey, 116
Mutesa, King, 87

Nägeli, Johann G., 94
Napoleon Bonaparte, 4
Naudé, Beyers, 270
Neill, Stephen C., Bp., xx, xxi, 6, 7, 50, 115, 120, 187, 191, 193, 194, 196, 197, 268
Netland, Harold, 258
Neuner, Joseph, 260
Newbigin, Lesslie, 101–2, 104, 111, 134, 189, 193, 194, 247, 250, 262
Newell, Marv, 159
Nicholai, Bp., 41
Nicholas, Daniel J., 159
Nicholls, Bruce, 138
Nicol, J. H., 168
Niebuhr, Reinhold, 232
Niklaus, Robert L., 203
Niles, D. T., 55, 103, 166, 167, 188, 207, 245
Nolde, O. Frederick, 221–23, 226, 228, 230–38, 240
North, Frederick, Lord, 5
Northcott, Cecil, 179, 180
Nurser, John S., 221, 229, 235, 236
Nyerere, Julius, 213

Oborji, Francis Anekwe, 272
Odell, Luis, 173, 174
Oduyoye, Mercy Amba, xxi, 150, 170
Oldham, J. H., 42, 49, 50, 51–52, 53, 57, 58, 66, 71, 163, 169, 173, 178, 223, 224
Oliver, Barry David, 95
Oliver, Roland, 87
Olonade, Timothy, 161
O'Sullivan, John, 20
Outterson, Hugh, 212
Oxnam, Bromley, Bp., 227, 230

Padilla, René, 145
Paine, Thomas, 5
Palmer, Edwin James, 215
Panikkar, Raimundo, 241, 260, 262, 263
Park, Sang Jung, 167
Parker, Michael, 38, 42, 59
Parker, Peter, 34
Pate, Larry D., 78, 155, 161, 162
Paton, William, 71, 225, 226, 228
Paul VI, Pope, 89, 112, 260
Payne, Ernest A., 8, 178
Peabody, Lucy Waterbury, 43, 64
Pentecost, Edward, 160
Petersen, Rodney L., 210, 214
Pfander, C. G., 15
Phiri, Isaac, 158
Pickett, J. Waskom, 63
Pierard, Richard V., 52
Pierce, Bob, 147
Pierson, Arthur T., 35, 36
Piggin, Stuart, 14, 15
Pius XI, Pope, 86, 259
Pius XII, Pope, 259
Plütschau, Henry, 7
Pope, Stephen J., 261
Pope-Levison, Priscilla, 110
Potter, Philip A., 60, 92, 104, 110, 177, 238, 239, 245, 248, 251, 270
Potts, E. Daniel, 10, 11
Pratt, Josiah, 25

Rafransoa, M., 170
Rahner, Karl, 262
Raiser, Konrad, 89, 93, 111, 120

Rakatoarimanana, Victor, 132
Randall, Ian, 30, 31, 138
Ranson, Charles W., xix, 72
Ratzinger, Joseph. See Benedict XVI, Pope
Rauschenbusch, Walter, 62
Reardon, John, 179
Rebmann, Johannes, 15
Reid, John R., Bp., 152–53
Reidy, Miriam, 169
Reuver, Marc, 91–92
Rhee, Jong Sung, 205
Rhoades, J. Benton, 69
Rivera-Pagán, Luis N., 109, 256
Robbins, Bruce W., 97
Robeck, Cecil, M., 79, 80
Robert, Dana L., 35, 38, 43, 64
Robertson, Edwin H., 146, 147
Robins, Raymond, 62
Rockefeller, John D., Jr., 62, 63, 164
Roosevelt, Eleanor, 235, 236
Rooy, Sidney H., 176
Ross, Emory, 201
Ross, Kenneth R., 50, 109
Rouse, Ruth, 3, 4, 12, 13, 24, 26, 29, 30, 31, 37, 39, 40, 41, 60, 137
Roy, Ralph Lord, 118
Runcie, Robert, Archbp., 131, 158
Rupp, Gordon, 133
Russell, C. Allyn, 118

Saayman, Willem A., 81, 86, 87, 93, 99, 139, 140, 141
Sabath, Bob, 215
Samartha, Stanley J., 195, 246, 247–48, 249–51, 253, 255
Samuel, Vinay, 79–80
Sandidge, J. L., 79–80
Santa Ana, Julio de, 151, 218
Scherer, James A., 123, 129
Schlatter, Wilhelm, 16
Schmidt, Martin, 25
Schmidt-Clausen, Kurt, 123, 128
Schroeder, Roger P., 261, 263, 271
Schutz, Roger, 215

Schwager, F., 30
Scopes, Wilfred, 195
Scott, Waldron, 142, 159
Scudder, John, 34
Selvanayagam, Israel, 255, 256
Semmel, Bernard, 4, 5, 8
Setiloane, Gabriel, 184
Sharpe, Eric J., 57, 123
Shaumba, Pierre, 203
Sheard, Robert B., 246, 251
Shedd, Clarence Prouty, 37
Shenk, Wilbert R., ix–xi, 17
Short, Frank, 184
Shorter, Aylward, 171
Silett, F. T., 157
Simons, Menno, 6
Slade, Ruth M., 201
Sleman, John B., 61
Smalley, William A., 24, 146
Smith, Fred B., 62
Smith, Gary Scott, 62
Smith, Gypsy, 61
Smith, Herbert, 201
Smith, Timothy, 77
Söderblom, Nathan, Bp., 57, 123
Speer, Robert, 35, 44, 49, 61
Stackhouse, John G., 258
Stafford, Tim, 148, 149
Stanley, Brian, 10, 49, 50, 65, 189, 196, 223
Steinkopf, Karl Friedrich Adolf, 16, 25
Stelzle, Charles, 62
Stettinius, Edward R., Jr., 221, 222
Stockwell, Eugene, 253
Stott, John R. W., 93, 111, 152–53
Stransky, Thomas F., 90, 142, 259
Stromberg, Jean, 253
Sundkler, Bengt, 57, 160, 189, 191, 193, 194
Swain, Clara, 34
Sykes, Norman, 7

Tatlow, Tissington, 57
Taylor, J. Hudson, 32, 35
Taylor, John Vernon, 157, 185
Teinonen, Seppo A., 223, 239

Name Index

Temple, William, Archpb., 58, 72–73, 178, 226
Tevi, Lorine, 171, 173
Than, U. Kwaw, 166
Thangaraj, M. Thomas, 210, 268–69
Thomas, M. M., 112, 166
Thomas, Norman E., 212
Thompson, A. C., 32
Thompson, E. P., 5
Thorogood, Bernard G., 14, 132
Tigert, John James, 146
Tillard, J. M. R., 86
Ting, K. H., Bp., 199
Tomkins, Oliver Stratford, 87
Tribhuvan, King, 155
Truman, Harry, Pres., 221, 222
Tsetsis, Georges, xxi, 186
Tsui, H. H., 197
Tucci, Roberto, 90
Turner, Nathanael, 32
Tutu, Desmond, Archbp., 115
Twaddell, Elizabeth, 25

Ury, Ruth, 69

Vajta, Vilmos, 130
Van Doorn, C. L., 157
Van Doorn-Snijders, W. S. F., 157
Van Dusen, Henry Pitney, xix, 85–86, 98, 99, 101, 122, 218, 227
Vandenburg, Arthur, 223
Vanderkamp, John T., 14
VanKirk, Walter W., 232
Vencer, Agustin B., 138
Venn, Henry, x
Vischer, Lukas, 87, 89, 90, 134–35, 183, 184, 186
Visser 't Hooft, Willem Adolf, xxii, 41, 42, 91, 93, 117, 179, 180, 232
Voskuil, Dennis N., 71
Wagner, C. Peter, 141
Wallis, James, 215, 216
Walls, Andrew F., 11, 13, 15, 26, 28

Wang Mingdao, 198
Wang, Thomas, 144
Ward, W. R., 12, 13
Ward, William, 3
Warneck, Gustav, 32, 44, 45, 46
Warnshuis, A. Livingstone, 71, 72, 229
Warren, Max, 102, 104–5, 154–55, 160
Washington, Booker T., 62
Watson, Charles R., 168, 234
Weber, Hans-Ruedi, 126, 163, 165, 168, 169, 173, 180
Wei, Francis, 243
Werner, Dietrich, 110
Wesley, John, 5, 8–9, 96
Westmeier, Karl-Wilhelm, 8
Whitefield, George, 8
Wickeri, Philip Lauri, 198, 200
Wickramasinghe, W. G., 133
Wilder, Robert Parmelee, 37
Williams, George, 37
Williams, Glen Garfield, 180
Williams, John, 32
Wilson, Woodrow, Pres., 240
Winter, Ralph D., 59, 103, 136–37, 153, 214, 266
Wishard, Luther D., 39
Wong, James, 160
Wong, Margaret, 71
Wood, Rick, 145
Woong, Ahn Jae, 167
Wright, J. Elwin, 137
Wright, J. Robert, 131

Xu (Tsu), Rulei, 200

Yannoulatos, Anastasios, Apb., 255–56
Yoder, Don Herbert, 21
Yoder, Howard W., 175
Yuzon, Lourdino A., 185

Ziegenbalg, Bartholomäus, 7
Zinzendorf, Nicolas von, ix, 7
Zwemer, Samuel, 60

PREVIOUSLY PUBLISHED IN
THE AMERICAN SOCIETY OF MISSIOLOGY SERIES

1. *Protestant Pioneers in Korea*, Everett Nichols Hunt Jr.
2. *Catholic Politics in China and Korea*, Eric O. Hanson
3. *From the Rising of the Sun*, James M. Phillips
4. *Meaning Across Cultures*, Eugene A. Nida and William D. Reyburn
5. *The Island Churches of the Pacific*, Charles W. Forman
6. *Henry Venn*, Wilbert Shenk (reprinted by Wipf & Stock Publishers)
7. *No Other Name?* Paul F. Knitter
8. *Toward a New Age in Christian Theology* Richard Henry Drummond
9. *The Expectation of the Poor*, Guillermo Cook
10. *Eastern Orthodox Mission Theology Today*, James J. Stamoolis (reprinted by Wipf & Stock Publishers)
11. *Confucius, the Buddha, and the Christ*, Ralph Covell (reprinted by Wipf & Stock Publishers)
12. *The Church and Cultures*, Louis J. Luzbetak, SVD
13. *Translating the Message*, Lamin Sanneh
14. *An African Tree of Life*, Thomas G. Christensen
15. *Missions and Money* (second edition), Jonathan J. Bonk
16. *Transforming Mission*, David J. Bosch
17. *Bread for the Journey*, Anthony J. Gittins, CSSp (reprinted by Wipf & Stock Publishers)
18. *New Face of the Church in Latin America*, Guillermo Cook
19. Mission Legacies, edited by Gerald H. Anderson, Robert T. Coote, Norman A. Horner, and James M. Phillips
20. *Classic Texts in Mission and World Christianity*, edited by Norman E. Thomas
21. *Christian Mission: A Case Study Approach*, Alan Neely
22. *Understanding Spiritual Power*, Marguerite G. Kraft (reprinted by Wipf & Stock Publishers)
23. *Missiological Education for the 21st Century: The Book, the Circle, and the Sandals*, edited by J. Dudley Woodberry, Charles Van Engen, and Edgar J. Elliston (reprinted by Wipf & Stock Publishers)
24. *Dictionary of Mission: Theology, History, Perspectives*, edited by Karl Müller, SVD, Theo Sundermeier, Stephen B. Bevans, SVD, and Richard H. Bliese (reprinted by Wipf & Stock Publishers)
25. *Earthen Vessels and Transcendent Power: American Presbyterians in China, 1837-1952*, G. Thompson Brown

26. *The Missionary Movement in American Catholic History, 1820-1980*, by Angelyn Dries, OSF
27. *Mission in the New Testament: An Evangelical Approach*, edited by William J. Larkin, Jr., and Joel W. Williams
28. *Changing Frontiers of Mission*, Wilbert Shenk
29. *In the Light of the Word: Divine Word Missionaries of North America*, Ernest Brandewie
30. *Constants in Context: Theology of Mission for Today*, Stephen B. Bevans, SVD, and Roger Schroeder, SVD
31. *Changing Tides: Latin America and Mission Today*, Samuel Escobar
32. *Gospel Bearers, Gender Barriers: Missionary Women in the Twentieth Century*, edited by Dana L. Robert
33. *Church: Community for the Kingdom*, John Fuellenbach, SVD
34. *Mission in Acts: Ancient Narratives in Contemporary Context*, edited by Robert L. Gallagher and Paul Hertig
35. *A History of Christianity in Asia: Volume I, Beginnings to 1500*, Samuel Hugh Moffett
36. *A History of Christianity in Asia: Volume II, 1500 - 1900*, Samuel Hugh Moffett
37. *A Reader's Guide to Transforming Mission*, Stan Nussbaum
38. *The Evangelization of Slaves and Catholic Origins in Eastern Africa*, Paul Vincent Kollman, CSC
39. *Israel and the Nations: A Mission Theology of the Old Testament*, James Chukwuma Okoye, CSSp
40. *Women in Mission: From the New Testament to Today*, Susan Smith
41. *Reconstructing Christianity in China: K. H. Ting and the Chinese Church*, Philip L. Wickeri
42. *Translating the Message: The Missionary Impact on Culture*, second edition, revised and expanded, Lamin Sanneh
43. *Classic Texts in Mission and World Christianity*, edited by Robert L. Gallagher and Paul Hertig
44. *World Mission in the Wesleyan Spirit*, edited by Darrell L. Whiteman and Gerald H. Anderson (published by Providence House Publishers, Franklin, Tennessee)
45. *Miracles, Missions, and American Pentecostalism: "These Signs Shall Follow,"* Gary B. McGee
46. *The Gospel among the Nations: A Documentary History of Inculturation*, Robert A. Hunt

www.ingramcontent.com/pod-product-compliance
Lightning Source LLC
Chambersburg PA
CBHW020109010526
44115CB00008B/762